# CAMPAIGNS AND ELECTIONS

# CAMPAIGNS AND ELECTIONS

## Issues, Concepts, Cases

EDITED BY
### Robert P. Watson
### Colton C. Campbell

LYNNE
RIENNER
PUBLISHERS

BOULDER
LONDON

Published in the United States of America in 2003 by
Lynne Rienner Publishers, Inc.
1800 30th Street, Boulder, Colorado 80301
www.rienner.com

and in the United Kingdom by
Lynne Rienner Publishers, Inc.
3 Henrietta Street, Covent Garden, London WC2E 8LU

**Library of Congress Cataloging-in-Publication Data**
Campaigns and elections : issues, concepts, cases / [edited by]
    Robert P. Watson & Colton C. Campbell.
        p. cm.
    Includes bibliographical references and index.
    ISBN 1-58826-120-4 (alk. paper)—ISBN 1-58826-144-1 (pbk. : alk. paper)
    1. Political campaigns—United States. 2. Political campaigns—
United States—Case studies. I. Watson, Robert P., 1962–   II. Campbell,
Colton C., 1965–
JK2281 .C354   2003
324.973—dc21                                        2002068270

**British Cataloguing in Publication Data**
A Cataloguing in Publication record for this book
is available from the British Library.

Printed and bound in the United States of America

5  4  3  2  1

# Contents

# Preface

The dawn of the twenty-first century is an exciting and important time to be studying campaigns and elections. In the wake of the historic 2000 presidential election, arguably the most intriguing and controversial contest of the modern era, a host of electoral reforms has been proposed and implemented across the country and in the nation's capital, from bans on "soft money" to the administration of local elections by nonpartisan supervisors to improved voting technology. So too have both the shortcomings and vitality of the electoral system entered the collective public conscience. November 2000 saw the U.S. public receive a valuable national civics lesson, not only on the importance of voting, but also on the workings of the intricate machinery of the Electoral College, vote recounts, voting machines, canvassing boards, and chads—be they hanging, pregnant, or dimpled.

In addition to the prospect of fundamental election reforms, important new issues and trends are redefining the style of campaigns and elections. Both the practice and study of this subject are dynamic endeavors, ever adapting to societal changes. So it is likely that within the next ten years, campaigns and elections will be different from those we know today. A number of forces at play are worth noting: possible political realignments, the rise of third parties, new media and communications technology, Internet voting and campaigning, demographic and racial shifts in the composition of the electorate, advances in polling and public opinion practices, more women serving in public office (including the first female president?), and an increasingly disenchanted voting public. Yet, age-old questions and problems continue.

In this volume, focusing on emerging issues and directions in campaigns and elections, we have selected timely, important, and controversial topics for inclusion. Every effort has been made to ensure that the book is accessible for students and practitioners, yet cutting-edge for scholars.

Along with thematic chapters, the volume also offers several behind-the-scenes case studies. These cases place concepts into perspective, helping to more fully explain the complexities of a topic or to illustrate real life effects, as well as to bridge the widening gap between theory and practice.

The cases on campaigns, for example, include a comparison of congressional races and a look at the role of ethics—in legal terms and in terms of the appearance of a candidate's conduct—in campaigns. The cases devoted to elections provide firsthand accounts of the recent controversial gubernatorial election in Mississippi and the 2000 presidential election (with the infamous vote recounts). Also a part of the volume are cases on voters and the candidates themselves, including a probing study of the third-party gubernatorial maverick, Jesse Ventura of Minnesota, and an examination of the closely watched New York Senate race between former first lady Hillary Clinton and former U.S. representative Rick Lazio.

As with any book on a topic so complex and multifaceted as campaigns and elections, the real challenge has been to compile a reasonably comprehensive yet concise study. We believe the respected and capable contributors to this volume met that challenge by exploring current themes and trends. The contributors' diverse backgrounds—in academia, public service, elections administration, and campaign management—along with their equally diverse perspectives on the subjects also strengthen the text.

The contents are organized into four sections, opening with an introduction that presents foundational concepts of the topics at hand to assist the reader uninitiated in the subject. The next three sections—current issues in campaigns, current issues in elections, and candidates and voters—constitute the core of the book. Each of these three major sections is divided into three essays followed by two case studies. The book closes with an examination of the 2000 congressional and presidential elections and their consequences for the future.

Our work in putting this book together was made easier by four factors, the first of which was that the topic lent itself, in our opinion, to an exciting study. Second, we were fortunate to have such capable colleagues who shared our enthusiasm for campaigns and elections. Third and relatedly, it was a pleasure to work with Lynne Rienner Publishers and its talented staff. So, Lynne Rienner, Leanne Anderson, Penny Monroe, Shena Redmond, Beth Partin, and Liz Miles, we thank you. Last, we acknowledge our spouses—Claudia Pavone Watson and Marilyn Lewis Campbell—whose support and patience are appreciated (and not contingent upon the success of this volume!); we are very lucky.

—*Robert P. Watson,*
*Colton C. Campbell*

# CAMPAIGNS AND ELECTIONS

# Introduction

## The Foundations of Democracy

The foundations of democracy are self-government and representative government, the functioning of which in turn is contingent upon citizen engagement in the political process. Two basic tenets of political participation are the right (and responsibility) to vote and the ability to participate in politics by seeking or holding public office. Indeed, the vitality of democracy is challenged by such occurrences as low voter turnout, a lack of real choices for voters in elections, fraudulent campaign practices, and poorly administered elections. But how many people run for office or work on campaigns? Do a majority of citizens cast a vote, much less an informed and enthusiastic vote in elections? Given that all these concerns have appeared in the political headlines in recent years, if the present state of campaigns and elections were the thermometer for the democratic experience, the diagnosis would be alarming.

Theoretically, campaigns and elections should promote democracy and encourage civic activism by, for instance, expanding citizen participation in politics, translating voters' preferences and choices into electoral decisions and government action, and ensuring accountability by elected officials and government. Because a small number of officials in a representative democracy cannot fully promote or serve the public will and interest, such involvement generally promotes accountability as well as provides a means to shape politics and public policy. Without input, however, elected officials might distort the public will or pursue self-interests.

Government, at times, will attempt to persuade or curb the influence of citizens, which makes it all the more important to promote participation and safeguard the integrity of campaigns and elections. Voting and participation serve important conceptual facets of democratic government by increasing the probability that the citizenry will participate on a regular and viable basis in politics, expanding the likelihood that citizens will affect public decisions, and reinforcing citizen independence of—or autonomy from—state control.

1

Increased activism in campaigns and elections democratizes citizen involvement while simultaneously offering a *controlled* means of participation. Here, a balance is sought between promoting maximum involvement for the populace while setting conditions on the format and eligibility for mass political involvement. Citizen participation in the form of voting and pursuing elective office promotes the democratic experience.[1]

## A Dynamic, Evolving Process

Campaigns and electoral systems have always been in a state of flux, influenced by a host of legal, political, and societal forces to such a degree that change and fluidity are defining characteristics of both processes. This is not to suggest, however, that some constants cannot be found. The strategy of "going negative," for example, has been a regular part of campaigns, the media have always covered elections, and voter decisions have always been about such concerns as partisan loyalty, policy issues, and the character of individual candidates.[2] Likewise, a basic framework governing elections is outlined by the Constitution, prescribing specific term lengths and the frequency of elections.

Yet, a near-constant stream of developments have left an indelible mark, dramatically altering the electoral landscape. Throughout the life of the U.S. party system, for instance, the coalition of voters who define the parties has been rearranged every generation or so by what is called "realignment," an electoral phenomenon that generally produces different parties with new bases of support, new policies, and new philosophies. Much debated by political scientists, realignments occur as major crises intrude on society or the economy and when major parties are unable to meet the expectations of large segments of society.[3]

The defeat of the Federalists by the Jeffersonians in 1800 has generally been considered the first of such realignments, signaling the meaningful rise of modern political parties.[4] Nearly three decades later, Andrew Jackson's presidential victory in 1828 and corresponding control of Congress by his party marked the end of an era of governance by the political elites, ushering in Jacksonian or "coonskin" democracy and a voice for the common person. A third realignment occurred during the outbreak of the Civil War and was highlighted by the demise of the Whigs, the new Republican Party gaining power, and, of course, the completion of the growing rift between North and South and the various political, social, and economic divisions between them. Another Republican realignment in the late nineteenth century would last until 1932, when the Great Depression and election of Franklin D. Roosevelt to the presidency brought a major Democratic realignment.[5] Such changing electoral outcomes, albeit less momentous, have continued to occur, each one marking a change in the political order.

Among the many institutional developments that dramatically altered the way in which campaigns and elections are waged, namely for the presidency, was the replacement of "King Caucus" by nominating conventions in the 1830s as the chief means by which parties would promote and select candidates for public office. Until then, presidential candidates had been nominated by their party's congressional delegates. This system was derisively known as "King Caucus" because candidates had to defer to the party leaders in Congress to win the party's nomination. Caucuses suited the interests of a handful of party elite who controlled the candidate selection process and directed party strategy and policy agendas from behind closed doors. This method of candidate selection at party nominating caucuses often included ambiguous—and, in some cases, nonexistent—rules, proxy voting at the discretion of party officials who frequently denied minority contenders any support, and meetings held without public notification or proper quorums. The rise of brokered conventions democratized this political process, with the intention of providing rank-and-file party members greater participation and influence in the selection of presidential candidates.

So too has the history of elections witnessed a tug-of-war between those seeking to expand the right of suffrage and those attempting to minimize or control who votes.[6] Indeed, many constitutional amendments directly pertain to voting rights and elections practices. The long struggle toward universal suffrage has also been shaped by court cases, civil rights movements, and social unrest.

Historically, in nations where democracy existed—albeit in a fledgling manifestation of its present form—the composition of the electorate was limited and regulated by government, insofar as property ownership was the chief precondition to voting. This system stemmed from the view among those making the laws that certain classes of people (those who did not own land) were ill-equipped to cast an informed vote. Voting subsequently was entrusted only to those likely to perpetuate the status quo. In the United States, the composition of the electorate has been restricted through the use of poll taxes, flawed voter registration lists, and a variety of other nondemocratic practices. For instance, voter registration lists were periodically purged in what was said to be an attempt to keep them up-to-date and accurate but with the unintended (or intended) impact of minimizing voting.

In general, today's citizens need only to register and show proof of identity, residence, and citizenship to exercise their right to vote. Ballots are printed in languages other than English, booths are accessible to the handicapped, and officials are available to provide assistance with voting. Voting registration is far less inconvenient today than in times past. Historically, voters could not afford to miss hours of work (and pay) in order to register, and the time frame for registration was so long before the date of the election that it often worked to the detriment of many would-be voters.

A major period in the expansion of suffrage occurred during Reconstruction at the close of the Civil War. Former slaves and free blacks were enfranchised in 1867 and 1870 through the adoption of the Fourteenth and Fifteenth Amendments, respectively providing for equal protection and the right to vote for black males. However, following the conclusion of Reconstruction in 1877, many southern states and communities employed an array of tactics designed to prevent blacks from voting. Known collectively as "Jim Crow" laws, such practices as imposing literacy tests, poll taxes, and grandfather clauses as well as intimidation and lynchings achieved their intended purpose.[7] A general contraction of voting rights for many racial groups resulted during this period and lasted through the 1960s. Similar practices were directed at individuals of Mexican descent, for instance, in Texas, and efforts at "Chinese exclusion" in California effectively disenfranchised many Asians, regardless of national origin.[8]

An exception to this general trend was the passage of the Nineteenth Amendment to the Constitution in 1920, which extended the basic right of voting to women. Ironically, in the period known as the Progressive Era in the early twentieth century, a range of plebiscitary reforms intended to democratize the political process, from the Australian ballot to direct primaries and registration requirements aimed at preventing double voting, produced an unintended drop in voter participation.

Civil rights gains of the 1960s occasioned important changes in voting rights and the rise of minority voting. The Twenty-fourth Amendment, passed in 1964, banned the use of poll taxes, and the 1965 Voting Rights Act provided mechanisms for addressing unfair elections administration practices directed at African Americans seeking the right to vote. This expansion of suffrage continued with the Twenty-sixth Amendment in 1971, which lowered the voting age from twenty-one to eighteen. Another step toward expanding suffrage was the much-debated and highly partisan 1993 "motor voter" bill, which eased the task of voter registration by allowing government offices to register voters who were applying for driver's licenses or public assistance. Although the law was vetoed by President George Bush in 1992, President Bill Clinton signed the measure into law the following year. Today, gains in voting rights by all races and groups of people have been assured by law, and an increasing number of women and minorities are seeking and winning elected office.

## Electoral Systems

Elections assume many forms, especially in the United States, where the constitutional principles of federalism and separation of powers allow for wide latitude in tailoring elections to fit state traditions, political conditions, and the preferences of voters. Democratic elections, as practiced currently in the United States and many other nations, provide a means for opposing political forces and interests to compete against one another and a process to replace current officeholders. In contrast, electoral systems in authoritarian regimes typically do not provide mechanisms to defeat sitting officials.

The electoral college is one of many such electoral systems, the genesis of which may be traced in large part to a concern by the Founders that common citizens were not necessarily competent to cast a vote; in addition, the Framers faced the challenge of conducting a nationwide election from a logistical perspective and believed that the electoral college would produce the best-qualified president, one not beholden to congressional leaders.[9] As such, the electoral college was formed as a group of electors chosen indirectly, who cast their votes for president and vice president. The vote recorded on election day by voters is therefore technically not the final word on who becomes president. Voters participating in presidential elections are not casting a direct vote for president, but rather they are casting a vote that will be considered by the electors.

This method for choosing the president was a masterpiece of political improvisation and compromise, rather than a formula based on any coherent political theory.[10] Each state is free to choose electors, who gather roughly one month after the presidential election. Historically, state legislatures selected presidential electors. Today, how someone becomes part of the eligible pool of electors is left to the discretion of the parties. They employ a variety of methods for selecting electors, such as state conventions, state political committees, primary elections, direct selection by a party, or some combination of methods. Most states use a method that benefits the dominant party in the state. By law, on the Monday after the second Wednesday in December, the electors convene in their state capitals and formally cast their votes, which decide the outcome of the race. These ballots and the certificates of their votes are then forwarded to Capitol Hill, where the votes are to be counted in the House of Representatives, with the president of the Senate (the vice president of the United States) presiding. So, although these electors pledge to support their party's presidential candidate, it is the electors and not the voting public who put the president in the White House.

Each state's allocation of electoral votes is determined by its representation in Congress, with the allocation of a state's electoral votes determined on the basis of a winner-take-all system. The candidate who receives a *plurality* of the state popular vote receives all of that state's electoral votes, no matter how narrow the candidate's margin of victory. Counting the three votes allocated to the District of Columbia, there are a total of 538 electoral votes. In this winner-take-all system, the presidential candidate who wins a state gets all the electoral votes of that state—the two exceptions to this system being Maine and Nebraska, who divide part of their electoral votes proportionally by district. A candidate must earn a majority of the electoral college's 538 votes to win the race.

As illustrated in the 2000 race between Republican George W. Bush and Democrat Al Gore, the candidate that wins the electoral college might not necessarily win the popular vote. For instance, one candidate (candidate A) might win a state with ten electoral votes by the slimmest of margins—say, less than 1 percent. But, that candidate gains 100 percent of that state's electoral votes. Whereas, the opponent (candidate B) might win another state—of nearly the same size—that has nine electoral votes by a landslide of 30 percent. In this scenario, candidate B—with one convincing win and one near tie—would likely have many more popular votes. Yet candidate B would lose the electoral college.

The controversy created over the 2000 presidential election between Bush and Gore and the ensuing debate over the merits of the electoral college are not new. The system failed to produce a clear winner in 1800 and 1824, when no one candidate received a majority of the votes. In 1800, Thomas Jefferson and Aaron Burr each received an equal number of votes. Ironically, Jefferson and Burr were running for president and vice president, respectively, from the same party. This situation was possible and at times even common because, until the passage of the Twelfth Amendment in 1804, the Constitution made no distinction between presidential and vice presidential candidates.[11] As per constitutional requirements, the tied election was thus decided in the U.S. House of Representatives where, with support from the opposition party—the Federalists—and their leader, Alexander Hamilton, Jefferson came out victorious.

Again, in 1876, the election between Rutherford B. Hayes and Samuel Tilden challenged the integrity of the electoral college. Hayes was declared the winner by a special commission after he failed to secure the majority of the electoral votes and even though his opponent captured more popular votes. In his bid for reelection in 1888, Grover Cleveland also failed to capture the majority of the electoral college, even though he took the popular vote. His opponent, Benjamin Harrison, was declared the winner.

Several other types of elections and rules exist for determining the winners of these contests. For instance, in single-member *plurality districts,* the candidate receiving the most votes—at least one more than the opponent—is the winner. In such elections, one does not need a majority (50 percent plus one) of votes to secure office. This system is common in state and local elections throughout the United States. However, a *majority system* mandates that a candidate garner a majority of all votes cast in an election to win. Although no longer commonly used, this method of election was historically employed in southern primaries. Oftentimes, such majority systems require that, if no one candidate receives a majority of votes, the two top vote getters compete in a "runoff" election to determine the winner.

A system prevalent in Europe is *proportional representation,* whereby legislative seats are allocated in approximate proportion to the percentage of votes a party receives in the particular election. For example, in the case of a political party earning 25 percent of the vote, that party then receives 25 percent of the seats in the legislative body. These systems are prone to benefit smaller, weaker third parties, in that the threshold for gaining seats is not total victory. In the United States with its winner-take-all system, it is difficult for third parties to muster enough votes to win even a single seat, regardless of whether they poll roughly one-quarter of votes in several races. In each of those races, they will still lose and consequently fail to capture even any seat.

Candidates for legislative office represent and run for office in electoral districts. That is not true for executive offices such as mayor, governor, or president, who serve the entire community, state, or nation. The question thus arises as to how such districts should be designed. The Senate was intended to add constancy, wisdom, and forbearance to the actions of the popularly elected House. Thus two Senate seats are allocated per state, so a senator represents an entire state. But members of the U.S. House of Representatives and state legislators serve specific districts, the composition and design of which are determined largely by population. (In addition to population, districts are technically to be designed according to community interests and contiguity, insofar as all the district lines must connect.) Every ten years, after the census is taken by the Commerce Department's Bureau of the Census, governments (in this case, state legislatures and boards) redraw or *reapportion* seats and district boundaries, according to shifts in the population.

Once the population figures from the decennial census are gathered, apportionment for congressional seats is derived by a mathematical formula called the *method of equal proportions*—the idea that proportional differences in the number of persons per representative for any pair of states should be kept to a minimum.[12] In the case of the U.S. House of Representatives, as the nation's population shifts, states gain or lose congressional representation (or seats); one state's gain means another's loss.

Historically, the designation of these districts has benefited incumbents or the dominant party. If Democrats control the legislature—and thus the reapportionment process—for example, they redraw seats to benefit their legislative member by pitting two Republicans against one another or creating "safe" seats for themselves by including a majority of Democratic voters in the district. In the South, reapportionment was a tool often used to prevent blacks from getting elected. Such reapportionment for purely political purposes is known as "gerrymandering," named for the former governor of Massachusetts, Elbridge Gerry, who in the early nineteenth century supposedly designed districts in the shape of a salamander (gerrymander) to serve the electoral interests of his party.

By law, districts must be roughly equal in population. But such population equality comes at the expense of other goals. Districts become artificial creations, the result of partisan, geographical, and racial politics that transcend city and county lines or ignore geographic and social lines.[13] A district representing a densely populated urban area, for example, will cover a small geographic region, but a rural, sparsely populated district might have to encompass a large region to contain an equivalent population base. The state of Wyoming, although large geographically, contains so few people that the whole state is a single-member district in the U.S. House of Representatives. However, large states like California, New York, Texas, Florida, and Pennsylvania carry many seats, and a large city such as Los Angeles incorporates several House districts.

## Current Trends in Campaigns and Elections

The modern campaign is analogous to a state of war.[14] These no-holds-barred contests for ideas and for the hearts and minds of voters have become longer and longer and increasingly sophisticated and have higher and higher price tags. With the high stakes of modern campaigns come growing staffs, pools of volunteers, interest groups lined up for and against every campaign, and hard-to-please voters.

Campaign strategy and the issue agenda used to belong to the political parties. But, by late 1960s and 1970s, the individual candidates were charting their own courses with the help of campaign professionals.[15] One of the defining traits of modern campaigns is the reliance on campaign professionals—individuals who work on a fee-for-service basis for more than one election cycle.[16] This increasingly sophisticated endeavor covers an ever-increasing array of services, from polling to opposition research to fundraising to media strategy and, more recently, the marriage of all these elements into an orchestrated, managed campaign. The contemporary campaign now incorporates all these elements plus get-out-the-vote efforts, scheduling and advance work to manage a jam-packed campaign season, legal counselors, press spokespersons, speechwriters, television commercial producers and media buyers to position the ad to the targeted market of prospective voters, and even image consultants. Teams of "hired guns" or "campaign warriors" offer a comprehensive array of campaign management services to candidates.[17] They find candidates eager to purchase the promise of victory these services offer. Indeed, it is almost unthinkable for a candidate for a national or statewide office today to not enlist the help of a team of professional campaign consultants.

Technological advances in communications, broadcasting, computer-based polling and survey research, and the Internet are ushering in a new era of high-tech campaigns. Because of the promise of faster services, the ability to reach more voters and targeted groups of voters, and a host of other benefits, candidates and campaign professionals are compelled to embrace these new technologies and practices.[18]

Media coverage of campaigns is sporadic and, at times, intensive to the point of saturation. The advent of the twenty-four-hour news cycle, "soft news" industry, rapid news production capabilities, and a proliferation of news outlets have increased the pace of campaigns. Candidates no longer have the luxury of responding to or discussing points on their own schedules. For perhaps all the aforementioned issues, the costs of campaigns have grown exponentially. This seemingly drives up the stakes of campaigns and causes a proliferation of well-organized and well-financed interest groups attempting to exert influence on campaigns. These examples are but a sampling of the many dynamic forces continuing to shape campaigns and elections.

Although certain core elements of campaigns remain, the approaches and methods used have changed dramatically, and new campaign tactics and techniques appear with almost every new election. These emerging trends, practices, issues, and important questions present themselves to students of campaigns and elections, campaign professionals, elections administrators, and elected officeholders. In this volume we examine several of these trends while putting them within the context of general campaign and election practices and scholarship.

In Part 1 of the book, "Current Issues in Campaigns," David Dulio and Stephen Medvic offer comprehensive assessments of the many roles and use of political consultants in campaigns and the practice of polling, respectively. Both Dulio and Medvic ponder the benefits and drawbacks of using consultants in modern campaigning, bringing a fresh perspective on the usual criticism of campaign professionals. Campaign consultants Joshua Whitman and Joseph Perkins then inspect the technological evolution of campaigns and consider, from their vantage point, the impact of these new practices. Part 1 concludes with two case studies. In the first, Robin Kolodny and Sandra Suárez compare two highly competitive recent congressional campaigns in Pennsylvania, offering the reader valuable insights from the races. Edward Yager then brings a career in local government and academia to his profile of an ethical and legal dispute in a recent local campaign, where even the *appearance* of an illegality is problematic for candidates. These cases offer the reader actual illustrations of some of the important issues defining campaigning today.

In Part 2, "Current Issues in Elections," Nicol Rae tackles the matter by discussing a collection of important trends defining modern elections. Two pressing issues in campaigns today, with significant consequences for the outcome of elections, are campaign finance reform and the Republican lock on the South. In an important chapter, Victoria Farrar-Myers examines various campaign finance reform proposals considered by Congress, along with their impacts. Matthew Corrigan sheds new light on the solid Republican South and chronicles efforts by both parties in this increasingly important region of the country for candidates for both Congress and the White House. The two cases at the end of the section provide behind-the-scenes accounts of two of the most controversial elections in modern times. Donna Simmons, a campaign consultant and senior political adviser, chronicles the 1999 governor's race in Mississippi, the outcome of which was thrown to the state House. The section closes with an examination of the infamous Florida election. Jane Carroll, the former supervisor of elections for Broward County, Florida, takes the reader on an insider's tour of the details behind Florida's contested presidential election of 2000, and Joan Karp, a chapter president of the League of Women Voters, provides an alternative look at the controversy.

Part 3 focuses on candidates for office and the voters, opening with a chapter on the experiences of women seeking elected office. Gary Aguiar provides his own insights into and interpretation of the various explanations for women's successes and failures in winning office. David Leal provides a comprehensive assessment of the state of minority voting and minority candidates for elected office. Stephen Stambough and Valerie O'Regan pick up on the theme of women in public office with an investigation of female candidates for the office of governor. Part 3 concludes with a case from Minnesotans Steven Wagner and Stephen Frank, who detail Jesse Ventura's maverick campaign, which captured not just the nation's attention but that of the two major parties as well. Jeffrey Kraus brings a wealth of insights to the 2000 U.S. Senate race between Hillary Rodham Clinton and Rick Lazio in his case study of this media frenzy in the Empire State.

The book's conclusion offers investigations of the 2000 congressional elections and 2000 presidential election. Both the chapter on the legislative race by Robert Dewhirst and Keith Gaddie and the chapter on the presidential race by Anthony Eksterowicz provide essential information from the 2000 election while keeping an eye on the future in pondering the consequences of these important, recent elections.

Despite scholars' best efforts to assess emerging trends in campaigns and elections, questions remain unanswered, such as what influences voters' choices and why individuals vote. Indeed, such factors as partisan loyalty, current issues and policy preferences, and a variety of characteristics of individual candidates weigh in on such decisions, as do the geographic, racial, income, and educational characteristics of voters.

Another central question that remains unanswered is the matter of whether elections matter. Arguments persist on both sides, and the question remains pertinent. Elections matter as meaningful vehicles for the public to exert their influence. Elections remain, in general, competitive, and voters have options. The public enjoys the freedom to choose and nearly universal suffrage now. Moreover, supporters maintain, most elections are competently and ethically run, and the ballot is an effective tool for protecting citizen interests and promoting their voices.

However, various critics allege that voting is ineffective.[19] They point out that most major issues in U.S. history have not been resolved through the ballot. Elections are not viable means of expressing views, when the voices of people are heard only once every other year in November, many do not participate, and the choices presented are not real. Such critics often maintain that other political activities are more useful in effecting change, such as writing legislators or organizing community groups. It might even be the case where elections condition the citizenry *away* from politics and away from other more promising social, political, and public activities.

Such challenges remain before us. At the dawn of a new century and after the most intriguing election of modern times, we face new challenges and the prospects of fundamental changes in campaign practices and electoral systems. Consider also that tens of millions of U.S. citizens fail to exercise their fundamental right to vote—presidential election turnout hovers at around 50 percent of eligible voters, and congressional races and state and local elections bring far less people to the polls. These eternally applicable and confounding concerns continue to pique our interest and warrant attention, especially given how little time and effort voting requires from us every two to four years. It is, therefore, an important and good time to study campaigns and elections.

# PART 1

## CURRENT ISSUES IN CAMPAIGNS

In a pure sense, campaigns present voters with information they can use to decide among potential officeholders and policies, whereas elections provide voters with a level of control over officeholders who make the rules under which democracy operates. The state of political campaigns is in constant flux, as the experiences of one election often define the next. The challenge for candidates, scholars, and voters is to stay abreast of the ongoing changes in campaigns and elections.

In the past, campaigns were contests driven in large measure by the political parties, where much of the campaign was conducted face-to-face, with volunteers and the local party supporting candidate activity.[1] Candidates were thus dependent on—and at times handpicked by—the parties. This situation changed with the advent of television and the growth in the number of eligible voters in elections, which spawned the mass media age of televised campaigning.[2] Television enabled candidates to take their messages directly to the voters, and the increase in the pool of voters forced candidates to appeal to a wider populace.

It has been suggested that political campaigns might be undergoing another dramatic change in the early twenty-first century, in the wake of the development of the Internet and its applicability to campaigns.[3] This is to be expected, as with every passing election cycle comes a different cast of candidates who seek public office, along with new campaign workers and consultants, new campaign techniques on both a tactical and strategic level, and new trends that influence candidates and the issues.

The form and substance of political parties has changed over time. As pragmatic and flexible entities, parties have altered their identities, structures, and operations to suit the needs of the contemporary electorate.[4] If one considers that political parties were formed to produce an efficient mass mobilization of voters for several levels of officeholders in their party, then who is to say that parties still do not deliver on their promises? However, modern campaigning has generally exceeded the institutional capacity of political parties.[5] As campaign techniques become increasingly more sophisticated, individual candidates in marginal races take advantage of these methods with or without the assistance and blessings of the party to finely target their efforts.[6] Political parties cannot always offer the specific information and persuasion techniques candidates believe are vital to their chances for victory.[7]

To many, the campaign consulting industry represents an unknown and frequently misunderstood component of political campaigns. Yet, campaigns have used consultants—both volunteers and paid professionals—since the early days of the nation. The first political consultants, for example, were most likely volunteers in the elections of John Adams and Thomas Jefferson, who gave their candidates advice about debating, circulating printed material, making speeches, and getting out the vote. Today, these "campaign warriors," as they are called, are major players in elections for every level of elected office.[8]

With the rise of candidate-centered elections, voters have moved away from partisan cues as the basis for voting, and for better or for worse, consultants have stepped in to fill part of the void. Campaigning and electioneering increasingly make a difference in election outcomes, and, accordingly, so does the profession of political consulting. Candidates and the political parties spend vast amounts of money to make sure that candidates are competitive and win. With each passing election, the consulting industry evolves and redefines itself. Nevertheless, as political scientist James Thurber observes, it is still essential to understand the individuals and their beliefs who play such a major role in the outcome of modern elections. Only by doing so can we understand their importance for modern U.S. democracy.[9]

In spite of the advantage in retaining office enjoyed by incumbents and a general cynicism by the voting public, many elections are close contests won at the margins, often by "niche marketing." This fact makes it all the more important for voters to follow campaigns and scholars to study them. The chapters that follow provide an insightful glimpse into how various methods of modern campaigning, such as polling, are used to carve out such "niches."

The activities of consultants deserve attention because much of what they do usually takes place out of public view. The growing importance of political consultants in campaigns necessitates scholarly study, as does the declining influence of political parties. Yet, it is important to note that consultants are working in tandem with political parties, transforming the way candidates communicate with voters and the way voters judge candidates.[10] David Dulio provides a thorough assessment of the rise of political consulting and its impact on modern campaigns.

In his chapter, Stephen Medvic provides a balanced assessment of the use of pollsters and polling. According to Medvic, it is not simply a matter of polls being used to manipulate the voter or as a replacement for bold leadership, as is often suggested by critics. Some of these allegations are valid, but the work of pollsters also allows elected officials to take the pulse of the electorate. Considering the plurality of opinions existing among the public and criticisms that public officials are out of touch with the public they serve, the value of this service is not to be minimized.

Another emerging force in campaigns and elections is advances in communication technologies. As modes of communication have evolved, so have the venues for campaign advertising, from newspapers to radio and television and the Internet. The number of media outlets for political advertising has expanded since the 1980s—and in so doing has created opportunities for candidates—but so have the range of services they provide and the number of groups using the media to convey information and advance their points of view. In 1934, for instance, voters hoping to turn the tide of the Great Depression backed an unlikely candidate for governor of California: Upton Sinclair, muckraking author of *The Jungle*. Alarmed at the prospects of the lifelong socialist being elected, Sinclair's opponents launched an unprecedented public relations blitzkrieg to discredit him. The result transformed the electoral process, ushering in the era of the "spin doctor" and the "attack ad."[11] The defeat of Sinclair sent a loud and clear message to candidates. Political advertising has become a pervasive medium for candidates, political parties, and special interest groups since Sinclair's gubernatorial campaign. Thus, it becomes all the more important to understand its role and impact on elections.

Computer technology marks another emerging force in campaigns and elections. As the use of computer-driven campaigns invades the electoral process, some candidates have seen fit to embrace it, wiring their campaigns to the information superhighway. Doing so has allowed them to interact with voters through Internet chat rooms, as well as to access an elite audience with high voting behavior. Such technology permits campaigns to efficiently target voters that may yield the most support per dollar spent, provided voters use the Internet for election purposes.[12] Perhaps the most familiar example of a successful use of the Web for electioneering purposes may be Senator John McCain's (R-Ariz.) 2000 presidential campaign, which raised more than $2 million and recruited 26,000 volunteers largely through the Internet.[13]

The Internet is also lowering the cost of entry into campaigns by allowing candidates to create "virtual" headquarters in cyberspace, substituting the expensive hardware of a traditional organization (offices, furniture, fax and copy machines, stationery, and postage). It has the promise to change the way campaigns are conducted and make them accessible to an ever-widening array of possible public servants. Yet, in may ways, the Web is an uncomfortable fit for voters, who still expect candidates to ask for their support, like to meet candidates (and not in cyberspace), and seem to be wedded to traditional forms of campaigning.

There are also challenges for the candidates. Unlike television or radio, for instance, it is difficult to use the Internet to seek out and activate a passive audience; on the Web the audience must already be motivated to search for information. With television and radio, voters do not have to search for a campaign message. But this emerging area of campaigning is still in its infancy, and one can expect new technology and applications to emerge to meet these political challenges. Some textbooks on U.S. politics and even some scholarly books on campaigns provide little, if any, discussion of emerging campaign technologies and the practices to which they give rise. This part of the book features the work of Joshua Whitman and Joseph Perkins, two experts on campaign technologies who have managed numerous campaigns throughout the South. Whitman and Perkins trace the historical evolution of campaign technologies and then offer a detailed lesson on both how to use emerging technologies and their impact on the increasingly scientific practice of campaigning.

The chapters and cases in Part 1 illustrate how the different "tools" of contemporary campaigns are deployed to affect fundraising, strategy, political advertising and communications, and polling. All these lessons and ingredients of campaigns are put together in a case by Robin Kolodny and Sandra Suárez. Kolodny and Suárez profile campaigns for a key congressional district in Pennsylvania and examine how incumbency, party support, issue advocacy, campaign funding, and other factors influence the nature and outcome of the campaign. What is often the ugly side of campaigning—scandal—is the topic of the other case. Edward Yager describes for the reader the political actions of a candidate for local office that resulted in a legal challenge of campaign impropriety. Yager considers whether there is a difference between actually doing the wrong thing in a campaign and giving the appearance of impropriety and documents how such a case comes about and is resolved.

This part of the book, with examples from federal, state, and local elections, shows that each campaign is unique, with its own critical decisions and turning points. Generalizations about campaigns elucidate discernible patterns and trends, but they cannot fully prepare a person for the frontlines of campaigns and elections. As such, the chapters on campaigns are supplemented with cases from real campaigns to give the reader a sense of the nuts and bolts of what occurs in contemporary campaigns.

# 1

## Inside the War Room: Political Consultants in Modern Campaigns

### David A. Dulio

In the fall of 1996, *Time* magazine called professional political consultant Dick Morris "the most influential private citizen in America."[1] Morris was one of the individuals behind President Bill Clinton's rebound after the crushing Republican victories in the 1994 congressional elections and the beginnings of the Whitewater scandal. He would later play a key role in Clinton's successful presidential reelection bid in 1996. Is the fact that a president's "hired gun"—such as Dick Morris—holds such influence an indictment of our electoral system or, more generally, our entire political system? No. Rather, Morris and other so-called "image merchants"—who are modern political consultants—are simply necessary byproducts of modern campaigning.[2] In fact, in some ways, consultants can even help encourage political debate during election campaigns.

## The Development of Political Consulting in the United States

Many students of electioneering and the history of political consulting consider a tandem of California-based political entrepreneurs to have been the first professional political consultants.[3] Clem Whitaker and Leone Smith Baxter started their firm, Campaigns, Inc., in 1933. Their first foray into electioneering was an initiative campaign to defeat a plan put forth by Pacific Gas and Electric, which would have destroyed a plan by the California legislature to create a project designed to control flooding and develop irrigation systems.[4] However, political consulting is much older than this; examples of it can be traced back to ancient Greece, where Quintus Tullius Cicero often provided campaign advice to his brother, Marcus Tullius Cicero.[5] Even in the United States, familiar signs of modern campaign advice and consulting date back many years. Some of the same techniques employed by political consultants of today were used long ago in one particular initiative and referendum campaign, but it was not run by Whitaker and Baxter.

The Federalists and Antifederalists, in their efforts to support and oppose the newly designed Constitution, relied on many of the same techniques that their modern counterparts would begin using over 200 years later. Both sides had advisers working on their behalf, creating strategic action plans to help spread what amounted to campaign messages and to build support up and down the Atlantic seaboard.[6] The Federalists became quite adept at using the "mass media" to spread their messages arguing for the adoption of the Constitution; the mass media at that time, however, simply meant newspapers rather than television and radio. The Federalists and Antifederalists also showed their abilities to run substantial get-out-the-vote (GOTV) efforts. However, their strategies were not focused, as today's GOTV efforts are, on mobilizing voters with rides to the polls or phone calls on election day. What amounted to get-out-the-vote efforts during the late 1700s employed postballot casting attractions. For instance, both Federalists and Antifederalists attracted voters with promises of refreshments after voting. Many times they consisted of rum punch, wine, and beer.[7]

Campaigning and electioneering have undergone serious changes in the years since the earliest campaigners, including a shift from a party-centered and party-dominated type of campaign to the more familiar candidate-centered system. Consultants were a reaction to this and other developments in electoral, political, and social practices in the United States. In particular, they filled a void that was created when parties lost some of their electioneering prowess. As both the electoral and social context changed in the United States, three major developments opened the door and set the stage for the modern consulting industry to take shape.

## From Party-Centered to Candidate-Centered Campaigns

The shift from a party-centered to a candidate-centered electoral order played a major role in the evolution of consulting. During their "golden age," parties controlled nearly all aspects of campaigning. It was party leaders who set campaign strategy and ran the campaigns organizationally. Parties "picked the candidates, gauged public opinion, raised money, disseminated campaign communications, and mobilized voters."[8] In addition, most campaigns were run in a similar manner—candidates and their surrogates campaigned on a face-to-face basis and asked for votes with a handshake. Even when individual campaign advisers began to appear, they were strictly from the party mold. As is well documented, parties have lost a good deal of their electoral power over time. The first blows to parties' electoral dominance occurred during the early 1890s with the rise of the Progressive movement, which, among other things, did away with the party patronage system and instituted the direct primary.[9] With a strong patronage system in place, the party had control not only of candidate recruitment and party elites but of the rank and file members as well.

In the aftermath of the Progressive movement, parties were "no longer able to distribute government jobs or contracts, . . . and had difficulty maintaining large corps of campaign workers."[10] The initiation of the direct primary, however, was an even stronger blow to party dominance because it took candidate recruitment away from the party elite and gave it to the rank and file, which by the 1920s did not have strong ties to the party because of the demise of patronage.

The impact of these reforms on the future of campaign consultants was great. Among other things, the reforms "encouraged candidates to develop their own campaign organizations" that were separate from the party structure.[11] Candidates saw that they needed to look elsewhere for help in their campaigns, marking one of the most important shifts toward the present candidate-centered electoral order.[12]

### Expansion of the Electorate

The second change in political practices that helped create a need for professional political consultants was the great growth in the electorate that occurred between 1932 and 1976. During this forty-four year period, the voting age population more than doubled, increasing from a total potential electorate of 75.7 million in 1932 to one of 152.3 million in 1976.[13] It meant that parties and candidates could no longer campaign the way they once did or in the ways that were familiar to them. "Party organizations, designed for campaigning to a limited electorate on a personal basis, were not an efficient means for reaching [the] . . . growing pool of voters."[14] By the middle part of the twentieth century, candidates found that they could not personally reach every potential voter. They had to look for a new way to talk to voters, and they had to look beyond parties for help and assistance in campaign communications.

This help came in the form of professional political consultants. After Whitaker and Baxter founded their business, "the campaign management industry grew rather slowly. A few companies went in and out of business shortly after World War II, and some public relations and advertising firms started accepting political campaign clients in the late 1940s. [But it was not until] the 1950s [that] there was a slow but steady expansion."[15] Generally, the growth of the industry tracked with the increase in the size of the electorate.[16] Thus the appearance of professional consultants was mainly a reaction to other contextual changes surrounding electioneering. In addition, consultants did not begin to appear in large numbers of races until after parties had lost some electoral power and left a void that candidates desperately needed filled.

### Advances in Technology

Not only were parties unable to meet the demands of candidates who now had to communicate with much larger numbers of voters, but they could not keep up with the technological advances that were finding their way into electioneering. The introduction of television in the 1950s had a tremendous effect on society in general, and it had a profound effect on the way elections were conducted from that point forward. The introduction of and subsequent domination by television in campaigns meant that candidate demand for technical assistance in their campaigns rose, and it was only outside professionals who could provide that advice and assistance.

The demand for the modern consultant with sophisticated technical knowledge and experience was enhanced by the fact that party organizations had neither the staff nor the skills necessary to help candidates when the new technology emerged. Parties were designed to and were successful at campaigning in a face-to-face manner; they were ill-suited for the mass media and mass communication–style campaigns that were developing. Those who could give candidates the help they needed were advertisers from Madison Avenue, who had been using the same kind of strategies to sell commercial products.

As one would expect, this style of campaigning and the use of specialized consultants began at the highest levels of elective office and spread to lower levels. President Dwight D. Eisenhower's 1952 campaign was the first to use television extensively, but it was not long after when all presidential candidates began to rely on it, as would many Senate candidates. From the early 1960s to the mid-1980s, the use of television and political consultants gradually expanded to where it is today, with a majority of candidates for federal and statewide office relying on television as the main medium for communicating with voters.

## Modern Political Consulting

Driven by the changes in electioneering that have taken place, especially since the 1950s, modern political consultants have become a fixture in campaigns. Elections are approaching a point at which no serious candidate at any level will embark on a campaign without having hired a consultant—or at least without specific plans to hire one in the near future. In fact, the presence of consultants in elections is increasing, as they are becoming involved in more races. But the modern political consulting industry is made up of more than just pollsters and media consultants, in spite of what conventional wisdom or popular press accounts would have us believe. Professional consultants today offer a wide range of services to their clients, who could be candidates, parties, or interest groups who run independent expenditure campaigns.

The services that the professional consulting industry offers are many, and the range of these services has expanded as consultants have become a more integral part of electioneering and technology has advanced. Many of the early consultants in the modern era offered general strategic advice to candidates because the party was no longer there to provide that kind of assistance. However, with the advent of campaigning technologies such as radio and then television, the development of scientific polling, and the use of computers to both identify and target voters, campaigning became more technical. As a result, "candidates began to turn to persons who possessed the requisite skills to market candidates through other media."[17] The general strategist needed help, and it "came in the form of specialized experts, and the evolution of campaign technology . . . witnessed an increasingly sophisticated craftsmanship."[18]

Today, candidates, parties, and interest groups can hire consultants who specialize in anything from media production, survey research, and direct mail voter contact to media buying (the placement of television advertisements), grassroots organizing, telephone banks, political website design, and many other services.[19] Therefore, a modern political consultant can be defined as an individual or firm that provides services and/or advice to clients on a fee-for-service basis (i.e., they are not permanent employees) during an election cycle and does so for more than one candidate, political party, or organized interest group over the course of more than one election cycle.[20]

There are three important parts of this definition. First, modern consultants provide specific services and are hired to do specific things for their clients. The industry is such that there are no more one-stop shopping alternatives for candidates. Second, modern consultants have longevity in the industry—the college professor who does a poll for a friend who is running for city council or the state legislature from his or her home office is not a professional. Third, the product that the consultant provides to the client can either be a tangible service such as a poll or television commercial, strategic advice for the campaign, or both. Consultants can be broken down into three rough categories—strategists, specialists, and vendors—based on their main service area.[21]

## Strategist Consultants

The most recognizable types of consultants are likely the strategist consultants, who are mainly media consultants, pollsters, and direct mail specialists, as well as general consultants, if one is hired. These professionals are political consultants in the truest sense of the term, for they are generally the ones who consult with the candidate and his or her campaign team on a regular basis. They are also the main creative and political minds behind a candidate's or an interest group's campaign, insofar as they are the ones who help to develop the client's strategy, theme, and message for the campaign. In other words, these individuals or firms provide both tangible services *and* strategic advice to their clients.

The specialization that has occurred in the industry does not mean that consultants who specialize in creating television spots do nothing else or that pollsters only conduct survey research. Consultants also offer their clients strategic advice on how best to win a campaign. For example, along with the candidate, campaign manager, and general consultant, the pollster often works with the media and direct mail specialists to craft the campaign's message. Specialist consultants do not simply provide the campaign with a product and then leave the candidate and campaign manager to put the different pieces together. Rather, the strategic consultants on the campaign team pool their collective thoughts and political expertise to craft and refine the campaign's strategy, theme, and message, and to make a plan on how best to disseminate that message during the campaign.

The move toward specialization is one of the most important developments in modern consulting. The earliest consultants focused mainly on strategic advice, and when they did offer services, they tended to do everything the campaign needed. For example, Whitaker and Baxter, the tandem who opened the first political consulting firm, also operated an advertising agency to place ads for clients, a political news bureau that maintained news contacts around the state, and a research wing that drafted preliminary research reports on candidates and issues. Consultants at this time offered a number of different services to clients. In other words, these consultants were the Home Depots of campaign services.

Modern professionals, however, cultivate a relationship with their clients that includes the provision of a very specialized product, as well as the advice on how best to use that product, whether it be a poll, television spot, or direct mail piece. But that was not the case as the move toward specialization developed. The first strategist consultants, who specialized in one area of electioneering, were strictly service providers, and "in some instances the professionals merely execute[d] the technical details of [strategies] decided by others."[22] For example, "Many [polling] firms [used to] simply supply statistical tables with little or no interpretation."[23] However, as the industry continued to grow in size and therefore competitiveness, firms found that they had to offer clients more. Many strategist consultants today market their firms as "full service." In today's context, however, full service does not mean one-stop shopping for all campaign needs; rather it refers to a consultant or firm that provides additional support to their product in the form of analysis or strategic advice. For example, the modern pollster not only writes a survey instrument and analyzes the data but also interprets the findings and talks to the other consultants and members of the campaign team about what aspects of the data are most promising for the campaign's message. In short, today's strategist consultants do not leave their clients blowing in the wind, trying to figure out what to do with survey data or film from a media shoot.

### Specialist Consultants

The second category of consultants—the specialists—are also integral to any candidate's or interest group's campaign but they are less likely to be involved in the planning and development of a strategy, theme, and message. Opposition researchers and fundraisers are certainly important to any campaign that is going to be successful, but they do not generally "form the strategic core of services."[24] The information and data presented to the campaign by the opposition researcher (many times, this function is performed by a political party or party committee) will likely be part of the campaign's strategy, theme, and message, but the individual consultant is normally not involved in the creative aspect of the message. Specialist consultants also provide campaigns with services such as telephone banks for voter identification and get-out-the-vote contact, and buy television and radio airtime for the campaign's commercials.[25]

### Vendor Consultants

Finally, there are the political vendors. These individuals and firms also provide critical information and data to campaigns, but that is all they do. One can argue that they are not consultants at all, given the fact that they contribute services such as printing campaign literature, compiling lists of voters that direct mail consultants will use in targeting specific groups of potential voters, and website design. Rather, these individuals and firms provide materials and services (voter files, websites, etc.) that strategist consultants need in order to craft and disseminate a campaign's message.

The fact that vendors do not have an integral part in deciding the strategy, theme, and message of a campaign does not mean that they are not essential to the campaign's success, however. For example, any hard-hitting comparative direct mail piece would be useless without a list with the names and addresses of potential voters in a district or state that is provided by a voter file vendor. In addition, polling data would not be readily available or attainable without the calling house that places all the phone calls and collects the data. Without vendors, other consultants could not do their jobs.

## The Work of Consultants

Of course, not all consultants fit nicely into one of these three categories. The duties of different consultants are more like a continuum on which different consultants range from strategist to vendor. Some may even change categories depending on the campaign and the services needed. For example, some campaigns may call on their media consultant to be more involved in the planning of the campaign, whereas others may want less input. Some campaigns may involve the opposition researcher in strategy meetings at the beginning of the campaign to get their input on the message the campaign will pursue. It all depends on the needs and wants of the individual campaign.

The consultants who make up a campaign's strategic core and those who work with the campaign on a regular basis also provide other services. Although the relationship that consultants build with candidates is only temporary, it does not mean that it is not an intimate one.[26] The relationship often moves beyond simple strategic advice: an additional "duty" for consultants might be to act as the candidate's "psychotherapist," as one Democratic media consultant described it.[27] Therefore, although the modern consultant has developed into a specialized service provider in one sense, the modern professional has also begun to offer clients a wider range of services, including some that would never have crossed the minds of Whitaker and Baxter in the 1930s.

The nonstrategic nature of many of the services delivered by vendors (or even some specialists) potentially allows many of them to work for clients on both sides of the aisle and increase their business volume.[28] However, a consultant who works for clients of both political parties is rare in the modern consulting world—Dick Morris is an anomaly.[29] That is only another reason *not* to consider vendors "consultants" in the truest sense of the term, as true consultants tend to stick with one party or the other, for the same reasons that candidates and elected officials rarely switch parties— they are ideologues who hold strong beliefs on issues and policies.

## Why Consultants Do What They Do

Empirical data on modern consultants show that consultants are driven by their own ideology and policy concerns. In a 1999 survey of the consulting industry, a majority (54 percent) of consultants reported that their main reason for getting into the business was their own political beliefs or ideology.[30] Another 8 percent said that they became consultants to help their party gain (or retain) majority status in government. The money that one might earn as a consultant was only mentioned by 11 percent of all consultants. These data contradict the conventional wisdom surrounding political consultants— much of which relies only on speculation rather than empirical data and is either dated or found in the popular press. These data also answer one of the loudest criticisms of modern campaign consultants—that these professionals are driven to a large extent by money and the opportunity to line their pockets.[31] Wealth and power do not draw most political consultants to the industry; they are motivated by issues, policy, and a desire to see their party control government.[32]

Further evidence of this motivation is provided by data that show that many consultants also take a candidate's politics into account when deciding whether to take him or her as a client. Consider the words of Republican consultant Robert Goodman: "I am interested in that candidate. . . . It is very psychological. . . . Election night is the worst night of the year for us unless all [my candidates] win."[33] A solid majority (60 percent) of consultants report that a candidate's political beliefs are very important when deciding whether to take on that candidate as a client. Nearly 40 percent reported that the candidate's ability to govern effectively once in office also mattered very much. Further, only 16 percent said that a candidate's chances of winning were very important to that decision. Consultants on both sides of the aisle report that their conscience influences their choice of clients. For example, Democrat Joseph Cerrell will not take a client that he would "have trouble voting for."[34] Republican Douglas Bailey turned down the chance to work on Richard Nixon's 1968 campaign for president, arguing that he did not want to work for a candidate he could not vote for; he also said that unless he "generally shared the candidate's philosophy, [he] would feel so uncomfortable [that] it would be a nonproductive and unpleasant relationship with the client."[35] Additionally, over half the consultants in the 1999 survey said that they had worked for a candidate they were eventually sorry to see in office, citing broken campaign promises, a changed position on an issue, or a new political philosophy once in office.[36]

## How Consultants Are Used in Campaigns

Professional political consultants have begun to find a place in campaigns of all shapes, sizes, and electoral levels. From campaigns for the presidency to the school board, consultants have made their presence felt, giving advice and helping candidates reach and communicate with voters. At the highest level of campaigning, consultants are seemingly omnipresent. Both George W. Bush and Al Gore assembled large teams of political professionals during the 2000 election: a total of twenty-six and twenty-one consultants or firms worked for the Bush and Gore campaigns respectively in some capacity.[37] These consultants ran the gamut from pure strategists (media, polling, mail, and general) to pure vendor consultants who contributed nonstrategic services such as telemarketing and help with filing Federal Election Commission reports.

Similar teams of consultants (although not nearly as large) are hired by nearly every candidate for federal or statewide office. Candidates for the U.S. Senate, U.S. House of Representatives, or governor assemble teams of consultants that usually consist of pollsters, media consultants, direct mail specialists, and fundraisers. Estimates of consultant use show that more and more candidates at the highest levels are seeking the help of professionals.[38] For example, Edie Goldenberg and Michael Traugott estimate that in House elections during the 1978 election cycle, only 9 percent of all candidates used a professional manager, and 39 percent hired a media consultant.[39] Compare these percentages to estimates from 1990, which suggest that 46.3 percent of all House candidates hired at least one consultant; that figure had risen to 63.7 percent by 1992[40] and almost 70 percent by 1998.[41]

Not all types of candidates are as prone to hiring a consultant. Those candidates in the most competitive races are more likely than those who are involved in a lopsided race. For example, open seat candidates, incumbents facing a tough reelection bid, and hopeful challengers hire consultants with greater frequency than do incumbents who run unopposed or with little competition or challengers with little chance of winning.[42] However, all serious candidates for office at the national level hire a cadre of consultants to run their campaigns. Even incumbent officeholders in safe seats or districts, who might not even have to campaign, often retain the services of a pollster so they can keep their finger on the pulse of their district or state.

In more recent years, candidates in down ballot races (state legislature, judge, mayor, city council, etc.) have found that they, too, can benefit greatly from the help of a political consultant. Today, candidates for mayor, state legislature, and city council also run professional campaigns that often employ pollsters and message delivery consultants (media or mail). Candidates of any kind can benefit from the assistance of a pollster, who helps them test and refine messages. Many candidates for down ballot races cannot afford to buy the television time necessary to wage an "air war" but turn to direct mail consultants to help them spread their messages. However, the candidates who can raise enough money—candidates for mayor of large cities or well-financed candidates running for state legislature—do utilize television commercials and turn to media consultants for their technical expertise and strategic advice.

For example, the well-known Republican polling firm of Wirthlin Worldwide (Richard Wirthlin was President Ronald Reagan's pollster) has done survey research for candidates running for sheriff in places such as Charlotte City and Palm Beach City, Florida.[43] Furthermore, "City council candidates in San Marcos, California, mayoral candidates in Huntsville, Alabama, and Warren, Michigan, and a circuit court clerk candidate in Chesapeake, Virginia, were assisted by professional consultants" in their recent bids for office.[44] In fact, there is such great demand at the local and state level today that some professional consulting firms deal solely in those types of races.[45] Some consultants look to down ballot races because they find the work more challenging and interesting, as "their focus is outside the beltway and the obsessively federal perspective" that is masked as "national" politics, says one Democratic consultant.[46]

## Political Consultants: Democracy's Help or Hindrance?

Although political consultants have begun to attract more attention from both scholars and journalists, much of this attention comes in the form of criticism. Consultants have been indicted for bringing about or exacerbating a number of problems surrounding elections in the United States:

> Political professionals and their techniques have helped homogenize American politics, added significantly to campaign costs, lengthened campaigns, and narrowed the focus of elections. Consultants have emphasized personality and gimmickry over issues, often exploiting emotional and negative themes rather than encouraging rational discussion.[47]

A full examination of these charges is beyond the scope of this chapter, but an empirical examination of many of these indictments shows that many of the claims are unfounded and that consultants are not the scourge on elections that their critics claim. Rather, in some ways, consultants can even benefit the electoral process.

Take for example the claim that political consultants have driven up the cost of campaigns. This criticism of consultants is based mainly on speculation. Although it is convenient to place the blame for rapidly rising campaign costs on political professionals by saying that they brought expensive techniques and tactics—mainly television but also computers, polling, and direct mail—to campaigns, the reality is that the move toward mass-media-based communications was inevitable. Not only were candidates and parties reacting to the growing electorate, but the nation as a whole was heading in this general direction. In addition, the first modern consultants did not impose technical communications and strategic techniques on candidates; there was a demand coming from candidates for these types of services. Again, it was a reaction to the changing context that surrounded elections in the United States.

More money is spent in elections today than ever before. During the 2000 election cycle, over $3 billion was spent by campaigners (candidates, parties, and interest groups).[48] By far the largest chunk of this pie was devoted to television advertisements—one estimate places the total spending on political advertising between January 1 and November 7, 2000, at nearly $1 billion.[49] Moreover, such spending is on the rise: "Political advertisers spent five times more on broadcast television ads in 2000 than they did in 1980."[50] Critics of consultants argue that much of this spending ended up in the pockets of media consultants in the form of fees or commissions. However, a careful examination of the spending illustrates nearly all of these dollars go *through* consultants, rather than *to* consultants. Some estimates find that more than 65 percent of a campaign's budget goes for advertising on television.[51] Granted, media consultants usually take a commission that ranges from between 7 and 15 percent on the advertising time that is bought for the commercials they make, but the lion's share of this money goes to television stations in the form of fees for airtime.[52]

Professional political consultants are also often saddled with much of the blame for the so-called negative tone of the political debate in the United States today. This charge is found mostly in the advertising that candidates, parties, and interest groups do over the course of a campaign. Critics have said that negative advertisements are "debasing democracy,"[53] and that if the trend continues, the "very future of democratic self-government may be threatened."[54] Claims like these have lead to "increasing worries that America's campaigns fall short of providing citizens with the information necessary to evaluate the merits of competing candidates and their policy proposals."[55]

It is easy to see how consultants' critics attribute the alleged consequences of negative campaigning to professional campaigners because this type of campaign is mainly associated with television commercials that are developed and made by political consultants.[56] Similarly, critics charge that "consultants have a tendency to foster ambiguity and symbolism rather than choice and accountability."[57] However, the blame on consultants is misdirected for two reasons. First, negative advertising has been around in the United States for well over 150 years. One need look no farther than the racist messages and antireligious tones in political cartoons of the mid-1800s (which were the equivalent of political advertisements during the times of partisan newspapers).[58] Second, by creating negative ads, consultants may be helping democracy by actually *lifting* the debate.

Conventional wisdom automatically assumes that, in the dichotomy of positive and negative advertising and campaigning, the former is more desirable than the latter. Recent scholarship has begun to challenge this dichotomy by arguing that there is a third category of advertisement defined as contrast ads, which are usually considered to be negative.[59] The messages consultants tend to help create during modern campaigns follow this comparative mold and try to highlight issues on which their candidate has a comparative advantage with the opponent.[60] Under the traditional dichotomy of positive and negative ads, these comparative ads are commingled with truly negative ads and linked to political consultants.

Although the definition of negative campaigning can be ambiguous, less debatable is the actual content of the ads consultants help to make. Recent work by Kathleen Hall Jamieson and her colleagues have argued that "attack is a useful component of political discourse and should be encouraged, not discouraged, as long as it is fair, accurate, relevant to governance, and accompanied by advocacy."[61] This work has shown that television commercials classified as "attack" and "contrast"—ads for which consultants are blamed and that are normally considered negative—actually contain and convey to viewers *more* useful policy and issue content than pure "advocacy" or positive ads.[62]

## Conclusion

Political consultants are here to stay, and they are likely only to become more important for and prevalent in candidates', parties', and interest groups' campaigns. Unlike the earliest political advisers and consultants, the modern professional has no ties to the party organization and is an independent businessperson. Political consultants today offer their clients a large array of services, without which many would not be able to campaign as efficiently or as effectively as they do. More and more candidates are recognizing this fact and turning to professionals for help in their campaigns.

# 2

## Campaign Pollsters and Polling: Manipulating the Voter or Taking the Electorate's Pulse?

### Stephen K. Medvic

*Today, the opinion pollster has become the strategic center of most campaigns.*

—Democratic pollster Pat Cadell

Polls are ubiquitous in U.S. politics today. They tell us where the people stand on the issues of the day, gauge the public mood, record the popularity and approval of elected officials, and identify the electoral preferences of "likely voters." In this chapter I focus specifically on polling in the context of election campaigns. Though seemingly every group with an interest in elections conducts polls—the media, candidates and elected officials, political parties, interest groups, and universities or research centers— I examine what are called "private" polls, those taken for candidates (and to some extent parties) rather than those conducted by the media or by universities (i.e., "public" polls).[1]

After tracing the historical evolution of polling in U.S. campaigns, I discuss the state of campaign polling. Among other issues, I address the types of public opinion research currently used in campaigns, the role of pollsters in setting campaign strategy, and future trends in polling. Finally, I turn to opposing perspectives on the impact of polling on the democratic process.

## A Short Historical Overview of Campaign Polling

In some respects, polling is still a relatively new addition to the campaigner's toolbox. It was not until the 1930s that systematic attention began to be paid to the public's attitudes, and even then the impetus came from the media and not from politicians. Around the same time, campaign management began to develop as a vocation. But it would be another three decades before these two activities merged into the industry that we know today as professional political polling. In order to review the historical development of polling in campaigns, therefore, it is necessary to briefly sketch the origins of scientific public opinion polling and professional political consulting.

### The Rise of Scientific Polling

The story of how public opinion polling came into existence is well known.[2] Prior to the 1930s, the most common way to measure public opinion was with a "straw poll." Straw polls are unscientific polls in which the pollster has very little or no control over who the respondents are. There can be multiple sources of bias in such polls, and there is no way to ensure that the poll results are representative.

Though straw polls were used as far back as 1824, the most famous was the *Literary Digest* poll.[3] First conducted in 1916, the *Digest* poll correctly predicted the presidential elections from its inception through 1932.[4] In 1936, however, the *Digest* incorrectly predicted a landslide for Alf Landon.[5] Explanations of the mistaken prediction are legion.[6] Though it is beyond the scope of this chapter to explore the problems in detail, suffice it to say that the *Digest* got responses from people who were not representative of the electorate.[7]

While the *Digest* was making a monumental error, three separate polls in 1936—by Elmo Roper, Archibald Crossley, and George Gallup—correctly predicted a victory for Franklin Delano Roosevelt.[8] In fact, using the same lists as the magazine, Gallup estimated in July 1936 that the *Digest* would predict Landon's share of the vote to be 56 percent.[9] Amazingly, Landon received 55 percent of the *Digest*'s sample. The ability not only to avoid the *Digest*'s 1936 error in one's own poll but to forecast that blunder made "scientific polling" an industry unto itself and obliterated all confidence in "straw polling."

The success of scientific polling suggested to some that polling was perhaps the most democratic method of arriving at the will of the people.[10] Further, the pollsters' correct predictions in the 1940 and 1944 elections convinced almost everyone that polling was an exact science. But disaster struck the polling world once again, when in 1948 the major pollsters predicted a win for Thomas Dewey over Harry S Truman.[11] Unlike the *Literary Digest,* which folded within two years of its error, the major pollsters stayed in business, learned from their mistakes, and strengthened their methodology. In fact, though most politicians remained skeptical about the value of paying for private polling, some candidates began using polls in their campaigns in the 1950s.

## The Emergence of Professional Campaign Management

Perhaps not entirely without coincidence, just as scientific polling was making its mark, professional campaign management began to emerge. The first campaign consultants, as we would call them today, began operation in California in the 1930s. Clem Whitaker and Leone Smith Baxter were hired to defeat an initiative drafted by the Pacific Gas and Electric Company.[12] Campaigns, Inc., the campaign management firm that Whitaker and Baxter created, went on to win seventy of the seventy-five campaigns they handled.[13] In doing so, they revolutionized the way campaigns were run. Specifically, they were the first managers to be hired from outside the party organizations.

By the early 1960s, a nascent political consulting industry had formed.[14] Over the course of that decade, political consulting rapidly became a full-fledged industry. Use of professional campaign services by candidates for the U.S. House of Representatives grew by 842 percent between the periods 1952–1957 and 1964–1969.[15] In 1970, no fewer than 150 House candidates hired professional management firms. The industry even created its own professional organization in 1969 (i.e., the American Association of Political Consultants). By the early 1990s, according to one estimate, nearly 63 percent of all House candidates would hire at least one professional political consultant.[16]

It has been argued that the major impetus for the growth of the consulting industry was the "decline of political parties" and the rise of "candidate-centered" campaigns.[17] This perspective maintains that, for a variety of reasons, parties became weak in the 1960s and 1970s and were unable to provide the level of campaign assistance they had in the past.[18] As a result, candidates became responsible for nearly all aspects of their campaigns. In order to fill the void, consultants emerged and soon became essential to candidates' campaign organizations. Though the argument is not without its critics, it seems clear that consultants offered candidates something parties could not, or simply did not, offer.[19]

In particular, consultants quickly became experts in campaign technology. Whereas early campaign professionals were "generalists" who could offer advice on all aspects of campaigning, consultants eventually specialized in specific areas of campaigns, such as advertising, polling, and fundraising. As campaign technology grew increasingly sophisticated, consultants became all the more indispensable.

### The Ascension of Campaign Pollsters

Given the nearly simultaneous rise of polling and of professional political consulting, it would appear inevitable that those two historical developments would culminate in the private use of professional pollsters in campaigns. What might not have been foreseen is the central role pollsters eventually assumed as campaign strategists. In this section, I briefly trace the confluence of public polling and professional consulting into private campaign polling.

To be sure, candidates have long found ways of taking the pulse of the public. In the early nineteenth century, party activists began carrying out systematic canvasses of voters in towns and districts throughout New England. "By the late nineteenth century," historian Richard Jensen notes, "the art of canvassing had been perfected and was widely utilized by astute politicians and major parties alike."[20] Of course, the focus of these canvasses was to gauge the electorate's voting intention—or what today is referred to as the "horse race"—and not to measure attitudes on key issues of the day.

As polling became more sophisticated, candidates began to realize that polls could assist them in their campaign efforts. Although some political operatives called for a greater use of polls in campaigns as early as the 1950s, most candidates remained skeptical until the 1960s.[21] In fact, according to the late pollster William Hamilton, pollsters were not routinely brought into campaigns until the mid-1960s.[22] Estimates by Louis Harris, however, suggested that many statewide campaigns were using pollsters by the early 1960s. Harris argued, "During the 1962 campaign it is likely that over two-thirds of the men running for the U.S. Senate had polls conducted for them, probably three-quarters of the candidates for governor employed polling from a professional organization, and about one congressional candidate in ten used survey research in his campaign for election."[23] In addition, a survey of elected officials involved in competitive races (i.e., those in which the opposition received more than 40 percent of the vote) in 1966 revealed the following: eleven of thirteen governors who responded hired independent professional pollsters, as did twenty-seven of thirty-two senators and fifty-nine of 135 members of Congress.[24]

According to Hamilton, 1967 marks the beginning of the first era of modern campaign polling.[25] What distinguishes this era, which ended in 1978, was the extensive use of pollsters by all candidates, not just incumbents or those for statewide office. In a study of eighty-six congressional campaigns in 1978, Edie Goldenberg and Michael Traugott found that 74 percent of incumbents, 61 percent of challengers, and 80 percent of open seat candidates relied either "very much" or "quite a bit" on polling data.[26] Though not all that polling was conducted by professional pollsters, Goldenberg and Traugott suggest that this level of usage was "much higher than observed in past studies, a sign of the increasing professionalism and sophistication of congressional campaign techniques."[27]

More important, by the end of this first era, pollsters "had won a seat at the strategy table."[28] I will have more to say about the strategic role of consultants in the next section of the chapter. For now, suffice it to say that prior to the 1970s, pollsters were simply number crunchers who provided analyses of raw data but had little say in the strategic implications of such analyses. That was because polls at the time took too long to conduct to be used for tactical or strategic modifications. Thus, all that polls could provide was a broad perspective on how the campaign was going at a given point in time. Once polls could be completed quickly, they could be used in something approaching an ongoing basis. That, in turn, meant that pollsters would have a more prominent place in campaign inner circles.

The current era of modern polling began in 1979. During this period of time, rapid changes in technology allowed pollsters to offer an array of information-gathering techniques (discussed below). As a result, the use of pollsters continued to grow. Paul Herrnson found that in the 1990s, 55 to 60 percent of all House candidates hired professional pollsters.[29] In addition to the increasing sophistication of the pollsters' craft and the growth of its use, the centrality of the pollster in the campaign has recently solidified. Today, serious candidates for major offices routinely hire pollsters even before announcing their candidacies.

## Current Polling Practices

Like most of what happens behind the scenes in campaigns, polling is shrouded in mystery. Most voters have never been contacted by a pollster, and few understand the mechanics of polling. Furthermore, even those who agree to answer a poll are unsure about how their responses will be used. In this section I explain what pollsters do and describe how polling is employed in campaigns.

### The Pollster's Arsenal

There are three types of polls conducted by pollsters for candidates. A "benchmark" poll is the campaign's first poll. It "gives a detailed analysis of the strengths and weaknesses, opportunities and dangers of the campaign ahead."[30] This poll is generally much longer (as many as 100 questions) and includes far more respondents than other campaign polls. William Hamilton and Dave Beattie suggest that the benchmark "should be conducted before communication with voters begins," or ten to twelve months before the election.[31]

Regardless of when it is done, the benchmark will consist of five essential elements: the political mood of the electorate, the voters' attitudes on important issues, the voters' attitudes on the candidates' personalities, perceptions of the sponsoring candidate's (i.e., the one paying for the poll) weaknesses, and reactions to potential arguments against the opponent.[32]

This information is then used to develop campaign strategy. The cost of a benchmark ranges from roughly $14,000 in a congressional race to $24,000 in a midsized statewide race.[33]

Here I would like to note that campaign pollsters are not interested in the responses of a random sample of the entire population or even of all eligible voters. Instead, pollsters "screen" potential respondents to identify "likely voters." They do so by asking a series of questions, which differ from pollster to pollster, about things such as the respondent's voting history, interest in the outcome of the upcoming election, level of attention paid to the campaign, and self-reported likelihood to vote in the election. Doing this allows pollsters to gathering information from a sample of people who the campaign can be fairly certain will vote on election day.

Along the way, the campaign will want to determine how the strategy is working or how to react to changes in the strategic environment. In these instances, "trend" or "brushfire" polls are conducted. These polls are shorter than benchmarks (no more than fifty questions) but have the same number of respondents. A typical campaign for statewide office will conduct between two and four brushfire polls at a cost of $12,000–$15,000 each; congressional campaigns will use one to two brushfires at a cost of $8,000 each.[34]

Finally, for campaigns that can afford it, daily "tracking" polls are used near the end of the campaign. Tracking often begins a month before election day and consists of short surveys (roughly twenty to twenty-five questions), with a fraction of the total sample interviewed each night. For instance, in a race for the U.S. House, the total sample size might be 400. Each night, 100 people would be polled and would replace the 100 who had been polled four nights earlier. The result is a "rolling average" that allows the campaign to track subtle changes in the electorate. These polls are particularly good for measuring the impact of campaign ads and other forms of campaign communication. For a statewide campaign (using a sample size of 700), the cost of tracking polls is roughly $9,500 per week; for congressional campaigns, the cost is approximately $6,000 per week.[35]

One of the advantages of polls is that they enable campaigns to generalize about the electorate as a whole. Snapshots of the electorate at any point in time, they offer a quantitative summary of where the campaign stands at that moment. But although the pictures polls provide are sweeping, they are not subtle. This is not to say they are not deep. As pollster Allan Rivlin has noted, polls can be like X rays; "an X-ray reveals the underlying structure—and that structure remains, even if the surface expression changes."[36] When polls "reach the level of deeply held beliefs and values that are durable," they can "lead to insights and strategies with lasting value."[37] Yet questions and responses on polls are written by the pollster, and respondents rarely get an opportunity to put things in their own words. To put a fine point on survey results or get a qualitative account of certain segments of the electorate, campaigns often use "focus groups."

Focus groups are made up of ten to twelve participants who are chosen based on some important characteristic they all share that is relevant to the campaign: race, ethnicity, sex, age, party identification, ideology, or vote preference. It is important to note that the focus group is not intended to be a representative sample of the entire electorate or even a representative sample of the group in question. It is simply a group of people with some relevant characteristic in common who are willing to express their opinions on a range of matters.

Campaigns conduct focus groups with those segments of the electorate they deem crucial to victory. Ideally, at least two sessions would be held with members of each targeted group. The total number of focus groups conducted is based on the size of the district or state, the number of targeted groups, and, of course, the amount of money the campaign can spend. Focus groups cost around $5,000, so the total can add up quickly.[38]

The goal of a focus group is to "determine what citizens know, what they comprehend, and the language that will fit their understanding."[39] Sometimes focus groups reveal preferences, attitudes, or values that were hidden from the pollster (or that need to be verified with a representative sample). More often, they indicate the way in which ordinary voters talk about politics. Thus, campaigns use focus groups in one of two ways—they can help the campaign decide where (or on what) to place emphasis, or they can help ascertain the most effective phraseology to be used in making campaign appeals. Of course, candidates and pollsters insist that focus groups do not, contrary to popular belief, determine the issue position of the candidate (nor, for that matter, do polls).

In addition to polls and focus groups, there are a few other ways to tap public opinion. One technique is called the "dial meter." These meters, which can be used in conjunction with focus groups but are more often used in "dial groups" of up to 100 participants, gauge reactions to campaign commercials and speeches. The device consists of a dial that is marked from 0 to 100 and is connected to a computer. As participants view an ad or listen to a speech, they turn the dial toward 0 if their response is negative and toward 100 if it is positive (50 is neutral). The computer aggregates the reactions and graphs the results, allowing the pollster to determine which parts of the ad or speech were viewed favorably and which were not (see Figure 2.1). Following the dial group, some pollsters conduct focus groups to determine why participants responded as they did.

There are classic examples of focus and dial groups influencing campaign decisionmaking. The 1992 Bush reelection team assembled a dial group in Chicago to view the president's State of the Union address. The group consisted of voters who supported Bush in 1988 but were undecided

**Figure 2.1  Hypothetical Dial Meter Results for a Speech**

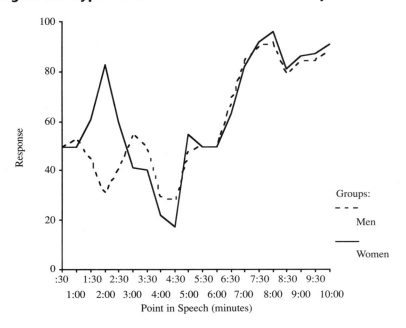

in 1992. According to one report, the speech's "most dramatic lines provoked little or no wrist action from the group."[40] Near the end of the speech, however, a line about government being too big and spending too much got an average response of 94, the highest in the entire speech. The next day, the Bush campaign shot a commercial with the president saying, "My [economic] plan will work without big government spending."[41]

The Clinton campaign that year was equally committed to focus groups. As the infamous Gennifer Flowers story broke, the campaign was caught off guard when reporters mobbed Clinton as he entered the front lobby of a factory. The resulting images on the nightly news appeared damaging. But when focus groups saw the stories, they appreciated Clinton taking on the media rather than avoiding it. The result, according to Clinton pollster Stanley Greenberg, was to adopt a "meet the press strategy": "We always went in the front door, not the back."[42]

Focus and dial groups are particularly useful for pretesting the impact of campaign ads. Participants viewing a spot before it runs can alert a campaign to potential pitfalls (e.g., misinterpretation or backlash) or to particularly ineffective ads. Because people have a tendency to say they dislike "attack" ads when asked directly, focus groups are best used with positive commercials or to guard against the use of a negative ad that produces extremely critical reactions.[43]

In addition to pretesting ads with focus groups, campaigns with considerable funds have recently turned to "mall testing" commercials. Here, campaign staff set up operations in a mall kiosk. When individuals agree to participate, they are asked a few preliminary questions, view various versions of ads, and complete a few follow-up questions. Responses, which can total upward of 200 at a single mall per evening, are entered into a computer, allowing for nearly instant analysis.[44]

The tools of the pollster's trade can be expensive. Yet public opinion research, according to Hamilton and Beattie, should account for between only 5 and 10 percent of the campaign's budget.[45] More than 10 percent would be "eating into [the campaign's] ability to communicate with voters"; less than 5 percent could put the campaign "in danger of communicating a flawed message."[46]

It might strike some readers as odd to mention communication so prominently in a discussion of the appropriate level of polling in a campaign. Yet polling is now at the strategic center of political campaigns, which are primarily about communication. As pollster Mark Mellman has acknowledged, speaking about his colleagues, "fundamentally, we're in the communication business."[47] Indeed, the pollster's input is as integral to the campaign's communication strategy as any other type of consultant's—if not more so.

### The Pollster as Strategist

The most important development in campaign polling over the last few decades has been the use of polls and pollsters in strategic (and tactical) decisionmaking. To be sure, some observers recognized quite early that information gleaned from polls could be useful in developing strategy. In 1963, for example, Louis Harris was able to predict, "The polltaker who is knowledgeable about politics will inevitably be invited to sit in on strategy meetings."[48] But, as has been noted, it simply was not technologically possible for pollsters to be of much value in this regard until the late 1970s or early 1980s.[49] Once such a role became possible, however, pollsters did not hesitate to take their seat at the decisionmaking table. They brought with them a wealth of data and a knack for transforming that data into usable information.

According to Hamilton, the key question every pollster has to answer is, "in order to win, what must be communicated directly to which group of voters (most of whom are not seeking the information) with a limited budget?"[50] That question entails two crucial elements of the campaign—the message and the targets. In fact, what Hamilton calls "message," others call "theme," and though the two are often used synonymously, they are conceptually different. Briefly, the campaign's theme is "the rationale for your candidate's election and your opponent's defeat."[51] The theme is relatively broad and can be used generally. A message, however, is more narrowly focused on appealing to a particular segment of the electorate. Thus, there can be multiple messages per campaign, though they should not contradict the overall theme. Part of the pollster's job is to help set the campaign theme, determine who the prime targets of the campaign are, and craft messages for those targets.

Determining whom to target is primarily based on the personal knowledge of the candidate and his or her advisers, in addition to basic group assumptions and voter canvassing, which can be done either door to door or by telephone. Ultimately, however, voters are placed in one of three categories—those who support the candidate, those who do not, and those who are undecided. The pollster can assist in targeting, not by identifying individual voters who are persuadable but by determining which groups of voters belong in which category. What, for instance, is the party identification of most undecided voters? How much support does the candidate have among his or her "base" (i.e., core support groups)? The pollster should be able to answer these and other key questions.

Once the campaign team members know who is for them, against them, and undecided—as well as the depth of support, opposition, and indecision—they can begin to craft a theme and messages. The theme, consisting as it does of a broad appeal, is developed by the campaign with some combination of instinct and research. According to Daniel Shea, "an appropriate theme is a combination of what the voters want, what the candidate has to offer, what the opponent has to offer, and other relevant contextual issues."[52] For our purposes, it is important that Shea notes, "Voter concerns are derived from polling data."[53] To use a tried and true example, if polling suggests that the electorate is unhappy with "the way things are going," a challenger may want to emphasize a theme of change. If, however, voters are particularly disgusted with an incumbent's personal character, the challenger may emphasize trustworthiness. At any rate, results from the benchmark survey will help in the development of the campaign's theme.

Campaign messages based on specific subjects (including matters of both policy and personality) are even more dependent on research than is the theme. If polling determines that suburban women are the largest group of undecided voters, a particular message will be crafted to appeal to them. Most likely, that message will include reference to a specific issue that is salient to that group. Voters have fairly well-defined perceptions of which party is better at handling various issues. These "party images" hold that Republicans, generally speaking, are more effective than Democrats at dealing with issues like crime, taxes, and national defense, whereas Democrats are better than Republicans at handling education, the environment, and jobs.[54] Party advantages and disadvantages constrain candidate options with regard to the messages they can successfully use. The campaign, therefore, must emphasize those issues that are salient to targeted groups and on which the candidate has an advantage over the opponent.

Suppose, for example, that suburban women are targeted by both campaigns as key swing voters. Suppose further that polling indicates that the top two areas of concern to these women are education and taxes. If the district follows typical patterns, the Democrat will be the preferred candidate on education, and the Republican will be seen as stronger on taxes. The strategy in this case is for the Democrat to tailor a message, consistent with the overall theme, that emphasizes education. The Republican candidate will do the same with taxes.

The strategic decisionmaking process is actually more complex than this brief discussion suggests.[55] Nevertheless, it should now be apparent that pollsters are crucial to this process. They not only gather the information upon which a communication strategy is based, but they help craft the theme and messages. In addition, they test the strategy's effectiveness and make suggestions about the way the messages are packaged. You would not be wrong if you guessed that media consultants often complain about pollsters encroaching on their turf.

## Dirty Tricks and Future Trends

This section would not be complete without mention of an unfortunate recent development in polling and of future trends in the field. "Push polling," which is not actually polling but is a "negative advocacy" telephone call in the guise of a poll, has recently garnered a great deal of media attention.[56] These pseudo-polls are "used to call tens of thousands or hundreds of thousands of voters to deliver a negative message about the opposition."[57] In a push poll, the caller will ask a respondent whom he or she supports in the upcoming election. If the respondent favors the opponent, the caller proceeds to give the voter inflammatory (and usually untrue) information about that opponent in the form of questions. The goal is to "push" the voter away from his or her original choice of candidates. For example, a voter may be asked, "Would you still support Candidate X if you knew that he uses cocaine?" The idea behind push polls is that outrageously negative attacks will be given credibility (and acceptability) by phrasing them in the form of research questions.

Complicating matters is the fact that campaigns often test negative messages using legitimate polling techniques. Here, campaigns call the normal number of randomly sampled voters (never more than approximately 1,500). Among dozens of other questions, the pollster will test the effectiveness of potential lines of attack against an opponent (as well as those that could be directed toward the pollster's candidate). For this purpose, the information is always factual. For instance, a voter may be asked if he or she would be more or less likely to vote for Candidate Y if he or she knew that Candidate Y supported a constitutional amendment outlawing abortion in all cases. Assuming Candidate Y does, in fact, support such an amendment, the results of the survey can help the campaign determine whether that fact can change votes. The difference between push polls and legitimate polls, then, should be clear. Glen Bolger and Bill McInturff identify a number of distinctions, the three most important being that scientific polls use relatively small samples, whereas push polls call thousands upon thousands of voters; that real polls last anywhere from five to forty minutes, whereas push polls often last under a minute; and that the purpose of a scientific poll is to obtain information in an unbiased manner, whereas push polls attempt to persuade voters using disinformation. Push polling has been condemned by numerous professional organizations, including the American Association of Political Consultants (AAPC) and the American Association of Public Opinion Research (AAPOR).[58] The AAPC also "called upon the news media and public . . . to refrain from characterizing persuasion or advocacy phone calling as 'polling.'"[59]

With respect to future trends in polling, one area that has been developing rapidly and has the potential to revolutionize the industry is Internet polling.[60] The use of answering machines and caller identification technology to screen incoming calls means that telephone polling is increasingly difficult to undertake. The resulting low response rates (which may or may not be problematic for polling) and potential for biased samples (given that those who do not screen have a greater chance of being included in the sample and may not be representative of the entire population) means that pollsters have to be creative in conducting scientifically sound polls. In addition, more and more pollsters realize that polls without focus groups (and vice versa) provide only one aspect of public opinion. Yet extensive use of polls and focus groups is prohibitively expensive for many campaigns. Internet surveys hold promise as a way to address these problems.

Methodology is developing to "conduct real qualitative research with quantitative support" on the Internet.[61] That is, pollsters are developing ways to generalize about qualitative information. To envision online focus groups, think of multiple chat rooms with large numbers of participants. Computer technology allows for rapid analysis of the content of these exchanges. Furthermore, online dial groups of potentially thousands of participants are now possible because of audio and video streaming technology. Currently, there are still problems. For instance, online focus groups are not yet fully interactive, and correlating opinions with demographics is difficult, at best.[62]

More generally, online polls face a self-selection bias. That is, because there is no simple way to access e-mail addresses, it is nearly impossible to get a random sample. Potential respondents have to voluntarily opt into Internet surveys. Even if, theoretically, one could randomly select respondents from a master list of e-mails, it is not entirely clear that Internet users are representative of the rest of the population (or of voters).[63] Nielsen/Net Ratings estimates that roughly 59 percent of the U.S. public currently uses the Internet.[64] Although that number is growing monthly, it certainly does not compare to the more than 95 percent who own telephones.

Harris Interactive, perhaps the leader in online survey research, is addressing these concerns. Though it is a "public" polling outfit, its practice with respect to online surveys is instructive. Harris Interactive has created a list of over 7 million potential survey takers who have registered with Harris Poll Online (HPOL), having been recruited from banner advertisements, online sweepstakes, and other sources.[65] From this list, samples for specific surveys are drawn and contacted automatically via e-mail. Respondents can then complete the survey online at their leisure (within a certain time frame). According to the Harris Interactive website, "All data are tabulated, checked for internal consistency and processed by computer."

Despite these bells and whistles, one might still object that the e-mail list consists of a self-selected group of volunteers. Recognizing the potential for bias in its samples, Harris Interactive "weights" the results of surveys by statistically adjusting them according to key demographic variables. Doing so allows Harris Interactive to generalize to the larger population. Although for most surveys, there is no reality check of the results—that is, the survey results cannot be compared to the distribution of opinions that actually exist among the population—election polls do have a moment of truth, namely, election day. In 2000, HPOL predicted that Al Gore would receive 47.4 percent of the vote to George W. Bush's 47.2 percent; in fact, Gore garnered 48.4 to Bush's 47.9 percent. That represents an error rate less than that for nearly all national telephone polls. The advantages of online polling should be obvious. Huge numbers of surveys can be processed in a short amount of time; questionnaires can be constructed using complex designs, allowing future questions to be determined by earlier answers; visual information can be used; respondents have flexibility with respect to their participation; and, since so much of the process is automated, costs can be held to a minimum.[66]

It remains unlikely that a private campaign poll could be validly and reliably conducted online because the lack of access to adequate numbers of e-mail addresses presents an insurmountable hurdle. Even if a private pollster maintained an e-mail list of many thousands of potential respondents, there may still not be enough in any given district to allow for Internet polling. Nevertheless, as e-mail becomes ubiquitous, the opportunities for online campaign polling will undoubtedly become available.

## The Normative Debate over Polling

No one would deny that campaigns today rely heavily on public opinion polls to make decisions during the course of an election. There is even a great deal of evidence that polling is used extensively in governing.[67] Yet there is little agreement as to the consequences of all this polling for elections and the democratic process. Though the arguments are numerous and fairly complicated, the debate can be summarized as one between responsiveness and manipulation.

In reality, few people today are as optimistic about polling's ability to enhance democracy as the pollsters of the 1940s were. But there are still those who argue that polling gives voice to people who would otherwise be shut out from forms of political participation that are dependent upon one's resources, such as wealth or education.[68] If a politician heard only from those constituents who showed up at town hall meetings or wrote letters, that politician would have a very skewed sense of the people's preferences.

One occasionally hears the argument that polling provides an unbiased sense of the will of the people, but more often the defenders of polling argue that it enables candidates and elected officials to be more responsive to that will. Defenders maintain that in a democracy, elected officials should, to a considerable degree, represent the views of their constituents. This view of representation is often called the "delegate" model. To the extent that the representative relies only upon his or her own judgment or, worse, upon the desires of special interests, adherents of the delegate model would find him or her unresponsive. Thus, as this argument goes, keeping tabs on public opinion—for which polling is perhaps the best method—is virtually required to maintain a democratic link between politicians and the people.

Think, for a moment, about the process of developing campaign strategy as discussed earlier. In its ideal form, this process begins with a benchmark survey, which the campaign uses to assess what the electorate believes to be important issues and where it stands on those issues. The campaign then crafts a theme and messages that will appeal to voters because they are based on what the voters themselves have said they want. Polling throughout the election merely serves to ensure that what the campaign is doing and saying comports with the voters' wishes. As pollster Frank Luntz concludes,

> This two-way feedback between candidates and their constituents, even if conducted through a third party [i.e., pollsters], contributes to maintaining a representative, democratic system. . . . Today, nearly all elected officials have the ability to ascertain public opinion on issues, making them better informed and more responsive legislators.[69]

From the perspective of the defenders of polling, candidates are simply following the lead of the people.

Critics of polling are more numerous, as are the arguments they make. One criticism is that constant polling leads to a decline in leadership. Following this line of reasoning, candidates and elected officials are to act as "trustees," doing what they think is right according to their own judgment, even if it means taking an unpopular stand.[70] Too often, however, politicians are tempted to conduct a poll to determine what position to take or decision to make. As Larry Sabato maintains,

> The concept of a *representative* democracy incorporates an essential acceptance of *trusteeship* as a legitimate and necessary element of rational government in a diverse, multifaceted society. Polls test, and possibly deny, the legitimacy of the trusteeship doctrine. They are fundamentally populist, purporting as they do to represent "the will of the people" and implicitly defying those in power to contradict the people's collective judgment and wisdom.[71]

The argument more often heard about the negative impact of polling in campaigns is that it helps candidates manipulate the electorate. What journalist Elizabeth Kolbert argues about focus groups has also been said of polling in general. Accordingly, focus groups "grow out of the assumption that Americans are fickle in their loyalties, that they don't completely understand their own political interests and that their opinions are easier to manipulate than to enlighten."[72]

Underlying the basic idea that polling leads to manipulation is the premise that polls uncover "hot button" issues that may be of little significance but have the power to move voters in one direction or another. One oft-cited example is the Bush campaign's use of the Pledge of Allegiance during the 1988 election. As governor of Massachusetts, Democrat Michael Dukakis vetoed legislation that would have required public schoolteachers to lead children in the pledge. That veto was used not only as an issue in the campaign, despite it not being one over which a national debate was taking place at the time, but also as a sign of Dukakis's general liberalism.

One of the most vocal critics of polling is essayist Christopher Hitchens, who argues that "polling is not a benign, detached mapping of the political landscape but, rather, a powerful means of cultivating and reshaping it."[73] One of the ways it does that is by inserting itself in the process at an early stage. Private polls are leaked, and public polls are given prominent coverage, and they influence not only which candidates opinion leaders support but where campaign money goes. This process influences perceptions, which in turn creates what has been called a "bandwagon effect." All this occurs, Hitchens notes, "before even one citizen's vote has actually been cast."[74]

For Hitchens, the problem is even worse, since polling involves a "dialectic of manipulation." Although obsessive polling helps candidates manipulate voters, it also forces candidates to "be ready at all times to assume the required shape and posture."[75] That is, when campaigns are so dependent upon polls for guidance, candidates' issue positions are likely to be swayed by the prevailing winds of public opinion.

In the end, critics of polling see the emergence of a "permanent campaign" in which the difference between campaigning and governing is blurred beyond the point of distinction. As Hugh Heclo summarizes, "The permanent campaign is a school of democracy, and what it teaches is that nothing is what it seems, everything said is a ploy to sucker the listener, and truth is what one can be persuaded to believe."[76]

As with many such debates, the truth may lie in the eyes of the beholder. Was Bill Clinton's support of welfare reform responsiveness to the will of the majority or sheer pandering? Is George W. Bush's position on a host of environmental issues leadership or unresponsiveness? With respect to manipulation, how could we ever know what a candidate honestly believes? And at what point does the attempt to persuade (which is, after all, what campaigns are about) become manipulative?

The health care debate in the United States illustrates how murky the role of polls can get. The issue got on the national agenda in large part because the underdog 1991 Senate campaign of Harris Wofford in Pennsylvania "found" the issue in focus groups and went on to win because of it. By the midterm elections of 2000, it was hard to find a candidate who did not support some version of a "patient's bill of rights" (not to mention a prescription drug benefit for the elderly). That caused great frustration for voters, who were left on their own to figure out which candidate was *really* for a patient's bill of rights and which was merely obfuscating. Health care highlights both the good and bad aspects of polling. Testing public opinion helped focus politicians' attention on a subject they might not otherwise have realized was a concern to average citizens (i.e., responsiveness). And yet the eventual popularity of at least one aspect of the issue forced politicians who are ideologically opposed to government meddling in the market to support legislation to do just that, however watered down their version might be (i.e., manipulation).

In the end, it may not be clear whether polling has, on balance, had a positive or negative effect on the U.S. political system. What is fairly clear is that its rise was probably inevitable. Beginning in the Progressive Era (i.e., the late nineteenth century to World War I) and accelerating through the 1960s, the people were given more and more power to hold elected officials accountable. As that power developed, it should have been obvious that politicians were going to find ways to keep abreast of public opinion. Indeed, in the midst of the Progressive era, James Bryce was prescient enough to conclude, "The longer public opinion has ruled, . . . the more are politicians likely to occupy themselves . . . in discovering and hastening to obey it."[77]

# 3

# The Technological Evolution of Campaigns: A Look at New and Emerging Practices

Joshua M. Whitman and Joseph W. Perkins Jr.

There is no escaping the technological upheaval that has dominated communication technology for the past quarter century. Rather than slowing, that upheaval is accelerating. Today's cutting edge will be rendered dull and ordinary in a matter of months by new hardware and software that will open heretofore unthinkable new possibilities for those involved in political campaigns.

Political communication is the battlefield where many technological innovations are tested and tried. Like real warfare, politics demands the use of every possible tool to gain the strategic advantage. The political campaign with the newest weapon may be able to launch a surprise attack, whereas the campaign that is ignorant of the latest technologies is vulnerable. It is virtually impossible to plan and execute successful political campaigns without knowledge of the available weapons offered by evolving technologies.[1]

It is easy to point to the birth of the computer as the beginning of the technological boom of the past half century. But it is the evolution of computer technology that is producing the accelerated change. Faster processors, better file compression, greater bandwidth, cheaper and better storage media, and, of course, the creation of the Internet have all helped elevate the computer from a supercalculator to a communication medium. Basically, knowledge is power, and it is by using that knowledge that politicos become better at the craft of politics. Today, it is possible to literally carry around in a briefcase all the data a campaign needs that, when used correctly, provide a very real strategic advantage over an opponent who is not versed in the ways of technology. As most of the world's financial markets will attest, this new technological medium possesses more potential for changing the world than any invention since Johannes Gutenberg invented movable type.

In this chapter, we present a snapshot of some of the ways new technologies affect the substance and process of political campaigns. Clearly, this snapshot is of change in motion. In a short time, the picture captured today will mutate into something many of us never imagined, but that change will likely be quantitative, not qualitative. That is, one can expect that in the short run technological changes will allow political practitioners to do what they do faster and more efficiently. However, experience tells us that the next major change in campaign crafts spawned by new technologies is probably just around the corner.

## Research

In the early 1980s, research was "nice if you could afford it," but today the first dollars raised in a political campaign are spent on research functions. Now more than ever, candidates and political practitioners are seeing the advantages of collecting and analyzing data. Through the advances in technology, it is feasible to collect more data faster than ever before, allowing for a potential campaign advantage.[2] The types and methods of research are vast, but the most common types are public opinion polling, focus groups, opposition research, media research, and policy research.[3] Indeed, when data are collected and analyzed correctly, they can play a vital role in even small local campaigns.

### Public Opinion and Polling

The heart of every campaign is the public opinion survey.[4] These polls are the beauty contests staged as much for public consumption as for strategic planning. Trying to run a political campaign without polling is like sailing the ocean without a compass, and new technologies have changed polling radically in recent years.[5]

Sampling affects both the application and quality of polling results. Techniques used for drawing a sample have improved over the years, as have the methods for collecting a sample frame. A poorly drawn sample or one drawn from a list not representative of those who will actually vote can render survey results not only useless but dangerous.

Electronic lists of registered voters are now available in most states. Because these lists are maintained on a daily basis by the state voter registration authority, these lists should be used whenever possible to draw a sample. Their use will ensure that only individuals who are eligible to vote are included in the sample employed to predict voter behavior on election day. Further, most registered voter lists carry other information about voters and their behavior that can prove to be extremely valuable during a campaign. Gender, race, age, voting precinct, and even some information about voting participation may be included on registered voter lists obtained from the state. And with the help of some database or geographic information system (GIS) programs, it is possible to overlay precinct or census block data on top of voter list information to provide even more flexibility and control of the sample drawn for research. These methods provide more accurate polling results.

For example, candidates can now visually identify those particular city blocks that voted for or against them or even gave money to them or to their opponent. Also, GIS software enables grassroots campaigning to develop an entirely new method of organizing and communicating the campaign message.

Lists are usually available in digital formats and can be imported into any number of database management software programs, such as Access and Filemaker Pro. There are a variety of options and degrees of complexity; these applications may be as complicated as a visual programming language or as simple as a spreadsheet. There are also specialized campaign software packages built to handle voter files, generate reports from these files, produce special lists, and generate polling samples.

Technological advances have also improved the methods of collecting data. Predictive dialers are the nerve center of most large telephone sales and polling operations. These computerized dialing systems automatically dial a preloaded list of phone numbers. The calls are dialed based on the average time a sales call or survey takes to complete. With this system, a bank of survey data collection personnel have no down time between calls. As soon as one survey is completed, the computer has another respondent from the list on the phone, saving the campaign time, resources, and money.

The data collection personnel are usually sitting in front of a computer terminal that contains not only the available and pertinent data about the respondent but also the entire survey form. This is an improvement over previous approaches, whereby the survey worker had virtually no information about the respondent and worked off a paper copy of the survey instrument. As the respondent answers the survey questions in this new technology, the survey personnel enter the answers directly into the computer. This method also allows for instantaneous analysis of the data, allowing the campaign to begin using the data collected upon completion of each phone call. Such advances are necessary in the hyperfast news cycles and limited response times that define contemporary campaigns.

This same survey data collection software can be programmed to vary the questions the respondent will be asked, depending on the answer the respondent gave to the previous question. As anyone involved in survey research will tell you, it is next to impossible to achieve the low error rates obtained by computer-aided telephone interviewing (CATI) systems when attempting to record data with pen and paper. Such systems allow for surveys to be tailored on the spot to the particular respondent.

Predictive dialing and data collection systems speed up the collection process and data entry and analysis while reducing the opportunity to inject errors into the data. Such systems therefore help to ensure that the conclusions drawn from the data collected are more accurate and representative. However, merely collecting accurate data does not guarantee that correct strategic decisions will be made with that data.

### Other Sources of Data and Data Analysis

The process of analyzing data obtained using the techniques discussed above has also become easier. "Data mining" describes the process of extracting useful and sometimes hidden information from raw data. A number of analytical, statistical software programs, such as SPSS, SYSTAT, and R, can be used to develop extensive descriptive and predictive analyses from data. These programs import data easily from spreadsheet or database programs, and they produce output in easy-to-read tables, graphs, and reports.

These analytical programs have helped eliminate the need for in-depth statistical training of staff so that they can extract usable conclusions from data sets. However, a fundamental understanding of descriptive statistics is necessary to avoid simple mistakes that can result in tragic outcomes.

Another method of obtaining a strategic advantage is to know what issues the opponent will hurl at the candidate and what issues the candidate will use to keep the opponent off balance.[6] In politics, the corollary of "know thyself" is "know thy opponent." Opposition research is essential not only to uncover things the opponent may have done or said, but also to understand how he or she thinks. Data storage and retrieval mechanisms have come a long way since 1980, and no longer do campaign researchers have to spend hours in newspaper morgues or scanning microfiche. Now, they can search digital databases for key words or phrases that may appear in the title or text of news stories. Lexis Nexis, West Law, and other online data services provide vast compilations of newspaper and other records from around the world. Even smaller newspapers that do not provide information online often have electronic databases of past articles available on CD-ROM; if not, the paper's archivists will conduct a custom search of their database.

Databases available on the Internet include tax records, campaign disclosure information, property records, lists of registered voters, legal filings, and others. Many state websites provide past election results that can be downloaded. There is also information available from state Web pages on corporations, their boards of directors and officers, and their majority ownership. The Securities and Exchange Commission has useful information about publicly traded companies and their leadership. Subscription services like Dunn and Bradstreet can also be helpful in obtaining a profile of an individual's financial background.

The court systems in many states provide information on cases through either free or subscription-based online systems. These services allow research on the parties involved in court filings and usually some indication of the disposition of the case. As a result, no longer can a candidate for office prevent others from learning about college-age indiscretions simply because the investigation is too time-consuming or difficult to undertake.

Media-monitoring services provide either video or audio files or transcripts of broadcast news coverage. An increasing number of states are broadcasting the proceedings of their state legislatures over the Internet, allowing anyone interested to listen to or record these proceedings. Availability of archival information from broadcast material offers the possibility of obtaining an individual candidate's position on an issue in his or her words, along with oral or visual documentation of the actual statement.

Electronic data storage and retrieval makes it possible today to conduct sophisticated background and opposition research without leaving the comfort of home. And with the increasing storage capacity of today's laptop computers, it is possible to carry all this research in a briefcase and have it at one's fingertips when campaign attacks demand an immediate response.

Another form of data collection that has made significant technological advancements over the years is the use of focus groups.[7] Asking people what they think about an issue and being able to listen to and statistically record the responses of a group discussing that issue helps to glean information that survey research can never touch. Today, focus groups can be used in ways never before possible. Dial systems provide each participant with a small electronic control that houses a dial or buttons or both. By turning the dial or pressing the buttons, depending on the system, respondents can register their response to or feelings about an issue. This system can also be used to test responses to media like television commercials. Throughout the thirty seconds of a sample commercial, participants can turn the dial left or right to indicate whether they like or dislike what they see and hear. This registers each millisecond response during the time the commercial plays. Because technological advances in media production have made testing of alternative commercials inexpensive and practical, focus groups can provide a valuable pretest of a commercial before thousands or even millions of dollars are spent to air it on television.

Every ten years, by constitutional mandate, the federal government conducts a count of every person living within the United States. One of the purposes of this count is to ensure equal and fair representation in the various elected offices throughout the country. Once the count is completed, the data are made available to state legislatures around the country, and those legislatures then have the responsibility of drawing new district lines that reflect the population shifts that have taken place over the previous ten years. Prior to the countrywide 2000 redistricting process, most legislatures drew new district lines using large maps, pencils, and calculators. The 2000 redistricting effort marked a tremendous leap forward in the methods used to draw new districts.

GIS technologies and applications are not new; they have been used by any number of engineering firms, utility companies, urban planners, and demographers for some time. Essentially, a GIS package allows a user to visualize data on a map for a certain geographic area. Therefore, the introduction of GIS technology into the redistricting and reapportionment arena enables elected representatives to more easily create and manipulate district lines.

However, with the completion of the 2000 census and the mandatory redistricting and reapportionment of state legislatures and Congress, GIS technologies will take on a whole new dimension in political campaigns. The demand to perform the tasks of redrawing governmental boundaries has created greater access to GIS software, along with technicians capable of using the software. GIS applications, such as AutoCAD Map, ArcView, or Maptitude, can be used to overlay numerous related databases at the census block or precinct level. Use of such software provides the political tactician the ability to look at voting populations in ways never before practical for most campaigns.

## Production

Technology has had the greatest impact on political campaigns in the area of media production. Whether direct mail, newspaper, radio, television, billboards, or any other medium, technological advances have changed production methods so much it is difficult to even compare them to those of a few years ago.

### Print Technologies

Historically, print media have required long lead times before distribution to produce the final printed communication piece. Today, however, one can proceed from initial idea to final print production in a matter of hours. Graphic design and layout programs like QuarkXpress and Pagemaker are very common and accessible. Typesetting (a term made antiquated by technology) can be done in a word-processing program or directly in the layout program. Art can be scanned from photographs or line art; downloaded on the Internet; produced in programs like Freehand, Illustrator, or Photoshop; or imported from art collections commercially sold and distributed on CD-ROM. High-quality photography and art images, clip art, and fonts may also be purchased from a number of commercial image databases, including eyewire.com and arttoday.com.

Some media producers prefer to shoot their own photographs for use in a print medium. Midgrade digital cameras now have resolutions beyond three megapixels, making digital photography one of the latest advances in print production technology. No longer does one have to wait for a film processor to develop and print photographs. High quality, high-resolution digital images can be captured and immediately placed in print media layouts.

These improvements in the production of print media have changed the strategic uses of the media. Increased speed and efficiency of production allow the easy customization of print messages to specific audiences. In fact, print has become the primary medium for "narrow-casting" messages in a political campaign. Through direct mail or other targeted delivery systems, it is easier to create specialized messages that drive directly at the interests and needs of voters in a specific precinct or even census block.

It is important to keep in mind, however, that the slowest portion of print production is still the process of putting ink on paper, but even it has made advances thanks to technology. Now photocopying techniques make production of small runs possible in a matter of hours. Even large color banners can be produced quickly at the local copy shop. Offset printing and other long-run print processes have also become faster because of advances in the computer technology that drives these multimillion-dollar machines.

For centuries, the graphic artist's final product was the boards—type and art pasted up on a board to be photographed by a printer for plate production. Today, the final product is a file that can be received by the print shop on disk or via the Internet. That file provides 100 percent digital, accurate input into the printing process for production of the final printed piece.

Because of the advances in newspaper printing technology, changes in production can be made until minutes before the deadline, such as a campaign rally. Once an ad is ready for insertion, it can be e-mailed to several newspapers at the same time without having to create separate boards for each paper. Typically, the ads seen in newspapers today never exist in a physical form until they are actually printed in the newspaper.

## Television and Visual Technologies

As the tools to increase efficiency and speed in newspaper production have grown, so too have the tools used to produce television advertising. No longer does mystery surround the production of a television commercial. The movie *The Blair Witch Project* has proven that it is possible to be a big-time producer without Hollywood overhead. High-quality digital cameras and desktop editing programs like Avid, FinalCut Pro, and Premiere can give anyone the ability to produce broadcast-quality media.

The ultimate video production versatility is realized when digital footage is edited on a laptop computer with the client looking over the editor's shoulder. When the commercial is finished, it can often be sent directly from the laptop to tape format for distribution to television stations. And eventually, transmission of that same thirty-second commercial will no longer need to be done via videotape but will take place via the Internet.

Those who choose to work with a high-quality production studio to perform the editing of the commercials will still be able to walk into the studio with a client-approved commercial in draft form. It is then possible to produce the final commercial in a much shorter time.

Technological advances have also increased the efficiency with which a campaign can work with a professional production and editing studio. No longer is it a necessity to fly to New York to edit a single thirty-second commercial. It is now possible to conduct a live edit session from a computer in, for instance, Alabama, with editors in a studio across the country. And once the editing session is over, a QuickTime file can be e-mailed to the client for approval, rather than having to wait a day for Federal Express to deliver a proof.

Another advancement in technology as it relates to television production is the vast amount of stock footage that can be obtained. Production houses around the country have opened their vaults of footage of everything from the perfect sunset to Martin Luther King Jr.'s "I have a dream" speech. This video can be purchased and inserted into a low-budget commercial in order to provide the excellent final product that every client desires.

### Radio and Audio Technologies

Like television and newspaper, radio is now a digital medium. Voice talent in New York can connect live to the producer and the client in a studio in Atlanta. Once the live edit session has finished and the final radio commercial has been produced, it is now possible to e-mail or post the spot on a Web page for radio stations to download. This advance is due to better quality and faster compression schemes that promise an excellent digital product that can go on the air to help influence the political landscape. As with video and print media, there are scores of digital databases for audio production materials. Background music, sound effects, speech archives, and other audio can be obtained through both public access and subscription services that are easily found on the Internet.

### Internet

Not only does the Internet aid in the production of the campaign message, but also it can disseminate that same message. Virtually every campaign today has its own Web page. The page usually includes a candidate biography, issues papers and position statements, a campaign calendar, and of course, a fundraising page that will allow supporters to charge campaign contributions to their credit cards. Currently, the designers of programs such as QuarkXpress and Pagemaker have produced computer applications that now make creating a Web page easier than ever before. Using these tools, the skills required to set up a Web page are similar to those required to produce a campaign brochure.

But the capacity of the Internet far exceeds the standard campaign Web page. It is now possible to form and organize a portion of a grassroots campaign online, using chat rooms and e-mail lists. And through these same chat rooms and other online communications, the candidate is able to connect more closely and directly than ever before with individuals who will cast a vote on election day.

## The Promise of Technology?

All this wonderful technology comes with a price. Technology has made it possible to manage information, conduct research, produce media, and manage campaigns better than ever before. It seems that anyone with enough processing power and the right software can be a political communication expert. But there is a problem that any campaign expert seeking success will recognize: owning a violin does not make that person a concert violinist. Along with these new technologies comes the corresponding need for campaign professionals who know how to use them, which, in part, helps explain the increasing use of professionals in campaigns.[8]

Technologies may appear to reduce the need for specialization and expertise in narrow areas of campaign activity. But technologies do not remove the impact of talent, training, and knowledge. Karaoke machines make it possible for anyone to sing along with great accompaniment, but that does not mean they contribute to the production of good music. Oftentimes, technologies make it easier to produce amateurish or inferior outcomes.

Similarly, because of the increased speed at which information flows in this new digital age, errors are magnified, and mistakes can easily be taken advantage of by the opposition. There once was a time that a campaign spokesperson could withdraw a statement given in haste, but that is no longer possible. Essentially, what professionals in politics have is a precision-guided weapon that is extremely effective when used correctly, but because of the weapon's very precision, any mistakes will be much more visible. Thus every serious campaign specialist must have a broad understanding of each weapon in the campaign arsenal.

The technologies discussed are merely the tip of the iceberg of what the future will hold in the ways of campaign communication. However, every advance in campaign technology will most certainly focus on the overriding goal of campaign-effective communication and persuasion to encourage individuals to select a certain candidate when they are behind the curtain on the first Tuesday following the first Monday in November.

# 4

## Case: Incumbency and Issue Advocacy in Pennsylvania's Thirteenth District

### Robin Kolodny and Sandra L. Suárez

In this chapter, we focus on the lessons that can be learned from a comparative case study of congressional district races in the same geographic district in two consecutive general election cycles. We were participants in a nationwide study that looked at the effects of issue advocacy campaigning by interest groups and political parties in 1998 and 2000.[1] This case study of Pennsylvania's Thirteenth District is an outgrowth of that project.

Before the 2002 redistricting, Pennsylvania's thirteenth congressional district was routinely one of the more competitive districts in the nation and one of the last few remaining "swing" districts in the nation.[2] That is, party control of the seat transferred back and forth with regularity.[3] Our study highlights the importance of incumbency, but not in the way that it is conventionally defined. The power of incumbency generally means that those already holding elective office are more likely to be reelected. The implications are that the incumbent needs the support of his or her party less than does the challenger. By the same token, the party helps challengers more than it helps incumbents. We found, however, that the power of incumbency in Pennsylvania's Thirteenth District meant that the incumbent was more likely to receive the support of his or her party.

Conventional wisdom also suggests that most interest groups become involved in campaigns because they are interested in securing access to politicians. However, we found that most groups were more likely to support a candidate that shared their beliefs, rather than the candidate that seemed more likely to win. Part of the reason may be that in a swing district such as Pennsylvania's Thirteenth District, it was difficult to determine which candidate was likely to win, but this uncertainty did not deter groups from becoming key actors in the electoral politics of the district. Moreover, it was found that most of the groups participating in the race were actively in favor of the challenger in 1998 but in favor of the incumbent in 2000.

Thus when it comes to the support of interest groups, the advantages of incumbency are not as absolute as they may seem, especially when organized interests are more likely to behave like ideological rather than access-seeking groups.

Finally, we learned that former House Speaker Thomas P. "Tip" O'Neill's old adage—"all politics is local"—requires some qualification. First, the electoral activities of national actors—political parties and interest groups—depended much more on national considerations, such as majority control of Congress and the fate of national public policy issues like Social Security, abortion, and the environment. Second, the campaign strategies followed by these national actors were informed more by a generic model based on television advertising, incumbency, and ideology than by local factors. And ultimately, although the activities of both national and local actors—political parties and interest groups—were sometimes helpful (and sometimes not so helpful), in most cases, the candidates followed their own instincts about how to campaign in the district. We concluded that it is the interplay of national and local concerns that explains the behavior of parties, groups, and candidates during the campaign, more so than the local politics of the district alone.

## The District

The thirteenth congressional district in Pennsylvania was one of the more competitive and unpredictable congressional districts in the 1990s. Republican candidates won the seat in 1990, 1994, and 1996. Democratic candidates won in 1992, 1998, and 2000. One-term Democratic incumbent Joe Hoeffel successfully defended his seat in 2000 over Republican challenger Stewart Greenleaf by 20,000 votes, a substantial improvement over his 9,000-vote victory in 1998. Hoeffel's victory also marks the first successful reelection of a Democrat "in a heavily Republican region in at least eighty years."[4]

Located in the wealthiest of Philadelphia's suburbs (most of Montgomery County, and parts of Bucks and Delaware Counties), the Thirteenth District has a relatively informed and active electorate. The Republicans enjoyed a 1.5 to 1 registration advantage over Democrats in Montgomery County in 2000, down from the 2.5 to 1 registration advantage in 1996. Lawrence Coughlin, a moderate Republican, represented the district for twenty-four years. When he retired in 1992, his open seat quickly became one of the most competitive in the country. The newly redistricted seat was still believed to tilt Republican, given the overwhelming partisan registration advantage. The race got even more attention when local television reporter (and wife of a former congressman) Marjorie Margolies Mezvinsky announced her intention to seek the Democratic nomination in the district. Her opponent was Republican Montgomery County commissioner Jon Fox. Despite Mezvinsky's fame, Fox was the favorite for the seat because of the Republican Party's registration advantage. However, a newly redistricted seat and a surge in Bill Clinton's popularity helped elect Mezvinsky by a 5 percent margin.

During the first year of the Clinton presidency, Mezvinsky broke a critical promise to her constituents. Despite campaigning heavily against new taxes, Mezvinsky changed her stance and cast the critical vote in favor of the president's economic package, as a result of enormous pressure from her party's leadership. The vote received considerable press attention—both for its consequences to the member and for the seemingly "strong-armed" tactics used to elicit it. It was Jon Fox's dream come true, and in their 1994 rematch, he defeated her by 4 percentage points. The fact that 1994 was a midterm election with a national Republican surge did not hurt Fox either, but residents of the district will always attribute Mezvinsky's dramatic vote change as the cause of her defeat.

In 1996, Fox faced a new Democratic challenger, Montgomery County executive Joe Hoeffel. Hoeffel had run for the seat previously against Coughlin in 1984 and 1986 but was not as well known as Mezvinsky. Hoeffel had a solid reputation for moderate stances and competence. Since 1996 was a presidential election year and Clinton was still popular in the district, Fox mounted a serious campaign. The year was also the first election cycle to see significant outside spending by interest groups, with the American Federation of Labor–Congress of Industrial Organizations (AFL-CIO) spending heavily on Hoeffel's behalf. Many thought this effort backfired as Hoeffel caught much of the blame for labor's negative campaigning. In the end, Fox held on to his seat by a record-breaking margin of only eighty-four votes, a "busload," as Hoeffel supporters called it.

The close race meant both sides almost immediately began plans for a 1998 rematch, the first of the two elections we studied in the district. Though the candidates were the same in 1998 as in 1996, the playing field had changed dramatically, as the idea of issue advocacy (by both parties and interest groups) became the norm in the nation's most competitive races. Ultimately, Hoeffel defeated Fox in 1998 by 5 percent.

In 2000, Fox declined to run again. This time, the Republican nominee was Pennsylvania state senator Stewart Greenleaf. A more moderate Republican than Fox, Greenleaf was believed to fit the district better, and thus it was felt that he would constitute a greater threat to Hoeffel. As we shall see, the political parties had a critical role here and changed the dynamics from what should have been a close contest to a relatively smooth victory for the one-term incumbent Hoeffel.

After the 2000 census, the state of Pennsylvania wrote a new redistricting plan, reflecting a loss of two congressional district seats for the state. One of these seats has been cut from the current allotment to the

Philadelphia area. The districts of Bob Borski (Third District) and Joe Hoeffel of Montgomery County were commingled, forcing Borski to retire rather than run against another incumbent. Consequently, Hoeffel's new district is more solidly Democratic than before.

## The Candidates

Political science literature has always made much of the "incumbency advantage" in elections, meaning that the incumbent member of Congress generally has more name recognition, positive evaluation by his or her constituents, media exposure, and campaign funds than the challenger. Sometimes, a high-profile challenger such as an actor, athlete, or astronaut will come along to neutralize the advantages incumbents normally enjoy.[5] However, such well-known challengers are the exception rather than the rule. Our comparative study points out one incumbency advantage that the literature does not stress: electoral support from the incumbent's political party.

At first blush, one might think that support from the officeholder's party is a given. However, until the mid-1990s, it can be said that the support parties gave to their candidates was helpful but not really a deciding factor in victory or defeat.[6] The advent of soft money spending gave the parties resources and options they did not have before. We found that in 1998, Jon Fox received a great deal of assistance from his party's congressional committee (the National Republican Congressional Committee, or NRCC), whereas Hoeffel received modest support from his party's congressional committee (the Democratic Congressional Campaign Committee, or DCCC). But in 2000, with Hoeffel as the incumbent, the tables were turned. The DCCC gave Hoeffel significant support in 2000, whereas the NRCC gave Greenleaf only token support. From the local perspective, a Greenleaf candidacy ought to have had more promise than Fox's. But the national perspective gave incumbent Hoeffel the advantage.

## Political Parties

Because of the political parties' mastery of soft money transfers in recent cycles, the true value of the political party presence in this race may never be known.[7] It is clear that in both 1998 and 2000, the party defending the incumbent spent the most money.

The parties reported very little in direct contributions and coordinated expenditures for each candidate in 2000. Joe Hoeffel received $4,175 in direct contributions and $10,702 in coordinated expenditures from the DCCC, well below the allowable amount of $67,560.[8] At first glance, the small amount of hard money in Hoeffel's race is surprising. However, sixty-seven current and former Democratic members of the U.S. House of Representatives donated a total of $61,550 to Hoeffel, which is further evidence of the party's hand.[9]

The Democrats spent approximately $1.4 million in soft money for Hoeffel on television advertising, direct mail, get-out-the-vote efforts (GOTV), and phone banks. Unlike in 1998, when the national committees of both parties placed ads and sent mail, in 2000, the national Democratic committees worked through the Pennsylvania Democratic State Committee. According to the DCCC, $1.2 million was spent on issue advocacy ad production and television airtime. The DCCC soft money ads aired early in the campaign cycle—just before Labor Day and throughout September. Though the party clearly thought Hoeffel's race important enough to deserve a million dollars in spending, campaign insiders doubted that the issue ads had a significant impact on the ultimate outcome. Hoeffel's principal campaign consultant, Neil Oxman of the Campaign Group, felt that these ads helped solidify Hoeffel's position in the race but did little to improve his lead over Greenleaf. Hoeffel's standing only improved once the candidate's own ads ran in October.[10] In addition to the television time, the Pennsylvania Democrats paid for six mail pieces on Hoeffel and one joint Hoeffel and Gore mail piece. The DCCC estimated its mail spending at $175,000.[11] One soft money mailer contained a factual error that hurt the campaign's momentum.[12]

Party hard money spending for Greenleaf was greater than for Hoeffel, but party soft money spending for Greenleaf was considerably less because no issue advocacy television ads were produced. Stewart Greenleaf received a total of $14,500 in party direct contributions: $4,500 from the NRCC, $5,000 from the Republican National Committee (RNC), and $5,000 from the Republican Federal Committee of Pennsylvania. He also received $62,577 in coordinated expenditures.[13]

At first glance, we might think that the NRCC supported Greenleaf more than the DCCC supported Hoeffel. However, the soft money spending for Greenleaf was reported to be zero. Though the NRCC promised to spend soft money on Greenleaf's behalf if the race remained competitive, it never followed through with this promise. We know that the NRCC transferred $1.2 million in soft money to spend on behalf of the candidates in three hotly contested House races in Pennsylvania. The Greenleaf campaign expressed frustration with the national party committees for failing to deliver on a promise of significant television time close to the election. According to Greenleaf's campaign manager, such assistance had been promised if the gap narrowed between the two candidates in the weeks before Election Day.[14] However, when the NRCC decided to pursue a television campaign, no time was left to buy in the already oversubscribed Philadelphia media market, where, in addition to the presidential candidates, U.S. Senate candidates in Pennsylvania, New Jersey, and Delaware were all buying time.[15] The DCCC also noted that although Hoeffel was listed as one of the NRCC's prime targets in 1999, its interest in the race seemed to fade over the summer, and its support for Greenleaf continued to be tepid through the general election crunch.[16] However, the DCCC's concern over Hoeffel's fate also waned in the campaigns' last few days. The Hoeffel campaign tried to get the DCCC to spend coordinated expenditure money (hard dollars) on last-minute radio ads to counter an effective radio ad campaign by Greenleaf, but its pleas were rebuffed on the grounds that the race was no longer considered close.[17]

In 1998, the NRCC spent heavily for Fox as part of its Operation Breakout issue advocacy program. Why did it not support Greenleaf to the same extent in 2000? There are a variety of explanations to consider: Greenleaf was more moderate than Fox, Republicans nationally were performing weaker than Democrats in legislative races, the NRCC believed that the race was no longer competitive, and in 1998 the party had the incumbent, but in 2000 it had the challenger. We believe the last of these is the most compelling explanation. Though it would seem that political parties should logically invest in challenger candidates on the premise that incumbents should be able to fend for themselves, when the margin between majority and minority control is slim, parties will protect incumbents first in an effort to pursue majorities.[18] Since the probability that incumbents will be reelected is quite high even in marginal districts, it makes more sense to invest in incumbents than in challenger candidates.

## Interest Groups

A similar case can be made to explain the variation in interest group activity between 1998 and 2000. There were clear differences in the level of group involvement and the type of group involvement in each cycle. Clearly, the most important explanatory variable for these fluctuations is the candidates involved in the race, followed by the party affiliation of the candidates in the race. Groups campaigned in Pennsylvania's Thirteenth District simply because they wanted to affect who controlled the U.S. House of Representatives, yet at the same time, they supported the candidate who best reflected their interests. That was true regardless of which candidate was perceived to be more likely to win.

Research on political action committees (PACs) suggests that business PACs are more likely than ideological PACs to follow an access-seeking strategy. That is, ideological PACs presumably are more interested in changing the composition of Congress and are more likely to support the candidate who is closest to their interests.[19] Although important, the behavior of ideological versus nonideological PACs can tell us very little about the interest group campaign in the Thirteenth District. Most of the groups involved in the 1998 and 2000 campaign behaved like ideological PACs.

The absence of access-seeking groups also challenges the presumption that incumbents are always in a more advantageous position than challengers. In our study we found that more groups mobilized in favor of Hoeffel than on behalf of the incumbent in 1998, although Fox had the support of many conservative social and economic groups. In 2000, more groups mobilized in support of the incumbent, meaning that Hoeffel benefited in both election cycles.

As in 1998, some of the issues emphasized by groups in their election advocacy included Social Security and Medicare, reproductive rights, and gay rights. In 2000, the environment also became a much more relevant issue. Among the groups involved in the Thirteenth District were four environmental groups: Friends of the Earth, the League of Conservation Voters (LCV), the Sierra Club, and Clean Water Action (through its local branch). All the environmental groups cited Hoeffel's past support for environmental causes as their primary reason for their involvement in the race. Compared to 1998, socially and economically conservative groups were absent largely because Greenleaf was considered more moderate than Fox. The lack of group support, in turn, contributed to the perception that Fox had been a stronger candidate than Greenleaf, making it even less likely that organized groups would support his candidacy.

The only group to use television for issue advocacy was the Sierra Club. Most voters were contacted via voter guides, literature drops, and phone banks. In-kind contributions in the form of staff or interns provided additional help to the candidates. By far, Hoeffel benefited the most from independent expenditures, issue advocacy, and in-kind contributions. Hoeffel had staff or interns on loan from the Human Rights Campaign, League of Conservation Voters, and Friends of the Earth. Preliminary data obtained from the Federal Election Commission (FEC) and during interviews with group representatives indicate that Hoeffel benefited from at least $380,961 in independent expenditures.

The Sierra Club television ads ran once in April and once in early September.[20] The issue ad, named "Strip Malls," praised Representative Hoeffel's leadership in protecting the environment and asked viewers to call Hoeffel to thank him and to ask him to vote in support of a bill "to help us control sprawl and protect our quality of life." The ad cost "about $70,000" to produce and broadcast. The group decided to run the ad in September, just before Labor Day "because it was a time when members [of Congress] were in their districts talking to voters."[21] As of October 2000, the group had also spent $3,086 in in-kind contributions of salary benefits in support of Hoeffel.

The LCV launched its "Environmental Champion" campaign in 2000 and put Hoeffel on its list, spending $177,232 to support his reelection.[22] It also polled Montgomery County voters in June and November to determine whether the environment was an important issue for the district. They found that "nearly 90 percent of voters said that clean air and clean water would play important roles in their voting decision. Forty-two percent said they would be primary factors."[23] LCV then spent $136,000 for 220,000 pieces of mail (five different pieces) sent to 60,000 district homes.[24] FEC data suggests that consultant fees and other miscellaneous expenditures in support of Hoeffel amounted to an additional $12,311.

Friends of the Earth, like the LCV, was not involved in the 1998 campaign, but in 2000 it sent a staff member to work on Hoeffel's campaign. The group got involved in 2000 because it "had established a good working relationship with Congressman Hoeffel during his two years in office" and "wanted to make sure that he returned."[25] Finally, a national group named Clean Water Action became involved through its local chapter on behalf of Hoeffel. The group targeted only its members in the district (8,000) through mail and a phone bank. The group's endorsement highlighted Hoeffel's defense of the federal Clean Water Act.

Hoeffel also benefited from the support of pro-choice groups, as he had in 1998, though both candidates in 2000 were pro-choice. Greenleaf's opposition to partial birth abortions explains why pro-choice groups worked for Hoeffel. The National Abortion and Reproductive Rights Action League (NARAL) became involved in the Thirteenth District race because Hoeffel was seen as a "vulnerable pro-choice incumbent."[26] The group had also been involved in Hoeffel's 1998 campaign and had a readily available list of voters identified as pro-choice. Although NARAL felt comfortable working with Greenleaf at the state level, his support for a ban on partial birth abortion was problematic.[27] In 1998, Fox had also suffered because of his lukewarm support for abortion rights. At the time he defined himself as a "supporter of *Roe vs. Wade*," yet pro-choice groups campaigned against him.

In 2000, NARAL's campaign strategy mirrored that used in 1998. The group conducted a phone survey to identify likely supporters. If voters were deemed unquestionably pro-choice, they were mailed a GOTV postcard in the days closer to election day. The postcard pointed out that Greenleaf had "sponsored legislation to promote and fund abstinence-only sex education" and "supports bans on safe, common abortion procedures throughout pregnancy, even when a woman's health is in danger." If the voters were deemed mildly pro-choice, then they received one or two get-out-the-vote (GOTV) phone calls. In addition, voter guides were sent with a list of national and state candidates endorsed by the group.[28] After the initial phone survey, the group targeted 15,000 pro-choice or likely pro-choice voters in the district. According to the FEC, NARAL independent expenditures amounted to $44,692 (phone banks and list processing).[29]

Another pro-choice group, Planned Parenthood, adopted a much more neutral and low-key approach. Planned Parenthood of Southeastern Pennsylvania also sent out a voter guide endorsing Hoeffel but noting that both candidates were pro-choice. The Human Rights Campaign (HRC) was also active in both 1998 and 2000. HRC started planning its 2000 campaign strategy at the conclusion of the 1998 campaign, working closely with its lobbyists to determine which members of Congress it should help reelect. According to HRC, Hoeffel had cosponsored the Employment Nondiscrimination Act and the Hate Crimes Prevention Act. In addition, Hoeffel voted to increase funding for housing opportunities for people with acquired immunodeficiency syndrome (AIDS) and supported programs for the "prevention, research, treatment, and care" of human immunodeficiency virus (HIV) and AIDS.[30]

Most of the HRC's activities targeted its members. In 2000 HRC members "received a voter card paid by the nonprofit side of the organization and recorded phone calls paid by the PAC."[31] It is important to note that the voter guide included a separate sheet of paper devoted solely to Hoeffel's "Record on Gay and Lesbian Issues" and emphasizing his HRC scorecard rating of 82 percent. In addition, HRC has a program called "Youth College," in which twenty young people are given campaign training and then sent to selected campaigns as in-kind contributions. Hoeffel's campaign benefited from this "donation."[32] According to FEC data, the group spent $1,709 in in-kind contributions in the period between August and October.

The National Education Association (NEA) Fund and its PAC, the NEA Fund for Children and Public Education, mailed three pieces advocating Hoeffel's reelection. According to FEC data, the group paid $89,202 for the independent expenditure mailing and a total of $110,700 for polling and research in support of Hoeffel.[33] The PAC mailing emphasized Hoeffel's support for Head Start, teacher training, and smaller class sizes. The NEA piece endorsed Hoeffel but did not specifically ask voters to support him at the polls. Neither of these groups mentioned Greenleaf. Finally, the National Emergency Medicine PAC of the American College of Emergency Physicians spent $2,000 in in-kind contributions to support Hoeffel.

Among the senior citizen groups, the National Committee to Preserve Social Security and Medicare and the American Association of Retired Persons (AARP) both sent issue advocacy mail. The AARP piece encouraged voters to log on to its website to get access to its voter guides. In addition, the AARP sent out a voter guide. Lastly, as in 1998, Handgun Control endorsed Hoeffel's candidacy. The group sent a postcard asking voters to support Gore and Hoeffel.

## Conclusion

Ultimately, political parties and groups protect incumbents fiercely, whereas challengers, especially those outside the partisan mainstream, have to hope for the best. The Democratic Party spent more money on behalf of Hoeffel than the Republican Party spent on behalf of Greenleaf in the 2000 race, whereas the Republican Party had been far more active on behalf of Fox in 1998 than the Democrats had been for Hoeffel that year. Interest groups were also more active in support of Hoeffel than Greenleaf in 2000. With the exception of the environmental groups, all the interest groups that actively supported Hoeffel in 1998 did so again in 2000. Given that the district has a majority of Republican voters, conservative economic and social groups were surprisingly absent that year. Part of the reason is that some conservative groups thought Greenleaf to be a weak challenger.[34] By contrast, during his two years in office, Hoeffel developed a strong working relationship with environmental, pro-choice, and education groups who wanted him to return to Congress. The events in Pennsylvania's Thirteenth District suggest that when a district is considered competitive, party and interest group activities are likely to contribute to the outcome.

What does an examination of the 1998 and 2000 races in this district tell us? First, candidates matter. The most powerful explanatory variable for differences in the campaigns is who the incumbent was and who the challenger was. The candidate's party, reputation, real or perceived issue stances, and experience all played a role in how other political actors responded to him and, in turn, to the outcome of the elections. Second, the incumbent will always be favored over the challenger for attention from the political parties and the voters. Even in an extraordinarily competitive district, the incumbent will receive preferential treatment. Finally, interest groups are, as might be expected, loyal to their issue stances. Thus, groups who were active for Hoeffel in 1998 remained active for him in 2000, whereas groups who were active for the more conservative Fox in 1998 did not come to Greenleaf's aid in 2000. Understanding political party and group behavior is important in an environment in which issue advocacy campaigns are unregulated and largely undisclosed.

# 5

## *Case:* Violating the "Appearance Standard": A Local Campaign Controversy

### Edward M. Yager Jr.

It has often been stated that "in politics, appearance is reality." This wise observation succinctly captures the ethical dilemma shared by two political antagonists in the city of Bowling Green, Kentucky—Mayor Eldon Renaud and Commissioner Joe Denning. Although both public officials would eventually be cleared by the Bowling Green Ethics Board of any wrongdoing on conflict of interest charges, they were nevertheless subject to public reprimands for violating the so-called appearance standard when the Ethics Board applied that standard to events related to Commissioner Denning's reelection campaign in November 1998.

In this case I examine the ethical and legal dispute between Mayor Eldon Renaud and Commissioner Joe Denning. The case spans a time frame of almost two years, from November 1998 through September 2000, and presents personalities and events not unfamiliar to other local jurisdictions across the nation. Other localities can learn from the experience of Bowling Green.

## The Appearance Standard

Public officials are held to a higher standard of ethical conduct than ordinary citizens. Not only are they required to avoid using public office for private gain, but they are obligated to avoid even the appearance of wrongdoing. The reasons should be obvious. The public views and evaluates public officials from a distance by reading newspapers, watching television, conversing with friends, and engaging in other information-gathering activities. Although a plethora of information is often available to the extent that it would overwhelm the average citizen, it is unlikely that most citizens will follow the news so closely that they will develop well-informed opinions on a variety of issues, including whether or not certain public officials are culpable of wrongdoing. Rather, most citizens draw conclusions about governmental affairs with incomplete knowledge; they often form opinions based upon appearances.

If the credibility of government is to be protected and maintained, then public officials have a duty to avoid even the appearance of wrongdoing. This duty begins during the campaign for public office and continues until the term of office expires. Unfortunately, Mayor Renaud and Commissioner Denning failed to subscribe to this higher standard. In the words of the public reprimands issued by the Ethics Board to both public officials, they "failed to maintain the highest standards of conduct for a public official by failing to avoid the appearance of impropriety."

## Background of the Case

The city of Bowling Green, Kentucky is located in south-central Kentucky, approximately 60 miles north of Nashville, Tennessee. With a population slightly under 50,000, Bowling Green is the fourth-largest city in Kentucky; home to Western Kentucky University; and the county seat of Warren County. The city has a council-manager form of government that provides a wide array of public services.

In the fall of 1998, six individuals declared their candidacies for the office of city commissioner for the city of Bowling Green. Two candidates were incumbents running for reelection, and four candidates were first-time challengers. All were competing for four seats on the City Commission. Commissioners serve two-year terms of office. Joe Denning was one of the two incumbents running for reelection. Denning had first been elected in November 1992 and was now running for his fourth term. On election day, November 3, 1998, Denning garnered 5,359 votes and placed third among the six candidates. The other incumbent, Jim Breece, collected 4,532 votes, placed fifth, and lost his seat. The election therefore produced a significantly reconstituted City Commission, with only Denning and Renaud as holdovers from the previous commission. Jim Bullington, Dan Hall, and Sandy Owen were all challengers who successfully captured commission seats; they were prepared to bring new ideas and plans to Bowling Green city government.

Newly elected commissioner Sandy Owen would be among the first to advocate change in the operations of city government. Shortly after taking her seat on the commission, Owen was appointed to the Bowling Green Municipal Utilities Board. This board oversees the operations of the public utility company, Bowling Green Municipal Utilities (BGMU), which provides water and electricity to the Bowling Green community. Other board members are also appointed by the mayor with confirmation by the City

Commission; only one seat on the board is reserved for an elected city commissioner.

Shortly after Commissioner Owen took her seat on the BGMU board, a dispute arose between Owen and other board members. Owen argued for greater public accountability of board decisions and proposed an ordinance that would provide greater City Commission and public oversight of the BGMU board. In spite of BGMU board opposition to Owen's proposed ordinance, the ordinance passed on a four to one vote. Only Mayor Renaud voted against the measure.

Shortly after the vote, on March 9, 1999, the BGMU board filed suit in Warren District Court, seeking to have Owen's new ordinance declared null and void; relations between certain commissioners and BGMU board members became increasingly strained. Owen wanted BGMU board members removed. In fact, on March 30, 1999, a letter to the BGMU board contained a request by Commissioner Owen (now Commissioner Jones, due to her recent marriage) that three BGMU board members—Bill Rabold, J. D. Droddy, and Edwin Wilbanks—resign from their positions with BGMU. In another move, a few days later, on April 9, the former chair of the BGMU board, Rabold, provided evidence that would lead to the mayor's ethics complaint against Denning and ultimately result in Denning's public reprimand by the Ethics Board.

## Issues in the Case

Within this milieu of political and legal conflict between the City Commission and the BGMU board, Mayor Eldon Renaud filed ethics complaints against Commissioners Sandy (Owen) Jones and Joe Denning on April 19, 1999. The mayor charged Jones with violating numerous sections of the city's Ethics Code. Most of the mayor's charges focused upon her alleged abuse of power by unduly politicizing the independent utility board. The Ethics Board heard the complaints against Jones and, after due deliberation, found no factual basis to support any of the charges. Commissioner Jones was exonerated.

The mayor also charged Denning with violating the city's Ethics Code. The mayor's principal allegation was that Denning sought and received preferential treatment from the general manager of BGMU, Eddie Beck, who allowed Denning to avoid making substantial payments on his overdue utility bill for more than two years, while at the same time continuing to receive electrical service. The Denning account was finally closed out in March 1998, but the outstanding $2,720 debt was not paid off by Denning, nor was the account referred to a collection agency, as is customary BGMU practice. Rather, the account was placed into inactive status, and Denning's electrical service was maintained but placed under a relative's name for billing.

In October 1998, the inactive (and unpaid) Denning account was discovered by Eddie Beck's successor, Bill Rabold. Less than one week after the Rabold discovery, Denning paid off the account with a cashier's check. Based upon these events, Mayor Renaud charged that Denning violated the city's Ethics Code by receiving preferential treatment by BGMU on his overdue utility bill. In his complaint against Denning, the mayor also raised a question about Denning using campaign funds to pay off the $2,720 debt owed to BGMU. In the transcript of the mayor's ethics complaint of April 19, 1999, to the Bowling Green Ethics Board, he stated:

> This being immediately before the election, the circumstances also raise questions regarding the source of the money for the cashier's check. Did his (Denning's) sudden acquisition of the funds to pay the account violate campaign finance laws? I have no answer to the question, but I suggest that an investigation into those circumstances is also a legitimate task of this committee, which might also consider turning the information over to the proper state authorities.

Denning initially responded to Renaud's charges through the local newspaper, the *Bowling Green Daily News,* and did not deny owing BGMU $2,720 for more than two years while continuing to receive electrical service. Denning did dispute, however, the mayor's charge that he received preferential treatment from BGMU. Denning observed that he was unemployed for ten to twelve months during the period in which his account was past due. Nevertheless, Denning claimed he set up a special payment schedule with BGMU and paid what he could to the utility during his period of financial difficulty. Denning stated in the *Daily News:* "I certainly don't think that I was given more of a preference than anyone else. . . . I was out of work and I had set up a payment schedule, which is done for anyone." Moreover, Denning was outraged that the mayor suggested a possible violation of campaign finance laws. Denning denied the charge, and on April 21, 1999, only two days after the mayor filed his ethics charges against him, Denning countered by filing two ethics complaints against the mayor.

Denning charged first that the mayor violated the city's Ethics Code by disclosing information with "reckless disregard for its truth or falsity," when the mayor suggested that Denning may have used campaign funds to pay off his personal bill with BGMU. Second, Denning charged that the mayor violated another section of the Ethics Code by arranging a meeting with J. D. Droddy, a member of the BGMU board, and Nicholas Brown, a member of the Ethics Board, to discuss procedures for drawing up an ethics complaint. This private meeting occurred at the mayor's house just a few days before the mayor, with assistance from Droddy, drew up and filed the April 19 ethics complaints against Jones and Denning. Brown and other Ethics Board members would ultimately hear the mayor's complaint against Jones and Denning, and so Denning charged that his ability to get a fair hearing before the Ethics Board was compromised by the mayor's meeting with Droddy and Brown.

The Bowling Green Ethics Board acted quickly, hiring legal counsel to represent the board and calling for hearings on the ethics complaints. Mayor Renaud's ethics complaints against Jones and Denning were heard first on May 6, 1999. Then, two weeks later on May 20, 1999, Commissioner Denning's ethics complaints against the mayor were heard by the same board.

## Adjudication of the Case

On May 6, 1999, the Bowling Green Ethics Board conducted a preliminary inquiry and heard testimony on the ethics charges brought by Mayor Renaud against Commissioner Denning. During his testimony, Commissioner Denning attempted to defend his actions. Denning stated that he had been unemployed for quite some time, had a medical condition that made it difficult to secure employment, and fell behind in paying his utility bill but had made special arrangements with BGMU to develop a schedule for paying off the $2,720 debt. Denning argued that he was being treated the same as any other Bowling Green citizen in the same situation and so no preferential treatment had been extended to him. Also, under questioning by his attorney, B. Alan Simpson, Denning categorically denied using any campaign money to pay his utility bill.

> Mr. Simpson: Did you use your campaign money to pay your bill?
> Mr. Denning: No, sir. Matter of fact, I doubt if my campaign had that much money in it.
> Mr. Simpson: Did the mayor ever ask you how you paid your bill?
> Mr. Denning: No, he did not.
> Mr. Simpson: To the best of your knowledge, do you know if he asked anybody else how you paid your bill?
> Mr. Denning: I'm not aware other than what I have read, and that is the accusation that there was a possibility that the funds came out of my campaign account.
> Mr. Simpson: Is that true or false?
> Mr. Denning: That is totally false.

An Ethics Board member, however, subsequently asked a key question about the timing of Denning's payment.

> Mr. Hohn: When you paid your—you paid the utility bill on October the 8th. Was that just a coincidence you paid it right before the election, or had you tried to get a loan earlier and couldn't get it? Is it just a coincidence?
> Mr. Denning: I think it's just a coincidence. I have found out in my very short number of years that it's easier to get a loan when you have a job than it is when you don't have one.

In spite of Denning's knowledge that the timing of the payment could surely appear suspect to some people, he nevertheless insisted that he had done nothing wrong. He seemed to be oblivious to violating the appearance standard, and his testimony revealed an insistence upon the rights of citizenship rather than the responsibilities of public office.

> Mr. Denning: I see myself as a citizen first. I should be entitled to any program that anyone else in the city of Bowling Green is afforded, and that includes a payment schedule. I should not be discriminated against because I'm a citizen that happens to be a city commissioner.

After hearing testimony and arguments by counsel, the board members deliberated and reached four findings:

> 1. The Board of Ethics determined that there was no factual basis for the allegation that you [Denning] used or attempted to use your official position as commissioner to secure special privileges, exemptions, personal or financial gain as set forth in ORD 25-4(6).
> 2. The Board of Ethics determined that there was no factual basis for the allegation that you accepted any valuable gift, in the form of service, loan, thing, or promise, from any person, firm or corporation which to your knowledge is interested directly or indirectly in any manner whatsoever in business dealings with the city as set forth in ORD 25-4 (4).
> 3. The Board of Ethics determined that there was sufficient evidence to conclude that you failed to maintain the highest standard of conduct for a public official by failing to avoid the appearance of impropriety. The Board of Ethics acknowledges that you were without employment for approximately ten (10) months and that this lack of employment caused you to become delinquent in the payment of several accounts or debts. These debts remained unpaid for an inordinate period of time and were paid in close proximity of time to the election and/or public's receiving information concerning your debts to the Housing Authority, on whose Board you sit, and to Bowling Green Municipal Utilities, a city entity overseen by the City Commission.
> 4. The Board of Ethics determined that there was sufficient evidence to conclude that you conducted yourself in a manner which failed to preserve public confidence in and/or respect for the government you represent by your conduct described in paragraph 3 above.

The Ethics Board concluded by observing that "contrary to your testimony, you are first a commissioner and second a citizen of Bowling Green, and as a public official you must maintain the highest standard of conduct. . . . Your elected position of public trust actually means that you must work harder than most citizens to avoid the appearance of impropriety. The Bowling Green Code of Ethics imposes this standard of conduct upon you as a public official." Based upon these findings, then, the Bowling Green Ethics Board issued a public reprimand to Denning on May 26, 1999.

On the same day, May 26, 1999, the Ethics Board issued two public reprimands to Mayor Renaud, based upon testimony heard on May 20, 1999. That testimony addressed the two ethics complaints Denning counterfiled against Mayor Renaud. The first complaint alleged that the mayor revealed a reckless disregard for the truth or falsity of his allegation that Denning may have violated campaign finance laws. Denning not only denied the mayor's charge but argued that the mayor was reckless in making the allegation. Under questioning by Renaud's attorney, David Broderick, Denning evaluated Renaud's allegation and raised his own question about not being contacted directly on the issue.

> Mr. Broderick: Now the comment was made—this being immediately before the election, the circumstances also raise questions regarding the source of money for the cashier's check. So the first complaint is you hadn't paid your bill.
>     The next complaint is now you have paid it in full, and the question is where the money came from. Is that a fair statement?
> Mr. Denning: That is a fair statement.
> Mr. Broderick: So the question that the mayor raised in his letter is did this sudden acquisition of funds to pay the account violate campaign finance laws. He didn't say it did. He has a question mark at that end, and says question, where did the money come from? Could it have come from campaign funds? Would you agree with that?
> Mr. Denning: I agree with the question.
> Mr. Broderick: Now, at that stage, tell me what is false about what we have covered so far?
> Mr. Denning: Well, as mentioned earlier, the mayor, if he had a problem with this, it would have been appropriate, I think, if he had approached me by it to see as to whether or not I used campaign funds in order to pay the BGMU bill, but the records reflect through other documents that is totally false even with the question mark I may have used campaign funds. We have proven that one is totally false.

Denning's second complaint focused on the meeting organized by the mayor to discuss the original filing of the ethics complaint against Commissioner Denning. On the weekend preceding the mayor's filing of the complaint, he invited J. D. Droddy and Nicholas Brown to his house to discuss the procedure for drawing up the complaint. At the time, Droddy was a member of the BGMU board, which was in litigation with the city; Brown was a member of the Ethics Board, which would hear any ethics complaint filed. Mayor Renaud was adamant that he did nothing wrong by organizing the meeting. Under questioning by Denning's attorney, B. Alan Simpson, the mayor insisted that he saw nothing wrong with the meeting.

> Mr. Simpson: Let me make sure I understand completely. You're telling this board today in this preliminary inquiry that you don't think it's

inappropriate to invite Dr. Droddy, who you knew at that time had
become an opponent of whatever nature of the commissioners of the
city of Bowling Green, and call him over to your house and call a member of this (ethics) panel over to your house to have a powwow? You
don't think that is inappropriate or doesn't even look inappropriate?
Mr. Renaud: No, sir.

Mr. Simpson also tried to drive home his point by describing an analogous
situation in which Mayor Renaud would likely object to a similarly
arranged meeting that worked against his interests.

Mr. Simpson: Well, if I had called Ms. Zoretic (Ethics Board chair) yes-
terday or the day before and invited her over to my house, and we
had sat out under the umbrella out back and had a glass of iced tea
and I had talked with her about all of these things, you would think
that was unethical, wouldn't you?
Mr. Renaud: Not if—not if somebody volunteered that information. You
wouldn't know unless I volunteered it. I'm just trying to do the right
thing.

Although the mayor felt he was only trying to do the right thing, the board
disagreed. On both counts, the board ruled against the mayor and issued
public reprimands. Specifically, the Ethics Board found:

1. As to the allegation and the ethics complaint that you [Renaud]
violated City Ordinance 25-13(9)(b)(1)(a), the Board of Ethics has determined that there was sufficient evidence to conclude that you disclosed
information with reckless disregard for its truth or falsity when you
specifically suggested that Commissioner Denning's sudden acquisition of
funds to pay his BGMU account may have violated campaign finance
laws and by suggesting further that the board should also consider turning the information to the proper state authorities. The board acknowledges that the timing of Mr. Denning's payment of his BGMU account
and the election was reasonable to present to the Board of Ethics; however, your complaint statement goes too far and was reckless.
2. As to the allegation in the ethics complaint that you violated City
Ordinance Chapter 25-3(1) by arranging a meeting between J. D. Droddy
and a member of this Board of Ethics, Nicholas N. Brown, the board has
determined that there is sufficient evidence that you failed to uphold and
maintain the highest standards required of a public official and that this
conduct is more likely to lead to the diminishing of the integrity, efficiency, or discipline of the city service.

This type of meeting gives the appearance of potentially influencing a
member of the fact-finding body, which is this Board of Ethics as a quasi-
judicial body. Moreover, this type of meeting is likely to cause any respondent to believe he or she might not or could not receive a fair hearing on an
ethics complaint before this ethics board. The board, however, does recognize and acknowledge that the Bowling Green Code of Ethics needs revision

including specificity as to the proper procedure for filing an ethics complaint, and the Board of Ethics considers this need for clarification of the Code of Ethics to be a mitigating circumstance in this matter.

Some had hoped that when the Bowling Green Ethics Board handed down its decisions on the ethics complaints, a sad chapter in Bowling Green politics would be over. That proved not to be the case. Less than one month after the Ethics Board issued the public reprimands, the mayor appealed to the Warren Circuit (County) Court, charging the board of ethics with "arbitrary and capricious" actions and seeking to have one of the two reprimands thrown out or vacated. Renaud chose to appeal only the first reprimand concerning his alleged "reckless" statement about Denning's possible payment of his BGMU account with campaign funds.

Legal briefs were submitted by attorneys for both the mayor and the Ethics Board to Judge John D. Minton Jr. of the Warren County Circuit Court for disposition. On September 14, 2000, Judge Minton issued his ruling, which vacated or dismissed the appealed public reprimand of Renaud. The judge found that "the Board misapplied the Code when it voted to reprimand Renaud specifically for a violation of Section 25-13 9(b)(1)(a) of the Code. . . . Quite simply, it is not a violation of the cited section of the Code to file a complaint even when the wording of the complaint may be 'reckless' or goes 'too far.'"

Mayor Renaud felt vindicated by the judge's decision. The mayor was quoted in the *Bowling Green Daily News* as stating, "I'm relieved that my name has been cleared. . . . had the ethics charge been allowed to stand, it would have 'tainted' the accomplishments of my administration over the past five years. . . . I was convinced I would find justice in Circuit Court once the ethics charge saw the light of day."

However, the Circuit Court ruling was only a partial vindication for Mayor Renaud. At the end of a very lengthy ethical and legal dispute, two public reprimands stood: one against Mayor Renaud and the other against Commissioner Denning. Both reprimands were issued by the Ethics Board for violations of the appearance standard—that is, the failure of a public official to avoid any appearance of impropriety. In addition, the Bowling Green community had been profoundly affected by the lengthy dispute. Media coverage of ethics and legal complaints among elected and appointed public officials left many Bowling Green citizens more cynical and less confident about Bowling Green city government.

## Conclusion

For many citizens who attempt to comprehend the milieu of political issues and events surrounding them, appearance is truly reality in their judgments and evaluations of issues, candidates, and public officials. Candidates and public officials therefore have a serious duty to recognize the significance of their actions according to the appearance standard. Even though their actions may be legal, candidates and public officials must constantly ask themselves how their actions might be perceived by citizens. It is unlikely that either Mayor Renaud or Commissioner Denning seriously considered this question. Their testimony reflects little attention to the appearance standard and how its violation adversely affected the Bowling Green community. Renaud and Denning deserved the public reprimands they received from the Ethics Board. The board's action carried no formal penalty or sanction but rather officially informed Bowling Green citizens of the unethical actions committed by the two public officials.

Candidates and public officials clearly have a higher standard than simply complying with the law. Even if their motives for an action are not culpable, they must be cognizant of appearances and willing to forgo an action that may look suspect. The alternative is to risk a violation of the public trust and an erosion of public confidence in government; and in this day when public cynicism of government is already much too high, candidates and public officials cannot simply appeal to the law and plead not guilty. They must take personal responsibility and adhere to a higher standard for the good of the American people and for the good of the republic.

# PART 2

## CURRENT ISSUES IN ELECTIONS

The controversy surrounding the Florida recount debacle during the 2000 presidential election exposed the organizational, technological, and institutional shortcomings associated with the way elections are run in the United States. How voters physically cast their ballot varies greatly from state to state and, within most states, from one local jurisdiction to another. It may seem odd to many people and appear confusing, but the highly decentralized nature of elections administration is rooted in the Constitution, which leaves the task to states that, in turn, delegate the implementation of elections to cities and counties. More often than not, any guidelines provided by the federal government and, more important, states, are vague and cover only the most rudimentary facets of election administration.

Up through the 1970s, nearly anyone could manufacture a "voting machine" and sell it to local election officials. Few states had any guidelines for testing or evaluating these devices. Local officials either took the vendor's word that the system worked or else depended on the opinion of colleagues who had already bought it.[1]

Today, Americans use a wide range of election technologies to record their vote, each type offering its own set of tangible benefits and problems. Paper ballots enable voters to record their choices, in private, by marking the boxes next to the candidate or issue choice they select, and then drop the voted ballot in a sealed ballot box. With mechanical lever voting, machines list the name of each candidate or ballot issue and assign a particular lever in a rectangular array of levers on the front of the machine. Voters pull down selected levers to indicate choices. "Punch card" systems use a card (or cards) and a small clipboard-sized device for recording votes, where voters punch holes in the cards (with a supplied punch device) opposite their preferred candidate or ballot issue. The "mark sense" system (optically scanned paper ballots) makes use of a ballot card on which candidates and issue choices are preprinted next to an empty rectangle, circle, oval, or an incomplete arrow. Voters record their choices by filling in the shape or by completing the arrow. All these traditional paper-based technologies, however, are prone to high rates of spoiled, or residual, votes.[2] The infamous "butterfly ballot"—a variation of the punch card system that had candidate names on both pages and punch holes down the middle—that was used in Palm Beach County, Florida, during the 2000 presidential election created a national controversy and introduced the public to a new election lexicon: punched, hanging, swinging, dimpled, and pregnant chads.[3]

The most recent configuration in the evolution of voting systems is known as "direct recording electronic" (DRE) voting. DRE is an electronic implementation of the old mechanical lever systems, in which the voter directly enters choices into electronic storage with the use of a touch screen, push-buttons, or similar electronic or computer devices. Arizona and California pioneered computerized voting in 2000, when they allowed various voters to cast their votes over the Internet in their primary and general elections. Arizona's experiment with Internet voting led voters to cast 40,000 votes—more than 46 percent of the total—through cyberspace, although it was quickly challenged in the judicial arena because it was believed to increase the electoral access of affluent persons (who owned computers) over poorer voters.[4] Electronic voting systems are also complex, and complexity can be the enemy of security and citizens intimidated by new technologies.

As is discussed in the cases in this section of the book, the voting systems used in certain counties in the state of Florida were part of the reason why the election of 2000 was so controversial. In part because of a flawed ballot design and antiquated machinery, it is possible that voters intending to cast a vote for Al Gore in the presidential race inadvertently voted for Patrick Buchanan. In addition, as is presented in the cases on the infamous Florida election and a recent gubernatorial election in Mississippi, elections are far from apolitical contests, and the science and politics behind administering an election are complex and demand highly qualified officials. Providing firsthand insights into the people, events, controversies, and results of the controversial elections in Florida in 2000 and Mississippi in 1999 are writers from the trenches of those elections. Donna Simmons, a former senior official in the Mississippi governor's office and campaign manager involved in the election in question, offers an account of the 1999 gubernatorial election. Two views of the momentous election in Florida in 2000 are provided by Jane Carroll, former supervisor of elections in Broward County, and Joan Karp, head of a chapter of the League of Women Voters in Palm Beach County. These two counties were at the epicenter of controversy in that election saga.

The variety of voting technologies used in the United States also raises issues about voting irregularities, the integrity of elections, and the issue of voting system standards. According to one study conducted shortly after the ballot battles, faulty and outdated voting technology that contributed to residual votes, together with registration problems, was largely responsible for the nearly 6 million votes lost in the 2000 election.[5] To be certain, close elections, problematic votes, and recounts occur in every election year. But in the 2000 presidential election, the winner's margin was less than one-half of 1 percent in four states: Florida, Iowa, New Mexico, and Wisconsin.[6] Simply put, questionable ballots affect electoral outcomes. It is, therefore, important to make sure elections work.

Voting system standards help state and local election officials ensure that the voting systems used by the public work accurately and reliably. Such standards and regulations could be cast in the form of documented agreements containing technical specifications to be used consistently as guidelines. They would ensure that automated voting systems (both those that use a paper ballot and all electronic systems) are accurate, reliable, and secure (e.g., the agreements would specify technical requirements for hardware, software, security, quality assurance, and documentation). Thirty-seven states make use of national standards recommended by the Federal Election Commission (FEC) or require testing against the standards before a system can be marketed within their boundaries, thus improving the integrity of elections in those voting areas.[7] The thirteen states that have not adopted these voting systems standards and likewise do not require the testing of systems against the standards by independent testing authorities are predominantly smaller, less populous states in the Great Plains region. Voting standards are not permanent, however. They must evolve with technological advancements, which can be cumbersome for less affluent areas, thus raising the issue of inequity between rich and poor.

With so much at stake, political parties have a vested interest in seeing their candidates win. From promoting election procedures and systems advantageous to their candidates to placing observers at polling sites, political parties play prominent roles in elections. Partisan politics continues to define elections, and election outcomes continue to transform politics in the United States. Dramatic shifts in power resulting from elections are traced in the chapter by Nicol Rae. Readers are provided with an historical account of such transformations and recent trends in elections.

Elections have produced divided government, whereby one party controls the Congress and the other controls the White House. The latter part of the twentieth century saw elections transform the South from the one-party domination by conservative Democrats to a Republican stronghold, both in state legislatures and in the state house across the region. The South suddenly emerged as a key voting block for Republican presidential candidates, who enjoyed overwhelming support in the region. However, the transformation continues and is analyzed by Matthew Corrigan, who suggests that Democrats are not doing as poorly in the region as expected. Corrigan also reveals survival strategies used by Democrats to remain competitive in the South.

Other great shifts in power resulting from elections include gains by Democrats in the wake of Watergate and President Richard Nixon's resignation from the White House in 1974 and Republican victories on the coattails of President Ronald Reagan's landslide in 1980. After decades in which the norm was Democratic control of Congress, in 1994 the Republican Party took over control of both houses in an election that produced the largest midterm loss for a party occupying the presidency since 1946. Not only did the Democrats lose fifty-two seats in the House and eight seats in the Senate (and then Senator Richard Shelby, a Republican from Alabama, switched parties), but the historic 1994 election brought to Congress a new crop of Republican revolutionaries, more conservative than their seasoned colleagues in the chamber and less interested in playing by the old rules. As was the case following Watergate, Reagan's election to the White House, and the 1994 Republican takeover of Congress, great shifts in power occur and produce changes in policy agendas and transformations in politics.

One of the seemingly enduring characteristics of campaigns and elections is the need for money. Candidates need money to employ new campaign techniques and technologies. And these new tools for winning office are increasingly expensive. It is rare for candidates to win major competitive elections without raising significant sums of money. Former senator William Proxmire (D-Wis.), who retired from the U.S. Senate in the 1980s without ever having spent $5,000 in a Senate race, was truly an aberration. Congressional candidates raised a total of $1.047 billion for the 1999–2000 election cycle and spent a total of $1.066 billion, according to a report by the Federal Election Commission.[8] These amounts were the highest recorded in any election cycle in the FEC's twenty-five-year existence.

The sources and strategies for funding campaigns are undergoing change and are worth our attention. Likewise, candidate loans and contributions to their own campaigns totaled $175.9 million, up 61 percent from the $107.2 million reported just two years earlier in 1997–1998. Much of this increase was fueled by one Senate candidate in New Jersey—Democrat John Stevens Corzine—who generated a record $63,253,520 in net receipts. Senate candidates used $107.7 million of their own funds, whereas House candidates used $53.6 million in candidate funds.[9]

Indeed, few changes have transformed U.S. elections and the pool of candidates more since the 1970s than campaign finance. It, in turn, has resonated—both positively and negatively—with voters. Incumbents gain financial and electoral advantages over challengers; wealthy contributors potentially buy influence through their donations, upsetting the balance of "one person, one vote"; and the integrity of the electoral system is put in question by the practice. Not surprisingly, then, campaign finance reform has been among the most highly politicized and controversial of all political issues in the United States. Questions need to be asked, such as why legislation has not done a better job of addressing the problems and what reforms are currently being considered. All the while, elections grow increasingly expensive, complaints of negativity abound, and low voter turnout continues to plague the process. The issue of campaign finance and campaign reforms is presented by Victoria Farrar-Myers, who unravels the complexities of the issue and explores the challenges of and prospects for reforming the system.

A system of competitive elections is at the heart of the nation's democratic experience. Ensuring the openness, fairness, and accuracy of elections, however, is easier said than done. This goal remains one of the most significant and complex challenges facing not only the United States but any democracy worldwide. Contrary to the barbs of critics and cynics, elections matter. Indeed, great shifts in power routinely occur when the people make their voice heard at the ballot box, and election outcomes continually transform the body politic. This part of the book examines the shifts in power and transformations resulting from elections, recent trends in elections, and the effort to reform the system. The cases concluding the section provide a behind-the-scenes look at the mechanics of administering elections, scandals that have defined some recent elections, and challenges to make sure the election does what it is supposed to do. Of course, in the end one would like to think that it simply comes down to the citizens getting out to vote for the best candidate.

# 6

# Partisan Politics in a Nonpartisan Society

## Nicol C. Rae

Close outcomes and an intensely high level of partisanship between the major parties have characterized recent national elections in the United States. These trends have been further reflected by increased partisanship in Congress and increasingly vexed relations between a Congress controlled by one major party and a White House controlled by the other. Yet, we have witnessed serious and significant "independent" or "third-party" campaigns and continuing apathy among the electorate. Even the intensely contested and controversial presidential elections of 2000 attracted only approximately 51 percent of the eligible electorate to the polls.[1]

In this chapter I suggest that an answer to the conundrum lies in the successful adaptation of the major parties (and closely related interest groups) to the post–World War II U.S. political universe, where television news has supplanted the parties' traditional role as the primary intermediary between voters and government. The apparent party "decline" and the rise of personality-oriented politics in electoral campaigns in the 1952–1976 period took place prior to the parties' perception of a possible new role in this "dealigned," "nonpartisan" political environment. Since the late 1970s, first the Republicans and then the Democrats have carved out such a new role for themselves in this "disaggregated" political universe, as purveyors of services to candidates (through creative interpretations of the 1970s campaign finance reform laws) and as coordinators of the campaigning activities of allied interests and political action committees (PACs). During the 1980s and 1990s, they have refined these activities to a fine art, although the focus on mobilization of the committed—in terms of both campaign resources and votes—has meant that the contemporary major parties are relatively uninterested in mobilizing the independent, the apathetic, or the uncommitted (still a preponderance of the U.S. electorate).[2]

Within this changed political universe of weak party loyalties and the permanent televisual campaign, traditional changes in voter alignments still occur, but they do not necessarily occur in harmony with campaign and election technology. As a consequence, the disintegration of the New Deal coalition and the rise of conservatism within the electorate was masked to some extent by the erosion of parties and the split-level voting alignments of the 1952–1976 period, and the shift did not manifest itself in the governmental dominance of the Republican Party, except in presidential elections. This prolonged realignment was largely completed by the early 1990s, however, and the Democrats and Republicans become clearly more "liberal" and "conservative" parties at all levels of electoral competition. With the end of the Cold War and the exhaustion of the conservative Reagan revolution, the national voting alignment between the major parties has become extremely finely balanced, and national elections have become highly competitive.

The modern period bears some superficial similarity to the late nineteenth century, which was also a time of intense partisanship and highly competitive national elections, with strong party leadership in Congress. Yet the late nineteenth century also witnessed unprecedented levels of party loyalty and voter mobilization in the United States, whereas the modern era has been a time of unprecedented dissatisfaction with national political institutions—particularly political parties—and widespread voter alienation and apathy. Social and technological developments have also driven the parties and their interest group allies toward a strategy of "selective mobilization" of the committed rather than competition for the votes of the uncommitted or nonpartisan.[3] The upshot of all these changes is a politics of intense partisanship in election campaigns and at all levels of government that continues, ratchetlike, to turn off an increasing number of voters, who—like Macbeth—see much of the overheated political rhetoric purveyed by politicians and the news media as "sound and fury signifying nothing." Before further explaining how Americans got to this pass, let us briefly discuss the political universe that preceded it.

## The Partisan Era: 1840–1948

Post–World War II U.S. history and political science have provided thorough and voluminous scholarship on the partisan era and the underpinnings of party machine politics.[4] In fact, there has been a tendency in some—but by no means in all—of this literature to romanticize the partisan century from 1840 to 1948, for despite the downside of corruption, ballot rigging, intimidation, and southern black disfranchisement, the two major parties during this period undoubtedly did succeed in mobilizing voters, not only in terms of electoral turnout, which soared above 80 percent in presidential elections, but also in terms of engaging voters in campaigns, no matter how banal the activities and slogans.[5] The residual strength of these voter loyalties was picked up by the authors of *The American Voter,* writing in the 1950s, when they found that intergenerationally transmitted partisan identification was by far the greatest single determinant of electoral choice among Americans.[6]

During the partisan era, Americans voted a straight party ticket at election after election. The overwhelming number of voters at this time identified with one or the other major party, and elections were largely an exercise in mobilizing the faithful. The job of parties was to contact voters, engage them in the campaign, let them know who the candidates were, and get them to the polls: all tasks that they performed in a most efficient fashion by all accounts.

When electoral and political change did occur, it did so in the form of voter realignments. They were engendered by an issue or event—slavery, the Civil War, free silverism, the Great Depression—so polarizing or traumatic that it could actually shatter deeply ingrained party loyalties and move voters (usually after the temporary expedient of a new but short-lived "third party") from one major party to the other.[7] Alternatively, it has been argued that such realignments were less a matter of conversion of voters than the mobilization of the hitherto unmobilized—immigrants, the younger generation, or voters in the newly settled western states.[8] Regardless, such periodic electoral shifts (1860, 1896, 1932) served as means for the resolution of political disputes at both the elite and mass level and encouraged necessary change in public policy and the nature of the political regime.

For a period of more than a century, then, parties and partisanship, with periodic realignments in which parties served as vehicles for political change, dominated U.S. politics and government and most emphatically campaigns and elections. After 1896, the party system become lopsidedly Republican nationally and in most regions of the country—with the exception of the even more solidly Democratic states of the defeated Confederacy. Partly in response to the need for electoral competition but perhaps more as a result of the development of mass newspapers, literacy, urbanization, economic growth, and a growing urban professional middle class, the Progressive movement embarked on a full-scale assault on the party machines via the direct primary, secret voting, civil service reform, and the initiative, referendum, and recall at the state and local levels.[9] Yet, although the Progressive onslaught marked the beginning of the long slow decline of the traditional party machines and entrenched partisan loyalties, it is testimony to the pervasiveness and resilience of machine politics and the loyalty it evoked from voters that the parties largely adapted themselves to the Progressive reforms without a notable loss in power, save for the newly settled western states, where the Progressive reforms snuffed out the potential for party development, and the Democratic South, where there was no serious party politics.

The partisan era continued beyond progressivism and through a final major electoral realignment in the 1930s. The New Deal realignment saw the Democratic Party build a large electoral and governmental majority of white southerners, immigrants, blue-collar workers, Catholics, Jews, and organized labor that effectively trounced the Republicans in the five subsequent presidential elections and established a dominance in Congress, state legislatures, and the major urban centers that persisted until the 1990s.[10] This broad coalition united in a consensus to extend the scope of federal government intervention in economic and domestic policy. In 1948, despite fraying at the edges of the coalition (in the shape of the Strom Thurmond and Henry Wallace third-party presidential bids), Franklin Delano Roosevelt's (FDR's) less charismatic successor, Harry Truman, was still able to achieve an upset victory over a moderate and highly regarded Republican nominee, Thomas E. Dewey.

The New Deal electoral world was still that described by the authors of *The American Voter* in the 1950s. Americans perceived the political world through the prism of partisan identities, and those identities still leaned heavily toward the Democratic Party, despite the comfortable presidential victories of Republican war hero General Dwight D. Eisenhower in 1952 and 1956. Yet, 1948 was the last classic old-style national election campaign pervaded by traditional partisanship and party loyalties. The 1952 Democratic National Convention would be the last to go to more than one ballot in choosing a president and in which the nominee emerged as the choice of party bosses at the convention itself in the classic manner of the partisan era. That election also demonstrated two new features that would characterize national election campaigns in the future: the significance of primary elections (especially Eisenhower's early win in New Hampshire) and the role of television (Richard Nixon's "Checkers Speech" and the "I like Ike" commercials). The 1956 election produced a victory for a president from one party together with a Congress where the opposing party at least controlled one house: an unusual circumstance in the partisan century but commonplace since (such an outcome has occurred in seven of the twelve presidential contests since 1956).

The election campaigns of the 1950s demonstrated two phenomena occurring simultaneously in U.S. politics: the gradual erosion of the New Deal electoral alignment and the gradual disappearance of traditional party-centered campaigns. Much of the confusion and volatility of U.S. politics in the following two decades can be explained by the concurrence of these developments.

## The Era of Dealignment: 1952–1976

During this period, it appeared that U.S. political parties were in inexorable decline and that single issues and candidate personalities had become much more critical in determining electoral choices among a much less partisan electorate. The New Deal electoral alignment was clearly in a state of atrophy, but voters appeared to be moving not between the parties but away from both of them. Moreover, it appeared that a whole new "baby boom" generation of voters remained unmobilized and perhaps unmobilizable by the traditional major parties.

Although previous realignments were characterized by voter shifts across the board at all electoral levels, the post-1952 period saw massive and unprecedented "ticket splitting," with different partisan outcomes at different levels of electoral competition, dramatic voter swings between parties from election to election, and the emergence of significant third-party challenges. Norman Nie, Sydney Verba, and John Petrocik's influential update of the *American Voter* study found that the intense party loyalties of the 1950s had eroded and that voters in the early 1970s were more influenced by personality, single issues, and ideology than party loyalties. They also found soaring levels of voters identifying themselves as "independents," especially younger voters.[11]

Within the major parties, the traditional party elites—state and local party bosses—found themselves dethroned in presidential nominating politics by insurgent grassroots movements of ideological activists galvanized by the polarizing national disputes over civil rights, the Vietnam War, and the so-called counterculture. The Republican eastern establishment, shattered by decades of electoral defeats, was ousted in 1964 by a national conservative movement led by the unrepentantly ideological Arizona senator Barry Goldwater, whose famous acceptance speech at the 1964 Republican Convention repudiated the central tenet of traditional party politics by stating categorically that he would rather be right on conservative principle than compromise to win at the polls.[12]

The Democrats' turn came in 1968, when insurgent antiwar candidates Eugene McCarthy and Robert Kennedy drove incumbent president Lyndon Johnson (LBJ) out of the race and dominated the presidential primaries. Nevertheless, state and local party leaders, following Kennedy's assassination in June, saw fit to nominate LBJ's handpicked successor, Vice President Hubert Humphrey, at the Chicago convention. Chaos inside and outside the convention hall indicated a party in disarray, and the insurgents turned temporary defeat into long-term victory after Humphrey's narrow defeat in the fall by instigating changes in the party's presidential nominating rules. The new rules stripped nominating power from the party leaders at the national convention and moved it to primary elections, where the mobilization of committed activists could have much more impact.[13]

Organizational disintegration made the national parties decreasingly adequate vehicles for electoral mobilization, yet beneath all the turmoil, a significant realignment of the electorate was underway: it was not a partisan realignment on traditional lines but an ideological realignment, reflected more in support for individual candidates and new social movements than political parties. While being hammered nationally by LBJ in 1964, Barry Goldwater succeeded in sweeping the Deep South states that had not gone Republican since the Civil War. In fact, the white backlash against the civil rights movement and the rise of the New South business class combined to put almost the entire region in the Republican column in presidential elections from 1968 onward. The new conservative ideological alignments among white southerners and the northern white middle class was further illustrated by the strong support for third-party conservative candidate George Wallace in both the South and sections of the urban North in 1968—Wallace won 14 percent nationally, the strongest third-party showing since 1924.[14] Similarly, black voters (many of them in the South, newly enfranchised by the 1965 Voting Rights Act) and northern, white, liberal, antiwar protestors lined up ever more strongly behind Democratic presidential candidates.[15]

Yet, in their traditional electoral bastions, both national parties held onto a large number of conservative southern Democrats and northeastern liberal Republicans, which confused the picture below the presidential level and combined with the more universal changes in voting habits and the communications revolution in election campaigns to complicate the situation. And in Congress, the persistence of Democratic loyalties beneath the presidential level in the South maintained nominal Democratic control, although both chambers were still dominated ideologically on many issues by the southern Democratic-Republican "conservative coalition" until the early 1970s. In fact, the prospects for a Republican congressional realignment to match the party's dominance in presidential elections since 1952 may well have been aborted by the Watergate scandal and the changes in campaign finance laws that followed. Many of the House Republicans defeated in the 1974 post-Watergate election were replaced by young liberal Democrats who brilliantly exploited the advantages of incumbency—primarily in media visibility and fundraising—in the new candidate-centered electoral environment to extend the Democratic House majority some two decades beyond its natural life.[16]

Watergate also led to the nomination and election of the consummate political outsider, former Georgia governor Jimmy Carter, as president in 1976. Carter typified the new politics. He won nomination as a complete political outsider by cultivating early primary election successes and a good television profile into such a degree of media momentum that he swept aside more conventional party favorites in the primaries. In fact, Carter ran almost as the "antiparty" candidate, promising a fresh start in the United States after the traumas of Vietnam and Watergate, with a "government of love." That year the Republicans almost nominated another outsider—conservative former California governor and movie star Ronald Reagan—over incumbent president Gerald Ford. Carter managed a narrow victory in

November with a semblance of the old New Deal coalition, but the major factors in his victory were the temporary electoral fallout from Watergate and the fact that his regional background helped him to become the first Democrat since FDR in 1944 to carry almost the entire South.[17]

In fact, Carter's presidency saw the beginnings of the clearing of the confused period of simultaneous realignment and party decline and the emergence of a new electoral order that still featured split-level electoral alignments and voter volatility, but all conducted within a much more partisan framework.

## The Return of the Parties:
## U.S. Campaigns and Elections Since 1980

The 1980 election marked the beginning of the new partisan era in U.S. politics, one in which political parties play a greater role in U.S. elections and government than at any time since the late nineteenth century but still fail to engage most voters or evoke anything like the loyalties of a century ago. Nevertheless, parties have carved out a critical role through adaptation to the late twentieth-century electoral universe and have provided leadership and direction to a potentially chaotic Congress of individual political entrepreneurs. There is nothing wrong with this in itself, but problems arise because political survival in this universe has driven the parties toward a degree of ideological and rhetorical polarization that creates problems for governance in the federal system, particularly when the considerably less partisan electorate continues to respond by dividing control of the executive and legislative branches between the parties.

The new partisan era really commenced in the late 1970s, when the Republican National Committee (RNC) under national chairman William Brock figured out that national party committees (the RNC plus the two congressional campaign committees—the National Republican Senatorial Committee and the National Republican Congressional Committee) could play a vital role in channeling funds to Republican candidates, recruiting congressional candidates, and providing services such as computing and polling to Republican campaigns.[18] The national committee also set up candidate and campaign manager training schools and a Republican journal of opinion. All this was possible because the national Republican committees were flush with funds brought in by successful use of small-donor fundraising via direct mail—using lists borrowed from conservative grassroots organizations and going back to the 1964 Goldwater campaign.

In the 1980 election, national party resources were used effectively by the Republicans to help elect Ronald Reagan—who ran the most partisan presidential campaign in years, even appearing on the Capitol steps with Republican congressional candidates—and to gain thirteen seats and take

control of the U.S. Senate for the first time since the 1950s.[19] Republican
national officials had also become adept at getting around the 1974 Federal
Elections Campaign Amendment Act (FECA) limits on party contributions
by channeling funds to their candidates through loopholes in the law that
left the parties free to raise and spend unlimited amounts for "party-building" or "advocacy" activities. The Republicans were thus the first to exploit
the so-called soft money loophole and make use of large donor fundraising
for the national party once again.[20]

In this new role, the national party did not usually intervene in primary
elections, as did the state party bosses of old, but concentrated on channeling funds to candidates already nominated. Yet, the new national largesse
undoubtedly did help to tie candidates somewhat more closely to the
party—particularly the national party, generally subordinate to state and
local organizations for most of U.S. history. The newly interventionist
Republican national party committees could also coordinate with sympa-
thetic PACs and pick out promising campaigns for the latter to support with
money and other campaign resources. In fact, the new role of the Republican National Committee was as a kind of "super PAC," tying the campaign
activities of a network of conservative organizations and PACs together in
a common cause: electing more Republican candidates to promote conservative causes in Washington, D.C. Despite the fact that significant numbers
of Republican officeholders and identifiers—never mind the general electorate—did not endorse their views, the national Republican Party and the
candidates it supported formed intimate ties with the antiabortion movement, the renascent religious right, and anti–gun control organizations.[21]
Republican party candidates increasingly relied on these groups for funding
and campaign services in primary and general elections. The fact that these
organizations had a core constituency of supporters likely to turn out in
increasingly low-turnout election contests made them all that much more
significant.

Although it took the national Democratic committees a decade to fully
catch up with the Grand Old Party (GOP), similar trends were in play on
their side as well. The difference was that, in the case of the Democrats, the
signs of party revival first appeared on Capitol Hill before their national
party committees began to copy the techniques of the Republicans.

Reforms of the congressional committee system in the 1970s, intended
to break the power of conservative, southern committee chairs and increase
the power of individual members, also enhanced the power of the party
leadership. Thomas P. "Tip" O'Neill was the first in a trio of stronger
Democratic U.S. House speakers, followed by Jim Wright and Tom Foley.
Although O'Neill did not get along well with the independent-minded
Democratic president Jimmy Carter, he was galvanized by the election of
Ronald Reagan, who constituted a major threat to the New Deal political
world that had nurtured O'Neill's political career. After Reagan wooed

conservative southern Democrats in the House to help pass his programs in 1981, O'Neill and his successors strove mightily to keep their congressional party united in defense of core Democratic programs and issues. They were also able to use their newfound control of the key Rules Committee to keep measures that would divide the Democratic Party off the floor of the House and the newfound power of the House Democratic caucus to remove committee chairs to keep the latter in line.[22]

More fundamental than the newfound muscle of the congressional Democratic leadership, however, was the continuing effect of the long-term secular post–New Deal realignment. As the Republican Party grew in the South, white southern Democrats were being replaced, either by Republicans or less conservative white Democrats who had to cater to the largely liberal political outlook of the new Democratic voter base in the South: African American voters. In much of the Northeast, many districts formerly held by moderate-to-liberal Republicans were taken over by liberal Democrats after 1974. The overall result of these electoral changes was to make the congressional Democratic majority more homogeneously liberal in ideology and the Republicans more conservative.[23] Increasingly, Democratic and Republican candidates throughout the nation found themselves seeking the same sources of support district by district for nomination and general election campaigns: minorities, gays, pro-choice groups, labor unions, trial lawyers, and teachers in the case of aspiring Democrats; and the religious right, gun owners, small business organizations, and antiabortion groups in the case of the Republicans.

These were the main forces driving increased party unity in Congress and the more and more heated partisan rhetoric being deployed by party leaders and followers. Ironically, the gap between the parties on traditional New Deal economic issues was narrowing as the Democrats moved right to encompass the new, more conservative economic consensus of the Reagan-Bush years. Similarly, the post-Vietnam gap between the parties on foreign policy intervention closed as the two conservative Republican Reagan and Bush administrations actually strove to wind down the Cold War in the wake of the collapse of the Warsaw Pact and the Soviet Union. But although the intensity of partisan rhetoric and bitterness appeared to be in inverse proportion to the real differences between the parties, the primary source of party cleavages in the United States since the 1980s has been that complex of cultural and lifestyle issues opened up by the civil rights revolutions and the new sexual freedom of the 1960s and 1970s—abortion, gay rights, feminism, the public role of religion, affirmative action, indecency versus civil liberties, and so on—moral questions that are notoriously hard to resolve. They are the issues that the most passionate adherents of the contemporary parties care most about, although it may not be the case with the public at large, perhaps explaining much of the disconnect between the intensity and fervor of contemporary partisans and much of the American public.

A final factor that has become increasingly important is the impact of the news media on the nature of political deliberation and debate. The point has already been made that television news, rather than the parties, now provides Americans with the bulk of their political information and that Americans "trust" television news far more than they trust politicians.[24] But television news is generally limited in the time it has to present information, and thus complex and sensitive moral questions—for example, abortion—have to be boiled down to relatively crude slogans—"the slaughter of innocent life" versus "a woman's right to control her own body," for example. The antagonists in the debate also have an interest in finding the crudest slogan to defame their opponents and try to "spin" the debate their way. Such a confrontation is likely to be far more dramatic than a nuanced discussion of the issue, and the fundamental role of television is to entertain. For reasons of time constraints and dramatic effect, then, debate between the parties or between interest groups on many issues boils down to rhetorical abuse, which makes bipartisan relations between the parties and efforts to resolve certain issues all the more difficult.

Most voters, of course, have mixed, complex views on many of these highly sensitive lifestyle issues, but public debate on these matters is framed by issue activists working through the national parties and the news media as between stark, polarized alternatives. What is highly surprising is that many voters split their tickets so that these forces cancel each other out in the national government. Voters have become "creative Madisonians" because the polarized partisan alternatives leave them with little choice.

## The Clinton Years: Partisanship in Extremis

The framework of U.S. politics in the 1990s had already been drawn by the conclusion of Ronald Reagan's second term in 1988. In the next decade, the tendencies already underway only intensified and were accompanied by a change in the partisan balances at different levels of electoral competition. Conservatism's ascendancy on economic issues became evident with the triumph of the neoliberal New Democrat Bill Clinton in 1992, yet the Republican presidential ascendancy was broken in Clinton's 1992 and 1996 victories and the dead-heat election of 2000. Perhaps even more surprising, the forty-year Democratic domination of the House of Representatives came to an end in 1994. All aspects of the national government were now closely contested between the parties. Yet, in contrast to the dramatically engaged electorate of a hundred years before, the closeness of U.S. elections in the 1990s might perhaps be attributed to fact that many, even among those who did choose to exercise their right to vote were impressed by neither of the two increasingly polarized ideological coalitions that still dominated national politics. Further evidence for this view was provided by the significant independent and third-party campaigns conducted by Texas billionaire Ross Perot in 1992 and 1996 and by Green Party candidate Ralph Nader in 2000.

The end of the Republican grip on the White House can be put down to two factors: the end of the prosperity of the Reagan years in the early 1990s recession and the end of the Cold War, which had given advantages to Republican candidates in presidential elections, since the presidential Democratic Party was captured by dovish forces during the Vietnam War. With the battle lines shifting to economic and domestic policy issues, the Democrats were much better placed to compete for the presidency, especially when led by the New Democratic southern governor Bill Clinton in 1992. Clinton was not untainted by the 1960s counterculture, but his support of the death penalty and welfare reform, in addition to his relative economic conservatism, reassured moderate voters that he was not a radical on social and cultural issues.[25] Republican conservatism seemed tired and exhausted, with no new ideas except to move further in a more radical direction than most of the electorate would want to contemplate; hence the adverse public reaction to the strident tone of the 1992 Republican convention given over to the forces of the religious right.[26] In office, after a difficult first two years, Clinton proved to be brilliant at the politics of "triangulation": paying enough lip service to the contemporary cultural shibboleths of the Democratic Party activists while making strategic moves toward Republican positions on some issues.[27] Although this tactic infuriated more militant leftists and drove Republicans into a frenzy of frustration, most Americans felt comfortable with Clinton's creative and continually evolving "centrism."

As far as Republican control of Congress was concerned, a series of factors in the early 1990s combined to give the Republicans a window of opportunity to grab control of the House of Representatives. That they took that opportunity was largely due to the foibles of the Clinton administration in its early years and some effective strategic leadership on the part of House minority whip Newt Gingrich. A prime factor in allowing the Republicans an opportunity to make significant House gains was the 1992 congressional redistricting. Traditionally, this process had helped to protect mostly Democratic incumbents, but a series of amendments to the Voting Rights Act and an alliance between the George H. W. Bush Justice Department and minority leaders in many states to create more minority districts worked to the Republicans' benefit. Many white conservative Democrats—particularly in the South—found themselves faced with a choice between a difficult primary election against a minority candidate or a difficult general election in a lily-white district against a Republican.[28] Many of them exercised a third option: retirement. Thus, there was a higher number than usual of new seats and open seats that might be potentially open to Republican capture. The congressional Democratic leadership was also embarrassed by a series of "scandals" that made them seem somewhat sleazy and arrogant from their years in power. Finally, the failure of the Democratic House and Senate majorities to pass President Clinton's much-vaunted health care program in 1994 also gave the congressional Democrats an image of ineptitude.

By astute use of the media, Gingrich was able to crystallize these issues and effectively nationalize the 1994 midterm elections into a referendum on Clinton and, by association, the Democrats.[29] The Republicans' focus group–tested manifesto, the "Contract with America," was designed to rally Republican activists and attract the attention of the news media. Moreover, Minority Whip Gingrich launched the contract at a large "made-for-TV" rally on the Capitol steps with Republican candidates, reminiscent of Reagan in 1980.

Gingrich was a pure creature of the new political universe of sound bites and strident rhetoric. Elected to the House in 1978, the Georgian had not been closely associated with any significant piece of legislation but had built his reputation by his bitter attacks on the congressional Democrats as "corrupt" and "unresponsive." In fact, Gingrich's attacks on the House floor and in the media were largely responsible for driving Jim Wright, a powerful and successful (in terms of legislative output) speaker, out of office. For that accomplishment, Gingrich was universally loathed by Democrats on Capitol Hill, yet he managed to rise to the leadership of his party by 1994. It is unlikely that such a polarizing figure would have been a congressional party leader in the age of Sam Rayburn and Joseph Martin—both highly partisan according to the old norms of partisanship in the New Deal era but also skilled legislative brokers.

Unfortunately for Gingrich, the polarized partisan politics of the 1990s had a habit of devouring its own children. Jim Wright had been hounded out of the speakership on ethics charges in 1989, with Newt Gingrich leading the Republican pack. Gingrich's own speakership was plagued by ethics charges from Democrats, and he too was forced from office after the GOP lost seats in the 1998 midterm elections. It was the first time a party holding the White House for six years—the Democrats—had gained seats in a midterm election since the 1820s.[30] A large part of the reason for the Democrats' success was the highly partisan impeachment proceedings against President Bill Clinton by the Republican House of Representatives in the middle of the election campaign.

The Clinton impeachment is a model example of the power of partisanship in contemporary U.S. politics. In the House Judiciary Committee, almost every significant vote fell along partisan lines, with Republicans voting to impeach the president and Democrats to drop the charges. The effort to impeach Clinton devoured Newt Gingrich and his designated successor, Robert Livingston. Why, against all electoral reason, did the Republicans persist?

They persisted because in fact in the 1990s political universe, it made eminent sense for all but five Republican House members to stick with the leadership line and impeach the president, even though they knew they had no chance of obtaining the necessary two-thirds majority for conviction in the Senate. Republicans were well aware that all the major interests that supported the party financially and organizationally were extremely hostile to the president. They also knew that, from coast to coast, these activists constituted the Republican electoral base and would be guaranteed to show up at the polls. In low-turnout primaries, a vote against impeachment might invite a conservative challenge: in a general election, an unenthusiastic base might contribute to defeat.[31] Similarly, on the Democratic side, all major party interest group allies and PACs were solidly behind the president.[32] Again, the politics of mobilization were crucial: those who show up at the polls (a diminishing proportion of the eligible electorate) have far more influence in current U.S. politics than those who do not, and one consequence of that simple fact was the impeachment (and later acquittal on largely partisan votes) of a president. Of course, the media had a field day, with the cable news channels competing with each other to offer more and more stories and endless panels of partisan antagonists rehashing the same arguments against or in defense of the president.

The irrelevance of the partisan antagonism to all but the committed was illustrated most dramatically by Ross Perot's two presidential candidacies: the first of which, launched on a cable TV chat show, garnered 19 percent of the national popular vote, the highest total by a third-party or independent candidate since Teddy Roosevelt in 1912. Interestingly, Perot's 1992 candidacy also probably contributed to the first significant increase in election turnout in decades. The appeal of Perot was that, for all his evident eccentricities, he seemed to be addressing a concrete issue that voters believed was the proper province of government—the massive federal budget deficit—rather than another battle over the culture war. The strength of Perot probably reinforced President Clinton's decision to give priority to dealing with the budget in his new administration, over other issues more dear to Democratic partisans. And although Perot appeared less credible and President Clinton's triangulation strategy had brought him closer to the center in 1996, the Texan still secured 8 percent for the presidential ticket of his new "Reform" Party.

The 2000 presidential election confirmed many of the truths of the preceding decade. Narrow margins of victory in the presidential and congressional elections confirmed the exceedingly close national electoral balance between the major parties at the turn of the century. Although neither of the two major party nominees could be described as "ideological" in style, they both were driven by the exigencies of nominating politics to cleave to their parties' activist base. When Republican frontrunner George W. Bush was upset in the New Hampshire primary by Arizona senator John McCain, he went straight to the party's base among southern conservative white religious voters, which would be absolutely critical in the following primary in South Carolina, including a notorious campaign stop at the controversial Bob Jones University. Similarly, to defeat a challenge by former senator Bill Bradley, Clinton vice president Al Gore associated himself with every one of the party's key interests and conducted a campaign that at least rhetorically seemed to run to the left of the administration he had served in for eight years.[33]

These close associations with their respective party bases surely help explain why voters were conspicuously unenthusiastic about both candidates. In the Republican primaries, Arizona senator McCain, campaigning on a platform centered on reform of the campaign finance laws to close the soft money loophole, did spectacularly well in early primary states where independents and Democrats could vote in the GOP primary. Green Party candidate and noted consumer advocate Ralph Nader also ran a significant general election effort that garnered 3 percent of the national vote and would have been higher, had his vote not been squeezed hard by the Gore campaign in the closing days. The disputed election result and the partisan furor that followed—again obsessively covered by the news media (particularly the cable channels)—only confirmed that the obsessions of the contemporary party elites were not the obsessions of "Main Street."

## Conclusion

As we enter the new century, partisanship remains the most salient feature of U.S. campaigns and elections. The forces that support each of the major parties in terms of finances and resources and the greater partisan commitment of those who actually show up at the polls determine this partisanship. National parties have become extremely effective at squeezing funds out of the committed and have used loopholes in the ostensibly tight campaign finance laws to channel money and services to candidates. National party committees also work closely with like-minded PACs to coordinate resources for election campaigns. Because these features are so crucial to modern campaigning, the focus of elections for the major parties is increasingly on mobilizing committed party and interest group activists, rather than the politically disengaged. These trends also influence government outputs at the national level—particularly in Congress—where party leaders and members have every incentive to satisfy certain electoral constituencies rather than uncommitted voters. The news media fuel partisanship, which, even if primarily rhetorical, provides drama and conflict, which in turn assist ratings. The advent of round-the-clock cable news networks in fierce competition has added another degree of intensity. Finally, the emergence of the Internet as a significant political medium appears so far to have encouraged the like-minded to congregate in cyberspace, reinforcing each other's commitments and precluding real civic deliberation and open dialogue.

The reaction to Senator McCain's candidacy in 2000 and the fate of the McCain-Feingold measure to eliminate soft money and reform the campaign finance laws to restrict the role of PACs are illustrative. The Republican Party establishment and conservative PACs opposed McCain and his legislation because it posed a direct threat to their fundraising network and their political power. And although congressional Democrats have paid lip service to the legislation, for tactical reasons they have been careful to craft versions that do not adversely effect their own electoral allies, such as organized labor. The bill ultimately passed.

The prevalence of significant third-party candidacies and the alienation from politics of the wider public indicates that they dislike the situation but cannot be mobilized in the current political universe to do anything effective about it except support third-party presidential candidacies, which seem to have become an endemic part of the contemporary political scene. Thus, the power of the contemporary parties comes from the campaign finance laws and the framing of issues and campaigns by the media as the primary conduits of political information. The intensely close, competitive elections of the late 1990s, with the parties more evenly matched in voter alignments than at any time since the late nineteenth century, have served only to intensify partisanship and have not succeeded in drawing more voters to the polls. Barring significant reform of those laws and the rise of alternative information sources for citizens, this situation seems likely to endure into the immediate future.

# 7

## Reforming the Reforms: Campaign Finance and Congress

### Victoria A. Farrar-Myers

The proposals are noble: leveling the playing field; encouraging more quality challengers; reducing the incumbency reelection rate; ridding the campaign and election system of corruption, or even the appearance of corruption; eliminating special interests; and making elections open to all. These are the ideas behind many of the campaign finance reform proposals that have been percolating ever since the original passage of the Federal Elections Campaign Act (FECA) in 1971. What current reformers hope to convey in advocating passage of additional changes to the campaign finance laws is all the positives the system can enjoy with the advent of new restrictions and disclosures.

What some of these advocates fail to acknowledge, however, is that this reform area has far-reaching and sometimes unintended consequences for campaigns, elections, parties, and representative democracy. Campaign finance reform for some may be only about who wins and who loses in the competition for dollars and votes, but it really is an issue that has deep roots at the very core of the U.S. political process.

## Campaign Finance and Reform: A Historical Look and Current Trends

When Congress passed FECA in 1971, it sought to limit the influence of wealthy individuals and special interests on the outcome of federal elections, to regulate campaign spending, and to mandate public disclosure of campaign finances by candidates and parties. This legislation was subsequently amended in 1974, in the wake of additional campaign finance abuses in the 1972 presidential elections.

The amendment set limits on contributions by individuals, political parties, and political action committees (PACs). It also provided public funding for presidential general elections, primaries, and nominating conventions and changed the landscape for how congressional and presidential campaigns were to be financed. In addition, the Federal Election Commission (FEC) was created to enforce the law, enable disclosure, and administer the public funding program for presidential campaigns.

In *Buckley v. Valeo* (1976), the Supreme Court upheld FECA's limitations on contributions as appropriate legislative tools to guard against the reality or appearance of improper influence stemming from candidates' dependence on large campaign contributions. However, the Court invalidated the act's limitations on independent expenditures, candidate expenditures from personal funds, and overall campaign expenditures. Through its ruling, the Court set into motion two conflicting principles—one that allows limits on contributions and one that finds mandatory limits on expenditures an unconstitutional limitation of free speech. These two principles led to legislation that attempted to control the corrupting influence of money in congressional elections through limitations on contributions by individuals, PACs, and parties. Further, campaign finance legislation was carefully constructed not to mandate congressional spending limits, although a few bills have proposed getting around this restriction by offering public funding or other incentives in exchange for voluntary spending limits. Following the Court's decision, Congress made further amendments to the FECA in 1976 to comport the legislation with *Buckley* and in 1979 to ease some of the act's administrative burdens.

Beginning in the 1980s and through much of the 1990s, two issues came to the forefront for those who studied the campaign finance issue: the rising costs of campaigns and the substantial reliance on PACs as a source of major funding. Figure 7.1 reflects the growth in aggregate expenditures by congressional candidates during this period. After slow but steady growth throughout the 1980s, the aggregate costs jumped in 1992 and have continued to escalate ever since then. During the 1999–2000 election cycle, total expenditures exceeded $1 billion for the first time. Similarly, Figure 7.2 reflects the growth of PAC contributions to House candidates from 1992 through 2000. By comparison, however, PACs generally have not increased their contributions to senatorial candidates during the same period.

Also of particular concern to political scientists studying congressional elections during the 1980s and 1990s were the additional issues of the advantages that incumbents held in elections and the lack of competitive elections stemming from challengers with inadequate resources.[1] As Figure 7.3 demonstrates, the cost of conducting a winning campaign for a House seat has more than tripled from 1982 to 2000 and more than quadrupled for the Senate. Prior to the 1994 election, Republicans and some scholars contended that the incumbency advantage contributed to what some believed would be that party's perpetual minority status in Congress.[2]

**Figure 7.1  Aggregate Spending in All Congressional Campaigns, 1982–2000**

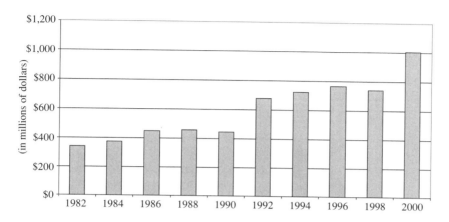

*Source:* Compiled from the Federal Election Commission news release, "FEC Reports on Congressional Financial Activity for 2000: Surpasses $1 Billion Mark," available at www.fec.gov/finance_reports.html.

**Figure 7.2  PAC Contributions to Congressional Campaigns, 1992–2000**

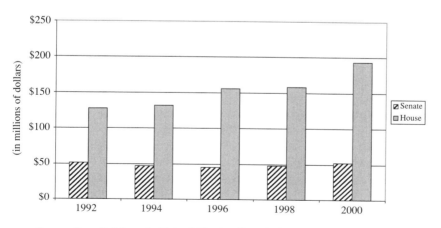

*Source:* Compiled from the Federal Election Commission news release, "FEC Reports on Congressional Financial Activity for 2000: Surpasses $1 Billion Mark," available at www.fec.gov/finance_reports.html.

**Figure 7.3  Aggregate Spending in Winning Congressional
Campaigns, 1982–2000**

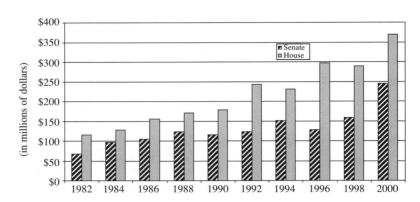

Source: Compiled from the Federal Election Commission news release, "FEC Reports on Congressional Financial Activity for 2000: Surpasses $1 Billion Mark," available at www.fec.gov/finance_reports.html.

Despite the GOP's success in congressional elections, starting with their taking control of the House after the 1994 vote, scholars still express trepidation over the incumbency advantage in congressional elections and fundraising.[3]

The growth of outside or special interests, such as PACs, in the electoral process caused grave concern for advocates of representative democracy. For instance, corporations and unions were thought by many to have an undue say in determining election outcomes. Further, office seekers were beginning to notice that their own messages were being drowned out by the advertising and policy positions of groups advocating a given candidate's election or defeat under the guise of providing the public with information (known as "issue advocacy" communications).

Many proposals geared toward improving the representative democratic feature of congressional elections focused on strengthening the political parties to help counterbalance the effects of these special interests. With the advent of candidate-centered campaigns, such reforms often became the standard mantra but provided very little relief. In addition, FEC regulations promulgated to assist parties with activities to revitalize themselves—namely get-out-the-vote (GOTV) drives and the like—were quickly becoming avenues for the proliferation of unregulated sums of money (known as "soft money").

Much like other actors in the electoral system, political parties have steadily increased their fundraising, particularly in terms of soft money, as seen in Table 7.1. Both parties have increased their share of federal money in both presidential and midterm election years since 1992 and have seen substantial growth in the amount of soft money that they have taken in. Although the GOP has maintained its traditional advantage in fundraising during the past decade, during the 1999–2000 election cycle, the Democrats raised almost as much soft money as the Republicans. Figure 7.4 reflects the flip side of the fundraising totals in Table 7.1; this figure shows party spending for each election cycle from 1982 to 2000. As one should expect, party spending is greater during presidential election years than in midterm

**Table 7.1  Party Hard- and Soft-Money Receipts, 1992–2000 (in millions of dollars)**

| Election Cycle | Democrats[a] | | | Republicans[a] | | |
|---|---|---|---|---|---|---|
| | Federal (Hard Money) | Nonfederal (Soft Money) | Total Receipts | Federal (Hard Money) | Nonfederal (Soft Money) | Total Receipts |
| 1991–1992 | 177.7 | 36.3 | 214.0 | 267.3 | 49.8 | 317.1 |
| 1993–1994 | 139.1 | 49.1 | 188.2 | 245.6 | 52.5 | 298.1 |
| 1995–1996 | 221.6 | 123.9 | 345.5 | 416.5 | 138.2 | 554.7 |
| 1997–1998 | 160.0 | 92.8 | 252.8 | 285.0 | 131.6 | 416.6 |
| 1999–2000 | 275.2 | 245.2 | 520.4 | 465.8 | 249.9 | 715.7 |

*Source:* Compiled from the Federal Election Commission news release, "FEC Reports Increase in Party Fundraising for 2000," available at www.fec.gov/press/051501partyfund/051501partyfund.html.

*Note:* a. Includes receipts for each party's national committee, senatorial campaign committee, congressional campaign committee, and state and local committees.

**Figure 7.4  Political Party Campaign Spending, 1982–2000**

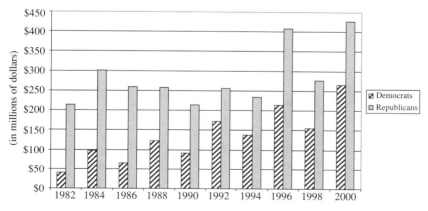

*Source:* Compiled from the Federal Election Commission news release, "FEC Reports Increase in Party Fundraising for 2000," available at www.fec.gov/press/051501partyfund/051501partyfund.html.

elections. But in both types of elections, the parties have continued to spend more and more.

In presidential elections, money has played an increasingly important role in the nomination process, where candidates' viability is often judged on how much money they can raise rather than their ability to govern and lead.[4] In presidential elections, the bar for how much a candidate needs to spend to make a splash in the primaries continues to be raised from the election before. Table 7.2 presents the funds raised by each of the candidates who sought the presidency in 2000. Of these, five candidates— George W. Bush, Al Gore, Steve Forbes, John McCain, and Bill Bradley— raised as much or more than Bill Clinton and Bob Dole did in 1996; and with Bush and Forbes also opting out of the public finance scheme established by FECA, the status of the presidential campaign public finance system also must be questioned.[5]

## FECA's Unintended Consequences

As noted above, campaign finance reform often has unintended consequences, and FECA set into motion several of them. First, candidates must spend more time and money raising contributions. This fact came about not only because of the restrictions placed on individuals and PAC donations but because of the growing costs of campaigns themselves. Candidates are forced to use television, which means campaigns can become very costly, as seen earlier in Figure 7.1. Second, because of this growing cost of campaigns, soft money has become a vital resource. Not only do the parties raise as much soft money as possible to help key races, but also corporations and labor unions are freely donating unlimited amounts of $100,000, $250,000, or more.[6] Thus, corporations, labor unions, and even wealthy individuals can have a large influence on the political process—more so than the average voter of more limited financial means.

Third, the appearance that special interests have more of an impact on politics than the everyday person leads to public distrust of politics and perhaps voter apathy. Although the Supreme Court in *Buckley* stated that money equals speech, most average voters feel that their small contributions will go unnoticed. More important, special interests that expend exorbitant amounts of money begin to feel as if they are making an investment in their interest or, even worse, attempting to buy influence and access.

Fourth, voters and special interests need not send their contributions directly to candidates or the political parties in order to have a loud voice in the electoral process. Instead, they can either spend the money independently or give it to an interest group to run so-called issue ads. These ads look like regular election ads, but they do not use "magic words" like

**Table 7.2  Candidate Receipts Through July 31, 2000**

| Candidate | Contributions from Individuals | Federal Matching Funds | Other Receipts | Total Receipts |
|---|---|---|---|---|
| **Democrats** | | | | |
| Bill Bradley | 29,270,589 | 12,462,045 | 409,931 | 42,142,565 |
| Al Gore | 33,871,206 | 15,317,872 | 13,667 | 49,202,745 |
| Subtotal | 63,141,795 | 27,779,917 | 423,598 | 91,345,310 |
| **Republicans** | | | | |
| Lamar Alexander | 2,301,747 | 0 | 783,884 | 3,085,631 |
| Gary Bauer[a] | 7,553,317 | 4,632,803 | (49,572) | 12,136,548 |
| George W. Bush | 91,331,951 | 0 | 3,134,390 | 94,466,341 |
| Elizabeth Dole | 5,001,635 | 0 | 126,197 | 5,127,832 |
| Steve Forbes | 5,752,150 | 0 | 42,392,826 | 48,144,976 |
| Orrin Hatch | 2,124,707 | 0 | 428,016 | 2,552,723 |
| Robert Kasich | 1,702,668 | 0 | 1,488,415 | 3,191,083 |
| Alan Keyes | 7,663,253 | 3,325,340 | 11,159 | 10,999,752 |
| John McCain | 28,143,613 | 14,467,788 | 2,436,536 | 45,047,937 |
| Dan Quayle | 4,083,201 | 2,087,748 | 146,746 | 6,317,695 |
| Bob Smith | 1,522,128 | 0 | 92,070 | 1,614,198 |
| Subtotal | 157,180,370 | 24,513,679 | 50,990,667 | 232,684,716 |
| **Total (Major Parties)** | 220,322,165 | 52,293,596 | 51,414,265 | 324,030,026 |
| **Other** | | | | |
| Pat Buchanan | 6,651,221 | 3,852,247 | 32,967 | 10,536,435 |
| Ralph Nader | 1,319,434 | 100,000 | 44,133 | 1,463,567 |
| Others | 5,291,555 | 1,498,507 | 143,774 | 6,933,836 |
| Subtotal | 13,262,210 | 5,450,754 | 220,874 | 18,933,838 |
| Total | 233,584,375 | 57,744,350 | 51,635,139 | 342,963,864 |

*Source:* Compiled from the Federal Election Commission website,
www.fec.gov/finance/precm6.htm.
*Note:* a. Bauer's reported value for "Other Loans Minus Repayments" was –$63,249.

"vote for" or "vote against." If an ad uses such words, under *Buckley,* the ad sponsor would be subject to FEC regulation; by not employing such words, however, the sponsor is free from regulation. As a result of the use of issue ads, much of the dialogue taking place in campaigns is outside the candidates' direct control.

Fifth, FECA has led to the formation of alliances between strange bed-fellows, in which traditional liberal groups, such as the American Federation of Labor–Congress of Industrial Organizations (AFL-CIO) and the American Civil Liberties Union (ACLU), and conservative groups, such as the U.S. Chamber of Commerce and the Christian Coalition, are fighting together to defeat campaign finance reform.[7] This alliance uses the First Amendment to smother any discussion of reforming the current process, which often leads to unproductive discussions and frustrated reform efforts.

## Congressional Attempts at Reform

### Shifting Focus: Campaign 1996 and the 105th Congress

After more than a decade of reform efforts that attempted to limit campaign spending, restrict contributions, and provide for public financing of congressional elections, the focus of reform following the 1996 election shifted to various perceived "loopholes" in the campaign finance system. Although many of these loopholes in the current law were a point of contention toward the end of the 1980s, concern escalated as the loopholes began to engulf the whole system. According to a key reformer in the House, Representative Christopher Shays (R-Conn.), the system began to "collapse on itself." The loopholes included:

1. *Bundling:* the collection of checks for (and made payable to) a specific candidate by an intermediate agent. Bundling allows PACs and parties to raise money in excess of what they can legally contribute and receive recognition for their endeavors from the candidate.

2. *Soft money:* money that may "indirectly influence federal elections but is raised and spent outside the purview of federal laws and would be illegal if spent directly on a federal election."[8]

3. *Independent expenditures:* money spent by individuals or groups on communications with voters to support or oppose clearly identified candidates. Such expenditures are considered independent expenditures and held constitutionally unregulated by *Buckley v. Valeo,* as long as there is no coordination or consultation with any candidate. Independent expenditures rose from $11.1 million in 1992 to an estimated $22.4 million in 1996.

4. *Issue advocacy:* groups may promote their views and issue positions in reference to particular elected officials, as long as the communication does not expressly advocate the election or defeat of a candidate by using the so-called magic words discussed above.

These loopholes began to overshadow PACs as the more severe threat to the campaign system. Although PACs were seen just a few short years earlier as the scourge of the electoral system, they were now considered one of the more legitimate forums for campaign contributions. PACs fall within FECA's scope, and thus they are regulated and their activities disclosed. The loopholes in the system, however, allowed interest groups and other donors to spend money and the political parties to receive certain funds free from federal campaign finance regulation.

Following the 1996 elections, campaign finance reform took on a new dynamic as the 105th Congress (1997–1999) began to debate the issue with the focus primarily on how to close some of these loopholes engulfing the system. The campaign that year at all levels, from President Clinton's

fundraising coffees down through the exorbitant levels of soft money contributed by corporations and unions to the outside groups' independent
expenditures for issue ads, set off warning bells for many reformers that the
campaign finance system was being pushed to the brink. In particular, soft
money and express advocacy issue ads, taken together, seemed to lead to
very egregious campaign finance practices in the 1996 elections. As a
result, reformers placed their focus on these "twin evils" in the congressional hearings that occurred in the wake of the 1996 elections.[9]

From the outset of the 105th Congress (1997–1999), the majority of
Republicans in both houses and their leaders opposed the idea of reforming the campaign finance system, particularly to address the twin evils.
Some opponents—led by Senator Mitch McConnell (R-Ky.), the self-
proclaimed "Darth Vader" of campaign finance reform—contended that any
restrictions on express advocacy represented an unconstitutional restriction
on free speech. This argument won the support of many conservative interest groups, particularly conservative religious groups; but McConnell also
garnered an unexpected ally when the normally liberal ACLU supported the
senator's position. Other Republicans cited concerns that federal legislation
banning soft money to state parties would violate the Tenth Amendment of
the Constitution, which reserves powers to the states. Finally, many Republicans contended that the only necessary reform to the campaign finance
laws was that of "paycheck protection," which would require unions to disclose their spending on political activities; some proposals even went further and would have required unions to receive membership approval
before spending their dues for political purposes.

The legislative journey for campaign finance reform during the 105th
Congress was a tortuous one, filled with unorthodox policymaking; emerging policy entrepreneurs; issue networks consisting of members of Congress, their staff, and public interest groups like Common Cause; and cross-
partisan efforts seeking bipartisan support.[10] It started in the Senate, where
reformers hoped that the McCain-Feingold bill, which targeted some of the
aforementioned campaign finance issues, would be able to garner enough
support for passage. Despite the fact that it had support from a majority of
senators, reformers did not have the sixty votes needed to end a filibuster
led by Senator McConnell. The bill went down to defeat not once but twice
in the Senate, the second time in February 1998.

At that point, many thought that the bill was dead. But reformers in the
House, led by Representatives Shays and Martin T. Meehan (D-Mass.),
took up the challenge of keeping the issue alive. The House reformers took
advantage of a number of events, including a legislative procedural device
called a "discharge petition," favorable news coverage from national papers
like the *New York Times* and the *Washington Post,* grassroots lobbying
efforts by their public interest group allies, and some tactical errors by former Speaker Newt Gingrich and the Republican leadership. As a result,

Shays was able to strike a deal with Gingrich that allowed the House to debate the issue of campaign finance reform. Reform opponents, led by Majority Whip Tom Delay (R-Texas), sought to bury the Shays-Meehan bill under an avalanche of amendments and substitute proposals, but reform supporters were able to fight off a series of poison pill amendments designed to break up the reform coalition.[11] The result of the extensive legislative wrangling was that the Shays-Meehan bill passed in the House by a vote of 252 to 179. Reformers hoped that this success would pressure the Senate in allowing McCain-Feingold, Shays-Meehan's companion bill, to come to a vote. But for the third time in the 105th Congress, the Senate sent campaign finance reform down to defeat. In the end, the 105th Congress failed to change any of the nation's campaign finance laws.

This abbreviated discussion of the campaign finance reform's legislative journey is useful for several reasons. First, it highlights the genesis of the current focus on the twin evils of soft money and express advocacy in reformers' efforts to change the campaign finance laws. Second, it provides a sense of both the fragility and resiliency of the issue in Congress. Campaign finance reform was left on the scrap heap of legislative proposals many times, only to be resuscitated by reformers time and time again. And even though the Senate finally ended reform efforts in the 105th Congress, reformers tasted enough success in the House to be able to keep the issue a viable one as Congress moved into its next session. Finally, the processes and interactions of the 105th Congress laid the foundation for the institution's subsequent consideration of the issue. It determined the roles for many of the participants, provided lessons for both sides of what to do and not do, and clarified what arguments by proponents and opponents were effective and which ones simply fell by the wayside.

### A New Clock: Efforts in the 106th Congress

The 106th Congress (1999–2001) began with a movement to pass the version of the Shays-Meehan bill that the House had approved at the end of the 105th Congress. On January 19, 1999, Representatives Shays and Meehan, along with Senators McCain (R-Ariz.) and Russell D. Feingold (D-Wis.), introduced companion bipartisan campaign finance reform bills in the House and Senate for the 106th Congress. As with their proposals in the previous term, the Shays-Meehan/McCain-Feingold legislation banned soft money—the unregulated contributions to political parties from corporations, labor unions, and wealthy individuals. In addition, the bills required special interest groups to pay for phony "issue ads" with money raised in accordance with federal campaign finance laws.

According to the president of Common Cause, one of the leading public interest groups that has been extremely vital in the fight for campaign finance reform:

Last year, the House Republican leaders did everything they could to delay House passage of reform, so that when the issue shifted to the Senate there was only weeks left in the 105th Congress. Early House action on the Shays-Meehan bill is a key test for Speaker Hastert and the new Congress. This decision will indicate if the Speaker will make good on his promise in January to "work together across the political fence" and "get down to business on legislation that addresses the problems that the American people want solved." Delay only serves to ensure that the current corrupt campaign finance system will continue into the future.[12]

The battle in the 106th Congress was no easier than in the 105th. The House Republican leadership made it clear that consideration of campaign finance reform was a low priority. The scenario in the Senate, however, had promise for a different dynamic. The seats of sixteen senators who voted against campaign finance reform in the 105th Congress were up for reelection in 2000, a fact that did not go unnoticed by supporters of reform.[13] Further, there were growing concerns about the vast sums that were being raised for the presidential campaign of 2000, sums that dwarfed the figures from 1996 and 1998.

Despite all the reformers' hope, however, the 106th Congress ended the way it began. The House's consideration of the Shays-Meehan bill, although not quite as complex as in the 105th Congress, was subject to a number of twists and turns and many poison pill amendments. Nevertheless, the House once again passed the Shays-Meehan bill (252 to 177). But as in the 105th Congress, when campaign finance reform moved to the Senate, opponents successfully filibustered the McCain-Feingold proposal, despite the fact that once again reform had the support of a majority of senators. Even though comprehensive campaign finance reform failed again, Senator McCain later successfully got an incremental piece of reform legislation through the Senate and eventually it became law. This bill narrowly targeted "527 groups," named so for a provision in the income tax code, but it still represented the first change in the nation's campaign finance laws since the 1970s.

At the end of the 106th Congress, the reformers' glass was both half empty and half full. It was half empty, of course, because for the second straight term, Congress did not pass comprehensive campaign finance reform that addressed the twin evils of soft money and express advocacy. But it was half full for several reasons. First, Shays-Meehan did pass the House, and McCain-Feingold did appear to have majority support in the Senate. Thus, campaign finance reform could remain a viable issue on the legislative agenda. Second, the passage of the legislation relating to 527 groups proved that reformers could get legislation past their opponents. Finally, most reformers hoped the next opportunity for reform would pose itself at the conclusion of the 2000 elections, in which soft money was again exploding—thus highlighting their claim of the need for reform. In addition, several presidential hopefuls, including Democrats Al Gore and Bill Bradley, were raising the issue to the public. Even presidential candidate George W. Bush said he would favor "some reforms." Most important, however, John McCain made campaign finance reform the centerpiece issue of his campaign for president. His success, both in terms of initially challenging the front-runner, Bush, in the Republican primaries and in energizing portions of the electorate who had heretofore not participated in the electoral process, bolstered his standing in the public eye.

### Current Process: The 107th Congress

In the wake of the 2000 presidential campaign, Senator McCain decided to make campaign finance reform his number one priority in the Senate during the 107th Congress (2001–2003). He used the public support he received during the Republican nomination campaign and the fifty-fifty partisan split in the Senate to put pressure on Senate leaders to consider campaign finance reform early on in the term. The dynamic this time had indeed changed. First, the fifty-fifty division between Republicans and Democrats left the Senate Republican leadership more vulnerable and less able to block consideration of the bill. Further, the continued rising cost of congressional and presidential campaigns spurred many to feel the trend would only get worse, thus needing some sort of reform now. The defection shortly into the 107th Congress of Vermont senator Jim Jeffords from the Republican Party to the status of independent aligned with the Democrats only enhanced this dynamic.

Even public opinion, which several years before seemed uninterested in campaign finance reform, appeared to see greater need for reform.[14] The *New York Times* reported in March 2001 that public opinion polling showed "that there is more unanimity on the need for campaign finance reform than on the need for a tax cut" as proposed by President George W. Bush (and later enacted).[15] Moreover, polling showed dissatisfaction and distrust with current campaign finance laws—56 percent in one poll were dissatisfied with the nation's campaign finance laws,[16] and 93 percent in another poll believed that elected officials returned campaign contributions with special favors.[17] Despite the public recognition of the apparent need for reform, the issue still remained of little salience to average Americans, who are skeptical that reform legislation actually would change special interests' influence.[18]

With the legislative dynamic more in his favor, Senator McCain was able to get the Republican leadership to agree to an early consideration of the revised McCain-Feingold bill for two weeks in March 2001. This measure included the following provisions:

- banning soft money contributions to the national political parties and prohibiting state political parties, which may be allowed to raise soft money under state law, from spending such money on activities related to federal elections;

- increasing the maximum amount an individual can contribute in regulated federal dollars to state parties for federal election purposes from $5,000 to $10,000;
- restricting "phony issue ads" sponsored by corporations and unions by making "electioneering communications"—that is, ads that clearly identify a candidate and appear within thirty days of a primary and sixty days of a general election—subject to federal regulation (this provision is known as the Snowe-Jeffords Amendment); in addition, any group that spends at least $10,000 in electioneering communications will be subject to certain disclosure requirements;
- strictly codifying the Supreme Court's decision in *Communications Workers of America v. Beck* (1988), requiring labor unions to notify nonunion employees that their agency fees can be reduced by the portion of those fees that are used for political purposes;
- strengthening the current law prohibiting foreign nationals from contributing to candidates for federal, state, or local office; and
- addressing situations in which groups other than candidates or parties spend funds directly, either in coordination with the candidate or independently.[19]

Just prior to the Senate debate in March, President Bush released his own set of campaign finance reforms. Among these reforms were a soft money ban on contributions from corporations and labor unions but not individuals and a requirement that corporations and labor unions get permission from shareholders and members before using any of their funds for political activities.

The debate in the 107th Senate originally appeared to promise a rerun of the processes in the 105th and 106th Congresses. This time, however, it was agreed there would be no filibusters in the Senate—just full debate. This agreement meant that Senator McConnell could not use his favorite weapon to prevent action on the McCain-Feingold bill. He would have to make an all-out case as to why limitations on campaign spending and fundraising are an infringement on First Amendment freedom of speech. In addition, a key opponent in the previous Congresses, Senator Thad Cochran (R-Miss.), joined the reformers, which sent a message that campaign finance reform had a real shot this time.

The dynamic in the 107th Congress also faced a new challenge. In the two previous Congresses, Democratic senators had been vocal supporters of the McCain-Feingold bill. But as seen in Table 7.1, with the two parties raising a roughly equal amount of soft money in the 2000 cycle, some Democrats had growing concerns about the bill's ban on soft money, particularly when the Republicans still enjoyed a vast lead in hard money fundraising.

During the 2000 election cycle, the Republicans raised over $190 million *more* than the Democrats in regulated hard money (see Table 7.1).

The Senate debate looked a bit like the House's in the 105th and 106th, with concerns centering around potential poison pills that threatened to cut into the majority needed to pass the reform bill. When the Senate debate began on March 19, 2001, the reform coalition faced its greatest poison pill amendment challenge from Senator Chuck Hagel (R-Neb.), who proposed an amendment to permit corporations, unions, and individuals to contribute up to $60,000 a year in soft money to the national party committees. The supporters of McCain-Feingold were successful in defeating this amendment on a vote of 60 to 40, arguing that this amendment would merely perpetuate the current problems with soft money.

A second amendment came from Senator Orrin G. Hatch (R-Utah) who tried to add a "paycheck protection" provision, which would require unions only to gain permission from their members before using any funds on political activities. This amendment too was defeated, 69 to 31. Senator Bill Frist (R-Tenn.) introduced a third poison pill that tried to make the bill "nonseverable." That meant that if the Court struck down one part of the bill, the other parts would fall as well. Once again, the supporters of McCain-Feingold were able to fend off this potential problem, winning the vote 57 to 43.

Despite these attempts to defeat reform, on April 2, 2001, McCain-Feingold passed the Senate by a vote of 59 to 41. This passage was considered a real breakthrough for reformers, who had been frustrated by the filibusters that prevented Senate action in the two prior congresses. Many hoped this would mean that campaign finance reform would pass this Congress. But the legislative dynamic had not changed only in the Senate—it had changed in the House as well.

Although the House has successfully passed campaign finance reform in the 105th and 106th Congresses, the reality that the Senate had passed reform meant that some "supporters" were rethinking their stance. Previously, House members had had a "free" vote, since they knew that the Senate would guarantee defeat of campaign finance reform.[20] This time their vote would count. Further, House Democrats shared the same misgivings that their Senate counterparts did. They were particularly concerned about the provision in the Senate-passed McCain-Feingold bill that raised the hard money limits for contributions from individuals to candidates.[21] Key Democratic campaign finance supporters Sam Farr (D-Calif.) and John F. Tierney (D-Mass.) sent a letter signed by thirty-five other House Democrats to the Senate indicating that raising the hard dollar limitations would place the House passage in jeopardy.[22]

Further, another set of key groups that could have made it difficult for reformers to pass the House companion bill, the black and Hispanic caucuses, had been openly discussing a "cap" on soft money instead of backing the all-out ban in the Shays-Meehan bill. This option made supporters concerned that they would lose a vast majority of supporters, or worse yet, pass a bill different from the Senate's, thereby forcing the bill into a conference committee, where such "gains" would be bargained out. Although this latter fear was somewhat mollified with the Democratic takeover of the Senate in 2001, meaning that reform opponents like Senator McConnell would be in a minority position, it still posed a threat to achieving the full extent of the reforms that both McCain-Feingold and Shays-Meehan were designed to achieve.

Despite the challenges facing reform supporters, Congress passed the McCain-Feingold/Shays-Meehan bill and President George W. Bush quietly signed it into law on March 27, 2002. When President Bush signed the new law, the Bipartisan Campaign Reform Act of 2002, he commented, "I believe that this legislation, although far from perfect, will improve the current financing system for federal campaigns."

A number of reasons might explain why reform proponents were able to pass legislation this time. For example, members of Congress may have wanted to distance themselves from the financial collapse of Enron, once the seventh-largest company in the United States and a major donor to candidates in both parties, including President Bush. Passing campaign finance reform thus offered an avenue for members to claim that they were attempting to reform the system. Further, the dreaded presidential veto, which was such a real possibility at the beginning of this Congress, seemed to fade as the connections were made between Enron, both in terms of donations and its operations, to the president and his administration. Although interest groups and reform proponents were quick to point out the Enron scandal, they also noted to members of Congress that if they supported this reform effort, they could claim in the midterm elections of 2002 not only a response to Enron but also a partial response to the cries for broader electoral reform that emerged from the 2000 election.

The most significant provisions of the Bipartisan Campaign Reform Act (BCRA) include the following:

- Bans national parties from raising and spending soft money.
- Prohibits federal officeholders and candidates from soliciting or raising soft money for political parties at federal, state, and local levels, and from soliciting or raising soft money in connection with federal elections.
- Prohibits state parties and local party committees from using soft money to pay for TV ads that mention federal candidates and get-out-the-vote activities that mention federal candidates. Permits state parties and local party committees to use contributions, up to $10,000 per donor per year, for generic GOTV activities and for GOTV activities for state and local candidates. Each state party or local committee must raise its own contributions and a portion of each expenditure must include hard money.
- Prohibits the use of corporate and union treasury money for broadcast communications that mention a federal candidate within 60 days of a

general election or 30 days of a primary and are targeted at the candidate's electorate. (Unions and corporations can finance these ads through their PACs.) Requires individuals and groups of individuals to disclose contributions and expenditures for similar broadcast communications.
- Raises limits on individual contributions to House, Senate and presidential campaigns to $2,000 and indexes for inflation.[23]

The soft money ban and other provisions of the new law will take effect November 6, 2002, and the changes in the contribution limits will take effect January 1, 2003. The new law also includes a severability clause, which means that if any provision of the bill is held unconstitutional, the remainder of the bill is not affected. This provision could prove critical in the court case that was filed immediately following the signing ceremony.

Senator McConnell and the National Rifle Association filed suit to challenge the new law's constitutionality—specifically, they argued that the issue ad provisions violate the First Amendment free speech protection. On May 7, 2002, the Republican National Committee joined the lawsuit, asking that the court also strike down the law's ban on soft money contributions. The outcome of this case will dictate the fate of other reform efforts. Currently, reformers are revisiting the discussion of public financing reform initiatives. This discussion could be easily quashed if reformers are forced to recast their efforts in the wake of a court defeat. Speculation regarding whether the Supreme Court will eventually remove the issue ad provision has both proponents and opponents of reform scrambling.

Other dynamics outside the legislative process also threaten to have a major impact on the likelihood of reform seeing the light of day. On June 25, 2001, the Supreme Court handed down its decision in *Federal Election Commission v. Colorado Republican Federal Campaign Committee* (2001). On its face, the decision was a victory for reform supporters, as the Court rejected the argument that restrictions on a political party's coordinated expenditures were unconstitutional. In a five-to-four decision written by Justice David Souter, the Court held such restrictions to be permissible, concluding: "There is no functional difference between a party's coordinated expenditure and a direct party contribution to the candidate." Given this conclusion, if the Court did not uphold restrictions on coordinated expenditures by parties, that decision would have the effect of undermining the scheme of campaign finance regulation that Congress has established.

But buried within the Court's decision is language that ultimately could harm reformers' efforts. The Court clearly distinguished between coordinated and independent expenditures, stating that a "party may spend independently every cent it can raise wherever it thinks its candidate will shine, on every subject and every viewpoint." The Court seemed to imply that parties could spend their money in any way they saw fit, free from regulation, so long as they did so independently of their candidates. By extending this logic, any independent expenditure should be free from federal regulation.

## Conclusion

With all this discussion of reform possibilities and BCRA's eventual passage, one must step back and ask some hard questions about what its effects really might be. More specifically, how will candidates, campaigns, elections, and parties be affected by campaign finance reform?

First, many of the reforms that were being debated in Congress would have had little or no impact on some of the most fundamental goals that campaign finance reform purports to achieve. For example, none of the primary reform proposals addresses the issue of candidate quality. Even with the passage of the BCRA, candidates will still be required to devote the bulk of their time to fundraising. In addition, nothing in the act seems to take away the benefit of name recognition or solve all the problems posed by wealthy candidates. Nor does it really address the issue of incumbency advantage, although perhaps a provision in an earlier version of Shays-Meehan dealing with the franking privilege, that is, the congressional perk of free mail, may have done so. Incumbents can still run candidate-centered campaigns; run against the institution, thus eroding its public support; and build huge amounts of campaign funds, known as "war chests," to scare away quality challengers.

Second, although the BCRA does address what to do with sham issue ads—assuming this provision survives legal challenges—it really does nothing to improve the content of campaigns. An earlier proposed provision dropped from the enacted bill that would have assisted with some media costs would have been a good first step, but it still would not have enabled candidates to take back the direction of their own message. Although reformers claim that the total ban on soft money from corporations, labor unions, and other special interests will enable the candidates to run their campaigns the way they see fit, nothing here provides an incentive for potential candidates to shy away from sound bite politics and move toward real issue discussions. Modern campaigns will still be tempted to use slogans and pithy sound bites to make it on the nightly news. Such lack of content does not foster informed voting or better democratic representation. In addition, special interests will still be able to do issue advocacy and express advocacy in an uncoordinated (albeit more public) manner, once again potentially drowning out the actual candidates; thus, in some instances, their actions may move the dialogue completely away from the candidates themselves.

Third, the jury is out about what effect reform will have upon political parties. Some argue it will hurt the national political parties because they will no longer have vital soft money funds to assist their candidates and to foster get-out-the-vote educational efforts. Skeptics state that current reform efforts do not discuss how the role for political parties in campaign finance might be expanded. If soft money is taken away, political parties might find themselves unable to adapt and become shells of themselves, active only in government (not in the electorate or as organizations). However, others argue that parties might have more of an incentive to assist their candidates, who would need grassroots efforts to make up for the lack of funds to reach voters in traditional ways (i.e., through costly television ads).[24] In addition, if the amount of coordinated expenditures that political parties are permitted to make for candidates were upheld by the Court, parties could still maintain a vital role. For example, future reforms could make political parties more vital in races that pitted a millionaire candidate against one who is not. In this scenario, party coordinate expenditures could be reduced for candidates who use more than, say, $50,000, in personal funds, thus giving the other candidate a fighting chance.

Fourth, the FEC will still be less effective than it might be. Although the BCRA provides for strengthening FEC enforcement power, it remains to be seen how this provision will actually play out. Further, the FEC, without additional appropriations, might find it even more difficult to keep up with the changing nature of campaigns and potential loopholes that can be extorted through other campaign provisions not addressed by either reform bill.

Fifth, the reform efforts did not address what to do with spending limitations. In the wake of *Buckley,* there will still be problems, for example, with getting presidential candidates to level the playing field when public funds are offered. Such was the case in the 2000 presidential election, in which, as noted above, candidates Bush and Forbes eschewed public funding and raised as much (in Bush's case, far more) than the other leading candidates who accepted public funding and thus were bound by its regulations. Further, with support for the tax checkoff system in steady decline, discussion of public funding still will require finding alternative sources of funds.[25] Some have suggested creating a fee on PACs or large corporations to provide some floor of public funds as an incentive to lowering campaign costs. Without this kind of reform, costs for presidential campaigns will continue to spiral higher with every cycle, thus calling into question whether the most qualified are really able to run for key electoral positions.

Sixth, the leading reform proposals did not address restoring the tax incentives for small contributors that existed prior to 1986. This reform may be essential if the system wishes to get away from "fat cat" contributors and tilt more toward the everyday voting individual. Certainly the fat cats would benefit from any tax deductions for campaign contributions, but they would make such contributions anyway. But a tax deduction might be enough of an inducement to get ordinary citizens to make campaign contributions. Nevertheless, without such an incentive, ordinary individuals will remain cut off from politics and continue to identify the process with "them," as opposed to "us."

Seventh, the enacted reforms will not significantly affect voter turnout. Although some reformers argue that ridding the system of unregulated funds will help the public believe that politics is not corrupt, reform does not go to the heart of the need to excite the body politic about partaking in this most basic civil right. Without some direct reforms to create incentives for ordinary voters to get involved, campaigns will remain of, by, and for the few.

Eighth, the BCRA does not address limiting the percentage or cumulative amount of contributions that could come from PACs. Thus there will still be a temptation for candidates to create their own leadership PACs or seek "bundling" through key PACs. Both of these activities are legal but circumvent the goals of campaign finance reform.

The question that remains is whether we will see some sort of comprehensive reform that will affect the way campaigns, candidates, and parties function in elections to come. With the passage of the 527 bill at the end of the 106th Congress and the BCRA in the 107th, Congress has already proven that compromise might be had over incremental reforms. In addition, Congress might more readily affect campaigns and elections through electoral reforms. After all, election 2000 demonstrated that U.S. elections are subject to possible discrimination and tampering.

Regardless of the passage of the BCRA, many difficulties in today's campaigns and election processes will go unaddressed, which raises the more significant question as to whether reformers are missing the mark. Perhaps they should be focusing their efforts on the issues addressed above instead of just money. As in many public policy problems, perhaps what is really wrong here is that reformers are addressing only the symptoms of a larger disease that threatens to affect the American political process: the threat stemming from the fact that democracy is of the majority and is only representative when the majority speaks. Enhancing participation, increasing turnout, and facilitating organizations that open the marketplace of ideas to the many seem like areas riper for reform in this instance than creating more regulations in which political actors likely will find loopholes.

# 8

## Democratic Survival
## in the Republican South

### Matthew Corrigan

By almost any measure, the 2000 presidential election in the South (defined as the eleven states of the old Confederacy) was a disaster for Democrats. The ticket of George W. Bush and Dick Cheney swept the South. Even with the disputed Florida election, the trend is clear: Democrats were hammered below the Mason-Dixon line. For Democrats in the South, the election brought back terrible memories of the Reagan sweep in 1984 and George H. W. Bush's overwhelming defeat of Michael Dukakis in 1988. The performance in the 2000 presidential race was another setback for Democrats, who once called the southern region "the Solid South" and where Republicans were described as merely ceremonial actors in the South's political system.[1]

### Why Study Elections in the South?

Analyzing the South as one social and political region has inherent dangers. With migration from other states and the increasing presence of suburbs near southern cities, the South is becoming more like the rest of the United States. Moreover, substantial variation is present within the South itself. Republicans from the Gulf Coast of Florida, for instance, have little in common with Republicans from rural Alabama.

However, examining the South as a distinct political unit is helpful for two reasons. First, in a complete reversal from the first half of the twentieth century, the South is now the foundation for the Republican Party in presidential elections and congressional elections.[2] Second, survey data reveal that southerners are more conservative on most issues than the rest of the country.[3] The South increasingly may be becoming less different than the rest of the country, but it is still *different*.

The Clinton-Gore ticket of 1992 and 1996 sought to make the South more competitive for Democratic presidential candidates. They were the

"New Democrats" who talked about personal responsibility, support for the police, and welfare reform. The Clinton-Gore campaigns did not plan on dominating the South; rather, they believed that if they displayed a more centrist message, they could bring a few of the southern states back into the Democratic column. This strategy had some success in the 1990s. Along with delivering Bill Clinton's home state of Arkansas and Al Gore's home state of Tennessee in 1992 and 1996, the Democrats won Louisiana and Georgia in 1992 and Louisiana and Florida in 1996. All these gains, however, were lost in the 2000 election, including the embarrassing loss of Al Gore's home state of Tennessee. Bush was so successful in the South that in six of the southern states, his margin of victory was greater than 10 percent (see Table 8.1).

With these stark numbers, the question is, Does the 2000 presidential election indicate that Republicans will completely dominate the region in the near future? Below the presidential level in the South, Republicans hold six of the eleven governor's offices and thirteen out of the twenty-two seats in the U.S. Senate. Also Republicans now control seventy-three out of 125 U.S. House of Representatives seats in the South. This majority status in House seats was achieved, in part, because helpful redistricting in the early 1990s created "majority-minority" districts and made surrounding districts more accessible for Republican candidates, who now ran in districts with very few minority voters, who tend to vote Democratic. All these advances represent substantial gains for Republicans since the 1970s and 1980s.

Yet, Democrats are competitive below the presidential level in the South. At the state legislative level as of 2001, Democrats had majorities in seven of the eleven Senate chambers and enjoyed the same advantage in House chambers. In 1998, Democrats took back the governor's offices in Alabama and South Carolina. In 1999, the Democrats managed to win back

## Table 8.1 Percentage of the Vote Won by George W. Bush and Al Gore in the 2000 Presidential Election in the South

|                | George W. Bush (R) | Al Gore (D) |
| -------------- | ------------------ | ----------- |
| Alabama        | 57                 | 41          |
| Arkansas       | 51                 | 46          |
| Florida        | 49                 | 49          |
| Georgia        | 55                 | 43          |
| Louisiana      | 53                 | 45          |
| Mississippi    | 57                 | 42          |
| North Carolina | 56                 | 43          |
| South Carolina | 57                 | 41          |
| Tennessee      | 51                 | 47          |
| Texas          | 59                 | 38          |
| Virginia       | 52                 | 45          |

*Source:* "CNN's All Politics," see Election 2000 archives at www.cnn/allpolitics.com_election2000archive.

the governor's seat in the shrine of southern conservatism, the state of Mississippi (see Chapter 9). In the past three years, Democrats have taken back U.S. Senate seats in North Carolina and Georgia and won open Senate seats in Arkansas and Florida. Do these statewide victories show how Democrats can remain competitive in the increasingly Republican South, or are they anomalies in an overall trend of Republican advancement?

In this chapter, I review some of the factors that brought about Republican advancement in the South, as highlighted by the 2000 presidential election. Four recent statewide races won by Democrats are then examined, including two governor's races from the Deep South—Alabama and South Carolina—in 1998 and two U.S. Senate races in the Border South—North Carolina in 1998 and Florida in 2000. In this chapter I seek to determine if these candidates and campaigns offer guidance for Democrats in responding to the issues and demographic trends that have propelled Republicans to majority party status in the South.

## Roots of Republican Advancement

The identification of the Democratic Party with the civil rights movement, dating back to Harry S Truman's desegregation of the armed services in 1948, initiated the rise of the Republican Party in the South.[4] With Democratic support for civil rights firmly in place by the 1960s and African American support along with it, the glue of segregation that held the conservative Democratic South together since the Civil War was gone. Republican Richard Nixon's "southern strategy," which separated white conservatives from the Democratic Party in the presidential election of 1972, helped bring about the competitive two-party South at all levels.

Observers are careful not to isolate race and civil rights issues as the sole causes for Republican advancement, however. A Democratic strategist and former chief of staff of the Democratic National Convention said in 1998, "LBJ and civil rights opened the door (for Republicans), but it was the McGovern to Mondale era that did us in."[5] Nevertheless, the link between the Democratic Party and the civil rights movement had lasting effects on southern politics. Since the 1960s, African Americans have been the most loyal voting block for Democrats in the South. This loyalty has developed to such an extent that in the 2000 presidential election, Democratic nominee Al Gore received over 90 percent of the African American vote. Democrats have to maximize African American turnout to be viable in most campaigns, but African American support alone will not elect Democrats in statewide races. Simply put, the true competition for votes in the South in recent years has been about capturing the vote of white southerners, and Republicans are winning this competition. For example, in Alabama, only 23 percent of white males supported the Gore-Lieberman ticket.[6]

In most southern states, Democrats struggled to get a third of the white vote.

Earl Black and Merle Black, in their seminal work, *Politics and Society in the South,* analyzed the demographic trends that shifted many white southerners away from the Democratic Party.[7] They found that demographic variables such as age, length of residency, education, and income were crucial in studying the migration of white southerners away from the Democratic Party. The scholars provided four areas to focus on with regard to these demographic trends: (1) a new southern generation of voters that had little attachment to the Democratic Party reached the age of active political participation in the 1970s and 1980s, (2) nonnative conservatives have moved to the South and brought an economic libertarian philosophy with them that aligns better with the southern Republican Party, (3) college-educated whites found that their economic philosophy was a better match with the pro-business Republican Party, and (4) middle- and upper-class southerners believed that the tax burden of the federal government was unfair and did not support what they saw as the Democratic Party's social welfare programs.

Additionally, other scholars have highlighted another important group among white southerners that has shifted toward the Republican Party: religious conservatives. Religious conservatives have rejected the national Democratic Party's more liberal positions on social issues, including abortion and school prayer, and have become an active force within the Republican Party in the South and nationally.[8]

Republican candidates responded to these changes by emphasizing issues in their campaigns that would resonate with these groups. Beginning with Ronald Reagan, the policies of low taxes, a strong defense, opposition to affirmative action, the promotion of conservative moral values, and opposition to welfare became the foundation of most Republican campaigns in the South. George W. Bush followed this game plan in 2000 with a strong emphasis on tax cuts, military preparedness, and less government regulation (especially with regard to the Second Amendment) in his campaign stops across the South. More important, Bush's campaign attempted to wrap all of these issues around a common theme of personal integrity and character. Although not directly addressing the subject of Clinton's impeachment, Bush's campaign believed the election would be won more on voters' judgment of the candidates' image and character than on the candidates' views on specific issues.

Exit polls confirm that southerners received these messages.[9] When asked about the personal candidate quality that mattered most in deciding how they voted, southern voters named honesty, leadership, and judgment as their top choices. Among the southern voters who named honesty as their first choice, 83 percent voted for George Bush. When asked, "Do you think Al Gore would say anything to get elected President?" 71 percent of southerners responded "yes"—only 49 percent answered yes about a similar statement referring to George W. Bush. Moreover, less than half of southerners approved of the way Clinton was handling the presidency, compared to his 57 percent approval rating nationwide (approval of Clinton "as a person" was low across the nation).[10] Finally, 44 percent of southerners thought Gore was "too liberal," whereas only 23 percent of respondents thought Bush was "too conservative." Clearly, Bush made the argument that even though Gore was from Tennessee, the Texan Bush was the true southerner.

In the wake of the 2000 electoral rout, is the situation as bleak as it appears for Democrats? The four examples that follow demonstrate that Democrats still can win in the South if they create unique, targeted campaigns that motivate their African American base without alienating moderate white voters.

## Four Statewide Races

### The 1998 Alabama Governor's Race: Democrat Don Siegelman Versus Republican Incumbent Fob James

Fob James, the Republican incumbent, was a living symbol of the strength of the Republican Party in Alabama. James was elected as governor as a conservative Democrat in 1978. He later switched parties and shocked observers with a come-from-behind win for governor in 1994, defeating Jim Folsom, the son of a legendary former Alabama governor. He strongly sided with religious conservatives on a range of issues, including the posting of the Ten Commandments in public buildings, fierce opposition to abortion, and the opposition to the teaching of evolution. Although these conservative religious stands helped to solidify his Christian conservative base, they also left Governor James open to political challenges from his own party and from Democrats.

Democratic gubernatorial candidate Don Siegelman was a career public servant and politician. He was elected to statewide office three times in Alabama before his gubernatorial effort in 1998 (he lost a bid for the governor's office in 1990). Siegelman understood Alabama's conservative politics, having served with former governor George Wallace. He focused relentlessly on one issue throughout the campaign: support for a state lottery that would fund education programs from kindergarten through high school.[11]

James was in trouble from the beginning of the campaign. With his provocative stands on social issues, some in the Alabama business community believed that he had embarrassed the state. James steadfastly supported a state judge who had hung the Ten Commandments in his courtroom.

James insisted that the national government, especially the federal courts, could not dictate laws and rights to the people of Alabama. He even threatened to use the National Guard to defend the hanging of the tablets. To some Alabamians, this action was too familiar to Wallace's stand in the schoolhouse door.[12] James also mocked the teaching of evolution by dancing around like an ape—a dance that was filmed by television crews and played over and over on news shows. These confrontational stands hurt James among a group that is critical to the rise of Republicanism in the South: the business community. Business groups believed that James was hurting the national and international reputation of Alabama with his strong religious views.

Because of dissatisfaction with James, business leaders backed James' opponent, Winton Blount, in the Republican primary. James won the primary by mobilizing his religious conservative base, but the primary drained resources from James's general election effort. Blount, along with other business leaders, then endorsed Siegelman.

Siegelman kept focused on his message of education. With support from business groups, Siegelman raised nearly $5 million after a year of fundraising and ran statewide commercials for five months before the November vote. His lottery and education message allowed him to appeal to voters that had abandoned Democrats in years past. His emphasis on a lottery to pay for new education programs appealed to conservatives who do not favor higher taxes. And his focus on education helped him with business leaders who advocated a greater emphasis on an educated workforce to help the state grow economically.

In addition, Siegelman was not cast as a liberal because he did not emphasize controversial social issues such as abortion rights that have doomed national Democratic candidates in Alabama since 1976. With support from African Americans and swing voters, Siegelman won a decisive victory, garnering 58 percent of the vote to James's 42 percent.

### The 1998 South Carolina Governor's Race: Democrat Jim Hodges Versus Republican Incumbent David Beasley

Another Republican governor in the Deep South—David Beasley—was challenged in 1998 in South Carolina. Beasley, a former Democratic state majority leader, had switched to the Republican Party in 1991. Initially, he was seen as a strong favorite for reelection in 1998.[13] However, Beasley alienated conservatives in 1995 when he reversed his position (citing a revelation from the Bible) and advocated the removal of the Confederate flag from the top of the South Carolina statehouse. Beasley, like Fob James, aligned himself firmly with the religious right in South Carolina. Because of his religious beliefs against gambling, Beasley also advocated banning video poker in gas stations, stores, and betting parlors across the state. Video gambling is a $2.4 billion industry in South Carolina, and the video game industry responded to this threat by launching a well-funded independent advertising campaign to defeat Beasley.[14]

Beasley's challenger, Jim Hodges, was a former Democratic state legislator who turned Beasley's opposition to gambling into his own issue. Like Don Siegelman of Alabama, Hodges advocated a state lottery to fund education. Hodges deftly turned the lottery campaign into one of regional rivalry. The campaign ran commercials touting a man named "Bubba" with a Georgia T-shirt who thanked David Beasley for opposing the South Carolina lottery, so South Carolinians would keep spending their money on the Georgia lottery and Georgia schools.

Hodges kept focused on the education issue, while Beasley struggled with his conservative base and the video gambling industry. Like Alabama, a lottery had appeal as a way of paying for new education programs without raising taxes. During the campaign, Hodges remarked, "South Carolinians are a conservative bunch, and they see a lottery as a voluntary tax that you pay only if you play."[15] Hodges even refused to discuss most other issues, especially social issues.

Hodges's campaign worked hard at mobilizing the African American vote. With African Americans making up 25 percent of the voting population in South Carolina, turnout among this group was crucial to Hodges's success. Democrats concentrated on transporting voters to the polls and the widespread use of absentee ballots for African American senior citizens

## Table 8.2  Racial and Ethnic Background and Overall Growth Rate for Southern States in the 2000 Census (in percent)

|  | White | African American | Hispanic | Overall % Growth Rate for State Population from 1990 to 2000 |
|---|---|---|---|---|
| Alabama | 71 | 26 | 2 | +10.1 |
| Arkansas | 80 | 16 | 2 | +13.7 |
| Florida | 78 | 15 | 17 | +23.5 |
| Georgia | 65 | 29 | 5 | +26.4 |
| Louisiana | 64 | 32 | 2 | +3.4 |
| Mississippi | 61 | 36 | 1 | +10.5 |
| North Carolina | 72 | 22 | 5 | +21.0 |
| South Carolina | 67 | 30 | 2 | +15.1 |
| Tennessee | 80 | 16 | 2 | +16.7 |
| Texas | 71 | 11 | 32 | +22.8 |
| Virginia | 72 | 20 | 5 | +14.4 |

*Source:* U.S. Census 2000. The Hispanic category represents ethnic background, not race. See www.census.gov.

(see Table 8.2).[16] This emphasis on turnout proved important because more than 90 percent of African American voters supported Hodges on election day. This level of support among African Americans marked a substantial improvement from the 75 percent support that the Democratic gubernatorial nominee received in 1990.

Hodges ran a campaign that motivated his base of African Americans and appealed to white moderates with issues like education. He won a close race by a margin of 54 percent to 46 percent.

### North Carolina's 1998 U.S. Senate Race: Democrat John Edwards Versus Republican Incumbent Lauch Faircloth

Lauch Faircloth was another conservative Republican from the South who was once a Democrat. After serving in North Carolina government and running a successful hog farm business, he was elected to the U.S. Senate in 1992. He beat a popular former Democratic governor, Terry Sanford, in a close election. Faircloth was a traditionalist in North Carolina politics, who combined conservative social values with a strong alliance with agricultural and business interests. He used the political network built by Senator Jesse Helms (R-N.C.) to solidify his conservative base.[17] Although some observers view North Carolina as one of the most progressive of the southern states, Faircloth targeted his campaign to traditional southern conservatives.

John Edwards was a political novice when he entered the Senate race in 1998. He was a successful trial lawyer who specialized in personal injury cases against insurance companies. He also possessed good looks and smooth television presence to contrast himself with the older and rumpled appearance of Faircloth. Edwards financed most of his $6 million campaign from his own personal wealth, while smartly turning his wealth into an asset by claiming that he was an outsider who was not beholden to special interests.[18] He built on this theme of being an independent outsider by focusing on the issue of reforming health maintenance organizations (HMOs), claiming that the insurance groups were not accountable to patients and that they cheated patients out of proper care by cutting back on medical services.

Faircloth hit back with a simple strategy, accusing Edwards of being a liberal who was connected with an impeached Bill Clinton. Helms spoke up for Faircloth and said a possible Faircloth defeat could "dash . . . any hope whatsoever of controlling the man [President Bill Clinton] who committed high crimes and misdemeanors of making the America the laughingstock of the world."[19] Faircloth's campaign even ran ads that morphed Edwards into a face of President Clinton.

Edwards rejected the label of liberal. He understood that North Carolina politics are a balance between progressive modernization and southern conservatism. This progressive modernization is exemplified by its highly rated universities (the University of North Carolina, Duke University, and North Carolina State University) and its advanced Research Triangle Park.[20] Its conservatism is showcased by the strong influence of traditional religion and its continuous support for the tobacco industry.

Edwards said he was a "different kind of Democrat" who understood North Carolina values and would not be captured by the liberal interests of the national party.[21] Edwards knew he needed to appeal to white moderate voters since the African American base was smaller in North Carolina than in other Deep South states (see Table 8.2). While Faircloth invited numerous Republicans from outside the state to campaign with him, including Robert Dole and Charlton Heston, Edwards isolated himself from the national party during the last weeks of the campaign.

By proclaiming his independence and offering a new image, Edwards beat Faircloth and Jesse Helms's political machine 51 percent to 47 percent.

### Florida's 2000 U.S. Senate Race: Democrat Bill Nelson Versus Republican Bill McCollum (Open Seat)

Senator Connie Mack's (R-Fla.) decision not to seek another six-year term in the Senate created a heated contest between former U.S. representative and Florida state insurance commissioner Bill Nelson and U.S. representative Bill McCollum.

Grandson to the famous Major League baseball manager whose name he shared, former senator Mack was a strong fiscal conservative on issues such as tax cuts, and he was also conservative on most social issues, including a strong pro-life stance. However, Mack recognized the tenuous nature of Florida politics by reaching out to swing voters on issues like protecting Florida's coastlines from oil drilling and giving vocal support for breast cancer research (which resonated with voters because he had been a cancer survivor).

To keep a majority in the Senate, Republicans were committed to retaining the open seat. Democrats also targeted this race as an opportunity to stay competitive in a state that now had a Republican governor (Jeb Bush) and a state legislature with a Republican majority.

Bill McCollum represented Florida's eighth congressional district, which encompasses Orlando. Best known for his conservative views on abortion and for serving as one of the House managers during President Clinton's impeachment in 1999, McCollum had secured the nomination for Senate when he convinced Republican state education commissioner Tom Gallagher not to run. Gallagher had won statewide office numerous times and was seen as more moderate than McCollum. However, McCollum made an early start in fundraising, and both Republican contenders sought to avoid a tough primary.

Bill Nelson was a veteran Florida politician who had served six years in the Florida House; twelve years in the U.S. House of Representatives, representing the state's nineteenth congressional district that includes Cape Canaveral, the home of NASA; and two terms as state insurance commissioner. Most notably, Nelson was a fifth-generation Floridian, a rare characteristic in a state noted for its transplants. Nelson's family history in Florida had shaped his political career; he was raised in the Florida Panhandle, the most conservative area of the state, an area that resembles rural Alabama or southern Georgia. Because of his ties to the space program, he was the last civilian to ride in a successful space shuttle mission before the Challenger disaster in 1986. His different experiences in two separate parts of the state served him well in the diverse state. Unlike many other politicians from his generation, Nelson stayed with the Democratic Party during the rise of the Republican Party in Florida in the 1990s.

The volatility of Florida politics reflects its growing population.[22] In every decade since 1950, the population of the state has grown by at least 20 percent. In two of those decades, the growth was near 50 percent. These new state residents have transformed politics in the Sunshine state. Retirees from the Northeast have settled in the southeastern part of the state and established a strong base for Democratic politics. Other citizens seeking economic opportunities and low taxes (Florida does not have a sales tax) have established successful business enterprises and supported the emerging Republican Party. Cuban immigrants and their descendants are particularly entrenched in the business and political life of southern Florida and generally favor Republicans. African Americans and non-Cuban Hispanics have maintained traditional ties with the Democratic Party.

To capture Florida, McCollum attempted to solidify the conservative base in northern Florida, including the Panhandle, as well as appeal to independent voters in central Florida near his congressional district. He attempted to paint Nelson as a typical liberal, saying his opponent would "tax everything that moves and some things that don't." Nelson rejected the liberal label and pointed to his years in Congress, when he had supported some of Ronald Reagan's agenda. Focusing his campaign on seniors, his advertisements and speeches continually mentioned Social Security, Medicare, and a prescription drug benefit. Nelson also sought to maximize the Democratic base in the southeastern part of the state, namely Miami-Dade, Broward, and Palm Beach Counties. Moreover, unlike other Democratic statewide candidates, Nelson did not abandon the northern part of the state and was able to compete for votes in the conservative Panhandle.[23]

In this tight race, both campaigns were at the mercy of the intense presidential race in 2000 in Florida. If the Gore campaign had not decided to compete for Florida, Nelson's campaign would have had a much more difficult task. The presidential contest was so competitive that it virtually drowned out the barrage of negative ads both the McCollum and Nelson campaigns were running. Unlike other southern Democrats, Nelson welcomed the Gore campaign to Florida, and it poured millions of dollars into boosting Democratic turnout. African American turnout increased dramatically because of the concerted efforts of the Gore and Nelson campaigns. They continually reminded the African American community that George W. Bush's brother, Florida governor Jeb Bush, had ended several affirmative action programs statewide. In effect, Nelson had the best of both worlds. He was able to profit from the Gore campaign's efforts but at the same time was not labeled with some of the image problems that Gore encountered nationally. With a huge turnout from the Democratic base and an appeal to swing voters in the central part of the state, Nelson won the race 51 percent to 47 percent.

## Conclusion

Do these four examples forecast a Democratic comeback in the South? More evidence is needed to make a firm rendering. Republicans have numerous advantages at the presidential and congressional levels. As stated above, the continued success of Republican presidential candidates in the South provides a huge advantage. With Texan George W. Bush in the White House, this success in the South is likely to continue into the near future. The redistricting process that aided Republican candidates in the early 1990s has begun again after the 2000 census. This time, Republicans have more seats and more influence in the governor's office and state legislatures (who control the redistricting process) across the South than at any time since Reconstruction. Republicans who long stayed away from local politics in the South because of Democratic control are now running for and winning local offices.[24]

However, the four races examined highlight the fact that Democrats are still a viable and competitive party in the region on a statewide basis. Although each race had its own particular circumstances, some common patterns are apparent. First, Democrats must pass a litmus test to show that they are not as liberal as national Democrats. In each race, the Democratic contender had to dispel this image quickly. As former senator Zell Miller (D-Ga.) remarked about Democrats in the South, "We have to prove that we will not raise taxes, let all the crooks out of prison, pour the public's money down a variety of rat holes, double everybody's welfare check, condone the burning of the American flag, let serial murderers escape the electric chair, confiscate everybody's guns and take down the Christmas tree at city hall."[25] The four Democratic winners all tried to move toward more moderate and conservative positions in their campaigns.

Second, Democrats can take advantage of Republicans who mishandle the mixture of religion and politics. Although religious issues play well in the South, southerners do have a saturation point for these appeals. If a candidate emphasizes conservative religious beliefs at the expense of all other policy issues, voters will rebel. The same is true of a few other issues. Governor Fob James's dancing like an ape to mock the teaching of evolution was viewed as a huge embarrassment to the state of Alabama. Governor Beasley's crusade against video gambling in South Carolina infuriated a well-funded industry and led to his defeat. Senator Lauch Faircloth's reliance on religious conservative voters led his campaign to ignore the progressive and moderate voters of North Carolina.

Third, Democrats can find specific issues that appeal to a wide spectrum of voters. In Alabama and South Carolina, Democratic candidates highlighted education. In North Carolina, John Edwards talked about HMO reform; in Florida, Bill Nelson focused on issues for senior citizens, including a prescription drug benefit. These issues appeal to Democrats, independents, and suburban Republicans. The candidates focused narrowly on these issues and did not allow themselves to be drawn into polarizing debates about social issues. A challenge for Democrats in the region is finding an acceptable method of raising revenue to pay for these programs. Governors Siegelman and Hodges offered lottery proposals (South Carolina approved a lottery, Alabama did not), but lotteries cannot provide all the monies needed for some of the programs offered by Democrats. Both Governor Siegelman and Governor Hodges lost very close bids for reelection in 2002.

Finally, Democratic candidates have to balance support among African Africans with support among white southerners. Democrats who run statewide campaigns realize that they cannot survive without the overwhelming support of African Americans in their state. At the same time, Democrats cannot win statewide contests solely with African American support. In Florida, Bill Nelson showed that a Democratic candidate could strongly support affirmative action but not be labeled as a liberal. This is a difficult balance for most candidates, including African American candidates. Focusing on issues like education—which is received well across party and racial lines—may be a way of achieving this balance. As the Hispanic population continues to grow in Florida, Texas, and other southern states, candidates will have to put together even broader racial and ethnic coalitions. However, if Republicans continue to dominate among white southerners, then their majority status will not be threatened in the near future.

# 9

## *Case:* The Contested Vote for Mississippi Governor

### Donna Simmons

A front-row seat to a dramatically close and historic election provided me with the unique opportunity both to participate in a successful campaign and witness the spectacle of democracy in action. It also offered an unparalleled learning experience, which is, along with some lessons picked up along the way, shared in the following narrative.

### Rule One: It's Never Too Early to Start

In 1997, two years prior to the statewide election cycle, Lieutenant Governor Ronnie Musgrove hired a full-time fundraiser and a full-time political consultant and rented an office on Congress Street in downtown Jackson, Mississippi, just a few blocks from the state capitol. The signs were clear and unmistakable—Musgrove would be running in 1999 and running hard, but for what?

Democratic attorney general Mike Moore sealed the state's high-profile tobacco lawsuit in the waning days of June and announced his success in early July 1997, making headlines on the Fourth of July. As part of the settlement agreement, the attorney general carved out a $62 million war chest for use over the next two years to establish community-based tobacco abatement and other related programs. Not surprisingly, the well-groomed attorney general quickly became the favorite to succeed two-term Republican governor Kirk Fordice.

Former governor William Winter had made it his business to groom four would-be career politicians during his term in office. The "four boys of summer" indeed became successful politicians, and, legend has it, they promised not to run against each other for governor. Rather, these four individuals—former governor Ray Mabus, former secretary of state and gubernatorial nominee Dick Molpus, state treasurer Marshall Bennett, and attorney general

Mike Moore—would run for the governor's office in turn. As the events of late 1997 and 1998 unfolded, the carefully crafted media presence of the lieutenant governor seemed to signal that he was contemplating a race against the reigning boy of summer. In what insiders called the campaign before the campaign, Musgrove and Moore squared off.

## Rule Two: Know the Terrain

The 1998 legislative session provided the battleground for the two unannounced candidates. The legislature faced the monumental task of appropriating the tobacco settlement dollars. Unlike in many states, Mississippi's lieutenant governor wields considerable power by naming all committees and committee chairs and referring each bill to committee. Wrangling over tobacco dollars continued throughout the session. During the final days, Musgrove negotiated directly with the state's speaker of the House, the state House's public health committee chair, and the state attorney general's most trusted political operative.

Much of the discussion centered on language buried in a number of other appropriation bills that ascribed power to the attorney general to fund a number of politically popular programs with tobacco dollars, thus stripping the legislative leadership of both influence and credit. After some discussion, the attorney general's operative stated simply that he did not need legislative permission to allocate the $62 million and that the language could be dropped from all the bills. The language disappeared. Around this time, the Partnership for a Healthy Mississippi was created, and questions continued to come from the legislature about the legality of the fund as well as the attorney general's control of such a large sum of money.

In a tribute to the attorney general's success, the Jackson County Democratic Party roasted him in his home county. Several guests spoke, including the attorney general's sister. She recounted a heroic story from their childhood, stating how proud she was of her brother for rescuing her once upon a time, particularly since the youthful Moore never liked confrontation. In late 1998, the attorney general gave every public indication that he would be running for governor in 1999 but failed to file the paperwork. Apparently, he reconsidered his decision, possibly because Musgrove continued to mount a sizable fundraising push. Musgrove's fundraising and Moore's actions at the time led someone associated with the attorney general's office to leak the story that Moore would soon announce his candidacy for reelection. Reached at home, Moore recanted his earlier statements, saying that after discussing the matter with his family and praying about it, he would not be seeking the governor's office in 1999.

## Rule Three: Create Distractions for Your Opponent

On the other side of the ballot, Republicans searched for a successor to the throne. Instead of uniting behind the next "Fordice," the Republicans found themselves staring at a ballot crowded with pretenders. Jimmy Heidel, the popular economic developer and odds-on favorite for the party's nomination, succumbed to a most disastrous scandal known as the "Magnolia Venture scandal." U.S. senator Thad Cochran (R-Miss.) disappointed state Republican Party leaders by announcing at the 1998 Neshoba County Fair that he would not seek the office. Mississippi first lady Pat Fordice reportedly tested the waters but perhaps found that her credibility among the voters was not on par with her popularity.

Thus, a field of four emerged for a bloody Republican primary: U.S. representative Mike Parker, a former Democrat; former lieutenant governor Eddie Briggs, also a former Democrat saddled with a 1995 defeat by none other than Musgrove; Dan Gibson, the religious right's representative; and state representative Charlie Williams. With the crowded field, it seemed certain that no one candidate would receive 50 percent of the vote, requiring a state-mandated runoff election between the two top vote getters. That was precisely what happened. Parker and Briggs continued the bloody battle.

The Democratic primary did not go as smoothly as the pundits had anticipated. A northern Mississippi judge and long-time "yellow dog" Democrat (a Democrat who tended to vote with Republicans), Jim Roberts, jumped into the fray. Roberts appealed to the good old boys, who vote in large numbers in Mississippi Democratic primaries, but who, in 1999, owed little allegiance to Musgrove. So, the overweight, balding judge figured he had a chance to knock off the moderate Democratic lieutenant governor, who had a propensity for using the state plane to be in all places at all times, including home.

Musgrove might have appealed to this core Mississippi voter base, but he did not. The starched suits, cufflinks, and spit-polished shoes hid Musgrove's upbringing as a North Mississippi country boy, raised by his mother following his father's death. Summers selling books across the country and working offshore on oil rigs to pay not only his way through school but also his older brother's way at community college did not make the connection with the public, possibly because of Musgrove's signature dark suits and prematurely gray hair.

Nonetheless, in early polling released to the public, Musgrove looked to be invincible. The misleading Mason-Dixon poll became the benchmark for measuring Musgrove's slide downward to election day. Internal polling, however, showed early on that, like most lieutenant governors, Musgrove was vulnerable to attack.

With very little message about what he would do as governor, Roberts took shots at Musgrove, with veiled references to the lieutenant governor's use of the state plane and travel in Mississippi Highway Patrol vehicles at state expense. A strong push by the Musgrove camp during the final weeks leading up to the primary put the votes out of reach for Roberts, but the damage had been done. In fact, Musgrove appeared to be bloodier than his eventual opponent in the general election, Parker, who survived the Republican runoff.

## Rule Four: Stay Focused

With little time for damage control, the Musgrove campaign took on the uphill task of demystifying a heretofore popular congressman with no record of doing anything. By doing little in Congress, Parker could create a superficial persona of the perfect leader. With the Republican state auditor continuing the assault on Musgrove's use of the state plane, Parker had the luxury of running warm, fuzzy, humorous ads featuring such memorable gems as armadillos and long-lost Musgrove relatives. Indeed, the Parker campaign gave new meaning to the popular sitcom describing itself as a show about nothing. Reporters such as syndicated columnist Sid Salter recognized this lack of substance but predicted its success against the policy-oriented Musgrove.

By taking issues like abortion and gun control off the table, the campaign was waged around personalities. Items such as Parker's meticulously groomed appearance and the fact that he never smoked in public seemed important. Conversely, Musgrove became the brunt of "training" attacks and was even asked if he had taken voice lessons to rid himself of his squeaky-sounding voice that voters remembered from earlier in his career.

With polling split and the undecided group growing smaller and smaller, the disciplined and determined Musgrove campaign stuck to a strong public education message and pursued guerrilla tactics with a twenty-first-century flair. While Parker carved away at the Musgrove base of supporters, the Musgrove campaign responded by expanding its base. Musgrove combined old-time strategies of one-on-one campaigning with new Internet technologies. Field workers used both the art and science of campaigning. For example, they employed traffic density maps to place yard signs, get-out-the-vote efforts targeted all eighty-two counties precisely, and the campaign never slept.

## Rule Five: Think

Mississippi law rotates the chairmanship of the state's Joint Legislative Budget Committee between the Speaker of the House and the lieutenant governor. In 1999, Musgrove chaired the committee. Having seen other politicians do a disappearing act in previous years when strapped with such labor-intensive duties, Musgrove vowed not to repeat the same mistake. Yet, for the entire month of September, Musgrove spent his days working on the budget, while Parker spent his days working the state's voters.

Fortunately for Musgrove, Parker was careless and made rookie mistakes that would ultimately undo his candidacy. From releasing a mailer on educational policy with a mathematical error in the cover photo to playing golf the last weekend of the campaign to leaving almost $500,000 in the bank, Parker hurt himself and appeared to quit before the game was up. Slowly and steadily, Musgrove passed him, seeking out Mississippi voters at events far and wide, even across the Mississippi-Tennessee line. He also used carefully constructed radio and television advertising to target voters prior to election day.

A series of ads in the weekly newspapers appeared before the Tuesday election, reminding the public of Parker's vote for the Balanced Budget Act and the cost in real dollars to the struggling local hospitals attributed to that legislation. The late release date prevented Parker from responding before votes were cast. These newspaper ads stirred a great deal of interest and generated more telephone calls to the Musgrove headquarters than any other single campaign message. While Parker played golf, Musgrove played politics.

## Rule Six: Be Ready to Win

Election day told the story. Efforts to suppress turnout and to confuse voters were clearly present, as non-Musgrove supporters wore T-shirts with Musgrove's name on them and made scenes near the state capitol—none of which could be directly linked to the Parker campaign. Misleading sample ballots were also spotted across the state, but it became clear that Musgrove's efforts to stir the bottom of the pot were working. Traditional strongholds for the Republican Party had felt the Musgrove presence, and he was winning some of that important vote.

With what would ultimately become a narrow victory by just 8,000 votes, the lieutenant governor was still short of the 50 percent plus one criterion for capturing the governorship. In this respect, Mississippi's gubernatorial election is similar to the presidential election in its requirement for victory. Also similar to the controversial 2000 presidential election, Musgrove's campaign recognized the importance of each vote and, accordingly, went into high gear to "lock down" the ballots. Attorneys monitored the ballots in courthouses in an effort to deter illegal activities that might jeopardize the fragile outcome. The Musgrove campaign, already exhausted from the hectic and demanding schedule of the days leading up to the election, put in yet another twenty-four-hour day, waking supporters and spouses at odd hours to ensure that eyes and ears were active and alert in every county. The effort paid off. At no point in time were ballot boxes lost or serious questions about foul play raised by either side.

## Rule Seven: Understand Perception

Parker sought to "let the state constitution work," but he never contested the outcome of the popular vote. As in the infamous 2000 presidential election, it is possible for one candidate to win the popular vote, while another candidate takes the electoral vote. The "third wave" of the 1999 election cycle centered on securing the electoral votes to be cast in the Mississippi House of Representatives on January 4, 2000. Even though Parker acknowledged he had lost the popular vote, he would not concede victory to Musgrove. Somewhat shell-shocked, Parker announced he would wait on the vote in the Mississippi House, choosing to let the antiquated state constitution decide the outcome of the close November election.

Mississippi's nineteenth-century constitution demands that if a candidate for governor or lieutenant governor fails to secure a majority of the popular vote and a majority of the electoral vote as ascribed by House district, it falls to the membership of the Mississippi House of Representatives to elect the governor in a public vote of the body. Although the constitution creates a mechanism for casting electoral votes based on the popular vote within a House district, the representative is not bound to vote the way of the district. The House member may vote at will, obviously to avoid a tie in that body.

With a popular vote victory to his credit and in his pocket, Musgrove wasted no time and crossed the state with his wife, Melanie, to thank the voters for their confidence and to remind them—delicately but firmly—that he had indeed won the people's vote. It was nothing new for Musgrove, and he was prepared for such a circumstance. In 1995, Musgrove had won the popular vote, but then lieutenant governor Eddie Briggs had won the electoral vote. Rather than pursue the contest in the House, Lieutenant Governor Briggs wrote a letter to the Speaker of the House removing himself from the race.

Before long, Parker's motives for staying in the race were called into question. The once calm, easygoing, smiling Parker was now portrayed as a disingenuous sore loser by the press. He was even under attack from members of his own party. Musgrove's strategy seemed simple and straightforward. His constituency was statewide. He won the statewide vote. Thus, the members of the House owed it to the state to ratify that vote, unite, and move the state forward to governing.

Although the sport of the impending House vote dominated the news, talk of the need for transition slowly bubbled to the surface. Parker's tactic eliminated time usually dedicated to transition activities: staffing the governor's office, planning inaugural activities, and readying the family to move to Jackson and into the governor's mansion.

## Rule Eight: Just Make It Happen

On January 4, 2000, Lieutenant Governor Ronnie Musgrove convened the state Senate. Speaker of the House Tim Ford was reelected by his peers and took the dais in the Mississippi House. Minutes later on this historic day— which also happened to be Melanie Musgrove's birthday—the roll was called. Campaign staffers, family members, and close friends of the effort gathered in state senator Hob Bryan's office on the second floor, listening to the House on the "squawk box." Bag lunches were handy, but very little was eaten.

As the votes were tallied, a message was delivered to Lieutenant Governor Musgrove at the podium: he had been elected by a vote of 86 to 36 in the House. Recessing the state Senate, Musgrove made his way to state Senator Bryan's office; he had already turned the lieutenant governor's office over to Amy Tuck, so that her transition into office could begin. A press conference was hastily called at which the governor-elect reacted to the House vote and promptly announced his selection of the inaugural chair and the transition chair. Work began immediately.

In seven days' time, both chairs would orchestrate what many said would be impossible. Phase 1 of the inaugural celebration went off without a hitch, and a skeletal staff assumed duties promptly at noon, January 11, 2000, on the twentieth floor of the Sillers Building, home to the office of the governor, Ronnie Musgrove.

## Rule Nine: The Campaign for
## Re-election Begins the Day After the Election

The final campaign for public support for a governor holding office without a firm public mandate was off and running immediately after the campaign for office ended. Every minute of every inaugural activity, every word of every speech, every press release—indeed, every action was measured against this need to build a mandate. Governor Musgrove's swearing-in ceremony was held on the grounds of the capitol, and many said it was the first to be open to the public. The crowds covered the grounds and listened to an upbeat message of hope for opportunity and prosperity, a message sprinkled with both humor and seriousness and punctuated with Musgrove's flair for the personal, the story, and the passion of his commitment to education and opportunity for each and every Mississippian.

Prior to the speech itself, the Mississippi Mass Choir performed as part of a multidenominational prayer celebration in the First Baptist Church of Jackson, another first. Bagpipes heralded the Musgrove family's walk to the capitol, which captured the front page of the only statewide newspaper the following day. A month later, Mississippi celebrated the new administration again with a parade, an open invitation to the governor's mansion to meet the first family, and an inaugural ball open to the public as well.

## Rule Ten: Do the Job, and Do It Well

The governor's staff operated in a parallel universe those first months, carefully planning the announcements of hirings and appointments, showing the open, inclusive face of the administration by pairing black and white choices. Challenged to build a legislative agenda after the session had begun, Musgrove used his first state of the state speech to unveil his agenda and list his priorities. Delivering on teacher pay became the single goal of this fourth campaign, both publicly and privately. Musgrove announced victory on the one hundredth day of the administration, as the legislature put a teacher pay package into law after the original legislation had died on deadlines. The measure would raise salaries to the southeastern average over just a few years.

Quickly, Musgrove moved to create anticipation for a new economic development plan and announced the ongoing activities of the Mississippi Public-Private Partnership for Economic Development. By early fall, the Advantage Mississippi Initiative was done, supporting legislation was passed, and Nissan North America announced plans to build its largest vehicle manufacturing facility in Mississippi, the state's first such facility.

Governor Musgrove and his team survived a hotly contested campaign, a rare and unique constitutionally mandated election decision in the state House, and the initial challenges of governing in the wake of such momentous events.

# 10

## Case: Two Views of the Florida Controversy

### View 1: What Happened in Florida on November 7, 2000?

#### Jane Carroll

What happened? That became the number one question for most of the United States as well as many other countries in November 2000. There are two very simple answers. First and foremost, Florida had a close election for the presidential electors. Second, the television network commentators changed their reports during the evening and misled the nation. Before the polls closed in Florida's Panhandle—which is in the central time zone—and while the actual results from the few precincts that had already reported to Tallahassee, the state capital, did show George W. Bush in the lead, NBC "gave the State of Florida to Al Gore!"

That was amazing to those of us still counting ballots and keeping up with the statewide results via the Internet. It was not yet 8:00 P.M., and we had hundreds of precincts still to be counted. Should we just go home and let the media have the final word, or should we do our jobs—we being the legally constituted canvassing board? As supervisor of elections for Broward County, I had to answer this question and had a front-row seat for this historic election. What follows is my story.

### Supervising an Election

#### Preparing for the Election

There is so much to do in preparing for and conducting an election in a large jurisdiction such as Broward County, with just under 900,000 registered voters. It is impossible to cover all pertinent tasks in a short case study, but a brief synopsis of the election of 2000 follows:

The election cycle consisted of three elections—held in September, October, and November—and began with candidates qualifying in July. Voter registration was an ongoing process. Since the inception of the National Voter Registration Act in January 1995 (a.k.a. "Motor Voter"), however, registration has not been as intense just prior to the "book clos-ing," which falls twenty-nine days prior to each of the three elections and marks the end of the period for registering to vote.

Ballot layouts for the 2000 election were completed immediately after candidates completed the qualification process. Printing followed, and absentee ballots were then available for persons choosing to vote in person, by mail, and through supervised nursing home voting.

Voter rolls—lists of eligible voters—were updated on a daily basis with new registrations, address changes, and absentee voting status. The precinct registers were printed as late as possible so as to include all changes and be as accurate as possible and were distributed to the precinct clerks the day before the election.

Voter identification cards were mailed to all new registrants, to those who made any changes in their registration, and to those whose polling place had been changed. The cards contained all pertinent information, such as the address of the polling place, voter information, and pertinent districts for congressional, state house, and senate for that particular voter.

A sample ballot booklet, formatted exactly as the ballot pages in the Votomatic would appear on election day, was mailed to each household in Broward County where there was a registered voter. (See the Appendix at the end of this chapter for pages from this book, an explanatory letter to the voter from the elections supervisor, and an explanation on using the voting equipment.) This mailing has taken place for all general elections since 1974, when the punch card system was acquired. The sample ballot has been very popular with Broward's voters and had proven to be a boon in expediting voting on election day.[1] Included on the instruction page (found in the Appendix) provided to voters was a note at the bottom of the page stating, "If you make a mistake, return your ballot card and obtain another." This statement was also posted in the voting unit at the polling place.

The sample ballot also had the following information: how to vote for a write-in candidate; an application to be a poll worker for future elections; and reminders that voters could find the address of their polling place on the voter registration card; that they would be required to show picture identifi-cation or, if they had none, complete an affidavit verifying their identity; and that all this information was available in other formats and in Spanish.

When a voter arrived at the polling place on election day, he or she was asked to observe a demonstration on the use of the voting system. After that, the voter was directed to the appropriate precinct register, which contained the list of all eligible voters. In a general election, the registers are organized in alphabetical order. There were also placards clearly directing the voter to the correct register. When the voter's name was found on the register, he or she showed a valid picture identification or used an affidavit and then signed his or her name or mark. If the signature matched the one preprinted on the register, the voter was issued a ballot with a gray security envelope that contained write-in provisions.

Precinct workers were instructed to ask if the voter still resided at the address on the register, as Florida law requires that the voter vote in the precinct in which he or she resides on election day. Address changes could be made on election day, and, if this was the case, the voter was directed to the proper precinct (the voter should have notified the elections office of the new address prior to election day).

If a voter's name did not appear on the register, a call to the elections office was necessary. Calling is difficult, however, on the day of a major election, such as the general election of 2000. It is next to impossible to have a phone system able to handle thousands of calls at a given time and have knowledgeable and competent people available to answer the calls. It is the responsibility of the citizen to keep records up to date so that only the truly unavoidable calls can be handled.

A somewhat related and increasingly important component of preparing for elections is voter education. For many years, Broward County has had extensive educational programs to encourage voting. In the mid-1970s, I instituted a program called the "Kiddie Ballot" for kindergarten through fifth grade. This program involved taking actual Votomatic machines to the classrooms with ballots containing issues suitable for the age group. A ballot focusing on issues of concern to middle school and high school students was later developed, as was a ballot with current events for high school students to use in conjunction with their annual voter registration drive. I started a voter registration program in 1972, when the voting age was lowered to eighteen. Through this program, several thousand seniors registered each year at their schools during April and May.[2]

Additionally, voting equipment and a display booth of printed materials were taken to many public events. Votomatic machines were available to adults, young people, and children for demonstrations and voting on current issues. Press releases were sent out with the results of this voting. In addition, the office's VoteMobile—a mobile educational display—visited shopping centers, fairs, and community gatherings to register voters and provide education.

*Poll Workers*

When the polls open at 7:00 A.M. on election day, everything is in the hands of the poll workers. For this reason, the Broward County Elections Office had made training a priority. Although many methods of training had been used and all have merit, during my tenure as elections supervisor, a state-of-the-art "Training the Trainer" program seemed to be most effective. Under this concept, through roundtable discussions with many precinct clerks in small groups, key leaders were asked to be what were called "regional clerks." Each regional clerk was assigned approximately fourteen precincts. His or her responsibility was to train all their poll workers. These training sessions were two hours long and were held prior to the September primary. If the regional clerk wanted a resource person from the supervisor of elections' staff, one attended. The regional clerks attended one-day workshops, in which they were trained by staff members and the supervisor of elections. The necessary materials were distributed to the regional clerks.

On election day, these clerks traveled to each of their assigned precincts, serving as a liaison between the election office and the poll workers. Poll workers fall into three general categories: demonstrators, precinct register workers, and workers at the ballot box. Each clerk had a cell phone and could be reached at all times by the elections office and sent to any precinct with a problem. Some precincts had several visits during the day from their regional clerk.

Feedback from the primary election was used to improve the general election by means of a second workshop, which was a half-day program for regional clerks. Problems were discussed and supplemental training inserts were distributed that covered differences between the primary and the general election. Enough materials were given to each clerk for him or her to provide copies to all workers, for whom mandatory training sessions were held before the general election.

The poll workers had a comprehensive workbook, which was used at their training session and also as a reference on election day. They had an operations checklist covering tasks before the polls opened, during the day, and after the polls closed. They were also furnished a supply list that they were instructed to check off. Troubleshooters were available to deliver anything to a precinct, should, for example, a call come to the voting equipment center about missing items.

The poll workers were responsible for setting up and checking the election equipment. The clerk in charge of each precinct assigned the remaining functions to his or her poll workers. Each of these workers also received "job aide cards."

If a voter needed assistance, he or she could bring someone to the poll or use the assistance of two poll workers assigned that task. Curbside voting was available if a voter needed it, and all polling places were accessible to those who needed special access. A wheelchair-accessible Votomatic was supplied to each precinct. Sensitivity training was also included in the poll workers' instruction book, and members of the Broward County Americans with Disabilities Act (ADA) Commission spoke to the precinct clerks at the training session.

When the polls closed at 7:00 P.M. on election night and the last voter had voted, the clerk and the assistant clerk brought the ballots—which had been placed in a numbered, sealed transfer case—to be counted at the central counting location. Any voter in line at 7:00 P.M. was allowed to vote.

## November 7, 2000: Election Day

"What a difference a day makes—twenty-four little hours," so goes the old song. Those words kept running through my mind as I drove home early on the morning after the election. Little did I know how many days of a contested election would follow and that actually none of them would turn out to make a difference. George W. Bush had won Florida that day, as would ultimately prove to be the case after thirty-six days.

Election day had not been unusual in Broward County. I had arrived at the office at 5:45 A.M., my usual time on election days. The poll workers had arrived at all 609 polling places, and all polls had opened on time at 7:00 A.M. The phones were busy after the polls opened, but that was to be expected.

Both Democrats and Republicans were active in last-minute campaigning for their presidential candidates, and rumors and imaginations were running wild. For instance, my office was getting calls from Democrats claiming that Democrats were not getting to vote and Republicans claiming that Republicans were not getting to vote. I began to think that we would not have any ballots to count!

### Counting Votes

Florida had been too close to predict, even on the eve of the election. That was not a source of grief to me, as I have never been a fan of polls. But the closeness of the polls and the number of supposedly undecided voters made the political parties paranoid about every story that reached their ears. After thirty-two years as the supervisor of elections, I knew that there were no unexpected or unusual concerns. As always, all reported problems were investigated and resolved by a very experienced and reliable staff.

Election day was a busy day—580,000 voters had cast their ballots. It now was time to depart for the voting equipment center, where these ballots would arrive for tabulation.

Both prior to the ballot count and immediately following it, a public test is performed on the tabulating equipment to verify that it is functioning accurately. The processing of the majority of the 50,000 absentee ballots began immediately because most had arrived prior to November 7. The ones that came in on election day had to be held until all precinct books were returned to the center in order to ensure that none had also voted at the polls. If that occurred, the absentee ballot was not opened for counting.

The precinct ballots began to arrive. More politicos came to observe the counting process than we normally encountered since the advent of the Internet and a direct real-time link to the tabulation equipment (with continuous scrolling of the results on all local public service cable stations).

During the evening, NBC reported that nine ballot boxes were lost in Broward County. Their local affiliate station was present at and broadcasting from our central election office. Even after repeated information was given to them that it was not true—no ballots were missing, nor had they ever been—NBC continued with its story. Later that night, I noticed that CNN commentator Bob Novak was saying something to the effect of, "What about those missing ballot boxes in Broward County?" By this time, local reporters were coming in to ask about the missing ballots. I assured them that all ballots were in. They replied, "But Tom Brokaw says they are missing." Somewhat irritated by this comment, I said, "Tom Brokaw is not here, I am, and all ballots are here at the counting center!" Operatives for both Gore and Bush were grasping at any and all straws by that time and making it difficult for those of us who were trying to finalize the count to do so.

### Recounting the Votes

Very early on November 8, when all unofficial returns were tallied by the State Division of Elections, we knew that Florida's mandatory machine recount would occur. A recount is triggered when the difference in outcome is one-half of 1 percent or less. So the Broward County recount was set for 1:00 P.M. on November 8.

Upon my arrival at the Voting Equipment Center at 12:30 P.M., I was greeted by the various members of the print, radio, and television media, as well as political activists, candidates, their representatives, and many individuals whose reason for being there was never determined. Elections officials were actually busy recounting three races. Not only did the presidential race fall in the mandatory recount amount, but also one of the four U.S. congressional races in Broward County and the county property appraiser races required recounts. Arguments soon broke out between the parties, attorneys, and candidates' representatives.

The work of the recount was overseen by the Broward County Canvassing Board. Each of Florida's sixty-seven counties has such a board. The three-member boards are chaired by the county judge. The chairperson of the County Commission and the supervisor of elections are the other two members. The judge and the commissioner are concerned only with the vote tabulation, whereas the elections supervisor has the total responsibility for the election. The commissioner and the elections supervisor are elected to their positions on a partisan basis for four-year terms. The judge is elected in nonpartisan elections but can have a party affiliation; however, this party affiliation cannot be listed on the ballot or used in campaigning. The canvassing board appoints as many agents as necessary to perform the election night tasks under its supervision. There were approximately 150 such people on hand in Broward County, Florida, the night of November 7.

All work of the Canvassing Board was always on view through glass windows, but only a reasonable number of people could actually surround the board. It was not a simple task to find out who represented whom and keep it to two observers for each party of interest. Microphones were set up so that observers outside the glass could hear our discussions.

The machine recount was completed by 6:00 P.M. After all 588,000 ballots were put though the tabulating equipment, the difference was a net gain of one vote for Bush (he had forty-four additional votes to Gore's forty-three additional votes). The reason for the slight change was the now famous "hanging chad," some of which had dislodged during the second count and thus become votes.

### The Hand Count

The board members departed the building thinking that the election was over. We were wrong! On November 9, the Gore forces called for a hand count. The chairperson of the canvassing board called a meeting at 10:00 A.M. on November 10 because Florida law calls for the canvassing board to meet with the person or persons making the request. It is within the board's discretion to grant or not grant the request. Arguments must be made as to the compelling reason to do a hand count. Broward County had only done one hand count previously and that was for a precinct city with fewer than 1,000 ballots, hardly the number of votes in a presidential election. The hand count in this one previous instance failed to reveal any "hanging chads," but the ballots had to be counted three times before accuracy was achieved. The outcome of the case in question was that the mayor had won by the same one vote margin he had achieved on election night.

At the meeting on Friday, November 10, Gore's representatives and the other two who had lost by less than one-half of 1 percent made their cases. The winning candidates also made their cases against the hand count. The board listened, discussed the various cases, and voted individually on each of the three. By a two-to-one vote, Gore's request was granted. I cast the one opposing vote and did so because punch cards were never meant to be hand counted. Human error far exceeds that of the machine. It is too subjective (a view that was certainly proven), and the more the cards are handled, the more they are subject to damage. The other two hand counts were denied by the canvassing board.

What has been underplayed in the discussion of Broward County's uncounted votes is that 97.6 percent were clearly voted and counted. A mere 1.3 percent overvoted (marked more than one candidate for a race), and 1.1 percent undervoted (failed to record a vote for a particular race), for a total of 2.4 percent. Broward County voters would get an "A" on anyone's grading scale.

Ironically, at the presidential election in 1996, Broward County had a 2.8 percent combined under- and overvote—four-tenths of 1 percent higher than 2000. Undervoting is not an unusual phenomenon in Broward County. In the 2000 election, 6,716 people undervoted the presidential race, 18,928 undervoted the U.S. senate race, and 41,902 undervoted in one of the congressional races. The large numbers in the other races make the 6,716 in the presidential race seem less significant.

The hand count for Gore was set for Monday, November 13, at 1:00 P.M. at the Voting Equipment Center. The deluge of people who had greeted me on November 8 seemed small compared to what awaited me that day. Florida law provided for certain procedures to be followed in a hand count. The candidate requesting it was allowed to select three precincts. The canvassing board then supervised the counting teams, each composed of two workers of opposite political parties. Each candidate was allowed one observer for each team.

The ballots for the three precincts selected were removed from the sealed cabinets in which they had been secured since the second machine count. Of course, the challenging candidate selected precincts favorable to him. In this case, the total votes in these three precincts were 3,557 for Gore and 133 for Bush. Even though Gore had carried Broward County by 67 percent, these precincts were not representative. In addition, Gore had only asked for hand counts in four counties that he had carried heavily. They were not representative of the entire state. In the long run, this factor was the most significant because all voters in Florida were thus not afforded equal protection. The entire state was not hand counted, and those counties doing hand counts did not have uniform standards.

At the conclusion of the hand count of the three precincts (at approximately 6:00 P.M.), Gore had gained four votes. They came from ballots brought to the canvassing board from the counting teams who had been unable to determine voter intent, again because of partially removed chads. The canvassing board had agreed on a standard of what constituted a vote prior to the count because Florida law was silent on what constituted voter intent. Our standard was that if a chad was hanging by one or two corners, it was to be considered a valid vote. A chad such as that can swing in or out, thus preventing the tabulating equipment from being able to read it when it swings closed, and constitutes voter error because it was not completely punched (not a tabulation error).

This distinction became very important in the ensuing votes taken by the canvassing board. As stated by law, when a manual count indicates an error in vote tabulation because of the system failing to count properly voted ballots, the canvassing board shall correct the error and then recount all precincts or request the Florida Department of State to verify the software or manually recount all ballots. I had requested an opinion from the Department of State, Division of Elections, on this matter because I anticipated that there would be varied opinions among the members of the canvassing board, as well as the many attorneys involved. The opinion was faxed to me at the counting center. It stated that unless the tabulating equipment had failed to count properly punched ballots, the county canvassing board was not authorized to conduct a manual recount of the remainder of the county or perform any action stated in this law.[3] The county attorneys concurred. Much discussion ensued, and finally a vote was taken. It was two to one to take no further action; therefore the vote count was over.

### Attorneys, Courts, and Sheriffs

Although the number of observers had increased, we used the same procedures as we had on November 8. After the vote was taken, chaos broke out. Sheriff's deputies escorted us to our cars and, once again, I left for home thinking the election was over.

On November 14, the attorney general of Florida wrote a conflicting opinion—one of many conflicts that were to occur in the election aftermath. It was highly unusual because he had not issued opinions on election matters since the legislature had given the Division of Elections (under the secretary of state) the authority to issue official election opinions. The secretary of state is the chief election official in Florida. The attorney general's opinion stated that the division's opinion was wrong in several respects. It was a lengthy opinion but finally concluded that the term "error in voter tabulation" encompasses a discrepancy between the number of votes determined by a manual count of a sampling of precincts and the number determined by the tabulating equipment. He did not directly state whether we should manually recount all precincts, but he said that the Division of Elections opinion stating that we should not do so was wrong.[4]

The courts had become involved at several levels on the same day. Attorneys were filing cases almost hourly. Our canvassing board reconvened at the request of the chairperson. We had further discussion after the county commissioner moved to reconsider. A circuit judge set a special hearing, and we recessed to attend. He listened to the attorneys for both sides and withheld judgment, stating that it was for the canvassing board to decide. We returned to the courtroom in which we had been meeting and decided not to reconsider our vote of November 13 (that is, not to continue manually recounting). Once again, I left sure that it was over.

Early on the morning of November 15, I received a call from my attorney that our chairperson had called the canvassing board back into session. We were to be in his courtroom at 10:00 A.M. When we reconvened, he stated that he wanted to reconsider. I knew then that the die was cast and that all 588,000 ballots were going to be manually counted. That is exactly what happened! The new vote was two to one but in the opposite direction of the original vote. Again, I was the dissenting vote.

The County Emergency Center was selected as the site, and 2:00 P.M. that day was the starting time for the manual recount. All ballots in the sealed cabinets were transported in the sheriff's moving van to the County Emergency Center, 10 miles west of our counting center. The facility was perfect for this recount. There were many tables and chairs and a press room with large picture windows looking into the counting room—the room where we, the canvassing board, spent sixteen or more hours a day. The ballots were guarded twenty-four hours a day by sheriff's deputies.

There were many times during the following days when I thought how much difference it would have made had I been able to get the county commission to take my advice in 1993 and purchase an optical scan voting system. I had tried to no avail for all the years after that, each time warning them about the "hanging chad" problem.

We started with a handful of teams but increased to as many as eighty teams at a time. There were 160 counters plus another 160 observers, one for Gore and one for Bush with each team.

Court cases abounded. The manual count continued. In spite of many delaying tactics and precincts that had to be hand counted again because of obvious errors, as was to be expected, Broward County completed the task. The certification was hand delivered to Tallahassee at the state Division of Elections prior to 5:00 P.M. on Sunday, November 26, as ordered by the Florida Supreme Court. This ruling stated that the secretary of state had to accept recounts up until 5:00 P.M on that date. Neighboring Palm Beach County did not make the deadline, and Miami-Dade County had stopped its count earlier in the week.

## Conclusion: A Solution?

Our involvement was over, but the rest of Florida and the country continued on until the U.S. Supreme Court made a final ruling on December 12. The country showed a new interest in elections. Task forces were formed. Legislation was proposed. As of this writing, it remains to be seen what the U.S. Congress will do: some reforms have been proposed, but few have been enacted. In 2002, 2004, and beyond we will find out if voters now know that one vote does matter.

As for Florida, Governor Jeb Bush appointed a twenty-one-member task force. It was composed of ten Republicans, ten Democrats and one of neither party. I was honored to be one of his appointees. It first met on January 8, 2001, with a deadline of March 1, 2001, for completion. Five public meetings were held in different parts of Florida. The task force decided on the following principles:

1. Voting should be simple and convenient.
2. A voting system should determine voter's intent.
3. A voting system should be uniform for fairness, reliability, and equal protection of voting opportunity.
4. Elections must achieve two competing goals: certainty that every vote counts accurately, and finality, so that elections end and governing begins.

To accomplish these principles, thirty-five recommendations were made. The most significant were:

1. Create and publish a voters' Bill of Rights (to be displayed prominently at polling places as well as being widely publicized). It also would list voters' responsibilities.
2. Recruit better qualified poll workers with better training.
3. Improve precinct communications.
4. Use nonpartisan election supervisors.
5. Stipulate that canvassing board members refrain from political involvement for that election cycle.
6. Develop a uniform and standardized voting system for 2002. (Decertify punch cards and central count mark sense systems.)
7. Develop uniform standards for recounts.
8. Provide a statewide online (real-time) voter registration database.
9. Provide provisional ballots at precincts.
10. Hold manual recounts of the entire jurisdiction in which a candidate was involved, that is, when the results of a statewide race are in doubt, the whole state, not selected counties, should be recounted.
11. Expand the time between elections.[5]

The Florida legislature met for its annual sixty-day session following these meetings. They passed an election reform act that included numbers 1, 2, 6, 7, 8, 9, 10, and 11 on the last day of the session, April 4. Needless to say, there was a great deal of testimony and many concessions between the Senate and House. The final product will do much to make Florida's elections the best in the nation.[6]

What have we learned from the 2000 election? Ideally, elections would be a 100 percent correct business all the time, and patronizing remarks that everyone's vote must be counted would never need to be voiced. But, realistically, we know that perfection eludes us in all phases of daily living. So, what have we really learned? I hope that all voters have learned the importance of voting carefully and understand that there may be unintended or unforeseen consequences if they do not. As election supervisors and administrators, we will provide the best possible voting system. We will hire the best people we can to work at the polling places. We will give the best instructions to the voters on election day and before. We will all do the best possible job we can.

## View 2: Election 2000—A League of Women Voters' Perspective

### Joan Karp

The voters of Palm Beach County, Florida, will not soon forget the year 2000—not because it was the turn of the century and start of a new millennium, nor because of the anticipation of Y2K problems with all our computer programs—but because it was an election year like none other in recent memory. In 2000, as in every election year, the League of Women Voters of South Palm Beach County (LWVSPBC) planned and executed various programs to educate citizens. The league's goal is good government through an informed electorate.

In addition to 2000 being a presidential election year, Florida voters had one senator and four contested U.S. representatives to elect. Palm Beach County voters also chose four state senators and ten state representatives; plus an array of constitutional officers: sheriff, clerk of the circuit court, tax collector, public defender; three school board members, and four county commissioners. Also on the ballot in November were four referenda: (1) a state question on high-speed rail, (2) two local-option questions on merit selection and retention of Circuit Court and County Court judges (elected positions that would be appointed if these passed), and (3) a Palm Beach County issue to raise the cap on the tax for Children's Services Council. The league also joined the People over Politics coalition and Common Cause of Florida to work toward creating an independent redistricting commission for the reapportionment that would follow the 2000 census. A very full plate, indeed, for the 2000 election.

## Reaching Out to the Voters

A lot of work goes into administering an election. Similarly, individuals and organizations—such as the League of Women Voters—dedicated to promoting the fair, competitive, and orderly administration of elections often spend months and devote considerable time and resources to making such a goal a reality. With all this territory to cover, the LWVSPBC used many avenues to reach out to the voters of southern Palm Beach County, Florida. The following list is designed to provide an idea of the type of work typically performed before and on behalf of an upcoming election:

• In the spring, LWVSPBC unveiled a new website that contained information about the league and links to various county and state government sites, as well as the sites for the League of Women Voters of Florida and the national League of Women Voters. When the referenda questions were finalized, they were posted on the site together with pros and cons for each issue.

• LWVSPBC visited high schools in the area and spoke to twelve senior classes about the importance of voting and the different races in Palm Beach County. Students who were age seventeen were registered to vote; they would be issued their registration cards on their eighteenth birthday. The highlight of the programs was student participation in the mock election using real voting equipment, which at that time was the punch card. The league chapter registered approximately 500 students.

• LWVSPBC's Speakers Bureau presented programs at thirty-eight different organizations to discuss the pros and cons of the referenda, the upcoming redistricting, and the league's goal of an independent redistricting commission. The speakers also emphasized the different elections to be held: both the primary elections and the school board election were in September; a runoff (second primary), if needed, was scheduled for October, followed by the general election and runoff for school board, if needed, in November. People new to the area are not necessarily aware of local elections, and it helps to remind them of such dates.

• Two League members were interviewed about the election issues on a talk radio show. The discussion was similar to the one given by the members of the Speakers Bureau. A call from a listener alerted the league to the problem that convicted felons who have paid their debt to society cannot easily have their voting rights restored in Florida. This issue became quite important to league officers after the election.

• Public voter registration drives were held by the league at Florida Atlantic University, at area green (farmer's) markets in two cities, and at art festivals in the county. Several corporations requested that LWVSPBC members come in and register their employees as well.

• LWVSPBC prepared a flyer listing the pros and cons of the referenda questions that was distributed at league speaking engagements, at general meetings, to all those receiving the league newsletter, and at the green markets.

• LWVSPBC participated in the Democracy Network (www.dnet.org), a website developed by the League of Women Voters of the United States in conjunction with Grassroots.com. (DNet is now wholly owned by LWVUS.) Voters simply need to type in their zip code, and the website allows voters to view all the candidates and issues in upcoming elections, from president down to local races. The southern Palm Beach County chapter contacted all local state representative and state senator candidates, as well as county candidates, with the goal of convincing them to add their biographies and opinions on issues to the site. The website and service provides something of a "one-stop shopping" source for voters and concerned citizens because all the candidates for each office and their positions are listed together. The process is similar to an online debate: anyone can suggest an issue, and the candidates can respond. Since the league was rather new at this and since some of the local candidates were not yet comfortable with computers, unfortunately, there was only about a 10 percent compliance rate from candidates. Those who did participate were very pleased. It did not cost them any of their hard-won campaign dollars and was effective in getting their messages out. The Sun-Sentinel, a widely read newspaper in the area, published a letter to the editor from the league president about DNet and its purpose.

• LWVSPBC held a well-attended public meeting on the issue of merit selection and retention of judges, with two members of the Florida Bar Association presenting opposing views. Curiously, the one who had run for an elected judge position and was defeated still favored elections for these judges.

• A Candidates Forum for the county offices of sheriff, clerk of the circuit court, public defender, and tax collector was sponsored by the league. An audience of 100 showed up for this forum.

• LWVSPBC participated in a Candidates Forum for U.S. Senate sponsored by the League of Women Voters of Florida. The forum was televised live on public television and available on the Internet. It was the only forum in which the independent party candidate was invited and participated, along with the Democratic and Republican candidates.

• A freelance writer interviewed the LWVSPBC president for an article published in the "Community" section of the Palm Beach Post newspaper. This article outlined some of the activities mentioned here.

• The chapter distributed several thousand issues of the special election edition of The Florida Voter, the LWV of Florida's newsletter.

• The chapter president published an op-ed piece in the Fort Lauderdale *Sun-Sentinel* on campaign finance reform.

• LWVSPBC participated in the national league's "Take a Friend to Vote" campaign, distributing bumper stickers and leaflets in an effort to get out the vote.

• A helpful videotape on clean campaigns created by the New York State League of Women Voters to be used as a public service announcement was acquired by LWVSPBC. Local public television aired it many times in the two months prior to the November election.

• Although it may sound trivial, LWVSPBC also prepared for the election by increasing the number of messages the league voicemail phone could hold in anticipation of increased calls. Hundreds of calls were received in the office, and in the days immediately preceding November 7, 2000, LWVSPBC responded to a few hundred calls.

In short, the LWVSPBC crew of volunteer women and men did everything possible to inform the voters and encourage them to go to the polls. Having done all this in anticipation of a smooth election, league members were ready and eager to cast their own votes and then relax and watch the returns come in on election day, November 7, 2000. However, what transpired that evening made history and was completely unexpected. Sadly, what was printed in the headlines was only part of the election story.

## November 7, 2000

Around midafternoon on Tuesday, Election Day, the phones started ringing with news of the difficulties with the Palm Beach County "butterfly ballot." This ballot, designed by the Palm Beach County supervisor of elections' office in an effort to produce a more voter-friendly ballot, actually ended up confusing countless voters and might have produced a large number of votes cast for the wrong candidate. Many people, including League of Women Voter members, who are well informed on how to vote, were unsure whether they had punched the correct place on the ballot.

For instance, some ballots had not been properly aligned in the machine, making it unclear as to which hole to punch for the candidate of one's choice. The presidential candidates were listed on two pages, but the holes were to the right on one page and to the left on the other page, interspersed with each other. As such, to vote for the candidate whose name appeared second on page one, voters would need to punch not the second hole, but the third hole from the top, as the second hole corresponded to the first candidate listed on page two. Only the voters who cast their vote for George W. Bush, whose name appeared first on the ballot (corresponding to the first hole on the ballot), were positive that their vote was correctly cast.

The initial reaction by many league members matched that of many voters in Palm Beach County and the various other counties in Florida where reports of voting irregularities and problems were reported. Because many league members serve as poll workers, they were at the polling sites where the alleged problems occurred, experienced some of the problems themselves when voting, and heard firsthand from confused and disgruntled voters. League members immediately began phoning one another to share their concerns. A formal meeting was held on Saturday, four days after the vote. By coincidence, this meeting had been scheduled before the election for the purpose of addressing new member orientation. However, that item never made it into the meeting agenda because, as might be expected, the problems with the election dominated the meeting's business.

The concerns of league members during and immediately after the election mirrored those reported by county voters. They included, for instance, the inability of poll workers and concerned citizens to contact the office of the supervisor of elections. Apparently, an insufficient amount of phone lines were available in the event of a problem, although it is supposed to be a common practice to add phone lines and a system for dealing with such emergencies during elections. When trying to notify election officials of the problems at the polling sites, answer questions from voters and poll workers, and remedy the situation, many poll workers, league members, and citizens were unable to reach the supervisor of election's office and staff.

Another problem was that insufficient measures were taken to provide provisional ballots for those having problems with their ballot or vote or those with difficulties verifying their voter registration. That too should have been planned and available for the election. The league heard from many citizens and its own members that poll workers and frustrated voters did not know that they were legally able to fill out an affidavit to vote when experiencing these problems. Voters must be better informed of their rights, and poll workers should have informed these individuals that there was a way for them to vote. Relatedly, many voters reporting problems when trying to vote stated that they did not know they could have asked for assistance from poll workers. Asking for and obtaining help might have alleviated many of the problems. For instance, those unsure if they had voted for their intended candidate or those who realized that they had punched the wrong hole could have voted again; by law, the voter is able to try three times to vote correctly. As such, their incorrect vote could have been discounted and a new ballot provided to the voter so that they might try again.

The primary problem appeared to be with the "butterfly ballot," which confused many voters and probably resulted in numerous incorrect or unintended votes. Several league members reported being confused by the ballot and uncertain as to whether they cast the correct vote. These reports came in immediately and remain to the present time. The supervisor of elections, Teresa LePore, had meant well and had made the controversial ballot available to the public prior to the election. However, two points are worth noting. One, because of the general public perception that elections were well run and experienced few problems, little concern was raised about either the ballot or the supervisor's readiness for the upcoming election.

Two, the sample ballot that the league examined before the election did not contain the holes in the middle of the two pages, the very feature that made the ballot so troublesome.

Fortunately for Palm Beach County, the issue of African Americans and others, mostly minorities, being turned away from the voting site did not appear to be a major concern. In Broward County, just south of Palm Beach County, and a few counties in the northern part of the state, numerous complaints were registered that African American voters were denied access to voting. Most of these complaints involved poll workers allegedly stating that they could not verify that the individual was registered to vote and African Americans being told that polling sites were closed even though they were legally supposed to be open. Still, like many African American voters around the state whose complaints often went unheeded, voters in Palm Beach County found many of their questions unanswered. Moreover, some election officials were hesitant, if not opposed, to working with the League of Women Voters in addressing the problem.

In the days immediately following the election, the league would have liked to reassure the public that the election was valid and that news of voting problems were unfounded, but that was not the case. Many members of the league found themselves just as uncertain as the voters and wondering whether the election was thrown into question. A full recount of the vote would have done much to reassure not only the voters of Palm Beach County but the nation, which, because of intensive and conflicting media reports, also began to question the validity of the election. The decision to recount votes in only a few sites did little to alleviate the growing doubts.

## Postelection Activities

While the authorities were wavering about whether to recount the Florida votes, the South Palm Beach County League chapter submitted the following letter to the editors of the area's three local newspapers. All three of them printed the letter in its entirety.

> The two Palm Beach County chapters of the nonpartisan League of Women Voters worked diligently to bring out the vote this year through candidate forums, speeches on ballot issues, the League-sponsored DNet website for candidate information, registration drives, publications and more. Through our "Take a Friend to Vote" campaign and our high school registration efforts, we emphasized that "one vote can make a difference."
>
> In Palm Beach County that thought has been proven. We urge the election officials and judiciary to include the thousands of ballots that have been thus far discarded and MAKE EVERY VOTE COUNT.
>
> As we move forward when election results are final, we plan to work with our state and national organizations to improve the election

process. For information on membership, call us at 561-276-4898 in South Palm Beach County or 561-965-4577 for the West Palm Beach Area.

> Joan Karp, President,
> League of Women Voters of South Palm Beach County
> Betty Hadden, President,
> West Palm Beach Area League of Women Voters

League members would soon find out that Palm Beach County was on everyone's mind. As they attempted to obtain information, they found themselves questioned by most everyone they encountered as to what really happened in the county. It was a strange predicament to be in. Everyone had a story to tell. It soon came to light that there had been problems with punch card voting for many years, but because previous presidential races were not close enough to be dependent on Florida's electoral votes, the problems were not seen as critical and not corrected. Moreover, several other Florida counties had problems that caused voters to feel they had been disenfranchised, such as the allegations by African American voters that they had been denied the opportunity to vote.

Suddenly, there was a surge of interest in the league. Over sixty people joined the LWVSBC chapter as a direct result of the election. The league was viewed as an organization that might be able to make something happen and improve the administration of elections. It became obvious that Florida—and the nation—were not finished with this election and that we all needed to find a way to contribute to changing the system. The election had the positive result of pointing out the importance of providing adequate funding for elections, something the state and county had neglected to do, as had much of the country. It also had the effect of emphasizing the importance of well-trained poll workers, election observers, and the role of organizations like the League of Women Voters.

Fortunately, the league was not alone in this thought. After the final results were in, Governor Jeb Bush created a task force to suggest reforms that would prevent another debacle like this one. The task force scheduled meetings throughout the state for citizen input. Recommendations were submitted to the Florida legislature by March 1, 2001, for action at the legislative session starting March 6, 2001.

## League Works for Election Reform

It was obvious to the directors of the LWVSPBC that the members wanted action on this issue and that input from the league was necessary. Accordingly,

LWVSPBC immediately formed a committee to get ideas from members, eighteen of whom came forward to participate. It was decided that a goal would be to present an opinion at the February 1, 2001, task force hearing.

The League of Women Voters of the United States and the League of Women Voters of Florida have long-standing positions on reforming elections, which are the result of local league study and combined consensus. These positions also allow leagues at all levels to lobby for reforms in all possible venues.

LWVSPBC started with the Florida League's established positions and decided to lobby on several. The LWVSPBC then broke into groups to allow for different discussions. When the working groups came back together, a prioritized list was developed that became a three-minute testimony and a slightly more detailed written version to submit to the task force. Other local leagues around the state as well as the State Board of the league testified at various hearings. The hearings were televised on C-Span, so the problems of the Florida election and effort to improve all elections remained in the public eye. Unfortunately, political leaders in Florida seemed less receptive to remedies and reforms than the citizenry.

League testimony concentrated on the following issues:

- developing statewide standardized equipment and ballot design, with market testing;
- ensuring equal access through accurate, up-to-date voter lists;
- developing new, more user-friendly registration application forms;
- eliminating the loophole in the Crossover Primary law that allows a write-in candidate to negate this law;
- prohibiting election officials from active participation in candidates' campaigns;
- electing supervisors of elections on a nonpartisan basis;
- decreasing of poll worker hours through job sharing and recruiting poll workers from a larger pool;
- automatically restoring felons' rights after the debt to society has been paid; and
- providing provisional ballots if eligibility cannot immediately be determined.

The LWVSPBC sent the following letter to area newspapers at the end of February 2001, chastising the Florida legislature for giving election reform a low priority even before the task force's report was due and the legislative session started:

> The legislature has yet to convene and the ink is not yet dry on the very thorough report of the Governor's Task Force on Election Reform, but

the President of the Senate and the Speaker of the House seem to have already decided that election reform has a low priority.[1]

To ignore the Task Force recommendations is an affront to the voters and to the 21-member bipartisan group who spent over two months traveling around the state interviewing many individuals and groups.

Contrary to what Mr. Feeney implies, the voters of Florida have not forgotten the issue, and will be reminded once again when they vote in Municipal Elections March 13.

Yes, we need to educate voters, and the League of Women Voters is in the forefront of that effort, but we must also educate the poll workers and election officials. And, we must give our Legislators an opportunity to discuss and decide on the merits of the Task Force's recommendations to reform the election system.

We urge voters to read the report of the Task Force on www.collinscenter.org (Click on Election Task Force), and then make their opinions known to their Representatives.

> Joan Karp, President
> League of Women Voters of South Palm Beach County

## End Results

After a very slow start, the league ended up being rather pleased in general with the reforms the Florida legislature ended up passing in the 2001 session. A short summary of the reforms follows:

- Punch cards, paper ballots, mechanical lever machines, and central count voting systems were prohibited. The two approved methods are now touch-screen and scanned ballots. (Palm Beach County decided on touch-screen ballots, and the county commissioners agreed to pay for them.)
- Money was earmarked for voter education and poll worker training. Poll workers must complete a specified number of hours of training. A manual of procedures is to be at each polling place.
- Absentee ballots become "convenience ballots"; that is, voters do not need a reason to vote absentee. The military and overseas ballot process was simplified.
- Provisional ballots will be available for those voters whose eligibility cannot be determined at the polls. Those ballots will be counted only if and when eligibility is determined.
- Statewide uniform procedures for recounts, certifications, and so on were required and established later by the Department of Elections.
- The second primary (or runoff primary) was eliminated for 2002 only. (This recommendation came from the legislature, not the task force.) The Florida legislature will determine whether it should continue in future elections.

In spite of this positive result, some of the task force's recommendations as well as the league's wish list were omitted:

- limiting political activity of members of local and state canvassing boards;
- holding nonpartisan election of supervisors of elections (the supervisors wanted this as well);
- allowing government workers to serve as poll workers;
- restoring the voting rights of ex-felons (Florida has an onerous process of application for rights restoration. The governor promised to make the process easier, but it is not yet in the statutes.); and
- changing public campaign financing by stating that campaign contributions from out of state would not count toward qualifying for matching public financing.

## Where Are We Now?

The league immediately began to focus on future elections and lobby the governor and Florida legislature to address some of the unresolved issues of election reform. It is not yet clear what the ultimate conclusion to this story will be, as the work of the legislature remains incomplete at the time of this writing and the results of the redrawing of legislative districts (reapportionment) remain contested. Whatever the new districts look like, the LWVSPBC will have more than the usual number of candidates and will be planning forums where applicable.

Palm Beach County purchased touch-screen voting machines and has already used them in local municipal elections. Although a few technical glitches and errors by poll workers occurred, it was a successful trial run. So too has the county been providing residents with the opportunity to practice voting and see the machines. Some of the main actors involved in the controversial election, namely Palm Beach County supervisor of elections Teresa LePore, former Florida secretary of state Katherine Harris, and other election officials from counties with voting problems remain very controversial figures in the state and have demonstrated at best mixed responses to overtures from the League of Women Voters to work together in addressing unresolved issues.

The supervisor of elections presented many opportunities for all the county voters to try out the machines and become comfortable with the new technology. The league, together with other organizations, is supplying volunteers to assist in the education effort. Additionally, the league has already been actively discussing the election reforms with various organizations and in public forums. LWVSPBC continues to lobby for an independent redistricting commission, which it hopes will be in place for the 2010 census reapportionment.

## About the League of Women Voters

The League of Women Voters is a national organization that has been in existence for eighty-two years and has a presence in all fifty states. Membership is open to all citizens, male and female. It is a grassroots organization. Each state has a state league, and within each state are local leagues. Dues paid to local leagues support the state and national organizations as well. The league's mission statement is as follows:

> The League of Women Voters is a nonpartisan organization that promotes political responsibility through informed and active participation of citizens in government and acts on selected governmental issues.

## Appendix

### Figure A.1 Voting Instructions

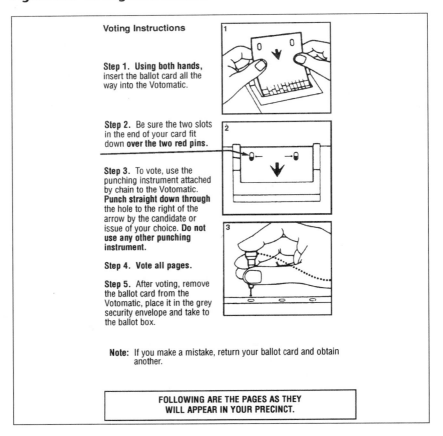

**Figure A.2  Letter from the Supervisor of Elections**

# JANE CARROLL
SUPERVISOR OF ELECTIONS
BROWARD COUNTY
BROWARD COUNTY GOVERNMENTAL CENTER
115 SOUTH ANDREWS AVENUE, ROOM 102
FORT LAUDERDALE, FLORIDA 33301
Phone: (954) 357-7050
Fax: (954) 357-7070

October 2000

Dear Voter:

Due to the fact that Broward County has eighty-eight ballot styles because U.S. Congressmen, State Senators, State Representatives, County Commissioners and School Board members are in single member districts and, therefore, do not run county-wide, we are sending you this sample ballot. This is the ballot as it will appear in your precinct. If you live in a city which has a special election on November 7, you will be able to vote that also on the same voting unit; however, we are unable to include that information on the sample ballot. You may notice some pages are missing. This is because you may live in an area not voting on the races or issue on that page.

It is our hope that by preparing this sample ballot for you, you will not find our different districts confusing. You will be able to study the ballot before you visit your polling place on November 7. You may also take this sample ballot to the precinct with you on election day if you would find it helpful.

The address of your polling place is printed on your blue voter information card. You will be required to show picture identification at the polls. **If you do not have picture identification, you will be required to complete an affidavit verifying your identity.**

Broward County uses a Computer Election System. The use of this system will be explained to you as you enter the polling place.

Please call our office at 357-7081, if you have any questions. At this time the phones are very busy. Please be patient.

Thank you and please vote.

Sincerely,

Jane Carroll
Supervisor of Elections

THERE ARE SEVERAL BRANCH OFFICES LOCATED THROUGHOUT THE COUNTY FOR
YOUR CONVENIENCE. PLEASE CALL (954) 357-7050 FOR THE LOCATION OF THE
OFFICE NEAREST YOU.

## Figure A.3  Broward County Ballot

| 1 | OFFICIAL BALLOT, GENERAL ELECTION<br>BROWARD COUNTY, FLORIDA<br>NOVEMBER 7, 2000 | | |
|---|---|---|---|
| **ELECTORS FOR PRESIDENT AND VICE PRESIDENT** | | | |
| | **GEORGE W. BUSH** - For PRESIDENT<br>**DICK CHENEY** - For VICE PRESIDENT | REPUBLICAN | 2➤ |
| | **AL GORE** - For PRESIDENT<br>**JOE LIEBERMAN** - For VICE PRESIDENT | DEMOCRATIC | 3➤ |
| | **HARRY BROWNE** - For PRESIDENT<br>**ART OLIVIER** - For VICE PRESIDENT | LIBERTARIAN | 4➤ |
| | **RALPH NADER** - For PRESIDENT<br>**WINONA LADUKE** - For VICE PRESIDENT | GREEN | 5➤ |
| | **JAMES HARRIS** - For PRESIDENT<br>**MARGARET TROWE** - For VICE PRESIDENT | SOCIALIST<br>WORKERS | 6➤ |
| PRESIDENT<br>AND<br>VICE PRESIDENT<br>(Vote for ONE Group) | **JOHN HAGELIN** - For PRESIDENT<br>**NAT GOLDHABER** - For VICE PRESIDENT | NATURAL<br>LAW | 7➤ |
| | **PAT BUCHANAN** - For PRESIDENT<br>**EZOLA FOSTER** - For VICE PRESIDENT | REFORM | 8➤ |
| | **DAVID MCREYNOLDS** - For PRESIDENT<br>**MARY CAL HOLLIS** - For VICE PRESIDENT | SOCIALIST | 9➤ |
| | **HOWARD PHILLIPS** - For PRESIDENT<br>**J. CURTIS FRAZIER** - For VICE PRESIDENT | CONSTITUTION | 10➤ |
| | **MONICA MOOREHEAD** - For PRESIDENT<br>**GLORIA LA RIVA** - For VICE PRESIDENT | WORKERS<br>WORLD | 11➤ |
| | To vote for a write-in candidate,<br>follow directions on the grey envelope. | | |

**Figure A.4  Palm Beach County "Butterfly Ballot"**

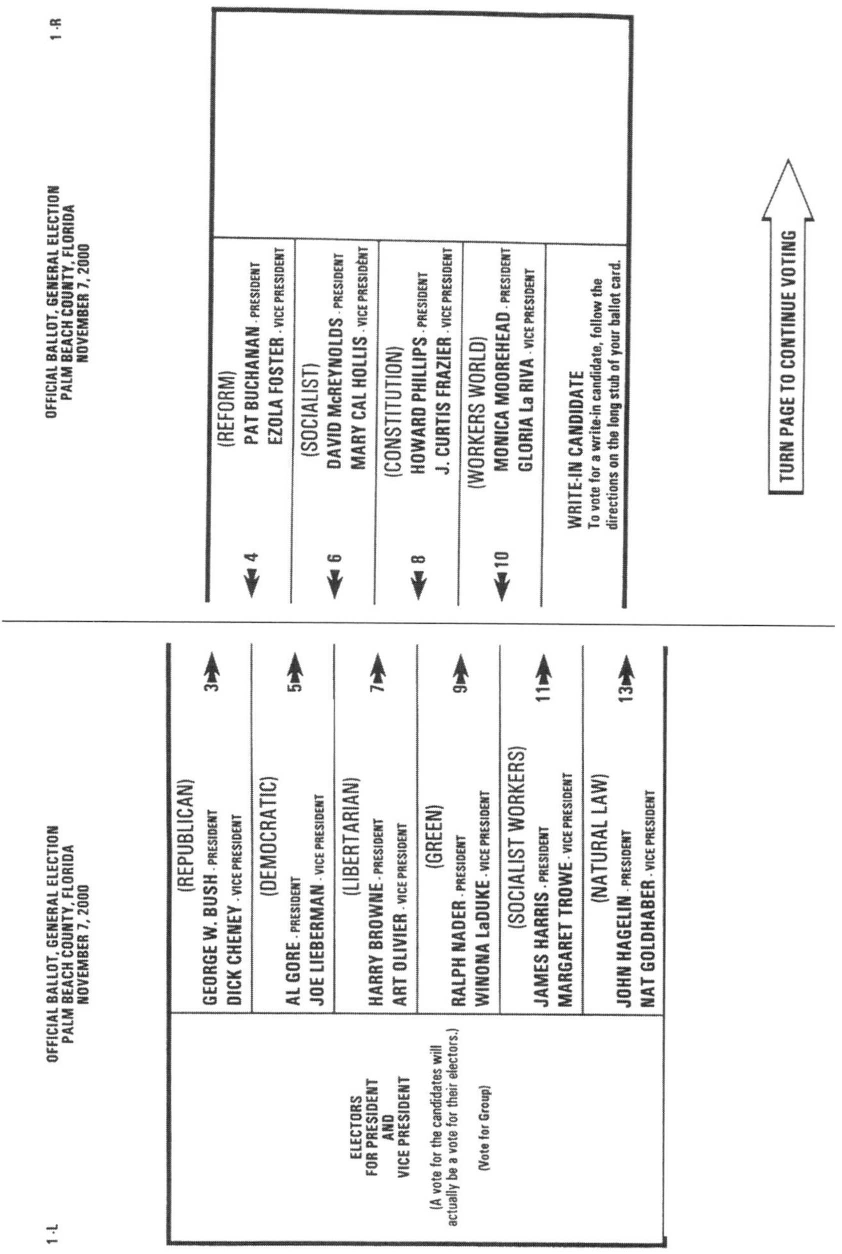

OFFICIAL BALLOT, GENERAL ELECTION
PALM BEACH COUNTY, FLORIDA
NOVEMBER 7, 2000

(REFORM)
PAT BUCHANAN · PRESIDENT
EZOLA FOSTER · VICE PRESIDENT

(SOCIALIST)
DAVID McREYNOLDS · PRESIDENT
MARY CAL HOLLIS · VICE PRESIDENT

(CONSTITUTION)
HOWARD PHILLIPS · PRESIDENT
J. CURTIS FRAZIER · VICE PRESIDENT

(WORKERS WORLD)
MONICA MOOREHEAD · PRESIDENT
GLORIA La RIVA · VICE PRESIDENT

WRITE-IN CANDIDATE
To vote for a write-in candidate, follow the
directions on the long stub of your ballot card.

4
6
8
10

1 -R

TURN PAGE TO CONTINUE VOTING

OFFICIAL BALLOT, GENERAL ELECTION
PALM BEACH COUNTY, FLORIDA
NOVEMBER 7, 2000

(REPUBLICAN)
GEORGE W. BUSH · PRESIDENT
DICK CHENEY · VICE PRESIDENT          3

(DEMOCRATIC)
AL GORE · PRESIDENT
JOE LIEBERMAN · VICE PRESIDENT         5

(LIBERTARIAN)
HARRY BROWNE · PRESIDENT
ART OLIVIER · VICE PRESIDENT           7

(GREEN)
RALPH NADER · PRESIDENT
WINONA LaDUKE · VICE PRESIDENT         9

(SOCIALIST WORKERS)
JAMES HARRIS · PRESIDENT
MARGARET TROWE · VICE PRESIDENT        11

(NATURAL LAW)
JOHN HAGELIN · PRESIDENT
NAT GOLDHABER · VICE PRESIDENT         13

ELECTORS
FOR PRESIDENT
AND
VICE PRESIDENT

(A vote for the candidates will
actually be a vote for their electors.)

(Vote for Group)

1 -L

# PART 3

## CANDIDATES AND VOTERS

In the absence of strong national political parties, it has been argued that the candidates themselves have triumphed in elections, aided by their issues and personalities.[1] No longer must entrepreneurial candidates pay heed to the parties' former power brokers to win nomination in primary elections. No longer can party leaders handpick their "favorite sons" for office outside of the purview of the voters. Candidates, instead, are self-sufficient professionals who choose their own set of policy choices; organize their own campaigns; and hire their own campaign managers, staff, and consultants.[2]

Candidates must employ a certain style and address issues in ways that have long appealed to voters of their districts or states. This is especially the case in less populous states, where political cultures can be distinct, and voter turnout is typically higher than the national norm. The continued existence of such truisms in campaigning exert influence on who runs for office and how they run for office. Alabama's political traditions, for instance, are colorful and hark back to a former time, whereas candidates and voters in New York indulge in an in-your-face style of politics.[3] Around election time, the stereotypical southern candidate's drawl thickens, his tailored suits are replaced by flannel shirts, and the Lincoln Town Car he used in Washington, D.C., is exchanged for a well-dented pickup truck. Likewise, the quintessential candidate from New York City may replace her conservative gray suit with an ensemble that is trendy and more colorful, but she is more likely to make her rounds in a taxicab than a pickup truck, and her odds of donning khakis and flannel are next to nil.

Subtle nuances in electoral systems, political culture, and voter behavior influence elections. North Dakota is the only state in the United States that does not require some form of voter registration. New Hampshire's voters demand that candidates endure the cold weather and spend time personally visiting with them in the state's many mom-and-pop coffee shops and lunch counters. In Hawaii, candidates are expected to participate in "signing"—that is, standing at intersections holding their campaign signs while waving to passers-by, who like to honk their horns and wave back. Even after the election, the fiftieth state's voters like to see successful candidates out along the roadside doing "mahalo waves" (Hawaiian for "thank you").

Although elected officials do not necessarily mirror their constituents in terms of demographic characteristics, the recruitment process and career ladder in politics has the effect of producing many who favor local views and prejudices. Contacts with voters throughout the campaign and while in office reinforce this convergence of views, as do representational norms adopted by most elected officials.[4] Whatever the reason, voters believe their views are shared by their elected officials. In turn, elected officials devote constant attention and effort to dealing with "the folks back home," in part to create the aforementioned effect. Simply put, local politics are ever present in the daily lives of incumbents seeking reelection and those challengers seeking to unseat them, irrespective of the many changes occurring in campaigns and elections.

Arguably the major factor influencing candidates and voters historically was the disenfranchisement of women and minorities. A bewildering array of institutional barriers, such as poll taxes, literacy tests, and restrictions on suffrage, were imposed on whole classes of people, preventing them from enjoying such basic rights as running for public office or voting. Former slaves and free blacks did not gain the right to vote until 1870, with the passage of the Fifteenth Amendment, but then the provision only extended to men. Still, even though this important obstacle to political enfranchisement had been lifted, it did not guarantee full participation in government and the political process by all blacks or minorities.

Old and bad habits die hard, and the entrenched views of many gave rise to an equally bewildering array of sociocultural pressures aligned against extending voting rights to minorities. In the South, in particular, "white primaries"—in which only whites could vote in primary elections, thereby ensuring "acceptable" white candidates on the general election ballot open to all citizens—the formation of white citizens councils, and outright acts of terrorism prevented many from voting. Chinese Americans in San Francisco, Mexican Americans in the border states, American Indians, and others experienced similar challenges to their political rights. In spite of the efforts of early suffragists dating to the Seneca Falls Convention in 1848, women would not secure the right to vote until 1920 with the passage of the Nineteenth Amendment.

Even today, the legacy of discrimination and disenfranchisement continues to affect the voting behavior of certain groups of people. Women and minority candidates still appear to face challenges in getting elected because of their sex or race. The questions of how representative of its people a democratic government should be and how best to ensure both equal political opportunities and elected bodies that resemble the full electorate remain unresolved. An increasing number of women and minority candidates are being elected to all public offices. The notable exception is the U.S. presidency, although such candidates as Shirley Chisholm, Elizabeth Dole, Jesse Jackson, and others have diversified the candidate pool.

This part of the book features three chapters that examine an array of issues facing candidates and voters from the perspective of race and gender. Gary Aguiar opens this section of the book with an examination of the many theories and challenges that attempt to explain why women are underrepresented in elected office. The next chapter, by David Leal, offers a comprehensive assessment of African American and Hispanic candidates and voting behavior. Although the United States is far from demonstrating political parity, progress has been made, and U.S. politics has been transformed along the way as a result of minority participation. Of great importance to candidates is how voters get their information. When that information passes through the news media, it is often filtered and altered. Indeed, one of the primary obstacles for minority and women candidates has been, at best, inadequate coverage from the media and, at worst, either no coverage or biased coverage. Stephen Stambough and Valerie O'Regan explore how newspapers cover candidates through a case study of a gubernatorial election. This campaign features a historic first, as one of the candidates was the first woman to pursue the state's highest office and thus offers the opportunity to also study the effect of gender in media coverage.

The case studies in this section of the book focus on some of the most intriguing candidates in modern times. Steven Wagner and Stephen Frank profile the candidacy of Jesse Ventura, a former professional wrestler who campaigned for the governorship of Minnesota, breaking nearly all the rules in his unconventional—if not outrageous—but successful campaign. Not only is Ventura a fascinating candidate to study, but his election and the case shed light on the voters of the state. The final case, written by Jeffrey Kraus, profiles the most closely watched contest outside the presidential race in the year 2000. The controversial and capable first lady Hillary Rodham Clinton squared off against former congressman Rick Lazio for a coveted Senate seat from the state of New York. The campaign was deluged by media coverage not only because of the importance of the office but because it provided a great human-interest story: popular and controversial former New York City mayor Rudolph Giuliani was Clinton's opponent until he withdrew from the race, and Clinton faced accusations of being a "carpetbagger" because she did not live in the state. But the campaign also makes for an informative case study. Clinton would go on to make history as the first former first lady to seek—and gain—elected office and the first woman to win a statewide race in the Empire State.

It must be remembered that at the core of the democratic experience are the candidates and the voters. Any election reform or, in most cases, even the fanciest campaign tactics will not work without the support of candidates and voters. And in the final analysis, it is the candidates who will govern and the voters who will make the decision of who will govern. The chapters and cases in this section explore that dynamic relationship between the candidates and voters, and the cases offer a glimpse into the challenges and experiences of candidates for public office.

A conclusion follows the essays and cases in this section of the book. It features an analysis of the 2000 congressional race by Robert Dewhirst and Ronald Keith Gaddie and a similar assessment of the 2000 presidential race by Anthony Eksterowicz. Both concluding essays place the campaigns and elections of the year 2000 in historical perspective while considering the significance of them with regard to the future of campaigns and elections.

# 11

## Women's Underrepresentation in Elective Office

### Gary G. Aguiar

In 2002, Congress set new records for the participation of women in its ranks. Former first lady Hillary Rodham Clinton joined three other new female senators for a record-setting thirteen women serving in the Senate.[1] Moreover, the House membership reached a new high of sixty women. Nevertheless, less than one-sixth of the members of Congress were female.[2] Given that they constitute a majority of U.S. citizens, women are vastly underrepresented in Congress.

By contrast, women made up more than one-quarter of the membership in eight European parliaments in 1998. In Sweden, more than 40 percent of the members of parliament were women; similarly high percentages existed in Norway, Finland, and Denmark.[3] Since many people of Scandinavian descent reside in large numbers in the upper Midwest, we might expect these states to elect many women to Congress. Yet of the thirty-nine senators and representatives sent to Congress by the six states of the upper Midwest (Iowa, Minnesota, Nebraska, North and South Dakota, and Wisconsin), only one was a woman.

Democrat Tammy Baldwin, as of 2001 the region's sole female member of Congress, represents Wisconsin's Second District, which includes Madison and several rural counties. In 1998, the Second District was assured of electing a female legislator because each party nominated a woman for the vacant seat. By all accounts, Baldwin was a highly qualified candidate because she had successfully won seats to the state assembly and the Dane County Board of Supervisors. Moreover, she was able to raise significant campaign funds from pro-gay groups. Thus, as an experienced campaigner and legislator, she was able to win election to Congress.[4]

Women do not serve in midwestern legislatures in great numbers either. In 2000, Minnesota ranked eleventh in the country.[5] According to the percentage of women in their state legislatures, the other midwestern states ranked much lower (see Table 11.1). The states range from Washington,

169

where more than 40 percent of the legislature is female, to Alabama, where women comprise less than 8 percent.

Why is there such a paucity of women elected to Congress from the upper Midwest? Why do women so rarely serve in midwestern state legislatures? First I review differences in electoral systems and political culture and then turn to a larger exploration of gender differences in the careers of elected politicians in Congress and midwestern state legislatures. Using, a "political opportunity" approach, I examine how candidates' backgrounds affect their likelihood of seeking and winning elective offices. I conclude that differences in men's and women's political ambition may explain why so few women seek elective office in the United States.

## Electoral Systems

Political scientists have hypothesized that the types of elections used by various democracies might explain the election of women candidates.[6] These studies of gender differences in electoral systems examine political parties' role in nominating candidates and the number of candidates elected from a district. The first major distinction in electoral systems is the extent to which the political parties control the nomination of candidates. We

## Table 11.1  Percentage of Women Serving in 2000 Legislatures

| Legislature | Total Number of Legislators | Percent Women |
|---|---|---|
| U.S. Congress | 540 | 12 |
| Iowa | 150 | 21 |
| Minnesota | 200 | 30 |
| Nebraska | 49 | 18 |
| North Dakota | 147 | 18 |
| South Dakota | 105 | 13 |
| Wisconsin | 131 | 24 |

*Sources*: Chester J. Culver. 1999. *Iowa Official Register, 1999–2000*. Des Moines, Iowa: Secretary of State; Hazeltine, Joyce. 1999. *Legislative Manual, South Dakota, 1999–2000*. Pierre, S.D.: Secretary of State; Alvin A. Jaeger. 1999. *North Dakota Blue Book, 1999–2000*. Bismarck, N.D.: Secretary of State; Mary Kiffmeyer. 1999. *The Minnesota Legislative Manuals, 1999–2000*. Saint Paul, Minn.: Secretary of State; Nebraska Legislature Online. 2001. "Senators of the Nebraska Legislature." http://www.unicam.state.ne.us/senators/senators.htm; Wisconsin Legislative Reference Bureau. 2001. "Wisconsin State Legislature." Madison, Wis.: Joint Committee on Legislative Organization, Wisconsin State Legislature, www.legis.state.wi.us; Michael Barone and Grant Ujifusa. 1999. *The Almanac of American Politics 2000*. Washington, D.C.: National Journal.

*Note*: These figures combine both houses for all legislatures, except Nebraska's unicameral legislature. Congressional data include the nonvoting delegates from the District of Columbia and four overseas territories. Wisconsin had one vacancy at time of publication.

expect that women are more likely to serve in legislatures where parties dominate the selection of nominees because parties are more likely to assemble a ticket that represents a broad range of interests.

The United States has a candidate-centered system of recruitment and selection. In other words, politicians are largely self-selected and self-elected; the political parties play a limited role in this process. Candidates typically must rely on their own efforts, resources, and social networks to win both the primary and general elections. In the United States, primary election voters, not parties, decide who will be the party's nominee. However, many European countries use a proportional representation (PR) system. In a pure PR system, voters cast a ballot for *a party, not a candidate,* and parties are allocated parliamentary seats based on the proportion of the vote they receive. Thus, voters typically do not play a role in the party's selection of candidates. Instead, each party prepares a list of candidates by ranking them for parliamentary seats. In two studies of advanced democracies, including the United States, Wilma Rule showed that PR systems explain much of the difference in women's representation in legislatures and concludes that "women are added to the lists as a means of broadening the general appeal of the team ticket."[7]

Moreover, even where parties do not possess exclusive control over nomination slates, they may recruit women candidates to produce a more balanced ticket to the extent the electoral system permits. In the United States, a few states elect legislators from multimember districts, where more than one candidate wins election. In one study of seven Wyoming elections, the researchers found that "larger multiseat election districts enhance the chances of women gaining legislative seats since more women run in larger districts and women get more votes in them as well."[8] Further, Susan Welch and Albert Karnig show that at-large races improve women's chances of being elected to city councils.[9]

Since electoral systems with multimember districts and PR systems are likely to produce more women legislators, perhaps party-centered political systems tend to produce more gender equity than candidate-centered systems.[10] This conclusion partially explains why fewer women are elected in the United States, where single-member districts predominate. However, both North and South Dakota legislatures elect their lower house members from multimember districts and have a low incidence of women in their legislatures.

## Political Culture

Some scholars have explored the extent to which political culture (i.e., the values and beliefs people hold about politics) might affect women's success in elective politics. One might argue that Scandinavian nations place a higher value on gender equity than other nations and, hence, are more successful in electing women.

Regional subcultures within the country account for some of the differences in women's election to state legislatures. In a study of sixteen states, Carol Nechemias found that states with a "moralistic" political culture—those that see politics as the community's efforts to work together to solve common problems—are likely to have more female members.[11] In a comprehensive study of women in state legislatures across time, Nechemias also found that traditional subcultures hurt women's chances of being elected.[12] In the old South, for example, politics was a field reserved for a small elite of wealthy white men. In turn, progressive states support women's candidacy greater than more conservative states. Women are also more likely to be elected in political contexts that favor greater aid to the poor.[13]

In a study of the "matrimonial connection" in Congress, Irwin Gertzog examined the incidence of widows who succeed to their husband's seat.[14] From 1916 to 1992, less than 16 percent of women who might conceivably have replaced their deceased husbands in Congress actually served. Important regional differences exist in widows' congressional service. In the South, widows who were nominated and elected to fill their husband's seat were often seen as mere caretakers, holding office for only one term until local elites could agree on which male candidate should take office permanently. Outside the South, widows who succeeded to office tended to be younger, more involved in their husband's career, and more interested in politics than southern widows. As a result, they were more likely to hold the congressional seat for a longer period of time and have a greater impact on substantive policy legislation.

Thus, regional differences in women's likelihood of being elected exist. However, these differences do not explain women's poor showing in the upper Midwest very well. The upper Midwest is usually described as moralistic in its political culture, which should translate into more women in their state legislatures. Of course, there is some variation within the region; Minnesota and Wisconsin, for instance, have a more progressive tradition than their neighboring states, which might explain the higher frequency of women legislators in those states.

## Voter Hostility?

Perhaps the most popular explanation among the general public is the hypothesis that some voters are unwilling to vote for female candidates. That is, an underlying voter prejudice may exist against female candidates, especially among male voters. A large number of researchers have explored this hypothesis extensively.

Many studies have looked at the percentage of votes received in general elections by candidates of each gender. These studies demonstrate no support for the hypothesis that voters are less likely to vote for women candidates. For example, congressional elections data from 1970 to 1974 indicate that candidate sex had little or no effect on election outcomes, controlling for incumbency and party.[15] The researchers concluded that the electorate is indifferent to the sex of congressional candidates. Another study examined state legislative elections from 1968 to 1980 in a conservative, traditional state: Oklahoma. These data suggest that when controlling for party and incumbency, "the vote-getting ability of women generally exceeds that of men candidates of the same status."[16] In a study of women as legislative candidates in Iowa, Nebraska, and four other states, Janet Clark and her colleagues found that after 1976, men did no better than women when competing for open seats and in incumbent races.[17] They contend that "today there is little difference in the voters' reactions to similarly situated candidates of both sexes."[18]

In a comprehensive study of candidates for all fifty state legislatures from 1986 to 1992 and all congressional and gubernatorial elections from 1972 to 1992, Jody Newman provided perhaps the most conclusive evidence to date.[19] Her key finding deserves to be quoted at length:

> When women run for office, they win . . . as often as men do. This study found no difference between success rates for men and women in general elections. . . . Based on the overwhelming weight of the data gathered, the conclusion is clear: a candidate's sex does not affect his or her chances of winning general elections. . . .
>
> Conclusion: The reason there aren't more women in public office is not that women don't win, but that not enough women have been candidates in general elections. When women run, women win as often as men.[20]

Finally, in an extensive review of the literature on voter hostility, Robert Darcy, Susan Welch, and Janet Clark found little to no evidence to support the hypothesis at the local, state, national, or cross-national levels with regard to the percentage of votes received in general elections.[21]

Lest one think that the problem then lies in getting women candidates to enter the race and win primary elections, several studies dispel this notion as well. In the six-state study of legislative candidates cited above, the findings indicate that "primary elections are not serving to deny new women their party nomination."[22] Further, in a pair of studies that examined open seat primaries for the U.S. House, Barbara Burrell found that voter prejudice is not a factor in the inability of women to secure congressional seats.[23]

In sum, none of these researchers found evidence of voter hostility to female candidates. Instead, these studies, when controlling for incumbency and party, provide conclusive evidence that voters are just as likely to vote for women candidates as for men. Indeed, a few of these results suggest that, on balance, voters may actually give a slight advantage to women candidates over similarly situated men.

## Political Opportunity Structure

The evidence reviewed so far suggests that electoral systems, especially PR and multimember districts, provide more hospitable environments for women candidates than primary elections and single-member districts. Also, political culture may explain some of the regional difference in women's success. However, neither electoral systems nor political culture provides a wholly satisfactory explanation for the lack of women in elected positions. Perhaps some other factor harms women's chances of being elected?

It can be hypothesized that women face a different environment than men that affects their likelihood of seeking and winning elective office. The political opportunity structure assumes that eligibility for public office is actually limited to a smaller set of people than the exceedingly large pool of candidates who simply meet the legal qualifications. Possibly, men have an advantage in their hunt for elective office because they possess certain privileges that are denied to potential women candidates. To further examine this possibility, three sets of political structural factors that have been suggested by scholars are considered: political party resources, the incumbency advantage, and candidates' experiences.

### Male Conspiracy?

First, some observers hypothesize that an elite male conspiracy in the United States discourages women from running for office. In particular, the explanation suggests that U.S. political parties fail to encourage or assist women candidates. Without a commensurate resource base, women may face more severe hurdles in organizing a successful campaign than men. Hence, they are less likely to run. First, it should be noted that this argument is contrary to the evidence presented above, which suggests that party-centered electoral systems (e.g., PR systems) are likely to produce more women officeholders than candidate-centered politics.

In a survey of women candidates in 1976, for instance, Susan Carroll found that party leaders were reluctant to initiate contact with women candidates.[24] Moreover, women candidates reported that party leaders seemed more likely to recruit them as "sacrificial lambs" in districts where the party was less likely to win and in single-member rather than multimember districts. Further, women candidates reported significant problems in raising campaign funds and attracting campaign workers. However, the latter challenges are faced by all campaigners; they are not unique to women.

Furthermore, Carroll's research design of surveying only women candidates means that we have no comparable data from men candidates.

Much evidence suggests that a male conspiracy against women candidates does not exist. In a study using campaign receipts of men's and women's congressional campaigns from 1972 to 1982, Burrell found that women candidates do raise less money than their male counterparts. However, controlling for incumbency and party, the data "suggest that candidate's sex is not a major factor in financial support."[25] Moreover, female candidates received campaign funds from similar sources—including large contributors—as men. In a similar study using 1980 U.S. House races, Carole Uhlaner and Kay Schlozman controlled for donors' interest in supporting powerful winning candidates (i.e., incumbents and committee chairmen) and found that "candidate gender had no independent effect on campaign receipts in 1980."[26] Moreover, when examining the forty-six races in which women ran against men, the relative amount of campaign receipts was more highly correlated with candidate status (incumbency and chairmanships) than gender.

In a review of the evidence on the male conspiracy hypothesis, Darcy, Welch, and Clark proved that women candidates for local office reported similar or higher levels of support from organizations, including political parties, labor, and business groups, than men.[27] Further, women legislative candidates in the traditionalistic political culture of Oklahoma raised and spent considerably more money than men in every incumbency and party category. Finally, in analyzing campaign receipts from the 1982 congressional election, the same researchers concluded that women candidates were not underfinanced compared to similar men candidates.

In sum, political scientists have been unable to locate evidence of a male conspiracy that hurts women's chances of winning elective office. Once we control for incumbency and party, women have at least equal access to important campaign resources. Indeed, in some cases, women have more access to campaign funds than similarly situated men candidates. Nevertheless, as Uhlaner and Schlozman suggest, regardless of the actual facts, if political elites and potential women candidates *believe* that women cannot raise sufficient campaign funds, then women may be less likely to run.[28]

## Incumbency Advantage

It is well known that incumbents have significant advantages in legislative elections at the state and congressional levels. Incumbents (those who currently hold office) are regularly returned to office. Upward of 90 percent of representatives and about three-quarters of senators have been reelected in the latter half of the twentieth century. A large majority of state legislators have also been reelected to office (albeit usually at somewhat lower rates than members of Congress).

Congressional incumbents have significant advantages over challengers, including name recognition, access to "pork barrel" programs, a full-time staff, and a government-subsidized publicity operation that might explain the phenomenon.[29] Moreover, strategic actors understand these advantages and are not likely to support challengers unless the incumbent faces a crisis (e.g., a scandal or an economy that favors the challenger's party).[30]

It is no surprise, then, that relatively few women are elected to legislative office; women, like other newcomers who challenge well-known, well-funded incumbents, are unlikely to win. Since most sitting legislators are men, incumbents possess these substantial resources that benefit them in their campaigns. Indeed, John Carey, Richard Niemi, and Lynda Powell suggest that term limits may assist women's chances to win office.[31] They report that, when controlling for structural and demographic factors, state legislatures with term limits are more likely than non–term limited states to elect women legislators.

It is impossible to understate the importance of incumbency as a factor in the lack of women's chances in legislative elections. Incumbency reduces opportunities for newcomers, including women, to gain elective office. Incumbents are able to raise tremendous sums of money; build huge war chests, and maintain both name recognition and the district's goodwill to scare away strong potential opponents. In ordinary circumstances, potential strong challengers refuse to run against incumbents and prefer to wait until the officeholder retires, dies, or seeks a higher office. Since these seats open up so rarely, they present relatively few opportunities for those seeking elective office to have a legitimate shot at election. Nearly every study cited above includes incumbency as a control variable because incumbency goes a long way to explain the lack of women legislators in the United States.

## Candidates' Backgrounds

Joseph Schlesinger suggests that the structure of political opportunity is a key factor in understanding the role of politicians in a democracy.[32] He argues that elections channel political ambitions into acceptable office-seeker paths; those who aspire to power must submit themselves to the electorate. Thus, a theory of political ambition requires an understanding of the backgrounds and experiences of elected officials. Since they have been elected, their characteristics present a fairly accurate portrait of qualified candidates. Thus, officeholders' characteristics may inform us about women's chances of being elected.

The data presented here have been collected from the most current sources of biographical profiles available, including the *Almanac of American Politics* and each state's official legislative manual or website (see

Table 11.2 for sources). Using these data, it is possible to compare the backgrounds of members of Congress with lawmakers from the upper Midwest. State legislatures are one of the primary breeding grounds for congressional candidates. Roughly half of each gender in the 106th Congress (1999–2001) had served in their state's legislature prior to being elected to Congress. So, if women are elected to midwestern legislatures in fewer numbers than men, we might reasonably expect that fewer quality candidates are available to run for the Congress from the region.

Increasingly, members of Congress have held no prior elective office. For instance, in the 106th Congress, more than one-quarter of both men and women were elected to Congress without holding prior office. Yet, from 1914 to 1958, only 8 percent of senators had never held a prior elective office; and 18 percent of the representatives serving in 1951 had no prior

**Table 11.2  Gender Differences in Composition of 2000 Legislatures**

|  | U.S. Congress | | Iowa | | Minnesota | |
|---|---|---|---|---|---|---|
|  | Female | Male | Female | Male | Female | Male |
| Dem. | 69 | 46 | 44 | 43 | 61 | 48 |
| College | 94 | 95 | 78 | 66 | 93 | 86 |
| Grad. | 55 | 70 | 41 | 33 | 49 | 46 |
| Attorney | 16 | 41 | 3 | 9 | 10 | 21 |
| Married | 64 | 87 | 78 | 90 | 92 | 94 |
| Over 40 | n.a. | n.a. | 91 | 71 | 75 | 60 |

|  | Nebraska | | North Dakota | | South Dakota | | Wisconsin | |
|---|---|---|---|---|---|---|---|---|
|  | Female | Male | Female | Male | Female | Male | Female | Male |
| Dem. | n.p. | n.p. | 50 | 32 | 36 | 30 | 38 | 50 |
| College | 78 | 65 | 73 | 55 | 50 | 62 | 75 | 69 |
| Grad. | 22 | 45 | 19 | 31 | 43 | 32 | 38 | 39 |
| Attorney | 0 | 28 | 0 | 4 | 7 | 9 | 9 | 12 |
| Married | 89 | 88 | 81 | 84 | 79 | 96 | 69 | 82 |
| Over 40 | 100 | 72 | n.a. | n.a. | 92 | 78 | 63 | 44 |

*Sources:* Chester J. Culver. 1999. *Iowa Official Register, 1999–2000.* Des Moines, Iowa: Secretary of State; Hazeltine, Joyce. 1999. *Legislative Manual, South Dakota, 1999–2000.* Pierre, S.D.: Secretary of State; Alvin A. Jaeger. 1999. *North Dakota Blue Book, 1999–2000.* Bismarck, N.D.: Secretary of State; Mary Kiffmeyer. 1999. *The Minnesota Legislative Manuals, 1999–2000.* Saint Paul, Minn.: Secretary of State; Nebraska Legislature Online. 2001. http://www.unicam.state.ne.us/senators/senators.htm; Wisconsin Legislative Reference Bureau. 2001. "Wisconsin State Legislature." Madison, Wis.: Joint Committee on Legislative Organization, Wisconsin State Legislature, www.legis.state.wi.us.

*Notes:* Figures report percentage of each gender for each variable.

Dem. = Democrats; College = earned a four-year college degree; Grad. = attended a graduate program; Over 40 = first elected to current office after age 40.

n.a. = The data are not available.

n.p. = The Nebraska legislature is elected on a nonpartisan ballot.

elective experience.[33] This restructuring of political opportunities might ease the entry of women into Congress by imposing fewer hurdles of earlier service. However, it probably also increases the number of men candidates who make a late-life transition to politics.

Moreover, more women members of the 106th Congress usually started from a lower elective office than their male counterparts. Nearly 40 percent of congresswomen were initially elected to a local office (i.e., municipal, county, and school boards), compared to only one-quarter of congressmen. Among Nebraska's forty-nine legislators, a majority of men (55 percent) had been elected to a local office.[34] Only three of the nine women legislators had held a prior office. Further, Charles Bullock and his colleagues indicate that women officeholders are becoming increasingly more common in county and school boards.[35] Perhaps women candidates must establish their credentials by holding local office before making a run for the state legislature.

It is helpful to consider a brief analysis of the role of political party affiliation in affecting women's chances of election. The much-publicized "gender gap" in voting and issue preferences indicates that more women agree with Democrats than men.[36] Moreover, left-leaning groups, like environmental and labor organizations, are more likely to recruit and support women candidates.[37] The well-known political action committee EMILY's List (early money is like yeast; it makes the dough rise) bankrolls pro-choice Democratic women.

Unsurprisingly then, more than two-thirds of congresswomen are Democrats, compared to a minority of men. In the five partisan legislatures studied here, the differences are not as large (see Table 11.2). In 2000, only Minnesota had more Democrats in the legislature than Republicans and closely resembles Congress in the partisan division of gender. In the other four state legislatures, however, more Republican women were elected than Democratic women. Although Republican women are more likely to receive votes in these largely Republican states, they are less likely to receive targeted assistance from liberal groups that champion Democratic women for Congress. The upper Midwest generates a smaller pool of eligible Democratic women, and hence, few are likely to receive national encouragement to run for Congress.

Party preferences, then, partially explain the lack of women candidates in the Midwest. Do socioeconomic differences explain women's difficulties in seeking elective office? A community's leadership usually rises from the higher strata of society. We normally expect those from higher social classes to seek and hold elective offices. In particular, individuals with higher educational attainment and those from the "speaking" professions (i.e., attorneys, educators, and journalists) possess the skills to communicate effectively with voters as well as the social networks to organize successful campaigns. To what extent, then, are women penalized by differences in their educational and occupational accomplishments?

Increasingly, women are becoming better educated. Nationwide, more than half of all currently enrolled undergraduates are women. Several dozen law schools now claim that a majority of their student body is female. However, it may take several decades of population replacement before these trends significantly change the overall educational and occupational pools.[38] In terms of the current composition of legislatures, it is reasonable to posit that women are likely to have similar levels of educational attainment as men. Indeed, to demonstrate their qualifications as legislators, women may need to possess higher levels of education. However, to the extent that attorneys are still prevalent in many legislatures, male legislators are probably more likely to have graduate school experience.

At the congressional level, the data largely bear out these expectations. Nearly all members of Congress, both men and women, possess a four-year college degree. Higher proportions of men have some graduate school experience; certainly a reflection of the large number of male attorneys in Congress. Four-tenths of congressmen are lawyers, compared to only 16 percent of congresswomen. However, we see dramatically different results in our sample of midwestern legislatures. Except in South Dakota, each legislature has a higher proportion of women who are college educated than men.[39] Moreover, among four of the six midwestern states, a similar or higher percentage of women legislators have graduate experience than men. In my recent survey of South Dakota's county commissioners, 70 percent of the women commissioners had at least some college experience, compared to only a bare majority of men.[40]

Thus, women candidates for state and local legislatures may need to achieve higher levels of education to appear qualified. Anyone who completes a four-year college degree is a better qualified candidate than a less educated individual; yet it may help women candidates more than men. Gender differences in education would generally appear to benefit women legislators from the Midwest in their quest for higher office.

Perhaps, women are less likely than men to run for political office if it places too great a strain on their families. For example, Nechemias found that women legislators are likely to have a shorter commute to their state's capitol than men.[41] Further, women who run for office may face additional questions about their family situation. In particular, married women with children may be asked about their child care arrangements. Some voters may assume that when a married father runs for office, his wife will be the primary caregiver. However, when a women runs, some voters may question her ability to balance obligations to her family and politics. Thus, we might expect that single women are more likely to seek and win office than men. The evidence in Table 11.2 demonstrates that marital status is related to gender in Congress; nearly nine-tenths of congressmen, but less than two-thirds of congresswomen, are married. In three of the midwestern legislatures, we find a similar pattern; higher proportions of men than women are married. However, in the Minnesota, Nebraska, and North Dakota legislatures, roughly equal proportions of each gender are married. Perhaps these legislators who are also mothers may be discouraged from seeking a seat in Congress.

## Age Structure

In an often overlooked passage, Schlesinger explains changes in the age structure of political opportunity over the course of the republic.[42] The data suggest that by 1957, most House members were elected in their late thirties or forties. In the first half of the twentieth century, senators were initially elected in their late forties or fifties. Two decades later, age at initial election to these offices had dropped substantially; representatives were in their late twenties and thirties and senators in their early to midforties at their first election to office. The increasing number of careerists who begin their service early and remained for a lengthy tenure reflects the professionalization of the institution in the second half of the last century.

Age may play a significant role in women's likelihood of seeking higher office. Women's traditional roles as wife and mother suggest that they are likely to be the primary care providers early in their children's lives. Women who accept these roles are unlikely to seek public office while their children are of school age. Hence, we expect that women are likely to delay the start of their political careers. In the 106th Congress, women were almost twice as likely as men to be first elected to Congress after age fifty (52 percent of women and only 28 percent of men). This gender difference in the age structure has a dramatic effect on the distribution of power between the sexes in Congress. In both houses, seniority is an important determinant of power in Congress, especially ascension to committee chairmanships. Since women tend to arrive at a later age, they are disadvantaged because they have fewer years left in their potential career. To date, no congresswomen has served as chair of a major committee in either house.

We find a similar pattern in the state legislatures. More women are first elected to the legislature after age forty than men (Table 11.2). Moreover, in my survey of South Dakota county commissioners, more than 85 percent of women respondents began their elective careers after age forty, compared to about 60 percent of men. Although seniority is less important in state and local legislatures than Congress, women legislators—who tend to be older at first election—have shorter political careers. As a result, women politicians have fewer opportunities to run for an open seat in Congress. In short, gender differences in the age structure is a significant factor in the lack of women in Congress.

To review, the structure of political opportunity offers three factors that might explain differences in the incidence of women officeholders. Although no evidence of a male conspiracy exists, it is clear that the incumbency advantage limits the occasions when eligible women candidates might move to higher office. Moreover, the characteristics of midwestern women legislators generally diminish their opportunities to run for Congress in three ways. First, the region produces a smaller pool of eligible Democratic women who might receive more national attention. Second, the age structure of political opportunity significantly limits possibilities for otherwise eligible women candidates. Third, since midwestern women legislators tend to start their political careers later in life, they have a shorter time frame in which to advance to higher office.

## Conclusion

Taken together, these factors offer a reasonable account of the lack of women's representation in Congress. Most impressive in this mound of evidence is the incumbency advantage and gender differences in the age structure of political opportunity. These disparate explanations can be united with a theory about gender differences in political ambition. Gender-based roles remain an influential source of differences that affect the chances of each sex seeking elective office. Although women may vote at a higher rate than men, their participation and interest in politics is lower than men. Generally speaking, girls have been socialized to be more passive and collegial than boys. A myriad of media and other cultural sources continue to remind girls that certain spheres, including politics, are less acceptable for women than men.[43]

The evidence presented in this chapter suggests that one of the main reasons women do not get elected to political office is that they do not run. The electorate never has an opportunity to vote for these unseen candidates. As a result of their differential political socialization, women probably have a lower desire to seek public office. For example, Carroll found relatively low levels of ambition among the women candidates she surveyed in 1976.[44]

A few scholars have studied factors that affect why some potentially strong, qualified candidates do not seek elective office. L. Sandy Maisel, Walter Stone, and Cherie Maestas use political "informants" in 200 House districts to identify potential candidates, whom they then interviewed.[45] These potential candidates report that besides a concern with their chances of winning, such matters as fundraising and separation from family are important factors in deciding not to run. Although they do not report gender differences, it is possible that family concerns may be more likely to dissuade potential women candidates than men.

Linda Fowler and Robert McClure employed the case study approach to explore the politics of unseen candidacy and political ambition.[46] They suggested that both the rhythms of elective careers and "the private side of congressional recruitment" affect the decision to enter a House race. First, a congressional vacancy must occur when a potential candidate has the necessary experience and qualifications to make a serious run. Second, some potential candidates fear that a move to Washington and the national arena will damage their family life through loss of privacy and reduced time with their children. Fowler and McClure also note that these two factors severely restrict women's likelihood of running for Congress: "The chance that a woman who has the credentials and desire to win a House seat will also reside in a district with a vulnerable or retiring incumbent is exceedingly small."[47]

Moreover, women who are involved in politics may see it in a somewhat different light than men.[48] For instance, much evidence suggests that women legislators approach lawmaking differently than men.[49] In twelve statehouses, women legislators tend to place a higher priority on legislation that relates to children, the family, or women than men.[50] Surveying state and local legislators in South Dakota, 83 percent of the women listed family and children's issues as a priority, compared to only 60 percent of men. In a survey of 3,000 California political activists over a twenty-year period, Edmond Costantini showed that women activists had different goals than men.[51] To that end, they were more likely to engage in activities that pursue broader policy-based outcomes.

Thus, compared to men, women activists are less likely to follow paths that lead to personal aggrandizement. These gender differences in political ambition suggest that women officeholders are less likely to use such male perspectives on politics as gamesmanship with zero-sum outcomes. In short, active women participants perceive the political world differently. As a result, the personal power that is attached to elective office may be less valuable to women than men.

# 12

## Minority Voters and Candidates: Tracking Trends

### David L. Leal

One of the key questions throughout U.S. history is how, and sometimes even whether, to incorporate minorities into the political process. This issue is becoming even more pressing as the Anglo (non-Hispanic white) percentage of the population continues to decline. Much of this decline is the result of the growth in the Latino population, which is reshaping the political and cultural dynamics of large swaths of the United States. As a result, our traditional and straightforward bifurcated paradigm on racial questions is now slowly changing into a more complex black-white-Hispanic perspective.

The 2000 census found that Latinos are now the largest minority group in the United States. Although the U.S. Census Bureau in 1999 estimated that Latinos would be 11.4 percent of the population in 2000, the census revealed that they are 12.5 percent, a figure Latinos were not projected to reach until 2005. This percentage may understate the true Latino population because the census is an actual count, not an estimate or statistical sample, and many Latinos are noncitizens with clear incentives to avoid contact with government agencies. These figures for the first time put Latinos ahead of African Americans, who are 12.1 percent of the population. Given the substantial levels of immigration from Mexico, the Latino population will only continue to grow.[1] Anglos currently constitute 69 percent of the U.S. population, and in some states they are transitioning from majority to plurality. Given these numbers, how well the United States incorporates Latinos, African Americans, and other minorities will determine to an extent the future health of the nation's democracy.

In this chapter, I discuss first the political history of Latinos and African Americans, particularly the changing formal and informal regulations over the right to vote. The elimination of de jure (legal) and de facto (informal but very real) restrictions are only part of the story, however. I also examine minority voting behavior, specifically whether African Americans and Latinos vote at the same rate as do whites and whether they support different candidates and parties.

Second, I look at the progress minorities have made in being elected to political offices. This issue is important because, as Roger Davidson and Walter Oleszek note, "When a member of an ethnic or racial minority goes to Congress, it is a badge of legitimacy for the entire grouping. Such legislators speak for people like them throughout the nation. Moreover, there can be tangible gains in the quality of representation."[2] In addition, the job of a national legislature like Congress is not just to serve particular interests but to legislate on behalf of the good of the entire nation. Political bodies likely serve this national interest best when they are a microcosm of the people.

## Historical and Legal Context

### African American Voting History

At the founding of the United States, the right to vote was limited along both racial and class lines. Most states allowed free males to vote only if they owned a certain amount of property, which excluded half of all men, all slaves and indentured servants, and all women. Free blacks could vote in the North if they met a state's other requirements. There were also religious restrictions in early America. Most colonies had Catholic and Jewish voting prohibitions, and some colonies prohibited Quakers and Baptists from voting. Rhode Island did not end the prohibition against Jewish voting until 1842. By the 1830s, most states had removed property requirements for white males. For African Americans, however, the right to vote contracted rather than expanded. By the start of the Civil War in 1861, all but six of the thirty-three states excluded all blacks from voting.

The aftermath of the Civil War changed this situation, but only temporarily. Adopted in 1870, the Fifteenth Amendment prohibited the denial of the right to vote "on account of race, color, or previous condition of servitude," and for a time this right was enforced. The postwar policy of Reconstruction meant that the northern army occupied the South and administered the former rebellious states. Blacks not only voted in large numbers but served as high-ranking federal and state officials. Congress also passed laws known as the Enforcement Acts to further protect black voting rights in 1870 and 1871, which were necessary because "from the outset, whites resisted enforcement of the Fifteenth Amendment. Violence, intimidation, and fraud were the primary means used initially to discourage blacks from voting."[3]

Several events eviscerated these new rights, however. First, the Supreme Court issued a series of rulings that strengthened the hand of "states rights" advocates in the South. For instance, the Court ruled in 1876 in *United States v. Reese* that Congress could not punish state officials for refusing to allow blacks to vote or for failing to count their votes. At the same time, a declining northern interest in Reconstruction and the "Corrupt Bargain" in the 1876 presidential election led to the end of Reconstruction and the withdrawal of Union troops.[4] The timing of the two above events may not be coincidental. Although some see the Supreme Court as the guarantor of civil rights and liberties, others argue that for much of U.S. history, it has followed public opinion.[5]

The southern states gradually devised a host of laws to disenfranchise blacks, collectively known as "Jim Crow" laws. One such law was the literacy test, which prohibited citizens who could not read (or whom a registrar of voters decided could not read) from voting. Whites were largely exempted from this test, either directly by law or indirectly by the "grandfather clause," which said that one could vote if one's grandfather had voted. Although some states outside the South adopted a literacy test at some time, it was not enforced in such a discriminatory way. The grandfather clause was overturned in 1915,[6] but the literacy test was not comprehensively banned until 1970.[7]

A similar tactic was the poll tax. Voters had to pay a fee to vote, which had a disproportionate impact on the relatively poor black population but also affected a large number of poor whites. Most states dropped this law by the 1930s, although it was still in effect in four states in 1960 and was not overturned for federal elections until the Twenty-Fourth Amendment in 1964.[8]

Yet another strategy was the "white primary," which allowed the Democratic Party to exclude blacks from voting in its primary. Based on the notion that a party was a private organization and could accept or exclude whomever it saw fit, this law was an especially effective means of disenfranchisement. In the one-party South, almost every elected official was a Democrat, and winning the Democratic primary was tantamount to winning the general election. It was not until 1944 that the Supreme Court in *Smith v. Allwright* overturned the white primary, which for two decades was a key target of the legal strategy of the National Association for the Advancement of Colored People.

A variety of extralegal obstacles were also placed in the way of black voters. Not only were violence, threats, and economic intimidation available to whites, but local voter registrars could refuse to accept or just throw away application forms filled out by blacks.

It is therefore no surprise that the number of registered black voters declined precipitously in the South after Reconstruction. "By the turn of the century, virtually all blacks had been disenfranchised in the South. Abandoned by the federal government, thwarted by the Supreme Court, and faced with a multitude of state laws designed expressly for the purpose of disenfranchising them, the majority of blacks in the South would not be permitted to exercise the franchise until 1965."[9] One historian noted that in Louisiana in 1904, for example, there were only 1,300 African Americans registered to vote.[10]

It was not until the civil rights movement in the 1950s that the situation began to change. The first legislative result was the Civil Rights Act of 1957, the first piece of congressional legislation on civil rights since 1875. It expanded the ability of the federal government to prevent interference with the Fifteenth Amendment and created the U.S. Commission on Civil Rights. The law had little impact because the Eisenhower administration grew reluctant to use it, so Congress passed somewhat strengthened revisions in 1960 and 1964. The Supreme Court upheld all three federal efforts, contrary to its actions in the nineteenth century.

Change was nevertheless slow, and black registration increased by only 36,000 in counties where federal suits were brought under the above three acts. Pressure for more significant change was generated by the continuing action of the civil rights movement as well as media coverage of the violent reactions by some whites. In an address before a joint session of Congress, Lyndon Johnson called for tough legislation ensuring the right to vote. According to Howell Raines, Johnson told his attorney general to draft the "toughest voting rights act that you can devise."[11]

The result was the Voting Rights Act (VRA) of 1965, the most important civil rights bill ever enacted by Congress. It ended literacy tests, provided for federal election supervisors in places of voting and registration where black electoral activity was low, created federal penalties for those who interfered with voting rights, and allowed federal officers to directly register voters and oversee elections.[12] To prevent southern governments from devising new and creative methods of disenfranchisement, the law required state and local officials to obtain federal approval ("preclearance") of any changes in electoral procedures. Although the VRA originally covered six southern states, it was eventually expanded to the entire South and a few other locations and reinforced by periodic revisions.

The results were dramatic. By 1969, black voter registration in the South increased from 35 percent to 65 percent. In Mississippi, the percentage shot up from 6.7 percent to 59.8 percent. More than 3 million African Americans were added to the rolls between 1965 and 1975.

## Latino Voting History

The first point to consider is that there is no one single "Latino" or "Hispanic" population. Instead, there are three primary national-origin groups and many smaller but growing populations. The three largest groups are Mexican Americans, Puerto Ricans, and Cuban Americans, and the number of people of Caribbean and Central American heritage is growing. Whether all these groups share enough common political and cultural values to be considered one group is debatable. For most political observers,

"Latino" is often used synonymously with "Mexican American," the largest of the subgroups.

A key event in Latino history is the Mexican-American War. The U.S. victory led to the annexation in 1848 of territory comprising all or part of the current states of California, Arizona, New Mexico, Colorado, Utah, and Texas. The Treaty of Guadalupe Hidalgo guaranteed Mexicans living in this territory the choice of moving to Mexico, gaining U.S. citizenship, or retaining Mexican citizenship. Forty thousand chose to remain on the U.S. side.

The subsequent political situation of Mexican Americans in these territories varied, however. In Texas, the Latino population was not large and had already seen a decline in status before annexation. The Texas Revolution of 1836 led to the independence of Texas, but control was assumed not by Tejanos (Texas Latinos) but the Anglo majority. Although Tejanos predominated in a few parts of the state and managed to retain power there for a time, the overall political and economic status of Tejanos quickly declined. Tactics such as literacy tests and poll taxes were used to disenfranchise Latinos, and violence and a variety of intimidation tactics were used against Tejanos. Annexation by the United States did not change the situation.

The state of New Mexico, by contrast, never saw the level of Anglo immigration that Texas did. In many places, particularly in the north, Latinos either retained their majority or were too numerous to ignore. Anglos were forced to cooperate politically, and Latinos thus preserved some political power at both the local and state levels. Until 1960, for instance, the only consistent source of Latinos in Congress was the territory and then the state of New Mexico.[13] This experience was not typical, however, and overall a combination of government neglect, declining population share, racism, poverty, and in some cases brute force deprived Latinos of a meaningful political voice in most of the Southwest.

At the turn of the century, the Latino population in the Southwest remained small. A major change that took place at this time was large-scale immigration from Mexico that would continue throughout much of the twentieth century. During the early decades of the twentieth century, not only was there a strong demand for labor in the booming U.S. economy, but the Mexican Revolution of 1910 and the resulting social disorder led many to move north. The border was largely open, and active efforts were made to convince Mexican citizens to immigrate. Demand for labor shrank during the Depression, and the U.S. government even organized mass deportations of Mexican citizens that sometimes ensnared U.S.-born Latinos.[14] World War II and the subsequent U.S. economic expansion reversed this trend, however, and almost continuous immigration from Mexico would be a familiar feature of the Southwest for the rest of the twentieth century.

The postwar years also saw renewed political activity by Mexican Americans. The many returning Latino veterans who fought for freedom overseas were disinclined to accept the usual barriers to full political and economic participation when they returned home. Several influential new organizations were founded at this time (League of United Latin American Citizens, American GI Forum), Latinos began to win a few consequential political offices, and the "Viva Kennedy" organization in 1960 saw the first large-scale Latino mobilization efforts in a national election.[15]

These beginnings were followed by the Chicano movement, a more radical effort that in some ways paralleled the African American civil rights movement. Disenchanted with Latinos' political, economic, and social status, a variety of protest movements began across the southwest in the 1960s. As Juan Gómez-Quiñones describes it, "confrontation politics and heightened ethnic consciousness characterized Mexican activity. Institutions were confronted through demonstrations, boycotts, strikes, sit-ins, and street fighting."[16] During this time, groups such as the United Farm Workers, the National Council of La Raza, the student organization El Movimiento Estudiantil Chicano de Aztlan (MECHA) and the Mexican American Legal Defense and Education Fund (MALDEF) were founded. The American public began to learn more about this population, in contrast to the "forgotten people" status that characterized Latinos for much of the nineteenth and early twentieth centuries. The confrontational style of the movement also differed from the more assimilationist tactics of previous Latino organizations.

Puerto Rico became a U.S. territory in 1898 following the Spanish-American War, and the Jones Act of 1917 granted Puerto Ricans U.S. citizenship. Puerto Ricans can move back and forth from the island to the mainland without any restrictions, and although many did live in New York in the 1930s, substantial immigration to the mainland did not take place until after World War II. The island became a self-governing commonwealth in 1952, but it does not send any presidential delegates to the electoral college and only sends a single nonvoting delegate to Congress.

The Spanish-American War also gave the United States possession of Cuba, but in 1902 an independent Republic of Cuba was formed. Cubans first came to the United States in large numbers following the overthrow of the Batista regime by Fidel Castro in 1959. Although many intended to stay in the United States only for a short time, the persistence of the communist Castro government meant that few returned to Cuba. Large numbers of Cubans were also flown to the United States in the mid-1960s and settled with substantial financial assistance from the U.S. government. Another period of significant Cuban influx was the Mariel Boatlift in 1980, in which 120,000 people, ranging from political activists to common criminals, were allowed or even encouraged by the Cuban government to leave. This group contrasted socioeconomically with the generally wealthier and better-educated initial immigrants. Politically, the Castro experience has given the Cuban community a strong anticommunist and pro-Republican character.

The VRA of 1965, as discussed above, was focused on African Americans and did not include any of the aforementioned Latino populations. When it came up for renewal in 1975, Hispanic (as well as African American) organizations argued that it should extend to them. It was not difficult to make the case that Latinos lacked full and equal access to the ballot box. As Chandler Davidson points out: "Both groups [African Americans and Hispanics] in Texas had historically been excluded from white primaries; both had suffered from the financial burden of the poll tax, from laws and practices that kept their candidates out of office, and from voter manipulation by Anglo-dominated machines."[17] The nation had also become more attuned to the Latino community since the passage of the original act because of the Chicano movement.

Under the 1975 extension, the VRA applied to regions if they had 5 percent or more of a language-minority group, if turnout of these groups in the 1972 presidential election was less than 50 percent, and if the election was conducted in English. It included Hispanics as well as Alaska natives, Native Americans, and Asian Americans. In doing so, the coverage of the VRA was extended outside the South to Arizona, Texas, Alaska, and parts of California, Colorado, and South Dakota. In practice, it required bilingual ballots and voting materials in these states and regions and subjected these areas to the "preclearance" requirements.

## Racial Gerrymandering

The membership of the Senate is predetermined by geography; each state, regardless of size, is allowed two senators. Some states have fewer people than the larger California counties, but Vermont and Wyoming each have the same voice as Texas and New York. The House is fixed in number at 435 districts, and each district elects one representative, but the boundaries and sometimes the locations of these districts change every ten years because each state is not given a permanent allocation of House seats. Instead, the seats are apportioned to the states depending on state size. The Constitution mandates that a census be taken every decade, and the results typically show that some states have gained in size and others have shrunk relative to each other. Seats from the latter are taken away and given to the former. For example, the state of New York had thirty-four representatives in the 1980s; that number declined to thirty-one in the 1990s and twenty-nine after the 2000 census. During this same time period, the number of Texas representatives increased from twenty-seven to thirty to thirty-two.

When the number of seats allocated to a state changes, district boundaries must be redrawn. In addition, because districts must be of approximately equal population, the changing distribution of populations within a state requires redistricting. This process is often controversial because legislators can draw boundaries that help one party over another. This process is called "gerrymandering" and sometimes results in districts of unusual shape, but they are generally acceptable as long as the districts are of approximately equal population size.[18]

Sometimes districts are created to maximize not the number of Democrats or Republicans but the number of minority representatives. By creating "majority-minority" districts, legislators can help ensure that a member of a particular group is elected. Without such a district, minorities have found it difficult to win elections. In addition, the minority population of a state has sometimes found itself the subject of negative racial gerrymandering. In this case, a minority population in one region may be intentionally divided among multiple districts, making them a majority in none, to prevent the election of a minority representative.[19]

The 1982 amendments to the VRA encouraged the creation of majority-minority districts, although the VRA noted: "Nothing in this section [of the act] establishes a right to have members of a protected class elected in numbers equal to their proportion in the population."[20] Then the Supreme Court ruling in *Thornburg v. Gingles* (1986) encouraged legislators to maximize the number of minority representatives.[21] This decision led to much racial gerrymandering, and a record number of minority representatives were elected in 1992.

In subsequent rulings, however, the Court has backed away from this decision. In 1993, the Supreme Court ruled in *Shaw v. Reno* that majority-minority congressional districts may violate the rights of white voters. Writing for the majority, Justice Sandra Day O'Connor wrote that voters may object to the districts based on the "equal protection" clause in the Constitution. She also wrote that such redistricting must be "narrowly tailored" to further a "compelling government interest," a standard that states traditionally have difficulty meeting. The case was brought in reaction to a North Carolina districting plan with two strangely drawn minority districts. Although the Court stopped short of saying that these districts automatically violate the Constitution, it seemed particularly suspicious of districts with odd shapes.[22]

Then in 1995 the Court ruled in *Miller v. Johnson* that race could not be used as the "predominant" factor in redistricting and threw out a Georgia redistricting plan. The Court, however, was again vague about how much race could be used as a factor in drawing lines.[23] This decision was a dramatic change from the 1986 ruling in *Thornburg v. Gingles,* and several states had to change their district maps. The results did not noticeably change minority representation in Congress, however, and the Court has even approved majority-minority districts in some circumstances.

The key point for the Court seems to be the oddness or "compactness" of the district. It is interesting to note, however, that no district has ever been declared unconstitutional, regardless of shape, if the drawing was done with partisan goals in mind. It is only when minorities are the intended beneficiaries that the Court has intervened. In fact, if a state can convincingly argue that a majority-minority district was drawn with partisan outcomes in mind, it can stand.

As Bruce Cain and Kenneth Miller summarize the current situation:

> Lower courts face two seemingly contradictory mandates: the legislative one stemming from the VRA to remedy situations of historic and persistent vote dilution and the constitutional one that treats race as a suspect classification, subject to strict scrutiny and narrowly tailored state actions. Neither the Supreme Court nor Congress has given the lower federal courts clear guidance in how to implement the VRA in light of these developments.[24]

An important debate to mention is whether the creation of majority-minority districts promotes the election of minority politicians but ultimately hurts the policy interests of minority communities. Such districts may elect more African American and Latino politicians, but they also lead to the election of more Republican officials in other districts. Because minorities are heavily Democratic, concentrating them together in sufficient numbers to elect a minority representative means withdrawing substantial numbers of Democrats from surrounding districts. These newly "bleached" districts may therefore be more likely to elect Republicans.

David Lublin finds that "Republicans conservatively won at least six more seats in 1992 and three more seats in 1994 thanks to racial redistricting . . . [which] made the House less likely to adopt policies favored by African Americans."[25] When one considers that a switch of only six seats would have changed House control from Republican to Democratic in 1998, these nine seats loom large.

There are other criticisms of the majority-minority redistricting strategy. Abigail Thernstrom argues that the act creates new racial and ethnic conflict because majority-minority districts provide an incentive for political appeals to be made on the basis of race and ethnicity.[26] She also suggests that minority politicians are better able than many think to win the votes of Anglos, which means majority-minority districts may not even be necessary to create diverse political bodies. Adolph Reed suggests that majority-minority districts provide largely symbolic political rewards and ultimately benefit only a small number of middle-class people, that the districts may convince Anglos that sufficient progress is being made on the race issue, and that they may discourage class-based alliances of people of different colors.[27]

One redistricting case of specific interest to Latinos is *Reynolds v. Sims* (1964). The Court decided that House districts must contain approximately equal numbers of inhabitants, not just citizens. Because the number of Latino noncitizens is relatively high, citizens may be a minority in some

Latino-majority districts. That can result in elections with very low turnout, which has attracted some criticism.[28] If the Court had ruled otherwise, however, there would be many fewer opportunities to create majority-Latino districts and consequently fewer Latino members of Congress.[29]

Applying the VRA to Latinos (and also Asian Americans) is not always easy, for it was understandably written with the African American community in mind. It was meant to address was the concerns of a large, coherent, and concentrated population that is eligible to vote but prevented by institutional barriers. Although the Latino population is large, it contains many noncitizens, is sometimes dispersed, and sometimes lacks pan-ethnic identity among members of the different Latino subgroups. In addition, the VRA is meant to remedy long-standing discrimination, and some have questioned whether its solutions apply to the large number of new Latino immigrants who have not been in this country long enough to establish a record of discriminatory electoral treatment specifically against them.

Finally, just because a district has a majority of nonwhite residents does not guarantee that a minority representative will be elected. Of the sixty-two majority-minority districts in 1998, Anglos represented eleven (18 percent). In addition, there were five African Americans and two Asian Americans elected from majority Anglo districts, so race is not the only factor in congressional elections.[30]

## Minority Voters

### Latino Registration and Turnout

Much attention has been paid to Latino voter turnout. Political scientists are interested not only in the percentage of the overall Latino population that turns out but also how it compares to that by Anglos and African Americans. Much of the research on Latino political participation is interested in explaining if, how, and why political participation has lagged among that group in comparison to the rest of society. Maria Calvo and Steven Rosenstone conclude that "Hispanics are less likely to participate in politics than are other Americans," a view that reflects conventional political wisdom.[31] Rodney Hero also acknowledges that Latinos have a reputation for low levels of political activity.[32]

Because we know that turnout is connected to factors such as age, education, citizenship status, and to a lesser extent income, an important question is how Latino turnout compares when such factors are taken into account ("controlled for," in the language of statistics). Because "Latinos are disproportionately younger, poorer and less educated than the general population," perhaps their participation does not lag when such factors are taken into account.[33] Carole Uhlaner, Bruce Cain, and D. Roderick Kiewiet argue that such intervening variables "fully account for lower Latino participation rates" and that "ethnicity per se has no independent effect" on differential participation rates.[34] Raymond Wolfinger finds that, although the turnout rate for Latinos lagged behind that for non-Latinos, the difference was not as large as many thought.[35] He also notes that when Latinos are registered to vote, they turn out at almost the same rate as non-Latinos.

One of the most important explanations for lagging voter participation is citizenship status. Almost 38 percent of Latino respondents in the Latino National Political Survey (LNPS, 1989–1990) identified themselves as noncitizens, and 40 percent is a commonly noted figure. Louis DeSipio found that 44 percent of Latino adults were noncitizens in 1994, with the figure reaching over 50 percent in some states, including California.[36] Scholars see lack of citizenship to be the most important reason for low Latino political participation.[37]

The reasons that the Latino population in the United States is composed of such large numbers of noncitizens include the long-standing and significant inflow of immigrants from Mexico as well as the long time it takes for Latinos to naturalize. As Michael Jones-Correa maintains, "it takes a generation for even half of the largely middle-class Latin American immigrant population in New York to become citizens."[38]

The mid-1990s did see an increase in both voter turnout and naturalizations in California that demonstrated the powerful political potential of Latinos. It was attributed by many observers to the anti-immigrant and, in the minds of many, anti-Latino Proposition 187 in 1994. California Republicans afterward suffered substantial political defeats at the polls, and some believe it will take years for them to recover from alienating much of this growing population.

When examining turnout data, it is important to differentiate between presidential and congressional election years because presidential elections generate saturation levels of media coverage; they are also more interesting to the public because they feature a relatively straightforward contest between (usually) two personalities for the right to live in the White House. Congressional elections, by contrast, feature hundreds of relatively disjointed campaigns, many candidates receive no media coverage, and the institution at stake is less well understood than the executive branch.

How does Latino voter registration compare with that of Anglos in more recent decades? From 1972 to 1996, 38 percent of voting-age Latinos were registered to vote in presidential election years, compared with 69 percent of whites, with an average gap of 31 percentage points. For congressional election years from 1974 to 1998, about 34 percent of Latinos were registered, whereas about 64 percent of whites were registered, for a similar gap of about 30 percentage points. In terms of actual voter turnout for presidential elections from 1972 to 1996, 31 percent of Latinos and 61 percent of Anglos reported voting, which again produces a gap of 30 percentage points. In congressional contests, the reported turnout of Latinos was 22 percent, and the turnout of Anglos was 47 percent, for a gap of 25 percentage points.[39] Again, one of the key reasons for these gaps is citizenship.

## Latino Ideology

Although one must be careful in making generalizations about large and complex population groups, Latinos are generally more liberal than Anglos. Latinos are much stronger supporters of the Democratic Party than are Anglos, both in terms of voting in presidential and congressional elections and partisan identification. Latinos are also more likely than Anglos to support an activist government and to differ from Anglos on language issues, such as making English the official language, requiring English in the workplace, providing public services in Spanish, and bilingual education. Latinos are also more likely to support affirmative action.[40]

This is not to imply that Latinos are monolithically liberal. There are well-known conservative strands within the Latino community: Latinos put a strong emphasis on faith and family issues and demonstrate lower support for abortion, and Cuban Americans largely oppose diplomatic relations with Cuba and support the Republican Party. Additionally, many Mexican Americans describe themselves as moderate or conservative, although their specific issue positions and voting behavior seem to belie these identifications. Republican Party officials therefore sometimes claim that Latinos have a high potential for conversion to their party. As Louis DeSipio, Rodolfo de la Garza, and Mark Setzler note, however, "Much of the talk of Latino conversion by Republican leaders is more rhetoric than reality."[41]

## Latino Partisanship

The Latino National Political Survey asked respondents to place themselves on a seven-point partisan scale, with the middle category representing independents and the extremes representing strong partisans. Among Mexican Americans, 66.8 percent identified in some way with the Democrats, 11.5 percent were independents, and 21.5 percent identified in some way with the Republicans. For Puerto Ricans, 71 percent identified in some way with the Democrats, 11.5 percent were independents, and 17.5 percent identified in some way with the Republicans. For Cuban Americans, a relatively low 25.5 percent identified in some way with the Democrats, 7.1 percent were independents, and a relatively high 68.8 percent identified in some way with the Republicans.

Then the survey asks, "Which party do you think has more concern for Latinos—the Democratic Party, the Republican Party, or is there no difference?" The only group that primarily answered "No difference" was Cuban Americans; 37 percent favored this option, versus 33 percent who preferred

Democrats and 19 percent who liked Republicans. Mexican Americans and Puerto Ricans thought the more concerned party was that of Bill Clinton and John F. Kennedy. For Mexican Americans, 42 percent chose Democrats, 11 percent Republicans, and 39 percent no difference; for Puerto Ricans, the results were 52 percent Democratic, a very low 6 percent Republican, and 34 percent no difference.[42]

To make some overall comparisons between races and ethnicities, we need to look at the questions from the *Washington Post,* Kaiser Family Foundation, and Harvard University National Survey on Latinos in America (2000). The survey asked respondents, "Overall, which party, the Democrats or Republicans, do you trust to do a better job in coping with the main problems the nation faces over the next few years?" In response, 45 percent of Latinos answered Democrats; 28 percent picked Republicans; and the remainder said neither, both, or do not know. For African Americans, 80 percent answered Democrat and only 6 percent Republican. For Anglos, 35 percent answered Democrat and 44 percent said Republican.

### Latino Voting

DeSipio, de la Garza, and Setzler bring together voting statistics from presidential elections from 1960 to 1996 and find that the average Latino Democratic vote was 73.5 percent. It ranged from a high of 90 percent in the 1964 Johnson-Goldwater election to a low of 56 percent in 1980, when Ronald Reagan defeated Jimmy Carter.[43] The figures from 1960 to 1972 include data only for Mexican Americans, however. This point is important because Cuban Americans are more likely to support Republican candidates. If we examine data from 1976 to 1996, we see that 68 percent of Latinos voted for the Democratic candidates, which is higher than the 40 percent of Anglos who voted Democratic during the same time period. In the most recent presidential election, Al Gore received about 66 percent of the Latino vote, whereas George W. Bush received 32 percent. Bush had 11 percentage points more than Dole did in 1996, which reflects Governor Bush's performance among Tejanos, who supported Gore over Bush by 54 to 43 percent.[44]

The LNPS asked respondents about their votes in the 1988 presidential and congressional elections. Examining the Latino subgroup preferences of those who did vote and recognizing that those who did not were a large population, the survey authors found that Mexican American voters supported Michael Dukakis over George H. W. Bush 63 percent to 37 percent, Puerto Ricans surprisingly supported Bush over Dukakis 52 percent to 48 percent, and Cuban Americans strongly supported Bush over Dukakis 86 percent to 14 percent. In congressional voting, Mexican American voters supported Democrats over Republicans 76 percent to 24 percent, Puerto Ricans supported Democrats over Republicans 65 percent to 35 percent, and Cuban Americans strongly supported Republicans over Democrats 79 percent to 21 percent.[45]

In the 2000 elections, 69 percent of Mexican Americans voted for Gore and 23 percent for Bush, 71 percent of Puerto Ricans voted for Gore and 19 percent for Bush, and 18 percent of Cuban Americans voted for Gore and 79 percent for Bush. Among other Latinos, 88 percent of Dominicans voted for Gore and 10 percent for Bush, 74 percent of Central Americans voted for Gore and 18 percent for Bush, and 69 percent of South Americans voted for Gore and 22 percent for Bush.[46]

### Assessing Latino Voting Behavior

To make some additional comparisons between races and ethnicities, it is helpful to look again at the questions from the 2000 *Washington Post,* Kaiser Family Foundation, and Harvard University survey. Respondents were asked how they voted in the 1996 and 1998 elections. In the 1998 congressional elections, 72 percent of Latinos voted Democratic, which is in between the 94 percent figure for African Americans and the 45 percent for Anglos. In the 1996 presidential elections, 78 percent of Latinos voted Democratic, which is again in between the 89 percent figure for African Americans and the 43 percent for Anglos. In general, Latinos fall in between Anglos and African Americans in their support for the Democratic Party. In this regard, the group they are most comparable to is Jewish Americans.[47]

### African American Registration and Turnout

The political participation of African Americans has increased dramatically in the last half of the twentieth century. Much of this change is due to the removal of the limitations on voting, as discussed previously. Other factors include mobilization by the civil rights movement and rising educational and occupational status levels.

How does African American voter registration compare with that of Anglos in more recent decades? For the reasons mentioned above, it helps to separately examine turnout in presidential and congressional election years. From 1972 to 1996, 63 percent of voting-age African Americans were registered to vote in presidential election years, which compares with 69 percent of whites, with an average gap of 6 percentage points. For congressional election years in the same time period, about 59 percent of African Americans were registered, whereas about 64 percent of whites were registered, for a similar gap of about 5 percentage points. With regard to presidential voter turnout from 1974 to 1998, 52 percent of African Americans and 61 percent of whites reported voting. Here we find a more substantial gap of 9 percentage points. In congressional contests, the reported turnout of African Americans was 39 percent, and the turnout of whites was 47 percent, with a gap of 8 percentage points.[48]

Some have suggested that African Americans participate more than Anglos once socioeconomic factors like education and income are statistically taken into account. One explanation is that group consciousness may help stimulate political involvement.[49] Sidney Verba and Norman Nie, for instance, saw it as an awareness of a shared and unjustly oppressed status, and another study described it as "a process through which dissatisfactions are aggregated across individuals and then politicized."[50] However, some argue that this statistically heightened participation was once true but is no longer operative.[51]

## African American Ideology

As shown in the section above on Latino voting behavior, African Americans are strong supporters of the Democratic Party. They are more Democratic than all the Latino subgroups and much more so than Anglos. In terms of ideology, they are likewise generally liberal. For example, they are more likely than whites to favor an activist government and redistributive programs and are also more liberal than whites on economic issues.[52] Kenny Whitby finds that although African American opinion varies, "In the main, however, blacks favor liberal policies. That is, black policy preferences, as expressed in public opinion polls, are skewed in the direction of affirmative action policies and programs that would assist the economically disadvantaged."[53] Nevertheless, as with Latinos, there cannot be one single ideology for a large and complex group. Carol Swain finds that "a strand of social conservatism runs through black America."[54]

## African American Partisan Registration and Voting

Although African Americans are today strong supporters of the Democratic Party, that has not always been the case. Until the New Deal in the 1930s, they were largely Republican. Economic factors moved them toward the party of Franklin Delano Roosevelt, as was the case with many Americans, but "Few could forget that the Democrat party was largely controlled by the South, which depended on lynching, supremacist violence, and legal devices to disenfranchise Blacks."[55] In the 1956 election, for example, Republican Dwight D. Eisenhower received about 40 percent of the black vote. The Eisenhower administration was concerned about losing these voters, and for this reason its Justice Department drafted what was to become the previously discussed Civil Rights Act of 1957.

In 1960, Republican Richard Nixon received about a third of the black vote in his campaign against John F. Kennedy. The watershed election for black party identification was 1964, which featured the presidential campaigns of Barry Goldwater, an unusually conservative Republican, and the more liberal Lyndon Johnson. Black identification with the Democratic Party reached 80 percent and has remained high ever since.

For instance, National Election Study survey data show that from 1952 to 1962, about 60 percent of blacks on average identified with the Democratic Party. From 1964 to 1996, however, this support shot up to over 81 percent. The change from 1962 to 1964 alone was 18 percentage points. Black support for Democratic presidential candidates from 1976 to 1996 has likewise been high. The average vote is 85.5 percent, compared to 40 percent for Anglos and 68 percent for Latinos.[56]

## Minority Politicians

### Latinos

Political scientists have developed a number of ways to think about the connections between voters and representatives. First, there is the idea of collective representation, whereby a legislature may represent the people as a whole even if there is no specific link between constituents and elected officials.[57] The second form of representation is what Hanna Pitkin called substantive representation, which occurs when a legislator votes in line with the interests of his or her constituents.[58] Pitkin contrasted it with descriptive representation, which takes place when voters elect a representative who shares key traits but not necessarily policy views. Substantive and descriptive representation are not mutually exclusive, but they are conceptually distinctive.

Latinos clearly have a deficit of descriptive representation. There are nineteen Latinos in the 107th Congress (2001–2003), not including the two nonvoting delegates from Puerto Rico and Guam, which comes to about 4.4 percent of the House. The 2000 Census shows that Latinos are 12.5 percent of the U.S. population. These members are largely from California and Texas, although they can also be found in Illinois, New York, New Jersey, Arizona, and Florida. All but three are Democrats. The two Cuban Americans are Republicans, which reflects the party registration statistics of this group, and there is one Mexican American Republican from Texas. Even when we account for about 40 percent of Latinos who are not citizens, there is still an underrepresentation of the population.

In all of U.S. history, only three Latinos have been elected to the Senate—all from New Mexico. The first Latino in the Senate was Republican Octaviano A. Larrazolo, elected in 1928. The next was Democrat Dennis Chavez, who served from 1937 until his death in 1962. Democrat Joseph M. Montoya was elected in 1964, and since his retirement in 1977, there have been no further Latino senators. The prospects for more in the near future do not appear bright, as New Mexico currently has two electorally secure Anglo incumbents.

In the House, the first Latino was elected much earlier. Upon the formation of the Florida Territory, Joseph Marion Hernandez was elected as a delegate from 1822 to 1823. He was later an unsuccessful Whig candidate for the U.S. Senate in 1845 and then moved to Cuba. As of 2001, just over sixty Latinos have served in the House.

After the extension of the VRA to Latinos, the number of elected officials increased. In the six states of Arizona, California, Florida, New Mexico, New York, and Texas, the number of Latino elected officials increased from 1,280 in 1973 to 3,592 in 1990.[59] The latter figure means that Latinos made up 4 percent of all elected officials in those six states, in comparison to a Latino voting-age population of 17 percent.

Overall, the National Association for Latino Elected Officials (NALEO) found that in 1985 there were a total of 3,147 officials, which increased to 4,004 in 1990 and 5,459 in 1994. Using a different counting methodology, NALEO found that in 2000 there were a total of 5,096 Latino elected officials across the nation. This number includes nineteen in the U.S. House, as noted above; 195 in state government; and 4,882 elected to county, municipal, judicial, school board, and other local offices.[60] Of the total number of elected officials in the United States (approximately 500,000), Latinos comprise just 1 percent.

## African Americans

The first African American to serve in the Senate was Hiram Revels of Mississippi, a Republican, in 1870. The first to serve in the House were Republican Joseph H. Rainey of South Carolina and Republican Jefferson Franklin Long of Georgia, both in 1870, in the 41st Congress (1869–1871). During Reconstruction, a total of sixteen blacks served in the Congress, including two in the Senate. They were all Republicans. On the state level, one black served as acting governor of Louisiana, and three states (Louisiana, Mississippi, and South Carolina) elected black lieutenant governors.

After the end of Reconstruction, white Democrats began to reassert control over federal and state offices through the legal and illegal means discussed previously. Over time, the number of black members of Congress declined, until by 1901 there were none. There would be no further black members of Congress until Oscar De Priest (R-Ill.) was elected in 1929.

In 2000, there were thirty-nine African American members of Congress, all in the House of Representatives. They comprise just over 7 percent of the Congress, although African Americans are about 12 percent of the U.S. population. The last African American senator was Carol Moseley-Braun (D-Ill.), who was defeated in 1998. In 1971, by contrast, there were only twelve African Americans in the House and one in the Senate.

The total number of African American elected officials has also grown over the last thirty years. In 1965, they numbered less than 100. By 1970, there were a total of 1,469, with ten at the congressional level and 169 at the state level. In 1980, there were 4,963, and in 1990 the total reached 7,335. By 1997, there were 8,617, with forty at the congressional level and 586 at the state level.

After looking at these figures in more detail, David Bositis finds that in the mid-1990s, most of the gains in the numbers of African American elected officials came from the South, particularly Mississippi and Alabama, whereas the western states actually saw a decline.[61] He also notes that women were a fast-growing presence in the ranks of African American elected officials and in 1997 constituted almost one-third.

Despite this improvement, African Americans are still not elected to office in proportion to their percentage of the overall population. In 1997, there were 500,000 elected officials across the country, so African Americans constituted only 1.7 percent. Blacks are almost 12 percent of the U.S. voting-age population, so the ratio of officials to population was only 0.144 (a figure of 1 would mean complete proportionality). This varies considerably from state to state, however. The ratio was 0.695 in Alabama, but only 0.071 in New York.

The relative political safety of African Americans and Latinos who occupy majority-minority House seats means that they are well positioned to enjoy long seniority. Because longer-serving members are more likely to receive committee chairs, this dynamic may work to increase minority political power in the House. As Hero notes, "Continuous reelection is central to gaining seniority and hence greater influence in Congress."[62] This fact is somewhat ironic because only a few decades ago, conservative white Democrats from safe southern seats used their seniority and chairmanships to block civil rights legislation.

In the 103rd Congress (1993–1995), African Americans chaired the Armed Services (Ron Dellums [D-Calif.]), Government Operations (John Conyers Jr. [D-Mich.]), and Post Office and Civil Service Committees (William Lacy Clay Sr. [D-Mo.]), and Latinos chaired Agriculture (Eligio "Kika" de la Garza [D-Texas]) and Banking (Henry B. Gonzalez [D-Texas]). These members held their positions in the era of Democratic House dominance, however, which is no longer the political reality. When the Republicans assumed control in the 104th Congress (1995–1997), there were no minority committee chairs.

Of the minority Republicans, the sole representative in the majority leadership in the 107th Congress was J. C. Watts of Oklahoma, the House Republican Conference Chairman who announced his retirement in 2002. Henry Bonilla of Texas is sixteenth in seniority on the Appropriations Committee, Lincoln Diaz-Balart of Florida is fifth in seniority on the Rules Committee, and Ileana Ros-Lehtinen of Florida is fifth on Government

Reform and ninth on International Relations. None are likely to become committee chairs in the near future.

## Conclusion

In this chapter I first outlined the historical and legal context of Latino and African American political participation. An ideal United States is one in which all citizens have equal political rights, and much progress has been made in that direction since the 1960s. Although there are many people alive today who can remember when minorities were denied the right to vote or otherwise meaningfully participate in political life, it is clear that political practice in the United States is moving closer to its political values.

I also pointed out substantial differences in the political behavior of Latinos, African Americans, and Anglos. In terms of voter registration, Anglos are the most likely to be registered, African Americans the second most, and Latinos the least. The same ranking applies for voter turnout. Nevertheless, there is far more registration and turnout today for members of both minority groups than before the VRA and other federal legislation were passed. In addition, when factors such as citizenship and socio-economic status are taken into account, scholars have found few differences in contemporary political participation.

In terms of partisanship, African Americans largely and Latinos mostly identify themselves as Democrats, and Anglos are most likely to identify themselves as Republicans. This trend also applies to voting in presidential and congressional elections. Because African Americans and Latinos generally take liberal positions on political issues and Anglos usually take more conservative positions, such partisan attachments come as little surprise.

Last, relatively few minority politicians are elected to Congress and other offices, although their share has risen in recent decades. Restrictions on the right to vote led to almost no minority politicians for long stretches of U.S. history, but this situation changed because of the VRA, as well as the creation of "majority-minority" political districts. The number of politicians of color has therefore risen but is still far short of proportionality. Although Latinos constitute almost 13 percent of the U.S. population, only 1 percent of elected officials are Latinos. African Americans are almost 12 percent of the population but constitute less than 2 percent of elected officials. I also noted the debate over whether the increasing number of minority elected officials (descriptive representation) has led to the advancement of policies important to the Latino and African American communities (substantive representation).

# 13

## Covering Candidates and Informing Voters: Newspaper Coverage of a Gubernatorial Election

### Stephen J. Stambough and Valerie R. O'Regan

Since the Year of the Woman in 1992, the face of politics seems to be taking on a more feminine look. One finds more female candidates and officeholders in leadership and representative positions throughout the country. As of 2002, women comprised 13 percent of both the U.S. Senate and U.S. House of Representatives.[1] Additionally, in 2002, female governors were leading five states and seventeen states had female lieutenant governors.[2] This increase in female representation and leadership, despite the fact that it has been slow in coming, is providing researchers with opportunities to examine elections involving female candidates. One topic of research that benefits from this growth in opportunities is the study of media coverage of campaigns by women, particularly those in high-profile elections. Another point of interest is the increase in women serving in statewide office and executive office, something that has occurred so infrequently during the history of the country that it has been difficult to study.

In the history of the United States, only nineteen women have served as governor of a state. Because this number is so small, the study of female governors and gubernatorial candidates is, not surprisingly, very limited. The few studies conducted on this topic deal with case studies of highly populated states, such as California, Texas, and New Jersey.[3] More specifically, certain variables that may be important to our understanding of female gubernatorial candidates are relatively constant in the states previously studied, begging the question of whether these findings are true for other female candidates for the office and prompting further research.

To date, little research exists that examines female gubernatorial candidates in detail for less populated states with different campaign norms, cultures, and political environments. Furthermore, little has been done to generalize the findings beyond the early 1990s in these few states. The limitations of the previous research leave scholars apprehensive about our under-standing of the political dynamics surrounding female candidates for the office of governor. These limitations are important not only in an academic sense but also in a practical sense. In 2002, many highly qualified women pursued the office of governor in a significant number of states to the extent that, if 1992 was the Year of the Woman in U.S. politics, then 2002 might be the Year of the Woman in executive politics. Although some of these states are highly populated and high-profile states like those previously studied, most of the female gubernatorial candidates, like former Maui mayor Linda Lingle in Hawaii and Kansas insurance commissioner Kath-leen Sebelius, ran in less populated states.

To gain an understanding of female gubernatorial campaigns in all states, it is necessary to expand the study of these campaigns to include interesting races in less populated states. In an effort to expand the litera-ture, in this study we examine whether knowledge of female candidates for governor can be generalized beyond the highly populated states to less pop-ulated states such as North Dakota. The focus in this chapter is on the media coverage during the gubernatorial campaign of 2000, when North Dakota had its first female candidate for the governorship. During 2000, Democrat Heidi Heitkamp ran against Republican John Hoeven to see who would lead North Dakota into the new millennium.

The purpose of this chapter is also to analyze and compare media report-ing of high-profile campaigns, such as a statewide gubernatorial election, when one candidate is female and the other is male. Existing literature sug-gests that media coverage may differ in various ways (such as likelihood of winning, issue positions, qualifications, and leadership traits) when dealing with female and male candidates. Moreover, because of the nature of a statewide campaign, media coverage is crucial for the dissemination of infor-mation regarding candidates and their campaigns.[4] As a result, the informa-tion conveyed by the media could have a significant effect on the perceptions and decisionmaking of voters. Therefore, determining the types of differences and extent thereof in media coverage is vital in the comprehension of the effect that the media has on electoral races, especially when one of the can-didates is female. We examine newspaper coverage throughout the different stages of the campaign by employing content analysis of the four major newspapers in the state. The intention of this chapter is to determine if press coverage of the candidates differed based on the gender of the candidates.

## Media Coverage

Over the years, the importance of media coverage during election cycles has been well documented.[5] Voters rely on the media to provide informa-tion about the candidates that they do not have the time or resources to collect on their own. Reliance on the media is especially important in high-profile, statewide races. This information can include biographical characteristics, issue positions, polling results, credentials, and expectations of success or failure. All this information is "framed" by the reporters or media executives to provide news accounts that are straightforward and interesting for their readers or viewers.[6] Voters who read or watch these reports use the facts provided by the media to make their voting decisions.

As one distinguishes between media coverage of female and male candidates, the framing of the news articles takes on additional significance if the framing differs because of the sex of the candidate. Framing of stories may have positive, negative, or neutral effects for the female candidates by reinforcing stereotypes and expectations.[7] Therefore, the type and focus of media coverage should be a significant consideration when examining the increasing phenomenon of women running for high-profile offices.

In the past, arguments have been made about the unequal treatment of female and male candidates in media reporting. A considerable amount of this research is done from a journalistic or descriptive style, providing news accounts that illustrate the differences in the coverage.[8] Although these accounts are important and beneficial to the study of the media and women in politics, they lack quantification of the differences in media coverage.

To offer a more quantitative approach to the subject, studies have been conducted using statistical analysis of the argument that media coverage of female candidates differs from the coverage of male candidates. Consistencies have been found in studies of women vying for a range of elected offices. Even in lower-profile campaigns, differences in newspaper coverage exist. For instance, research on the press coverage of female state legislative candidates found subtle differences in reporting.[9] As such, references to incumbency status appear more often for male incumbents than female incumbents; this subtle difference offers males, more often than females, the advantage of name recognition and expertise that is implied by the status.

In high-profile elections, less subtle differences in press coverage of female and male candidates have been found. Kim Kahn, for instance, found that in both senatorial and gubernatorial races, female candidates receive less issue attention than their male opponents do.[10] This discrepancy in issue coverage may be detrimental to female candidates as they attempt to communicate their issue agendas to the voters. In addition, female senatorial candidates receive less all-around campaign coverage than their male rivals do, and in many cases the coverage they receive questions their viability to win the election.[11] Research has also found differences in the viability assessments of female gubernatorial candidates running for open seats; in these races women are portrayed by the press as less likely to get elected than their male opponents.[12] Since a substantial percentage of the female gubernatorial candidates run for open seats, the differences in press reporting are an obstacle for them.

In addition to these findings, scholars contend that the press has held women to different standards than their male counterparts[13] and that the focus of the press tends to be on "style over substance" for female candidates.[14] News stories about female candidates have stressed their familial roles or spouse's business dealings, described their appearance and personal traits, and focused on the novelty of their candidacies. In contrast, stories on male candidates focus on issue agendas, stereotypical traits such as leadership qualities and rationality, business and military experience, and competitiveness as a candidate.

Despite studies that media reporting disadvantages women, other findings are more optimistic. According to pollster Celinda Lake, "press coverage of women candidates has grown more favorable over time, even if it still has a long way to go."[15] As more research is being done concerning the media's treatment of women running for office, other assessments of the treatment are being presented. Some suggest that during the 1990s, press coverage of female and male candidates is becoming more similar. There is little if any evidence of bias against female candidates as far as the quantity of coverage, and issue coverage has become "roughly equal."[16] As the political role of women has expanded, especially in the 1990s, gender-based press coverage is less obvious and not always an obstacle for women. Media treatment may still differ, but these differences point out the advantages of electing women and demonstrate that women are being taken more seriously as candidates. Yet others contend that although press coverage has been negative for certain female candidates, the negativity was due to their badly run campaigns and the issues they addressed rather than their gender.[17]

## Questions About the Nature of Media Coverage

Although these findings are encouraging, questions remain. Is the press coverage of female candidates significantly different from the coverage of their male opponents? If it is different, how is it different? If the press coverage is different, is it a disadvantage or an advantage for female candidates?

Although other scholars have addressed these questions, we propose that the earlier studies have not analyzed the differences in coverage over an extended period of time. The bulk of the existing literature focuses on the time period after Labor Day (the "post–Labor Day stage").[18] These studies exclude the early stages, when the party organization is working behind the scenes to determine the party nomination (the "metacampaign stage"); the stage just prior to, during, and immediately following the party conventions (the "nomination struggle stage"); and the stage following the formal announcement of the candidates by the parties ("the postnomination stage"). As a result, existing research does not offer a thorough analysis of the differences in media campaign coverage of female and male candidates during the entire campaign. We expand the available analyses of media coverage by searching for differences in press coverage during *all* the campaign stages. Consequently, an additional question is asked: Does press coverage differ throughout the entire campaign period or only during the period following Labor Day?

In addition, the uniqueness of the campaign in this study allows for the opportunity to ask questions regarding the effect of an illness on press coverage during a high-profile campaign, more precisely, a "women's illness" facing the female candidate. On September 22, 2000, Heitkamp announced that she had been diagnosed with breast cancer. After two weeks away from the campaign trail and a modified radical mastectomy, Heitkamp resumed her quest to become North Dakota's first female governor. Although tragic, the cancer announcement allows scholars the chance to examine how the press covers the disclosure of a candidate's serious illness. Did the press coverage of Heitkamp take on a more negative tone following the announcement? Did the press coverage become more personal after her cancer announcement?

## Women and the Governorship

As mentioned in the opening, there have been relatively few female governors in the United States. Of the nineteen that have held this top state post, seven of them gained their seat by either succeeding their husbands for different reasons or finishing their predecessors' terms. The first female governor was Nellie Tayloe Ross of Wyoming, who won a special election to fulfill her deceased husband's term. She was inaugurated on January 5, 1925. Later that same day, the second female governor also took office in Texas: Miriam "Ma" Ferguson, who was elected as a surrogate for her controversial husband, who was forbidden from running for office again. The first female governor to get elected based on her own qualifications and support was Ella Grasso of Connecticut in 1975.[19]

Over the years, both Texas and Arizona have had two female governors each. Besides Ma Ferguson, Ann Richards was elected and served in Texas from 1991 to 1995. In Arizona, both female governors—Rose Mofford and Jane Dee Hull—assumed the office to complete the terms of their predecessors. Of those women who have been governor, the shortest term in office was held by Nancy Hollister of Ohio, who served for just nine days. The nine-day period fell between her predecessor's resignation to serve in the U.S. Senate in December 1998 and the inauguration of the governor-elect in January 1999. The longest term in office for a female governor was held by Christine Todd Whitman of New Jersey, who served from her inauguration in January 1994 until January 2001.[20]

Despite the low numbers overall, more and more women are leading their states as governor. As of 2002, there was a "record" number of five female governors serving their respective states, along with a female governor in Puerto Rico. Although there have been relatively few female governors, the number of women seeking this coveted position has increased over the years. Examining the period between 1970 and 2000, one finds 1986 to be a breakout election for female gubernatorial candidates, when a total of eight women ran for the office nationwide. In the sixteen years before 1986, there had been only ten female gubernatorial candidates in all. One other point of historical significance regarding the 1986 election was the fact that the state of Nebraska had two women running against each other for the governorship.

Following the path of the 1986 election, the year 1990 demonstrated that this increase in women running for the governor's house was not a fluke; that year, there were eight female gubernatorial candidates nationwide. Looking at the two election periods in 1994 and 1998, one sees further growth in the number of female gubernatorial candidates; during both elections, a total of ten women ran for the office across the country. This trend is both continuing and growing. As mentioned earlier, a significant number of women pursued the office in 2002, many of whom were well known and highly qualified candidates. The 2002 cohort of female candidates included two lieutenant governors, three state treasurers, two state attorneys general, and multiple members of state and local public and legislative offices. The characteristics of this group indicate a corresponding growth in the number of women running for and being elected to statewide office, something that both might be a result of the advances made by women seeking the governorship and might in turn produce more likely candidates for governor.

As the number of female candidates increases, it is believed that the opportunities to elect more women to the governorship also expand.[21] It appears that as the number of lower-level offices held by women increases, so too does the candidate pool of women with ample political experience to run for governor and mount viable campaigns. Finally, given that four of the past five presidents came directly from the governor's house—Jimmy Carter, Ronald Reagan, Bill Clinton, and George W. Bush—the prospect of electing more women to the governorship might increase the prospect of one day electing a female president.[22]

As previously mentioned, studies of the media coverage of female candidates have developed from a descriptive style into more statistical analyses of the differences between coverage of female and male candidates. Kahn's research on female candidates for high-profile offices provides strong evidence of differences in press coverage of female and male candidates.[23] However, more current research suggests that women and men are being treated more equally, and if there are differences, they may not harm women.[24]

In narrowing our focus to studies of women candidates for executive office, we find that the amount of research is even more limited. Research addressing differences in media coverage of female and male presidential candidates during the 2000 presidential primary campaign supports the early findings of gender differences in overall press coverage.[25] According to the authors of these studies, Elizabeth Dole received less overall coverage than George W. Bush and John McCain in spite of the fact that public opinion polls ranked her as the second most popular Republican candidate. The research also showed that the content of the coverage probably differed based on the gender differences of the candidates; more attention was given to Dole's appearances and personality traits in comparison to the male candidates. In addition, differences could be found in the tone of the coverage; these differences tended to favor the male candidates.

When focusing only on female candidates for the governorship, research demonstrates that although the amount of coverage seems to be equal, other gender differences surface.[26] Similar to the study of female and male presidential candidates, article content reflected candidate gender. Articles in the media about female gubernatorial candidates were more likely to deal with their personal lives, appearance, or personalities. In contrast, media coverage of male candidates focused on the candidates' positions or records on the issues and tended to provide evidence or reasoning supporting male candidates' remarks.

## Stages of a Campaign

One of the contributions of this research is that media coverage of the campaign is extended to the early stages of the campaign. It is often said that the traditional beginning of a campaign occurs on Labor Day weekend. We know that is not true. Campaigns are not events; they are processes. Much of this process takes place beneath the radar screen, out of the public view, and long before Labor Day. At the presidential level, this process never really stops. Potential candidates are visiting Iowa and New Hampshire in 2002 in anticipation of a 2004 presidential race. At the state and local level, this type of preparation may not be the norm, but even in the glare of the public spotlight, there is often significant campaign activity and campaign coverage long before Labor Day.

The obvious starting point for coverage of a campaign occurs when the candidates formally announce their candidacies. At this stage, much of the campaign work is aimed at lining up endorsements, volunteers, a campaign staff, and financial donors. The announcement is the first time a candidate is introduced to the public as a candidate for this office. It is also the time for candidates to set the early tone for their campaigns, along with what they believe will be the winning campaign theme. This period is the later stage of what has been referred to as the "metacampaign."[27] For the purposes of this chapter, it is interesting to note how the local media frame the coverage of the candidates at this stage of the campaign.

The next identifiable period of the campaign is the nominating process. In most states, it happens during the primary election campaign. In the 2000 North Dakota gubernatorial campaign, however, the true nomination struggle did not occur during the primary election in June but at the party conventions in April. It is possible for a candidate who did not receive the party endorsement at the convention to challenge the endorsed candidate during the primary election. That type of challenge only occurs during the unusual circumstance of a deeply divided party. These divisions often hurt the general election chances of the eventual nominee; thus party unity is a key goal during the nomination stage.[28] Divided parties were never a concern in the 2000 gubernatorial race in North Dakota, since both the Democratic Party and the Republican Party quickly rallied around their nominees without serious divisions. During the nomination coverage, candidates need to show a united party, introduce a platform, present themselves as leaders, and begin the campaign as their party's nominee. At this stage, we expect an increase in both personal and issue coverage while news organizations cover the conventions.

The next stage is often a quiet time in campaigns. Before the traditional beginning of the campaign over Labor Day weekend but after the nomination struggle is a period when people pay little attention to politics. At this time, a decline in media coverage of the campaigns is expected.

The final stage of the campaign comes after the Labor Day holiday. Campaigns need to begin the final push toward election day with a strong organization and prepared events. Campaigns need to focus on the positive personal characteristics and campaign issues they want the voters to think about. Because of the increased campaign activity during this period, one might expect an increase in coverage at this time.

For this chapter, we included an additional campaign stage unique to this race: the period after the cancer announcement. This is not the first time candidate health has been an issue, nor was it the only race in the 2000 election cycle that included an element of candidate health (Senator William Roth's age became a significant issue in Delaware following a public dizzy spell), but there is little research on the effect of such a personal revelation during a campaign. Because of the inherently personal nature of this issue, we expected an increase in coverage of Heitkamp's personal characteristics during this stage. Furthermore, we expected that this coverage would not be predominantly negative (for fear of sounding insensitive) but would more likely be mixed in nature.

## Content Data

By looking at newspaper coverage of the 2000 gubernatorial campaign in North Dakota, we investigate any differences in the coverage of the two candidates. Specifically, we analyze any differences to determine whether these differences are consistent with our expectations of a female-male election.

Our data for this research come from content analysis of the *Bismarck Tribune, Fargo Forum, Grand Forks Herald,* and *Minot Daily News.* These four newspapers are used because they are the newspapers of the four largest cities in the state. Furthermore, by including papers from various sections of the state, we are able to capture a more comprehensive understanding of the media coverage of the election.

## Findings

The first item investigated was whether candidate gender was a factor in coverage about candidate viability. As discussed earlier, previous research suggests that female candidates receive less favorable "horserace" coverage than their male counterparts. Like the races previously studied, this contest was an open seat election. In contrast to these earlier studies, Heitkamp (the female candidate) did not receive significantly less favorable coverage than Hoeven (the male candidate). Of the modest amount of horserace coverage throughout the campaign in the four papers, the coverage was relatively balanced between the two candidates, with a slight edge to Hoeven. Out of the sixty-seven articles that discuss candidate viability, fully thirty-one listed both candidates as equally competitive. By examining the frequency data in Table 13.1, it is apparent that there are few differences in terms of the coverage, except that Heitkamp's campaign viability was mentioned in seven more articles than Hoeven's campaign viability. In these articles, the coverage was generally positive for both candidates. The only difference is that of the little coverage that listed either candidate as declining or a sure loser, four of these articles listed Heitkamp as such, compared to only one article about Hoeven.

These findings are in contrast to previous research about open seat gubernatorial races but are not surprising in this case. Heitkamp held statewide elective office for more than a decade in her service as North Dakota attorney general and tax commissioner. In the previous election cycle, she won reelection as attorney general with 64 percent of the vote. By all measures, she would be considered a quality candidate with significant prior political experience. Prior to the campaign, John Hoeven was not very well known to the average voter throughout the state and had only

**Table 13.1  Horserace Coverage of Candidates by Gender and
Viability Rating**

| | | | Hoeven | | |
|---|---|---|---|---|---|
| | | No Mention | Likely Winner | Competitive and Gaining | Competitive | Competitive but Declining |
| Heitkamp | No mention | 380 | 4 | 1 | 0 | 0 |
| | Likely winner | 5 | 1 | 0 | 2 | 1 |
| | Competitive and gaining | 1 | 4 | 0 | 4 | 0 |
| | Competitive | 6 | 1 | 2 | 31 | 0 |
| | Competitive but declining | 0 | 2 | 1 | 0 | 0 |
| | Sure loser | 0 | 1 | 0 | 0 | 0 |

*Note:* Cells indicate number of articles.

appointed political experience, having served as the president of the State Bank of North Dakota—one of the state's many throwbacks to its populist roots. Although he previously considered seeking elected political office (ironically for governor as a Democrat in 1996), his first attempt was his 2000 candidacy for governor as a Republican. Until Hoeven had a chance to demonstrate an appeal to North Dakota voters, Heitkamp, as a proven vote getter, was generally seen as the clear favorite.

The second item analyzed was the issue coverage each candidate received in the media. As we looked at the issue coverage in the press, three noteworthy differences were apparent. First, in analyzing the amount of total issue coverage throughout the campaign, it is apparent that Heitkamp received more issue coverage, measured by number of articles and number of paragraphs. Overall, there were 360 articles devoted to Heitkamp's issue positions and 320 articles devoted to Hoeven's issue positions. Additionally, there were 722 paragraphs that dealt with Heitkamp's position on the issues, as opposed to 571 paragraphs dealing with Hoeven's issue positions. These findings are contrary to the literature arguing that female candidates receive less overall issue coverage.

The second interesting difference was found when we divided the issue coverage into two categories: traditionally female issues (see Table 13.2) and traditionally male issues (see Table 13.3). The traditionally male issues are composed of economic development, agricultural issues, and employment and salary levels. Education, teacher pay, and health care make up the traditionally female issue category.[29] According to the tables, Heitkamp received greater coverage for both female and male issues for both number of articles and number of paragraphs. Among the female issues, Hoeven did receive greater paragraph coverage for educational issues, but this advantage was overshadowed by Heitkamp's greater advantage in coverage of

**Table 13.2 Newspaper Coverage of Female Issues by Candidate and Article Tone**

| | Educational Issues | | | Teacher Pay | | | Health Care | | |
|---|---|---|---|---|---|---|---|---|---|
| | Heitkamp | Hoeven | Diff. | Heitkamp | Hoeven | Diff. | Heitkamp | Hoeven | Diff. |
| Positive articles | 12 | 7 | +5 | 5 | 6 | −1 | 9 | 5 | +4 |
| Positive paragraphs | 30 | 14 | +16 | 9 | 10 | −1 | 29 | 15 | +14 |
| Negative articles | 2 | 1 | +1 | 1 | 0 | +1 | 0 | 0 | 0 |
| Negative paragraphs | 2 | 4 | −2 | 1 | 0 | +1 | 0 | 0 | 0 |
| Mixed articles | 15 | 12 | +3 | 16 | 13 | +3 | 11 | 3 | +8 |
| Mixed paragraphs | 19 | 38 | −19 | 35 | 26 | +9 | 24 | 3 | +21 |
| Neutral articles | 33 | 34 | −1 | 26 | 22 | +4 | 15 | 10 | +5 |
| Neutral paragraphs | 57 | 70 | −13 | 55 | 34 | +21 | 31 | 16 | +15 |
| Total articles | 62 | 54 | +8 | 48 | 41 | +7 | 35 | 18 | +17 |
| Total paragraphs | 108 | 126 | −18 | 100 | 70 | +30 | 84 | 34 | +50 |

**Table 13.3 Newspaper Coverage of Male Issues by Candidate and Article Tone**

| | Economic Development | | | Agricultural Issues | | | Employment and Salaries | | |
|---|---|---|---|---|---|---|---|---|---|
| | Heitkamp | Hoeven | Diff. | Heitkamp | Hoeven | Diff. | Heitkamp | Hoeven | Diff. |
| Positive articles | 17 | 19 | −2 | 15 | 8 | +7 | 13 | 19 | −6 |
| Positive paragraphs | 35 | 37 | −2 | 67 | 19 | +48 | 22 | 31 | −9 |
| Negative articles | 2 | 0 | +2 | 1 | 0 | +1 | 2 | 0 | +2 |
| Negative paragraphs | 3 | 0 | +3 | 3 | 0 | +3 | 8 | 0 | +8 |
| Mixed articles | 16 | 21 | −5 | 14 | 9 | +5 | 21 | 19 | +2 |
| Mixed paragraphs | 42 | 40 | +2 | 28 | 13 | +15 | 35 | 25 | +10 |
| Neutral articles | 36 | 43 | −7 | 29 | 30 | −1 | 49 | 39 | +10 |
| Neutral paragraphs | 63 | 61 | +2 | 58 | 70 | −12 | 66 | 55 | +11 |
| Total articles | 71 | 83 | −12 | 59 | 47 | +12 | 85 | 77 | +8 |
| Total paragraphs | 143 | 138 | +5 | 156 | 102 | +54 | 131 | 101 | +30 |

teacher pay issues and health care issues. For male issues, Hoeven received more article coverage for economic development issues, but the coverage of Heitkamp's issue positions on agricultural issues and employment and salary issues was enough to give her the overall edge for male issues. Again, these findings contradict previous research that suggests male candidates receive more issue coverage than female candidates[30] or that issue coverage is approximately equal for both female and male candidates.[31]

By examining the tone of the articles, a few patterns emerge. First, of the traditionally male issues, agricultural issues appear to be an outlier. For the other two traditionally male issues, Hoeven received more positive issue coverage and less negative issue coverage. For agriculture, however, Heitkamp received substantially more positive coverage than her male opponent received. Although this conclusion is counter to previous findings, it is not surprising in the context of this campaign. Heitkamp is from rural North Dakota, whereas Hoeven is from one of the cities. In terms of overall coverage of traditionally male issues, Heitkamp clearly received more coverage of agricultural issues and employment and salary issues. For economic development issues, however, Hoeven received more article coverage while receiving less paragraph coverage. It is not surprising that Hoeven received greater article coverage of economic development issues than Heitkamp since that was the centerpiece of his campaign and was tied directly to his political biography as head of the State Bank of North Dakota. The fact that Heitkamp received more paragraph coverage, even on this issue, provides further evidence suggesting that the female candidate was not disadvantaged as far as issue coverage in the media. That is counter to previous findings cited above.

Although Heitkamp received more coverage regarding male issues than anticipated, Hoeven received considerable coverage of his positions on one of the female issues. Contrary to expectations, Hoeven received more paragraph coverage of educational issues than his female opponent received. When measured as the number of articles, Heitkamp received greater coverage on this issue, but the difference was not as great as expected. Consistent with expectations, Heitkamp received more coverage for both teacher pay and health care issues.

When coverage of female issues was analyzed for article tone, we saw a difference between the coverage of educational issues and teacher pay issues for the candidates. On educational issues, Heitkamp received more purely positive coverage, but Hoeven's coverage was more likely to be mixed or neutral. For teacher pay issues, Heitkamp received more mixed and neutral coverage, but there was little difference between amounts of positive coverage for the candidates.

A possible explanation for these findings might be found in how these issues were framed. Debates over designing a strong educational system with good results followed the traditional lines that are associated more positively with female candidates. The issue of teacher pay was framed differently. Both candidates proposed increasing teacher pay by roughly the same amount. The debate centered on funding mechanisms, especially potential tax increases and the autonomy of local school districts. Hoeven charged that Heitkamp would raise taxes for teacher pay increases and dictate the policy from the capitol. Hoeven proposed more flexibility at the local level for policy implementation. The debate quickly became one not of whether teachers should be paid more—both agreed—but of local versus state government and taxes. Therefore, this shift in the framing of the policy debate made the issue of teacher pay look more like a traditionally male issue of economics and government power instead of a traditionally female issue of education.

Finally, as we separate issue coverage of the traditionally male and female issues into the five distinct stages of the campaign (see Table 13.4), the third interesting difference in news coverage is revealed. Upon examination, it was found that the campaign stages that were omitted from the earlier studies show significant differences in the press coverage of the candidates, especially during the postnomination stage. During the metacampaign stage, Hoeven received slightly more coverage in paragraphs about traditionally male issues. There also appears to be a difference in the amount of coverage during the nomination struggle stage, when Heitkamp received more coverage of traditionally male issues and slightly more of traditionally female issues. It is important to note, however, that during this stage, there was practically no coverage of female issues for either candidate. During the postnomination stage, both candidates received significant coverage of male and female issues, with Heitkamp receiving more for both types.

## Table 13.4 Newspaper Coverage of Issues by Candidate and Campaign Stage

|  | Heitkamp Articles | Heitkamp Paragraphs | Hoeven Articles | Hoeven Paragraphs |
|---|---|---|---|---|
| Traditionally male issues |  |  |  |  |
| Metacampaign | 4 | 16 | 8 | 24 |
| Nomination struggle | 13 | 69 | 10 | 39 |
| Postnomination | 49 | 189 | 44 | 143 |
| Post–Labor Day | 12 | 46 | 9 | 30 |
| Postcancer story | 40 | 110 | 42 | 113 |
| Total | 118 | 430 | 113 | 349 |
| Traditionally female issues |  |  |  |  |
| Metacampaign | 11 | 23 | 4 | 5 |
| Nomination struggle | 7 | 13 | 3 | 4 |
| Postnomination | 43 | 170 | 37 | 133 |
| Post–Labor Day | 8 | 30 | 8 | 32 |
| Postcancer story | 22 | 57 | 29 | 58 |
| Total | 91 | 293 | 81 | 232 |

The most significant finding about these first three stages is not in the differences between the candidates but in the fact that the majority of the issue coverage occurs during these times. As discussed earlier, previous studies focus on coverage following Labor Day, and some are limited to only the last month of the campaign. These findings suggest that this type of focus misses much of the coverage that can be vital to understanding the media treatment of the two candidates.

In the post–Labor Day stage, more paragraphs were dedicated to Heitkamp's positions on traditionally male issues than Hoeven's. However, both received an almost identical amount of paragraph and article coverage on traditionally female issues. During the postcancer stage, we find that both candidates received approximately the same amount of article and paragraph coverage of both types of issues, which is consistent with the research done by others, namely Kevin Smith.[32]

The final aspect examined in this research involved the coverage of personal characteristics of the two candidates in the media. Based on prior research, it was expected that the female candidate would receive greater emphasis on her personal characteristics than her male counterpart. The data reported in Table 13.5 support this expectation. Two-thirds of the total mentions of personal characteristics were for Heitkamp. This result signifies a substantial difference in the treatment of the two candidates.

The story goes deeper than just total numbers, however. By analyzing total number of mentions by campaign stage and by tone of the article, we found a few other patterns. First, there appears to be a substantial increase in references to personal characteristics of Heitkamp after her cancer announcement. Although there is no research that addresses this relationship, the result is not very surprising. This story was a very personal story about a candidate as a human being. Many stories surfaced concerning her toughness, commitment to family, and her physical ability to do the job—both as a candidate and as a potential governor. Although there were concerns relating to her health and ability to remain in the race, the newspaper coverage was seldom completely negative. Only one story that contained a personal reference was classified as negative. Twenty-five of the references were found in stories that were coded as positive.

The interesting and important finding, however, is that most of the coverage of Heitkamp after the cancer announcement was either mixed or neutral. Much of the coverage during this time could be characterized as "Heidi is tough and energetic, but . . . ." This type of "compliment, but . . ." coverage mirrored what would become one of the dominant issues at the end of the race. The Heitkamp campaign charged that the Hoeven campaign was engaged in a "scare campaign," including using precinct walkers to tell potential voters that her health was much worse than she was admitting and that she would probably be dead within a year. There was no concrete link of these rumors to the Hoeven campaign, and their source may have just

**Table 13.5  Tone of Articles Mentioning Personal Characteristics of Candidates in Newspaper Coverage**

| Campaign Stage | Positive Coverage | Negative Coverage | Mixed Coverage | Neutral Coverage | Total Coverage |
|---|---|---|---|---|---|
| Coverage of Democratic Candidate Heidi Heitkamp | | | | | |
| Metacampaign | 6 | 9 | 9 | 5 | 29 |
| Nomination struggle | 9 | 5 | 11 | 1 | 26 |
| Postnomination | 22 | 25 | 45 | 18 | 110 |
| Post–Labor Day | 8 | 0 | 4 | 3 | 15 |
| Postcancer story | 25 | 1 | 25 | 26 | 77 |
| Total | 70 | 40 | 94 | 53 | 257 |
| Column (percent) | 27.2 | 15.6 | 36.6 | 20.6 | 100 |
| Total (percent) | 18.1 | 10.4 | 24.4 | 13.7 | 66.6 |
| Coverage of Republican Candidate John Hoeven | | | | | |
| Metacampaign | 11 | 0 | 18 | 4 | 33 |
| Nomination struggle | 10 | 0 | 1 | 5 | 16 |
| Postnomination | 26 | 11 | 9 | 20 | 66 |
| Post–Labor Day | 0 | 0 | 0 | 1 | 1 |
| Postcancer story | 3 | 1 | 7 | 2 | 13 |
| Total | 50 | 12 | 35 | 32 | 129 |
| Column (percent) | 38.8 | 9.3 | 27.1 | 24.8 | 100 |
| Total (percent) | 13.0 | 3.0 | 9.1 | 8.3 | 33.4 |

been a few overzealous Hoeven campaign workers acting on their own. The controversy escalated, however, when outgoing Republican governor Ed Schafer uttered his own "compliment, but . . ." comment during a call-in radio show. He talked about how physically grueling the job of governor could be and that he worried Heitkamp—no matter how strong she is— would not be able to physically handle the job while undergoing treatment. The Heitkamp campaign protested this comment, but in doing so committed a common error in campaign strategy. In spending so much time responding to these statements and rumors, her message during the last few weeks of the campaign became "cancer shouldn't matter," while her opponent could stay above the fray and reinforce his message, "I'm for economic development and higher teacher pay."

Table 13.5 shows that the distinction between predominantly positive coverage and mixed coverage was important not only during the postcancer stage but throughout much of the campaign. In addition, analyzing by campaign stage suggests an important difference in negative coverage as well. During the first three stages of the campaign, Heitkamp received significantly more purely negative coverage of personal characteristics than Hoeven did. After Labor Day, however, the amount of negative coverage was equal. Studies that only examine post–Labor Day coverage would have completely missed this difference. The importance of this distinction is that during the early stages, when the candidates are framing their campaigns and introducing themselves to the voting public as gubernatorial candidates, Heitkamp was painted in a negative light, whereas Hoeven was portrayed in a positive light. These early impressions were never challenged later.[33]

There is also a considerable difference for positive and mixed coverage: 27.2 percent of Heitkamp's personal coverage was predominantly positive, whereas 38.8 percent of Hoeven's personal coverage was predominantly positive. The comparable numbers for predominantly mixed coverage are almost a mirror image. Heitkamp received 36.6 percent mixed coverage, but only 27.1 percent of Hoeven's coverage was classified as mixed.

## Conclusion

The 2000 gubernatorial campaign in North Dakota, which was won by John Hoeven, was historic for the state in that a woman was a major party nominee for the first time. Although it was a first for North Dakota, it was not a first in U.S. history. Previous studies of female gubernatorial candidates provide a guide for what to expect from media coverage in this race. These preliminary data suggest that some of these expectations were met; others were not. The female candidate did receive greater attention from the media about her personal characteristics than her male opponent. However, she also received greater attention about her issue positions than her opponent. The counterintuitive findings for issue coverage suggest that previous findings may no longer be true or that they cannot be generalized to races such as this one. Further analysis of a wider variety of female-male elections is warranted to assess the generalization issues and the accuracy of past research, now that female candidates are less of a novelty.

In addition, we demonstrate in this chapter that research on media coverage must begin before the post–Labor Day period to capture a complete picture of the differences in media coverage. Except for the coverage of Heitkamp's personal characteristics after the cancer announcement, there was little personal or issue coverage for either candidate after Labor Day. By ignoring the earlier campaign stages, researchers overlook much of the important coverage of candidates and therefore risk presenting an incomplete description of media, women, and politics.

Finally, the truly unique aspect of this campaign was the cancer announcement and its effect on media coverage. With this research, we hope to begin to understand this relationship. Further research comparing such personal matters—like health revelations—of male and female candidates is needed to determine whether gender plays a role in this coverage. Currently, there are few cases that can be used for comparison. Most of the cases involving male candidates are of older male candidates in which age and fragility become an issue. This type of health matter is not ideal for comparison because age is a known factor when entering a campaign, as opposed to an unexpected health concern arising during the campaign. However, case studies such as this one lay the foundation for comparative research when other, more comparable cases develop.

This particular case study tells a story not only about the 2000 North Dakota gubernatorial campaign but also about media coverage in general. The first lesson is that framing matters. Not only does framing matter, but it occurs early in the campaign. Most of the issue and personal characteristics coverage was printed long before Labor Day—the traditional start of the campaign season. This finding makes sense, considering that the whole concept behind framing is to establish a context through which we interpret future activities and stories about the campaign and the candidates.

A second lesson is that issue coverage during campaigns is important to analyze. Transmitting candidate messages about issue positions provides a significant amount of information that voters rely on to help them make choices between candidates. If the media portrays one candidate as more or less capable in dealing with an important issue, based on the sex of the candidate, this difference can influence voter support. However, given the results of this study, the differences in coverage of issue positions may not be consistent. One explanation may be that campaigns and candidates really do matter. The amount and focus of issue coverage may differ among the various races where female and male candidates vie for elective office because of the campaign style of the candidates. If female candidates emphasize their concern or expertise about traditionally male issue areas or male candidates highlight their concerns about traditionally female issue areas, then media coverage may reflect these positions. Furthermore, expectations about issue positions can differ according to the background of the candidates. Regardless of their sex, candidates raised in rural areas may be viewed as more capable of dealing with agricultural issues, and candidates from urban areas are expected to be more competent dealing with issues affecting cities.

The third lesson learned from this case study concerns political media coverage of the personal characteristics of the candidates. Based on past research, it is expected that the female candidate will receive more coverage of her personal characteristics than her male counterpart. That was true in this case, but it represents only part of the story. The other important parts of the story involve the timing and tone of the coverage. Most of the coverage of personal characteristics occurred during the postnomination stage. This timing is important because it ties directly into the important time for the framing of the campaigns. This is the period when the candidates try to set the tone for the campaign and to introduce themselves to the entire electorate—especially the independents and peripheral voters, who paid little attention during the nomination stage. In this case study, the most significant findings about personal characteristics are that Heitkamp received twice as much negative coverage during the postnomination stage than Hoeven did during the *entire* campaign and that she received significantly more "mixed" coverage throughout the campaign. By examining both the timing and the tone of the coverage, this study and future studies can better understand the importance of media description of the candidates as well as how the media communicate normative evaluations of the candidates.

A final lesson that can be learned from this chapter confronts the notion that women are still viewed as novelties in the political world and thus are treated differently by the media. We suggest that the novelty factor still exists, but to a lesser degree. As more women run for elective office at the local, state, and national levels, this notion may become increasingly outdated.

# 14

## *Case:* The Maverick Campaign and Election of Jesse Ventura

### Steven C. Wagner and Stephen I. Frank

Initially, almost no one took Jesse Ventura's candidacy to become Minnesota's thirty-eighth governor seriously. No one thought a former professional-wrestler-turned-gubernatorial-candidate for the Reform Party had any chance to beat Hubert H. Humphrey III, the very well known Democrat-Farmer-Labor (DFL; Minnesota's Democratic Party) Party candidate, or Norman Coleman, the Republican Party candidate.

Jesse Ventura is the first Reform Party candidate to win a major public office anywhere in the country. How did he win? He is not a liberal, a conservative, or even really a centrist in the true sense of the term. As a candidate, he never stayed "on issue" and always deflected tough questions about policy positions from his competitors and the media, offering very little in the way of specifics. Nonetheless, Ventura obtained 773,713 votes (37 percent); Coleman received 717,350 votes (34 percent); and Humphrey ended with 587,528 votes, or 29 percent of the total.[1]

We suggest that Ventura won because of several factors: the increase in the numbers of independent voters, public campaign funds, high voter participation, same-day voter registration, weak or injured opposition candidates, and a terrific media campaign.[2]

## More Independent Voters

In Minnesota and elsewhere, more and more voters are seeing themselves as independent voters. The Minnesota Poll reported that about 20 percent of Minnesota voters in the mid-1950s saw themselves as independents.[3] However, the St. Cloud State University (SCSU) Survey reports that about 40 percent of all Minnesotans see themselves as independent voters today.[4] This doubling of self-identified independents since the 1950s has significant consequences for the state's elected offices and helps explain

Ventura's election. Be that as it may, as is true of most independents across the county, independents usually vote Democrat or Republican in elections.

Voters in Minnesota have a long history of voting for candidates running under a label other than Democrat or Republican. In recent years, independent Minnesotans have supported Reform Party candidates. In 1992, Ross Perot captured 24 percent of the presidential vote, and in 1996, he obtained 12 percent of the vote in the state.[5] Particularly important for Ventura's candidacy was who voted for Perot. In 1992 and 1996, alienated middle-class voters and young, male voters living in suburban areas supported Perot. These voting blocs, in turn, became important constituencies of Ventura's campaign.

## Campaign Finance

In Minnesota, similar to what we find in approximately twelve other states, candidates for state office have the option of accepting partial public funding of their campaigns. If a candidate accepts public funds, he or she must adhere to spending limits. The candidate's party, however, may freely spend to assist the election of its candidate.

Humphrey and Coleman, Ventura's two opponents in the gubernatorial race, both agreed to the spending limit of approximately $2 million. Coleman's share of available public funds was $559,670, and Humphrey's share was $603,544.[6] Ventura also accepted the spending limits, but his share was $308,840.[7] Although Ventura received less public money than either Humphrey or Coleman, the spending limits imposed on Humphrey and Coleman ensured that they would not grossly outspend Ventura, giving him a fighting chance.

## Voter Participation

If there is one politically oriented activity that is easy to do in Minnesota, it is voting. State law has made registration easy and voting simple. Thus, turnout in Minnesota tends to be high compared to averages in other states. Average turnout for a presidential election is 65 percent. Turnout for Ventura's election was 61 percent, the highest in the nation for a nonpresidential election year. Relatively high levels of education and competitive political parties in Minnesota also positively influence voter registration and turnout.

Many in Minnesota argue that voter turnout is high simply because registration is easy. For instance, candidates and parties may go door-to-door with voter applications and even help people fill out the forms.[8] Minnesotans may register when they apply for their driver's license or when paying annual income taxes. In the case of college students, they may register when they pay their tuition.[9] Finally, Minnesota even allows voters to register to vote at the polls on election day. In the 1996 presidential election and the 1998 gubernatorial election, approximately 15 percent of the voters registered on election day.[10] This percentage was slightly higher than the average of past elections, possibly because of Ventura's candidacy.

An important linchpin in Ventura's gubernatorial campaign strategy was his ability to excite newly eligible and alienated voters both to register and actually vote. Ventura had previously shown his ability at capturing new voters. In 1990, when he ran and won the Brooklyn Park (a suburb of Minneapolis) mayoral race, his election was due to the turnout of new voters. Approximately 20,000 people voted in that election. This number compares to the 2,600 votes cast in the previous mayoral election.

## Republican and DFL Candidates

Although the Republican Party and the DFL Party nominated what initially seemed excellent candidates, both candidates were rather bland campaigners, committed several tactical campaign errors, and eventually became what can be described as straight men for Ventura's populist campaign. The Republican Party nominated St. Paul's incumbent mayor, Norman Coleman. Although Coleman once was a DFL member and was initially elected as St. Paul's mayor as a DFL candidate, he had switched to the Republican Party three years before the gubernatorial election and quickly adopted conservative policies. But the staunchly loyal and conservative members of the Republican Party did not completely trust Coleman. These individuals tended to see Coleman as an East Coast liberal and former Humphrey employee. We suggest that Coleman was a wounded candidate from the beginning of the general election campaign.

The winner of the DFL Party primary was Hubert H. Humphrey III. Humphrey had obvious name recognition and had served the state for the past sixteen years as Minnesota's attorney general. As a champion of Minnesota consumers, Humphrey had just won a $6 billion settlement from the tobacco companies, which remained fresh in the minds of voters. Overall, Humphrey was a social liberal.

The Republican Party nominated a pragmatic conservative. The DFL Party nominated a pragmatic liberal. The two parties saw their candidates as safe bets. Coleman could easily appeal to conservative Minnesotans, and Humphrey, with probably the premier name in the state, could easily appeal to liberal Minnesotans.

## Candidate Jesse Ventura

Jesse Ventura entered the gubernatorial race because he thought a growing state budget surplus belonged to the voters. He argued that the established political forces were either too conservative or too liberal. According to Ventura, the bipolar Republican and DFL Parties had forgotten the more moderate voters like himself. He saw himself as a regular "working stiff" whom entrenched politicians had forgotten. He suggested then that most Minnesotans shared his fiscally conservative and socially liberal views.

Ventura is a self-defined libertarian. He argues for individual liberty, free choice, less government regulation, and lower taxes. At the same time, Ventura is clearly not a pure libertarian. He is a strong supporter of public schools and believes in government support of urban mass transit.

Ventura is also a populist. He sees himself as a reformer of the establishment and an adherent of good government practices. He promotes open political participation and shuns special interest control of governmental processes. Also important is that Ventura is an entertainer. Thus, he was able to approach the campaign as an entertainer, catching the attention of the media, while Humphrey and Coleman played a traditional game of politics. Joseph Kunkle suggests that Ventura's candidacy fit into an increasingly potent trend in U.S. politics.[11] As parties weaken and the media coverage of campaigns becomes more pervasive, the field is wide open for entertainers to break into politics and redefine the rules.

Ventura ran as an outsider, lacking a party, well-developed ideology, or even the political background earlier entertainer-turned-politicians have had.[12] Ventura was clearly aware of the potential his entertainer and celebrity status held for his candidacy, and he milked that status for all its worth. He approached the campaign as the heir to the character Howard Beal in the movie *Network,* who shouts, "I'm mad as hell, and I'm not going to take it any more!" Ventura had the ability to tap into the mother lode of popular culture at the national level, jump across the boundary from entertainment to politics, and persuade enough voters that they had nothing to lose by him winning. Finally, it was clear that Ventura would stand out from the Republican and DFL candidates. Ventura has a very distinct speaking style and deep voice, a shaved head, and is 6 feet, 4 inches tall, weighing approximately 250 pounds. Not the average politician.

## Campaign Strategy, Issues, and Debates

Ventura's campaign strategy was rather simple. Early in the campaign, his advisers decided to seek free publicity and make heavy use of the Internet. The campaign targeted the greater Twin Cities area because half of all eligible voters reside in that part of the state. Accordingly, the major Twin Cities media outlets reach about 80 percent of the state.

Ventura campaigned as a classic outsider. Initially, it appeared Ventura could not possibly win the election. Polling data from a statewide survey taken in mid-September showed Humphrey with a substantial lead. Approximately 50 percent of likely voters indicated a commitment to voting for Humphrey.[13] Norm Coleman had the support of 29 percent, and Ventura had a lock on only 10 percent in that same poll.

However, a candidate outside the major parties, with no apparent chance of winning, is given extraordinary latitude by the voters, other candidates, and media. Ventura took full advantage of this opportunity. It was easy, given his persona. He embraced his outsider status and was irrepressible and outrageous. He was often loud, confrontational, and brash but always newsworthy and memorable. Ventura made heavy use of props—his military experience, leather coats, and his body. Without a doubt, Ventura provided voters with a candidate that contrasted with "politics as usual."

Ventura's campaign style and his policy positions showed he understood the importance of using pop culture to attract young voters. A typical campaign event had Ventura quoting late rock-and-roll singers Jim Morrison and Jerry Garcia. Ventura poked fun at DFLer Humphrey and Republican Coleman by giving them street gang names, the "ReBLOODicans" and "DemoCRYPTS."

A key element in Ventura's success was making inroads with middle-class, moderate voters. As it turned out, Ventura was immediately able to connect to the middle class. He argued that he could represent the average taxpayer because he was an average taxpayer. At campaign events, Ventura spoke with candor and compassion. He offered an antiestablishment message that voters sought. Importantly, Ventura attacked taxes, the bane of the middle classes. Completely without any details, Ventura suggested that property taxes be frozen, property tax assessors be eliminated, and previous state budget surpluses returned to the taxpayer. What is remarkable about these statements is how grand they were, but neither Humphrey nor Coleman called attention to the fact that most of previous budget surpluses were returned and those dollars not returned were expended on education and transportation. They failed to address this opportunity to minimize Ventura's thunder.

One of the problems Ventura faced early in the campaign was the "gender gap." It was clear that males, especially those in the eighteen- to twenty-six-year-old age group, who were white suburbanites, easily related to Ventura. His persona as a "bad boy" former professional wrestler with a fondness for personal watercraft and motorcycles fit nicely with his appeal to males. However, Ventura's advisers expressed some concern that this persona might be a double-edged sword, working against his ability to attract female voters. Thus, early in the campaign, Ventura chose as his running mate Mae Schunk, a sixty-four-year-old public schoolteacher.

If there was a single, identifiable turning point in the campaign, it came when Humphrey insisted he would not debate Coleman without also including Ventura. Humphrey thought it was a stroke of genius. But he incorrectly thought that, if Ventura appeared raw and uninformed, the voters would stay with a safe, professional politician. As it turned out, the strategy was a major error. Ventura's socially tolerant views attracted Humphrey supporters. His fiscally conservative views attracted Coleman supporters. Most importantly, inclusion on the stage with Humphrey and Coleman told everyone that Ventura was a legitimate candidate.

All three candidates participated in nine debates. Three received statewide coverage. Normally, debates reinforce the existing attitudes and opinions of likely voters. But in this case, the large number of debates attracted an unusual amount of attention and better than average broadcast and print media coverage. Thus, voters and those otherwise unlikely to vote paid attention to the debates more than might be expected, for three reasons: One, there was not an incumbent governor. Incumbents have an unusually high chance of reelection. Thus, all three candidates appeared as likely winners of the debates and the election. Second, the tracking polls suggested likely voters were fluid in terms of which candidate they intended to support. Thus, voters were more attentive to the debates as a source of information about the candidates. Third, Jesse Ventura was an unknown commodity that Humphrey insisted be included in the debates. Thus, the media and the voters paid attention to the debates to see the show Ventura was likely to offer.

Throughout the debates, Humphrey attempted to convey the image of a decent individual. He may have succeeded, but it also became clear that he lacked imagination and personality. Coleman also attempted to appear as a nice guy. Perhaps he did, but he also conveyed the image of an extreme fiscal and social conservative. While Humphrey and Coleman fought over policy positions and ideology, Ventura continuously told everyone that his campaign was about rejection of politics as usual, as seen in the behavior of his two opponents.

Using his theatrical skills to entertain the crowds, Ventura quickly became the star. He was funny and proved to be a plain speaker of personal or homespun wisdom. Indeed, he appeared raw and often uninformed. He even conveyed a certain pride in not knowing policy details. His ignorance became an asset and helped to immediately connect with the voters, who often do not know minute details of tax and spending policies.

Coleman and Humphrey committed an error by not attacking Ventura, because they thought he would fade and both could then capture his supporters. They accepted the "wasted vote theory" that suggested supporters of independent candidates would eventually vote for main party candidates once they realized their candidate could not win and thus, their vote would otherwise be wasted.

The Minnesota Poll tracked voter support of the three candidates throughout the campaign and in October reported that Ventura had climbed to 21 percent support.[14] Humphrey's support had dropped from 53 percent in September to 35 percent, and Coleman was at 34 percent. Ventura's advisers were becoming confident their candidate had a real chance of winning.

## The Internet

Ventura used the Internet because it was an inexpensive and efficient use of valuable campaign resources. It also allowed Ventura to broadcast his message without interference. If a problem arose, his home page provided a place to make immediate clarification.

Ventura's "Geek Squad" volunteers maintained the site. They videotaped campaign events and downloaded them almost immediately. The volunteers also constructed and maintained the "JesseNet," an electronic mailing list of 3,000 names. The list enabled quick fundraising and campaign rally organization capability. The most effective use of JesseNet occurred before the "Drive to Victory Tour," a seventy-two-hour recreational vehicle tour of Minnesota to rally voters and get them out on election day. The Internet also provided the communication device the campaign used to send instructions to the drivers and other volunteers. Potential voters unable to participate in the tour were able to watch almost on a real-time basis. The geek squad traveled with the tour, taking pictures and immediately loading them on the home page.

## The Media

The campaign's resources did not allow Ventura to begin media advertising until September. At that time, the campaign ran four different television advertisements. The first advertisement was soft. A picture of the U.S. flag appeared on screen and the voice-over told voters that Humphrey and Coleman's partisan fighting was hurting Ventura's efforts at unifying the people of Minnesota. The second advertisement reinforced Ventura's message that he, with Minnesota, was standing up to special interests. It pictured two child action figures. The Ventura figure, appearing in a business suit, argued with the second figure, dressed as the Evil Special Interest Man, who tried to give the Ventura figure money. The Ventura figure responded, "I don't want your dirty money" and then socked the Evil Special Interest Man.

The third advertisement, once again, made use of the action figures. This time the ad featured them preparing a war wagon for the Drive to Victory

Tour. The fourth advertisement ran the Sunday before the election and is sure to become a classic political campaign advertisement. Once it became apparent that Ventura might actually win, Humphrey and Coleman began to point out that Ventura lacked the education and experience to prepare him to govern. In response, the fourth advertisement showed Minnesota voters that Jesse Ventura was no longer Jesse "The Body" Ventura but now he was Jesse "The Mind" Ventura. The advertisement had Ventura sitting on a rotating pedestal, with his back to the screen. Slowly the pedestal rotated until he faced forward. At that point, it was clear Ventura simulated Auguste Rodin's statue *The Thinker*. Once he had fully turned to the screen, he winked.

Sure enough, on Tuesday, November 3, 1998, Ventura won the election to be Minnesota's governor with 37 percent of the vote. As he put it, "We shocked the world."

# 15

## Case: Showdown in the Empire State—Clinton Versus Lazio

### Jeffrey Kraus

With the words, "I surely will miss it, but there are other things to do in life and there comes a time," retiring U.S. senator Daniel Patrick Moynihan (D-N.Y.) triggered what would turn out to be the most-watched Senate race in 2000.[1] Moynihan, who had been elected four times, announced his departure almost two years before the election. Moynihan's decision, announced three days after then-Representative Charles Schumer (D-N.Y.) defeated three-term Republican senator Alfonse M. D'Amato, brought an end to an era in New York politics. For almost twenty years, Moynihan and D'Amato were New York's political odd couple. Moynihan, a former Harvard economics professor, focused on a variety of policy issues. D'Amato, the one-time town supervisor of Hempstead, earned the nickname "Senator Pothole" by concentrating on constituent service and funneling federal projects and programs to New York.

Over the course of the next twenty-four months, the senatorial contest would take a number of what seemed to be unpredictable turns—only to be overshadowed by a presidential election that would take more than five weeks after election day to decide. Moynihan's initial announcement resulted in immediate speculation as to who would compete for the first open Senate race in New York in more than four decades. Among the candidates mentioned for what appeared to be a wide-open field were several Democrats: U.S. Housing and Urban Development secretary Andrew M. Cuomo, son of former governor Mario M. Cuomo; Robert T. Kennedy, son of Robert F. Kennedy, who had held this seat at the time of his assassination in 1968; Westchester representative Nita Lowey; State Comptroller Carl McCall, and U.S. Health and Human Services secretary Donna Shalala. On the Republican side, the potential candidates were New York mayor Rudolph W. Giuliani, Long Island representative Rick Lazio, and the vanquished D'Amato.[2]

## Clinton Enters the Race

This wide-open field eventually winnowed, but not without a stunning development. Representative Charles Rangel (D-N.Y.) suggested that First Lady Hillary Clinton become a candidate for the seat.[3] Senator Robert Torricelli (D-N.J.), the chair of the Democratic Senate Campaign Committee, also floated the idea in a conversation with NBC's Tim Russert before an appearance on "Meet the Press."[4] Russert then reported that Torricelli had told him "that, if he had to guess, he believes that Hillary Rodham Clinton will run."[5] The Rangel and Torricelli pronouncements fueled speculation that the first lady would run. Clinton's spokesperson did nothing to discourage the talk, stating that the first lady was "certainly flattered by the speculation" and adding, "at this point, she has no plans to run for elective office, but she hasn't ruled it out. . . . I can tell you that she does like New York."[6]

Clinton then began a round of consultations with New York political operatives regarding the race. Beginning with Harold Ickes, the deputy chief of staff in President Clinton's first administration and a veteran of New York politics, Clinton went on to meet with politicians, union leaders, and political strategists to determine whether her candidacy would be viable. In March 1999, Clinton spoke at a New York fundraiser sponsored by the Women's Leadership Forum, where she suggested why, after eight years of investigation and scandal, she might be willing to subject herself to a Senate campaign: "We cannot drop out of the political process and leave the arena to those with very specific agendas. . . . You can say all you want about the flaws of our political system, but when it comes right down to it, somebody is going to make the decisions."[7]

Over the next few months, Hillary Clinton would move (not always smoothly) toward announcing her candidacy. When the New York Yankees appeared at the White House after winning the World Series, the first lady (a Chicago native) wore a Yankees cap and claimed to have been a lifelong fan of the team (a contention believed by no one). She purchased a home for herself and the president in Chappaqua, a suburb in Westchester County, New York, and then embarked on what she called a "listening tour," to learn more about the state and the problems of its people.

In August 1999, Clinton had to sidestep a controversy created by her husband. President Bill Clinton offered clemency to sixteen convicted terrorists from the Armed Forces of National Liberation (FALN), a Puerto Rican nationalist group. The move was depicted by Republicans as an effort by the president to win Latino votes for his wife among New York's large Puerto Rican community. To make matters worse for candidate Clinton, her husband's decision was opposed by the Federal Bureau of Investigations (FBI) and the Federal Bureau of Prisons, as well as a number of law enforcement groups. Three weeks after the president's offer of clemency, Clinton came out against it, arguing that the prisoners had taken too long to renounce violence, a condition for their release. Her position won her a few friends in the law enforcement community but also managed to anger a number of Latino politicians.

Hillary Clinton managed to alienate another key voting block in New York, Jewish voters, through her own actions (or, it can be argued, inactions). Traveling to the Middle East in her capacity as first lady, she visited Israel—a prerequisite for any candidate interested in running for office in New York because of the state's large Jewish population. As a means of providing balance to the trip, she also decided to visit the portion of the West Bank controlled by the Palestinian Authority.

At Ramallah, she joined Suha Arafat—wife of the Palestinian leader— in dedicating a new maternal health care program that had been financed by the United States. In her remarks, Arafat stated: "Our people have been subjected to the daily intensive use of poisonous gas by the Israeli forces, which has led to an increase in cancer cases among women and children."[8] Clinton failed to immediately condemn Arafat's statement, triggering a firestorm of criticism from pro-Israeli interests. She was denounced by Jewish leaders and Republicans for standing by silently in the face of Arafat's comments. Her explanation for her inaction—that the translation had been faulty—failed to satisfy her critics.

Clinton's missteps were characteristic of first-time candidates. As former representative Mickey Edwards (R-Okla.) observed, "This is what happens when you can't keep your mouth shut. . . . you get in trouble. . . . I call it bubble-gum mouth. You put in a nickel, and something comes out. It's just like they feel compelled to talk."[9] In February 2000, more than a year after the idea was first floated, Hillary Clinton formally announced her candidacy for the U.S. Senate from New York. With her husband seated onstage, the first lady declared, "I am pleased to announce my candidacy." It was expected that she would face Rudolph Giuliani, the term-limited mayor of the city of New York in the general election.

## The Giuliani Candidacy

Rudy Giuliani had considered running for this Senate seat years earlier. After he led the successful prosecution of Bronx Democratic leader Stanley Friedman for political corruption in 1986, speculation began as to what the then U.S. attorney would do next. When asked about a possible Senate race against Senator Moynihan in 1988, Giuliani told the *New York Times,* "I think I'd be very good," adding that "I don't have any question that I could do the job in an innovative and creative way."[10] However, Giuliani decided to remain U.S. attorney after he and Senator D'Amato could not agree on a successor.[11]

Giuliani found himself in a similar situation for 2000. Because he was term-limited, there were questions as to how the mayor would continue his political career. Between December 1997 and December 1998, Giuliani visited twenty states, suggesting a presidential or vice presidential candidacy. Moynihan's decision to leave the Senate created an opportunity for the Republicans to take back a Senate seat that had been in Democratic hands for twenty-four years, further cementing their control over the Senate. Giuliani, who had managed to become mayor of heavily Democratic New York City a few years prior, was perceived by many as an attractive candidate, despite lingering questions about his loyalty to the Republican Party. As a result of intense pressure from national Republican leaders, Governor George E. Pataki dropped his opposition to Giuliani and announced his support in August 1999. Pataki's decision forced Lazio from the race, opening the field for Giuliani.

For the next seven months, Giuliani would raise millions of dollars; poke fun at Hillary Clinton's "listening tour" and lack of New York roots, and shift some of his positions in order to make his candidacy more palatable to upstate voters. During this time, he never moved beyond a statistical dead heat with Clinton. It appeared that New York would witness one of the costliest and most contentious Senate races in U.S. history.

Then, Giuliani's campaign took some unexpected turns. On March 15, a young security guard named Patrick Dorismond was killed in an altercation with undercover police officers. The mayor and his police commissioner launched a campaign to discredit Dorismond by releasing his criminal record. Dorismond had been arrested twice as an adult for assault and gun possession and also had been arrested as a thirteen year old. In making that information available, the police released a sealed juvenile record. Even Giuliani's supporters were critical of his decision to demonize the unarmed Dorismond. "Rudy Giuliani has screwed up, and screwed up big time," a *New York Post* columnist wrote.[12] In the wake of the Dorismond incident, a New York Times/CBS News poll found Giuliani's approval rating had dropped to 32 percent.[13] The same poll showed Clinton ahead of Giuliani, 52 percent to 42 percent, with the two in a statistical tie in upstate New York.

Giuliani's prospects were further undermined by a potential challenge from the right. Joseph DioGuardi, a former member of Congress representing the Westchester area, announced that he would seek the Conservative, Independence, and Right to Life Party nominations. Such a candidacy would siphon conservative votes from Giuliani, ensuring a Clinton victory.

Two personal matters also had an impact on the mayor's Senate bid. First, in late April, Giuliani announced that he had prostate cancer. The mayor said that he would continue his campaign while considering various treatment options. When asked how this illness would affect his Senate campaign, the mayor said, "I have no idea."[14]

Less than two weeks later, Giuliani's personal life was shattered. He announced that he and his wife of sixteen years, Donna Hanover, were filing for a legal separation. He said that the announcement was prompted by press reports of his relationship with a "very good friend," Judith Nathan. Although separations and divorces in U.S. politics are no longer taboo, Giuliani's announcement differed in two respects. First, his wife learned of the news with everyone else—through a televised press briefing. The second difference was his wife's reaction. Shortly after the mayor's press conference, Donna Hanover made a statement in front of Gracie Mansion, the official residence of New York City mayors. She accused Giuliani of having a longtime relationship with another woman, an unnamed staff person: "I had hoped that we could keep this marriage together. . . . Beginning last May, I made a major effort to bring us back together. Rudy and I reestablished some of our personal intimacy through the fall. At that point, he chose another path."[15]

Within days of this turn of events, Giuliani announced that "this is not the right time for me to run for office."[16] He said that his pending treatment for prostate cancer meant that he could not mount an effective campaign for the Senate. Instead, Giuliani committed himself to completing his term as mayor.

Giuliani's departure paved the way for Rick Lazio to return to the contest. Lazio, the Long Island lawmaker whose voting record was described by Michael Barone and Grant Ujifusa as being "in the middle of the House," quickly picked up the support of Governor Pataki, the national Republican establishment, and the Conservative Party, as well as the "anti-Hillary" vote.[17] In a poll taken less than three weeks after he entered the race, Lazio and Clinton were tied at 44 percent.[18]

## The Issues

The campaign was less about specific issues and more about the messages and images that each candidate attempted to convey about the other. The Lazio strategy was an attempt to duplicate Pataki's successful 1994 campaign against then governor of New York, Mario Cuomo: Like Pataki, Lazio sold himself as an uncontroversial, pro-choice Catholic who could win by not being a hated liberal icon. Lazio's campaign also emphasized the "carpetbagger" issue and what its managers portrayed as the "sleaziness" that surrounded the first lady and the president.[19]

The Clinton campaign depicted Lazio as a Newt Gingrich conservative while presenting plans on education, health care, and the upstate economy. This focus on issues salient to New Yorkers was designed to overcome her lack of experience in elective office and to shift the focus of the campaign away from her personality.

Some issues did emerge in the campaign. Lazio made campaign finance an issue when he challenged Clinton, during their first debate, to agree to a ban on "soft money." After some postdebate haggling, both sides agreed to the ban. Although Lazio may have pushed the issue, it probably had little positive effect on his campaign. He would probably have benefited more from soft money spending because of the Republican Party's greater capacity to raise funds, as well as the political right's antipathy toward the Clintons. Also, as Matthew Carolan and Raymond Keating observe, "Lazio wasted time on campaign-finance reform—an issue few voters care about or understand."[20] Some voters may have been repelled when, during their first debate, Lazio marched over to Clinton on the other side of the stage and demanded that she sign a pledge to ban soft money. This gesture helped boost Clinton's support among women voters.

In New York, with its large population of Jewish voters, the Middle East is always an issue. Both Clinton and Lazio aggressively courted the Jewish vote. Clinton's embrace of Suha Arafat was resurrected, as was her one-time support for a Palestinian state. Lazio attacked President Bill Clinton for not condemning Yasser Arafat for his role in encouraging civil disorder on the West Bank and for failing to move the U.S. Embassy to Jerusalem. Lazio criticized Hillary Clinton's acceptance of $50,000 from a fundraiser held by the American Muslim Alliance (her campaign returned the contribution after it was reported by the news media). In the days before the election, a State Republican Committee telephone campaign linked Clinton to terrorist groups like those responsible for bombing the naval ship, USS *Cole*. Criticized for this tactic, after some delay, Lazio said: "I would have preferred that that would not have been mentioned in those calls. Those were not done out of my campaign."[21]

The Clinton campaign countered by using a picture (that had been released by the White House) of Lazio warmly shaking Arafat's hand while visiting the Middle East. They were also able to produce a fundraising solicitation letter from Lazio to the same Muslim group that had donated money to the Clinton campaign. Hillary Clinton also campaigned extensively in Jewish neighborhoods and among Jewish groups. In a letter to the Orthodox Union, a Manhattan-based organization, Clinton wrote: "You can be sure that I will be an active, committed advocate for a strong and secure Israel, able to live in peace with its neighbors, with the United States Embassy located in its capital, Jerusalem."[22] Although Lazio made some inroads with conservative orthodox Jews, Clinton was able to hold this traditionally Democratic voting bloc. A Marist Institute of Public Opinion poll found Clinton leading Lazio among Jewish voters by a margin of 67 to 29 percent.[23]

Although the Middle East was a major issue in New York City and its suburbs, the condition of the economy was a salient issue in upstate New York. As Barone and Ujifusa stated, "While much of inland industrial America has revived in the 1990s, Upstate New York remains in deep trouble. Upstate no longer has central transportation arteries as in the days of the New York Central's water level route, and so is off the beaten path; its population has not risen much since the 1950s."[24] Clinton campaigned extensively in this traditionally Republican area and made the region's economic revitalization a major theme of her campaign, claiming at one point that it was "the most important issue in this race."[25] Her proposals for economic recovery included lower utility rates and taxes, financing for technological development, entrepreneurial incubators, a technology extension program, and support for the region's tourism and agriculture. In contrast, Lazio contended that the region had "turned the corner."[26] Joseph Dolman wrote that "for all his ordinary-guy pretense, Lazio just doesn't seem to understand upstate New York or its protracted economic troubles. He seems more eager to prove that he is not Clinton."[27]

The abortion issue, although not as prominent, also had an effect on the race. Both candidates were pro-choice, but an exchange during their second debate on the issue may have been decisive. Clinton stated that she would not vote to confirm a Supreme Court nominee who opposed *Roe v. Wade.* Lazio answered by stating that he supported abortion rights but that he would vote for "the most experienced, qualified" nominee.[28] According to Clinton's pollster, "the choice issue was really galvanizing for suburban women."[29]

## The Outcome

Hillary Clinton defeated Rick Lazio by 55 to 43 percent. Clinton carried New York City by a three-to-one margin. Outside New York City, Lazio received 50 percent to Clinton's 46 percent. But that margin was not enough to overcome the Democratic plurality in New York City.

Why did Clinton win? A large voter turnout in heavily Democratic New York City and Clinton's strong showing in traditional Republican areas carried her to victory. Her willingness to campaign in upstate New York, an area ignored by most statewide Democratic candidates, was critical to her success. Her showing indicates that an aggressive Democratic campaign in traditionally Republican areas can attract votes to the Democratic column, suggesting an erosion of party loyalty. This lesson was not lost on Governor Pataki who, in early 2001, began to court a number of key constituencies in New York City in an effort to counter Democratic inroads in upstate New York. The most visible manifestation of this change in strategy was the governor's visit to Vieques, Puerto Rico, and his subsequent statements urging the Navy to end its use of the area for target practice, a position designed to court the city's Puerto Rican voters.

Lazio failed to mobilize the Republican base. He never articulated an argument for his candidacy. Instead, he attempted to make the election a referendum on the first lady and the president. Although a similar strategy may have worked for George Pataki in 1994, it failed miserably in this race. By 1994, Governor Cuomo had worn out his welcome after twelve years in office. On the contrary, President Clinton and Hillary Clinton remained very popular in New York. The "anti-Clinton" approach might have worked in a number of other states, but not in New York. Lazio also attempted to distance himself from George W. Bush's flagging campaign in the state. Rather than support Bush's tax cut proposal, Lazio instead presented a more modest tax reduction plan. The failure to create an identity or at least align himself with his party's standard-bearer resulted in a confusing message to the electorate. Lazio attempted to define himself by who he was not rather than who he was.

It can be argued that Representative Lazio never had the opportunity to develop a message. Clinton spent 489 days campaigning and visited every one of New York's sixty-two counties; Lazio had less than six months to present himself to the voters. "If he would have had a year, Hillary Clinton would have been dust," said Michael Long, the chairman of the state Republican Party. "We did the best that we could. We were not only fighting Hillary Clinton, we were fighting the White House. We were fighting the President of the United States," Long added.[30] It turned out to be a very expensive fight. According to documents filed with the Federal Election Commission (2001), Lazio spent more than $40 million and Clinton nearly $30 million. Add to this the nearly $21 million expended by Rudy Giuliani, and the total spent on the New York Senate race exceeded $91 million, making it the most expensive Senate campaign in the country during the 2000 election cycle.

## Postscript

Immediately after the election, Hillary Clinton attempted to make the transition from first lady and celebrity candidate to one of 100 senators. Her task was complicated by the controversy surrounding the last-minute pardons by President Clinton of more than 140 individuals, including the fugitive financier Mark Rich. She also came under fire for the lease on her Manhattan office. At over $514,000, the rent was the highest paid by any U.S. senator. This problem was compounded by the criticism of her husband's decision to spend $800,000 on a penthouse suite in midtown Manhattan for his postpresidency office. President Clinton would eventually decide to relocate his office to a less expensive space in Harlem.

A Marist College Poll conducted in the wake of these controversies in 2001 found that only 30 percent of the respondents thought that Senator Clinton was doing an excellent or good job, whereas 42 percent did not rate her job performance positively. An April 2001 Marist poll placed her job approval rating at 35 percent. The same poll found that 48 percent of the respondents believed that she was doing a fair or poor job.[31] For most of

2001, the media covered each historic first for the new senator with fascination, and her swearing-in ceremony was a lead story.

With time, the media's focus on Clinton tended to reflect her position as a U.S. senator, and references to her first ladyship grew less prevalent. Hillary Rodham Clinton took a seat on the Budget Committee, Environment and Public Works Committee, and Health, Education, Labor, and Pensions Committee, where she pushed a host of legislative initiatives from minimum wage increases to loans for women entrepreneurs. Her historic first as the first former presidential spouse to be elected to public office was replaced with the historic first of becoming the first woman elected statewide in New York.

Lazio, after being briefly encouraged to run for Nassau County executive, has (like many other former members of Congress) become afflicted with "Potomac fever." In May 2001, he was named president and chief executive officer (CEO) of the Financial Services Forum, a public policy group made up of the CEOs of twenty-one financial services companies. Lazio's salary was $250,000 annually for his work as a lobbyist. At the time of this writing, speculation continues to swirl over whether he will reenter politics. In addition to saying that it was "possible but unlikely" that he would lobby Congress for the group when the one-year prohibition on lobbying by former members ends, Lazio has made overtures indicating his interest in running for office.[32] The Republican Party has also shown interest in having him pursue his old congressional seat from Long Island, which was held by Democrat Steve Israel after Lazio vacated the seat to run for U.S. Senate. Still remaining unresolved—and a reason to run again, should the party help address the problem—is roughly $750,000 in campaign debt from his failed Senate race.

As for the two other major figures in this race, Mayor Giuliani stayed to finish out his second term as mayor. His personal life continued to be a public spectacle. The cover story of the May 21, 2001, edition of *People* magazine was titled "The Mayor, the Wife, the Mistress." The story dealt with efforts by Donna Hanover, the mayor's wife, to bar his "very good friend," Judith Nathan, from Gracie Mansion. Despite their separation, the mayor and his wife had continued to live at the official residence, and Hanover sought to keep Nathan out so that the mayor's two children would not meet her. A judge granted Hanover's request. The mayor then stripped Hanover of her duties and the title of "first lady," reassigned members of her personal staff to other city agencies, and reduced her security detail.

The tragic terrorist attacks on New York City on September 11, 2001, lifted Giuliani's public stock, however. The mayor's calm and confident handling of the crisis was praised.

After leaving office, Giuliani remains a popular and controversial figure. The former mayor battled cancer and questions surrounded the use of and access to his mayoral papers, which upon leaving office he placed in the Rudolph W. Giuliani Center for Urban Affairs, a nonprofit organization. Several major talk shows and international documentaries focusing on the terrorist attacks centered on Giuliani, and several books and movies—including one featuring celebrated actor James Woods in the role as Giuliani—were put in production in the months after his mayorship. As of this writing, there continues to be talk of Giuliani pursuing another public office or taking a position with the television networks or another prominent endeavor.

Daniel Patrick Moynihan, whose decision to retire triggered this contest, resumed his academic career by becoming a professor at Syracuse University's Maxwell School of Government. On the day that Lazio was hired by the Financial Services Forum, Moynihan was named by President George W. Bush as co-chair of a national commission to study Social Security.

# PART 4

## CONCLUSION

# 16

## The Congressional Elections of 2000: Tradition Meets Competition in the New Age

### Robert Dewhirst and Ronald Keith Gaddie

Despite being lost in the saturated media coverage of the contest to determine the new occupant of the White House, the closeness and intensity of the 2000 election contests to determine the balance of power on Capitol Hill on the other end of Washington, D.C.'s famous Pennsylvania Avenue was equally dramatic and close. Among the particularly noteworthy and possibly even spectacular congressional contests that year were several classic Senate elections. The nationwide struggle to control the upper chamber included the much publicized first-time election of a sitting first lady, the election of another senator who spent almost $60 million of his own money to assure victory, the triumph—through the election of his spouse—of a Senate candidate who died several weeks before the election on November 7, and the election of another candidate determined only after the last mail-order ballot was counted many days after the polls closed.

The 2000 congressional elections renewed many of the traditions found in most preceding elections throughout the second half of the twentieth century. However, they also produced some distinctive findings and accelerated some recent trends, which for some might suggest the start of a new era in national politics in the United States. At least five noteworthy characteristics emerge from an examination of the 2000 congressional elections.

First, the 2000 elections did nothing to ease the precariously close balance of power between the two parties within both chambers on Capitol Hill. Second, the priority of winning "open seat" contests involving no incumbents—increasingly the most competitive battlegrounds in the second half of the twentieth century—attained new levels of intensity in 2000. Third, the financial arms race to fund political campaigns continued to escalate to record-setting levels. Fourth, incumbents seeking reelection again racked up high success rates, with senators doing well overall and representatives, again as usual, much better still. Finally, the impeachment and acquittal of President Bill Clinton failed to affect congressional elections to any apparent degree.

In sum, while individual candidates, particularly incumbents, continued their tradition of doing well electorally, there did not appear to be a national consensus and hence no governing mandate over what should be done. In the year 2000, a public, lacking any overarching issue burning across the political landscape, appeared to be largely content with the overall peace and prosperity found around the nation and generally unmoved by the frequently intense partisan battles waged throughout the lengthy campaign.

## An Even Closer Balance of Power

Incredibly, the 2000 election returns produced a Congress whose balance of power was even closer than before the election. This development most certainly frustrated leaders on both sides of the political aisle and left Republicans and Democrats alike both nervous about prospects for governing and scheming to gain leverage to win future battles. At the beginning of the fall campaigns for the House, that chamber had 222 Republicans to 209 Democrats, with two independents and two seats vacant. Following the elections, the Republicans held 221 seats, the Democrats had 212, and two seats were captured by independents. In sum, in the House, only seventeen seats changed partisan hands following the election; nine of these were open seats. As noted by Gary Jacobson, this seat exchange record was tied for third lowest among the past twenty-seven congressional elections.[1] For the third consecutive election, Democrats gained seats in the House, having picked up a net of thirteen seats since the watershed 1994 election.

Meanwhile, contrary to widespread political insider expectations, the 2000 elections generated more change on the other side of Capitol Hill. The balance of power in the Senate in the 106th Congress (1999–2001) was fifty-four Republicans and forty-six Democrats, with the election day producing a new chamber of fifty members from each party. This outcome surprised many pundits and prognosticators, who spent most of the election season describing the vulnerability of the Republican House majority while paying relatively little attention to the control of the upper chamber.

As has so often been the case, the setting for the 2000 elections could be said to have largely determined the outcome of the contests. To begin with, neither party benefited from the political setting in 2000.[2] For more than a decade, the number of voters who identified themselves as Democrats remained only slightly more numerous than their Republican counterparts. Perhaps even more significantly, there were no issues churning the electoral waters to favor either party and activate its faithful while simultaneously attracting the support of the uncommitted.[3] Hence, it appears that a relatively equal political hand dealt to each side produced a relatively equally distributed outcome.

In addition, there was widespread optimism about the state of the nation's economy. Economic growth, begun around the time President Bill Clinton came to office, continued at an incredibly healthy pace as the 2000 election campaign season approached. The gross domestic product remained high, the unemployment rate was exceptionally low, and the legacy of the record deficits of the Reagan-Bush years became a bad memory as lawmakers debated how best to handle anticipated surplus revenues. In sum, voters had plenty of reasons to be happy maintaining the status quo and few, if any, good reasons for wanting change. So incumbents, Democrats and Republicans alike, tended to benefit from peace and prosperity. And since there were slightly more Republican incumbents running, one might speculate that their party benefited slightly more from the status quo during the election.

## New Heights of Intensity in Open Seat Contests

The composition of the House of Representatives in particular is largely dependent on open seat elections. Nearly three-quarters of the members of the House were initially elected via an open seat or special election. Those seats are far more competitive than incumbent elections and thus attract far more resources from both parties than incumbent elections.[4] Open seats typically constitute less than 10 percent of contests in a given election cycle but are often critical to the long-term control of Congress. In 1994, for instance, when Republicans made their epic fifty-two-seat gain in the House, eighteen of those seats gained were previously Democratic open seats. Republicans won 75 percent of open seats that year, by far their best performance since 1972. It was the success rate of Republicans in the open seats that provided the critical seats to control the House.[5]

In 1996 and 1998, the Democrats and Republicans essentially split in the open seats, as both parties confronted similar numbers of retirements. This pattern of little net movement in the open seats continued into 2000, with the Republicans gaining one seat. That one seat and the domination of Republicans in open seat contests were important to the continued maintenance of the shrinking Republican majority.

Republicans entered the 2000 election at what appeared to be a decided disadvantage. Of the thirty-two contested open seats that resulted from the departure of incumbents, twenty-four (75 percent) were held by the Republicans entering the election. Only eight Democratic seats came open. The last time the balance of House retirements was so skewed was in 1994, when Democratic seats accounted for over 60 percent of all open seats, and Republicans gained eighteen seats in the open constituencies. Other research indicates that overexposure, through excessive retirement, often bodes poorly for the party with more retirements. So, on the surface, the open seat trends would have indicated an opportunity for the Democrats to reclaim control of the House.[6]

The results of the 2000 election contradicted that expectation. Of the thirty-two true open seats, Republicans actually retained one more than they started with, taking twenty-five of thirty-two seats. Why was this the case? Closer examination of the pattern of retirements in 2000 versus 1994 reveals why the Republicans might have won.

In 1994, Republican gains came largely in districts where the party had a strong base of national support for the president but previous congressional success was somewhat lacking. Disproportionate numbers of Republican pickups in 1994 were in the South. In 2000, of the five Republican pickups, only one—Virginia's second congressional district—was in the South. The remaining four pickups were strewn across the highly competitive industrial belt—West Virginia's Second, Michigan's Eighth, Missouri's Sixth, and Pennsylvania's Fourth Districts. And of the five Republican pickups, Virginia's Second District was the only congressional district where the Republican normal presidential vote was over 50 percent.[7] In the other districts, Republicans won open seats by running ahead of the historic presidential performance.

Democratic pickups were similarly distinct. Three were on the coasts where the Gore-Lieberman ticket ran strong—New York's Second, Washington's Second, and California's Fifteenth District. One, Oklahoma's Second District, was in the Border South. In all four districts picked up by the Democrats, the Republican normal presidential vote was less than 50 percent, indicating that they were districts where Republican incumbents had survived on personal advantages while the support for the national ticket was not a majority.

Taken together, these switches of seats around the margins led to a net gain of one for Republicans in the open seats. Typically, such a shift would be inconsequential and of little real importance in determining control of the House. In 2000, that seat was nearly critical, as Republicans held their tenuous majority by the narrowest of margins. A more typical pattern from the previous two decades would not have boded nearly so well for Republicans. Between 1982 and 1998, Republicans won 51.2 percent of the 365 contested open house seats, gaining a net margin of nine seats. At that rate of success in 2000, Republicans would have lost a net of eight seats and, holding incumbent success constant, forfeited control of the House.

This exercise, however, does not recognize the ability of parties to generally retain their seats. About one in three open seats will switch parties, but most stay with the incumbent party.[8] From 1982 to 1998, Republicans successfully defended about 70 percent of their open seats while taking about 40 percent of Democratic seats. If we apply those rates of success to the types of open seats in 2000, we see that the Republicans enjoyed exceptional success. Based on the tendencies of open seats since 1982, the Republicans should have expected to retain seventeen of their twenty-four open seats and capture three of eight Democratic seats for a total of twenty seats and a net loss of four. Holding other effects constant, that would have resulted in a breathtakingly close Democratic plurality of one seat in the House.

So what happened in those open seats? Conventional political science would expect that the party with the better partisan base would win. But what happens when the constituency is closely divided? In such cases, spending, candidates, and campaigns take on even more critical importance. When we look into the more competitive districts—which we define as open seats where the Republican normal presidential vote is between 45 percent and 55 percent (known as "marginal districts")—we see that the Republicans won thirteen of the fifteen most competitive districts. The only losses were in West Virginia's Second District and Washington's Second District.

Was it spending that made the difference? To be sure, the party spent a great deal of money in the open seats, averaging just over $1 million per race in the fifteen most marginal open districts. However, the Democrats were similarly well-heeled in these constituencies, spending on average nearly $900,000 per district when one excludes the $5.5 million spent by Democrat James Humphreys in West Virginia's second congressional district. Republicans had the spending advantage in only eight of these fifteen districts. In the two Republican districts picked up by Democrats inside the marginal box—close races decided by a few percentage points and/or swing voters—the Democratic candidate outspent the Republican nominee. Both parties fielded largely experienced candidates in these districts; only two districts had no candidate with prior elective experience on the ballot. Democrats were more likely to field experienced candidates than Republicans, both in general and in marginal districts.

The only possible explanation is the campaign itself. Republicans running in these competitive districts were freed from any direct responsibility for the impeachment of President Clinton. They were running in districts where Ross Perot had run well (the average 1992 Perot vote inside the margin box was 21.1 percent, and Perot ran ahead of his national showing in ten of these fifteen districts in 1992 and 1996). To go into those individual campaigns requires more space than is available in this chapter, but the individual campaigns must matter, if only because these Republicans ran only slightly ahead of or behind their national ticket, and they ran in districts where the party was competitive and where voters recently demonstrated strong independence in choosing a president. Republican candidates needed only to capitalize on their partisan base and a small body of swing voters who, in the past, had not warmed to Bill Clinton, Al Gore, or the Democrats in Congress.[9]

This close congruence between past presidential voting, as represented through the normal vote measure, and the vote for the House is what is interesting about the open seats in 2000. Congressional elections continued to become more partisan, almost rigidly so. When political scientists initially developed multivariate models of district-level incumbent congressional elections in the late 1970s, financial data, incumbency controls, and candidate experience data contributed substantially to explaining election outcomes, beyond any influence by coattails or other measures of district partisanship.[10]

An examination of even the open seat contests of the 1970s and 1980s reveals only a loose positive relationship between the normal presidential vote and the congressional vote. Absent incumbents, House elections from 1972 to 1990 were only loosely structured by party. In the 1970s Republican candidates for Congress often ran as much as fifty points behind the normal presidential vote in open seats, and even in the 1980s the typical Republican candidate ran about ten points behind the normal presidential vote. The presidential to congressional connection was severed even in the districts without incumbents. Much of the lack of structure came from the South, where presidential realignment (the change from Democrat to Republican) preceded congressional realignment by two decades. Even outside the South, throughout the 1970s and 1980s Republicans in open seats ran behind the normal presidential vote (see Table 16.1).

Entering the new apportionment cycle in 1992, the Republican congressional vote formed a strong linear relationship to the normal presidential vote. But again, the presidential vote was typically higher in most districts. Starting in 1994 and continuing through the end of the decade, the House Republican vote closely aligned with the presidential vote, on a 1 to 1 basis (slope) running generally out of the origin or even slightly above it. The relationship continued into the 2000 election, with open seat Republicans actually running slightly better than the normal presidential vote.

Ironically, a consequence of the new partisanship in congressional voting is the slipping away of the Republican majority. Although the House appears to be immune to a Democratic takeover in the short term (unlike the Senate, as we have already seen), the possibility of unexpected vacancies threaten this majority. Republicans already faced the loss of two members from safe districts in the fall of 2001—Representatives Steve Largent (R-Okla.) and Joe Scarborough (R-Fla.). Although Republicans held both of those districts in special elections, the party holds many districts that, in the absence of an incumbent, are potentially among the most competitive in the nation.

If, for instance, one notes what Ronald Gaddie and Charles Bullock consider to be the forty-three most competitive districts in the United States—districts that, when open, are estimated to be decided by less than 1 percentage point—thirty of those seats are held by Republicans.[11] Death

**Table 16.1  Winning Inside the Margin Box: Republican Success in the Most Competitive Open Seats**

| District | Incumbent Party | GOP$ | Dem.$ | GOP Vote | Dem. Vote | Normal Vote |
|----------|-----------------|------|-------|----------|-----------|-------------|
| AZ1 | Republican | 441,962 | 40,565 | 52.60 | 43.40 | 52 |
| FL12 | Republican | 844,508 | 490,117 | 57.00 | 43.00 | 55 |
| IL10 | Republican | 1,358,668 | 1,613,438 | 51.10 | 48.90 | 49 |
| IL15 | Republican | 1,302,567 | 753,532 | 53.20 | 46.80 | 49 |
| IN2 | Republican | 920,342 | 290,090 | 50.90 | 38.80 | 53 |
| MI8[a] | Democrat | 1,226,815 | 1,709,379 | 48.80 | 48.70 | 46 |
| MO2 | Republican | 623,813 | 635,344 | 55.30 | 42.40 | 54 |
| MO6[a] | Democrat | 625,230 | 594,895 | 50.90 | 46.80 | 46 |
| MT1 | Republican | 1,628,663 | 1,547,115 | 51.40 | 46.20 | 50 |
| NJ7 | Republican | 1,877,098 | 1,603,303 | 49.50 | 47.10 | 48 |
| OH12 | Republican | 1,609,422 | 452,414 | 53.00 | 43.70 | 50 |
| OK2[a] | Republican | 698,393 | 822,481 | 41.80 | 54.90 | 46 |
| VA2[a] | Democrat | 642,108 | 771,352 | 51.90 | 48.00 | 54 |
| WA2[a] | Republican | 704,945 | 1,191,173 | 45.80 | 50.30 | 46 |
| WV2[a] | Democrat | 983,409 | 5,477,724 | 47.50 | 46.60 | 46 |

*Note:* a. District changed parties.

or sudden resignation in any three of these districts holds open the possibility of a Democratic takeover of the House. (Since 1982, the highest number of special elections held has been seven.) Such a result is highly unlikely, but it does indicate further the tenuous nature of the Republican hold on power in the House. Their dependency on incumbency and the judicious use of money (discussed further below) in an environment in which party voting is on the increase allowed Republicans to retain their majority in 2000. That majority, however, is quite vulnerable, and it was only through exceptional performance in the open seats that Republicans retained the House.[12] Such performances were required again in 2002, when there were around fifty open House seats.

## The Pursuit and Expenditure of Campaign Funds

The pace of the arms race of massive campaign fundraising and subsequent expenditures—a major characteristic of U.S. politics in the last several decades of the twentieth century—increased at an accelerated pace in 2000. After the last dollar had been spent, the elections established an array of records, spanning virtually every category in which such records were kept. In the Senate, a pair of East Coast races in neighboring states accounted for more than $137 million in campaign contributions and expenditures. A wealthy Democrat, John Corzine, spent $62 million of his own money to win a Senate seat from New Jersey, defeating Bob Franks, a Republican who raised about $6.4 million. Meanwhile, another spectacularly expensive Senate race occurred in neighboring New York, where Hillary Clinton received nearly $30 million in donations to defeat Representative Rick Lazio, a Republican who raised $38.9 million. Individual and contest records were also set by House candidates. In California, a Republican, Representative James Rogan, raised more than $6.8 million in an unsuccessful effort to defend his seat against Adam Schiff, a Democrat who raised $4.3 million.

Overall, in 2000 as in the past, candidates—normally the incumbent—who won the fundraising contest were more likely than not to win the election too. In the Senate, the twenty-nine incumbents raised more than $118.4 million, as opposed to the $62.5 million given to challengers. House incumbents outraised their challengers by an even larger margin. However, the power of fundraising was further illustrated by victorious Senate challengers; they outraised their vanquished incumbents by an average of $6.7 million to $7 million.[13]

### Joint Fundraising Committees

The 2000 election campaign featured the continued escalation of the use of joint fundraising committees, which merged the efforts of congressional candidates and party committees to help finance party-building activities. Used extensively in previous races as joint fundraising efforts by national and state committees, by 2000 both parties began linking individual candidates with party committees. This new technique allowed candidates to slip by Federal Elections Campaign Act limitations on contributions given directly ("hard money") to candidates themselves. The joint committee would either share funds raised with the candidate or donate the money entirely to the campaign. This tactic was particularly popular with Senate candidates embroiled in expensive and highly contested races.[14]

Joint committees presented many benefits to linked candidates. The primary benefit was providing a method for bypassing existing campaign contribution limits. In addition, joint committees gained access to extensive donor lists while also enabling candidates to receive additional money from faithful individual and political action committee donors who previously provided the maximum amount of funds allowed by law. Anthony Corrado reported that with six months remaining before the fall 2000 elections, at least eighteen such committees had already raised about $13 million.[15] The thirteen Democratic committees had collected about $10 million, with the remaining $3 million gathered by the five Republican committees. Although this technique provided an edge to Democratic candidates, Republicans were busy honing their own special fundraising tools.

## The Candidates Themselves as Donors

In 2000 House Republicans established a fundraising program termed "Battleground 2000." Party leaders from each chamber and other members from electorally safe seats were asked either to donate funds themselves or solicit them from loyal supporters. The contributions went to a separate fund to help finance campaigns of party nominees locked in thirty-five close contests. By the middle of October, party leaders announced their project had generated $17.5 million in additional revenue.[16]

## Issue Advocacy and Party Soft Money

As in the past, interest groups were extensively involved in financing the 2000 congressional elections. However, the massive amount of funds interest groups raised and spent in connection with "issue advocacy" efforts in 2000 were particularly noteworthy. Issue advocacy, as defined in a 1976 U.S. Supreme Court ruling, *Buckley v. Valeo,* involves any communication that does not specifically call for either electing or defeating a candidate. Hence, under these guidelines there were no limits placed on interest groups to collect and spend money to try to influence the outcome of federal elections. Interest groups did not get involved in this tactic extensively until 1996, when labor unions launched a $35 million advertising campaign directed at defeating incumbent Republicans.

However, David Magleby reports that during the 2000 election campaign, interest groups spent an estimated $347 million on issue advocacy advertising plus an additional $487 million of political party "soft money" to finance advertisements seeking to defeat candidates.[17] Such funds are noteworthy for many reasons, not the least of which is that they were bound neither by donor disclosure requirements nor maximum contribution limits. Moreover, Magleby notes that such funds were especially important in 2000 because they were targeted to fund the few competitive congressional campaigns that year.[18] Particularly noteworthy is the finding that in several contests, "outside" money expenditures surpassed funds collected and spent by the candidates themselves.

# The Incumbency Factor—Still Supreme

Despite all the talk of intense partisanship and the closeness of the balance of power on Capitol Hill in 2000, in the end, the year's election returns once again reaffirmed the ability of incumbents to win reelection, regardless of such noteworthy factors as party affiliation, region of country, seniority, or chamber membership. The generally high success rate of incumbents, particularly those in the House, tended to follow patterns found in most previous elections in the second half of the twentieth century.

For example, in the House, 394 of 403 incumbents running for reelection won. Of the nine unsuccessful incumbents, three lost primary contests, and the remaining six lost in the general election. Moreover, the margin of victory of those incumbents tended to follow traditional patterns. More than 85 percent of the House incumbents and about half of their Senate counterparts were running in uncontested to lightly contested races. Election returns revealed only ten incumbents winning with less than 55 percent of the major two-party vote and only sixteen capturing less than 60 percent of the vote. Hence, as in so many previous elections, large numbers of House incumbents won reelection by comfortably large margins.

However, as has also been the case historically, incumbent senators in 2000, although successful overall, tended not to fare as well as their House brethren. The success rate of incumbent senators in 2000 was 79 percent, but their House counterparts were reelected at a whopping 98 percent rate. Both return rates generally were in line with previous elections, although Senate incumbent success rates have been much more likely to vary from one election to the next than House contests. Of course, several incumbent senators were freshmen up for their first reelection try after storming to victory in the wake of the 1994 election, the outcome of which enabled Republicans to capture control of both chambers of Congress for the first time since the early 1950s. These freshmen incumbents campaigned under additional news media scrutiny, and another large class of Republicans confronted the electorate in 2002, gaining seats in both the House and Senate.

## The Unsuccessful Attempt to Remove President Clinton and the 2000 Election Outcome

Likely because it had been more than a century since the Senate had held an impeachment trial of a president, no official or observer really knew just how such an event would affect subsequent elections. To be sure, opinion polls concerning the impeachment and trial of Clinton consistently revealed, by ratios of two-to-one or more, a public overwhelmingly critical of the move and wanting the entire process to end quickly with an acquittal. One obvious speculation could be that the act helped fan partisan fires already blazing in many quarters. That, in turn, could have fueled the increased campaign donations outlined here previously.

Another possible impeachment outcome, which was closely watched nationally throughout the campaign, was the fate of Republicans prominently involved in the effort. Under particular scrutiny were the thirteen representatives who presented the House impeachment case before the Senate. Although most of the managers were carefully chosen because, in part, they came from electorally "safe" districts, two members did not. One impeachment manager, Representative Steve Chabot (R-Ohio), logged 55 percent of the vote against a weak challenger. However, the other Republican manager from a marginal district, Representative James Rogan (R-Calif.), lost his reelection bid in one of the most expensive and closely watched contests in House history. By October 17, Rogan's campaign expenditures had surpassed the $5.7 million mark, and his challenger, state lawmaker Adam Schiff, had spent more than $3.3 million. Throughout that campaign, it was widely acknowledged that partisans on each side wanted to make the contest a political test of the failed impeachment effort. Hence, Republican and Democratic faithful alike opened their checkbooks, seeking to assure victory for their side.

In the end, perhaps Jacobson provides one of the more astute observations about the politics at work here when he speculates that the Republicans were not punished electorally because their effort failed in the end.[19] The worst case for the Republicans was that three of their four defeated House incumbents represented swing districts carried previously by President Clinton. The politically marginal electoral composition of their districts meant that they were always vulnerable to attracting strong and politically experienced challengers, which each did in 2000. But the impeachment effort perhaps also attracted much more campaign funds than they should otherwise have expected to receive.

## Conclusion

Regardless of how one analyzes the congressional elections of 2000, the overarching conclusion has been that the elections certainly were not dull. Indeed, the intense drama of the elections seemed to continue throughout the early days of the 107th Congress (2001–2003). The precarious fifty-fifty division in the Senate necessitated a lengthy negotiation between Majority Leader Tom Daschle (D-S.D.) and Minority Leader Trent Lott (R-Miss.) to agree to the terms of governance. Although the Republicans would have the ultimate upper hand in organizing the chamber because Vice President Dick Cheney would break any ties in their favor, Daschle managed to win several important concessions. For example, the Democrats gained parity on committee membership and staff assignments. However, the Senate's delicate balance soon tipped in the Democrats' favor after Senator James Jeffords of Vermont bolted the Republican Party and declared himself an independent who would vote with the Democrats to organize the chamber. By the start of the 107th Congress in 2001, it seemed almost as though the closeness and partisanship found in the 2000 elections were so well established that they would continue through the contests in 2002 and in the years well beyond.

From a long-term perspective, we must consider the place of these elections in the larger context of the definition and perpetuation of the party system. The 1994 election has been hailed as a realigning event that brought southern politics into a coherent shape and destroyed the remnants of the New Deal coalition. Certainly, the cursory evidence from the open seats indicates not just coherence in southern politics but in congressional and presidential politics across the nation. What is not clear is what the fundamental issues are that define the politics of the day and will serve as the basis for crafting a new, lasting majority. Neither Republicans nor Democrats campaigned to distinguish themselves from each other on pressing issues, and such circumstances usually benefit congressional incumbents by tempering the tides of national politics. And this phlegmatic period in U.S. politics comes with the parties evenly divided across the national electoral institutions. It was a perfect tie, an election that failed to produce a mandate on which to govern.

When last the Congress was so evenly divided, Dwight D. Eisenhower reigned as the U.S. political ideal, and Republicans enjoyed a presidency without congressional control. From 1951 to 1959 was the last period in which the House remained so closely divided for so long, with the Democrats holding an average of 228 seats to the Republicans' 206 seats (Republicans held an eight-seat majority in the House from 1953 to 1955). It was a period of subsumed issues, and it followed an era of Democratic hegemony in Congress. The close division was finally broken by economic distress (the 1958 recession), which produced the election of a Democratic congressional majority that would hold an average of 62 percent of House seats until 1995.

Given the degree of professional development and organization of both major parties, we should expect shifts in seats to be small for the near term, absent a pressing or important issue. Should that next issue come, it will likely be one that reflects poorly on the incumbent presidential administration, and it will cut deeply into the seats of one party or the other, much like the elections of 1958, 1974, 1980, and 1994. What remains to be seen is which party will be punished and when.

# 17

## The Significance of the 2000 Presidential Election: Institutional Impact and Possible Reforms

### Anthony J. Eksterowicz

*Just moments ago, I spoke with George W. Bush and congratulated him on becoming the 43rd president of the United States, and I promised him that I wouldn't call him back this time.*
—Vice President Al Gore's Concession Speech
December 13, 2000

The most remarkable thing about Vice President Al Gore's concession to George W. Bush for the presidency was the date—a full thirty-six days after the November 7 election. From election day through Thanksgiving and beyond, both candidates battled through the courts for the presidency in a rare and historic postelection period. The nation watched mesmerized as U.S. politicians, interest groups, state and national judges and courts, media reporters, commentators, and academicians all sailed through uncharted historical and constitutional waters. It was as though someone had declared overtime for one of the most coveted positions in U.S. politics, the presidency of the United States.

The election was essentially a tie, with Vice President Gore winning the popular tally by approximately 530,000 votes and George W. Bush ultimately being awarded a slim electoral victory of 271 to 267 by a slim five-to-four majority decision in the U.S. Supreme Court. This was not only overtime but a last-second victory in overtime. Such an election was bound to have an impact upon U.S. political institutions and processes and specifically on the winner, President George W. Bush, as he attempted to govern.

To better understand the impact of this election, the 2000 presidential election is initially and briefly described in its various phases: nomination; general election; and postelection period. I then analyze the impact of the election on various U.S. institutions and processes. Finally, a few lessons that have been or should be learned from this historic election will be suggested. Such lessons are still evolving, as our institutional structures and processes prepare for the next national congressional election and future elections. It is to be hoped that a broad set of reforms will emerge from these lessons.

## The Nomination Phase

### The Democratic Race

For the Democrats, Gore was considered the front-runner early in the nomination phase. His early rival, Representative Richard Gephardt of Missouri, the House Minority leader, decided in February 1999 to work for a new Democratic majority in the House. Doing so would ensure his election as speaker of the House. The vice president held advantages in media coverage, familiarity with the voters, fundraising, and political endorsements, especially from the party faithful. He also enjoyed the advantage of economic prosperity and budget surpluses that the Clinton administration helped cause.

However, Gore was not without weaknesses. He was closely associated with President Bill Clinton and therefore with all of President Clinton's troubles, from Whitewater and Monica Lewinsky to the unsuccessful attempt to impeach President Clinton. In addition, the vice president was vulnerable on the issue of fundraising, especially concerning Chinese contributions. The media often referred to Gore's participation in fundraising in a Buddhist temple, making it a rather well known liability for the candidate.

These vulnerabilities led to a challenge from former senator Bill Bradley of New Jersey. The issue was trust and character. Senator Bradley pledged to set a new tone in Washington by honestly dealing with the problems besetting the country. He was the only candidate not frightened by the huge amounts of money raised by the vice president. Bradley had his own sources of money, including lucrative donors from the National Basketball Association, which allowed him to compete in the early 2000 primaries.

Bradley also had vulnerabilities. His campaigning style was stiff and wooden. It was also a problem for the vice president, but next to Bradley, the vice president looked comfortable and in command. Senate friends often described Bradley as aloof or a loner. On the stump, Bradley was clearly uncomfortable explaining his positions on issues or responding to Gore's accusations or attacks. The result of this battle was a decisive victory for the vice president. Senator Bradley did not win a single primary election. By March 7, 2000, his campaign was over; he conceded two days later, lending his support to Vice President Gore.[1]

*The Republican Race*

The Republican nomination race appeared all but won in the early stages of the battle, until Senator John McCain challenged Governor George W. Bush and exposed his vulnerabilities. Early in the Republican nomination race, there were many contenders, such as Elizabeth Dole, John Kasich, Patrick Buchanan, Steve Forbes, Dan Quayle, Gary Bauer, John McCain, Orrin Hatch, Alan Keyes, and Lamar Alexander. Many of these candidates dropped out of the race early. Perhaps the primary reason was the enormous sum of money that Governor Bush raised.[2]

Very few candidates could match this effort except Steve Forbes, who had access to virtually unlimited funds because of his family's wealth. A second related reason was the Republican Party's early acceptance of the Bush candidacy. The party faithful quickly closed ranks around the front-runner. By the end of 1999, three viable candidates remained—Bush, McCain, and Forbes—and the race quickly evolved into Bush versus McCain.

Both candidates had vulnerabilities. McCain highlighted Bush's vulnerabilities by concentrating his effort upon three states—New Hampshire, South Carolina, and California. McCain won a decisive victory in New Hampshire. He demonstrated that the Bush fundraising effort could be neutralized by hard work, at least in New Hampshire. Republican party regulars were worried that Bush had wasted their money and was not working particularly hard.[3] After New Hampshire, the hunt for money by the Bush campaign assumed a new urgency. Bush forces concentrated upon McCain's vulnerabilities. Senator McCain was perceived (and portrayed by the Bush forces) as an obstructionist in Senate Republican Party circles. He was considered to be a loner and aloof like former Senator Bradley. There were also innuendos about his temperament and temper.[4]

Despite their reservations concerning his work ethic, the Republican Party closed ranks around Bush. Although Senator McCain won primaries in New Hampshire, Michigan, Connecticut, Massachusetts, Rhode Island, and Vermont, these victories were not enough to offset Bush wins in other states, especially South Carolina. With the exception of New Hampshire, McCain won the states carried by Gore in the general election. This fact might reflect McCain's relative independence from the Republican Party. In Michigan, for instance, McCain was aided by the crossover votes of Democrats and independents allowed to participate in that state's Republican primary. Despite his victories, by March 9, 2000, McCain's fate was evident. He conceded and grudgingly, over time, supported Governor Bush.

No one can deny the tenuous relationship between the two generated by these nomination battles. Front-loaded primaries aided Bush and Gore. Front loading is the positioning of many state primaries early in the election year. This schedule helps the candidates earn money and status within their respective political parties. Only those successful candidates can compete in many places at once.[5]

## The General Election

Both candidates looked forward to their respective nomination conventions. The Republicans went first in Philadelphia. The drama revolved around the selection of a vice presidential running mate and the Bush campaign's handling of Senator McCain. Governor Bush selected Dick Cheney, a former member of the House of Representatives, Ford administration chief of staff, and secretary of defense under the first Bush presidency. Most commentators applauded the choice because Cheney's prior experience would complement Bush's lack of national and international experience. Senator McCain was handled about as well as could have been expected, given the great antipathy between these two men. Governor Bush led in the election polls both before and after the convention.

Vice President Gore had to deliver the convention speech of his life to regain a lead in the polls. As with the Republican convention, there was intense speculation concerning Gore's vice presidential selection at the Democratic convention in Los Angeles. Gore chose Senator Joseph Lieberman of Connecticut, a devout Jew with high moral credentials. Gore felt he needed to counter the Clinton "character" problem, and Lieberman allowed him to do just that. He also needed to show his compassion and commitment to values and morality. He did this by delivering what most commentators conceded was his finest speech.[6]

Symbolism overtook substance a bit when the vice president walked up to the podium and planted a long (some would say very long) kiss on his wife's lips. The media coverage was exceptional and the result was one of the largest postconvention bounces in the national public opinion polls in modern times.

Political scientists predicted a Gore victory of 3 to 5 percentage points based upon their economic election modeling. If the economy was doing well, the models predicted, the present party and administration would benefit by winning the election.[7] However, as Figure 17.1 shows, daily tracking polls continued to indicate a close race.[8] Gore was ahead in the polls from the Democratic convention until the beginning of October. The figure also shows Gore beginning to surge during election week, which would explain his popular vote victory but not the electoral loss. Candidate strategy helps explain the electoral loss.

Both candidates understood that the race would be close. Gore lost, but we must inject a note of caution here. Gore won the popular vote, and by some analysis, he actually may also have won the electoral vote; a host of voting irregularities in the state of Florida made it impossible to tell.[9] The

**Figure 17.1  Daily Polls, September–November 2000**

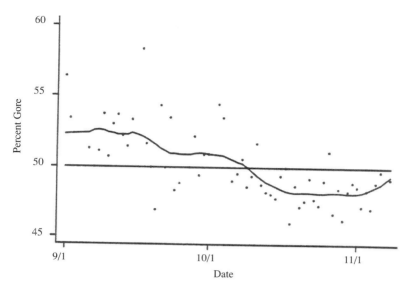

*Source:* Robert S. Erikson. 2001. "The 2000 Presidential Election." *Presidential Studies Quarterly* 116: 40. Reprinted by permission.

press and public have treated him as the loser because he is not the current president. One such analysis focuses largely on his problems. For example, soon after the election, the centrist wing of the Democratic Party argued that Gore ran a campaign that tilted too far to the political and ideological left. However, the left wing of the Democratic Party argued that his campaign was too centrist.[10]

Both wings are correct. Both candidates adopted remarkably similar textbook strategies. Both Bush and Gore sought to shore up their base. For Gore this meant speaking to women, union groups, working people, minorities, and the elderly, which he did quite effectively while on the stump addressing large targeted audiences. His strategy was decidedly populist. However, when addressing a wider audience like those generated through national debates, Gore was much more muted, emphasizing moderate themes and policies in both substance and tone. The theme was now the middle class working together in a unified fashion, without the fiery us (the poor) versus them (the rich) rhetoric of the Gore stump speech.

For Bush, the strategy was similar. On the stump, to selected audiences, he could be as assertive as Pat Robertson, assailing the country's lost morality; championing the right to life, faith-based initiatives, and the rights of gun owners; and proclaiming his religious-based morality as a personal story. During the debates, the nation witnessed a more muted Bush, who seemed moderate on most public policies. He differed with the opposition candidate not on fundamental issues but on the means to achieve ends. They were different, but they were the same.

Their strategies were simple and similar. Both Bush and Gore wanted to solidify their own party base to energize their party faithful and then move to the center of the political spectrum to attract the necessary number of independent and undecided voters to win the election. Perhaps both strategies worked. However, when these general campaign strategies combined with an electoral college strategy, trouble was bound to follow for one of these candidates.

Both candidates targeted their campaigns to the electoral battleground states because neither could afford to compete nationwide. Efficient targeting may have worked for both candidates. As Robert Erikson notes:

> We offer a speculative explanation for the concentration of Gore's gain in nonbattleground states, which is interesting in its potential implications. Both campaigns focused their attention solely on battleground states, leaving much of the nation with virtually no campaign ads or candidate appearances.
>
> By the final week, voters in the battleground states had enough information to figure out whom to vote for. Meanwhile, in the uncontested nonbattleground states, voters had little information. Many made up their minds at the last minute, generating late decisions for Gore.[11]

Such decisions would explain the late Gore surge in the polls illustrated by Figure 17.1. It could also explain the electoral college vote because in a close election, both the popular vote and electoral vote become a bit arbitrary.[12] In addition, in a close race, all the imperfections inherent in the U.S. voting system become apparent and are magnified, simply because every vote counts a bit more in such elections. Both candidates pursued strategies, either purposefully or by accident, that would cause such results.

Both Bush and Gore successfully divided the nation. Table 17.1 illustrates some problems, however. With respect to income, the vote of people making under $50,000 and those making over $50,000 is split down the middle, as are the votes of males and females. The numbers for gun owners and nongun owners are a bit farther apart. Other categories of voters show similar splits, except among white Protestants and Catholics and regarding beliefs concerning the role of government.

Splits in the popular vote reflect splits in the electoral vote. Figure 17.2 indicate the states that went for Bush in 2000 and Dole in 1996, Bush in 2000 and Clinton in 1996, and Gore in 2000 and Clinton in 1996. The states in gray represent new states for George W. Bush. In addition, although third-party candidates Ralph Nader and Pat Buchanan did not receive many votes, their impact in Florida was eventful. As Gerald Pomper notes:

**Table 17.1  2000 Exit Polls—Gore vs. Bush by Selected Voter Categorizations**

|  | Percent of all Respondents | Percent Gore | Percent Bush |
|---|---|---|---|
| Income |  |  |  |
| Under $50,000 | 47 | 52 | 44 |
| $50,000 and above | 53 | 45 | 52 |
| Protestant vs. Catholic |  |  |  |
| White Protestant | 47 | 34 | 63 |
| Catholic | 26 | 49 | 47 |
| Gender |  |  |  |
| Male | 48 | 42 | 53 |
| Female | 52 | 54 | 43 |
| Marital Status |  |  |  |
| Married | 65 | 44 | 53 |
| Unmarried | 35 | 57 | 38 |
| Religious attendance |  |  |  |
| At least once a week | 42 | 39 | 59 |
| Less than once a week | 56 | 55 | 43 |
| Gun ownership |  |  |  |
| Gun in the house | 48 | 36 | 61 |
| No gun | 52 | 58 | 39 |
| Role of government |  |  |  |
| Should do more to solve problems | 43 | 74 | 23 |
| Leave to businesses, individuals | 53 | 25 | 71 |
| Abortion rights |  |  |  |
| Should be legal all/most cases | 56 | 65 | 32 |
| Should be illegal all/most cases | 40 | 27 | 71 |
| Stricter gun legislation |  |  |  |
| Support | 60 | 62 | 34 |
| Oppose | 36 | 23 | 74 |

*Source:* Robert S. Erikson. 2001. "The 2000 Presidential Election." *Presidential Studies Quarterly* 116: 40.

The close national division was reflected in some of the states. A shift of merely a quarter of 1 percent of state votes—an infinitesimal . . . total of 17,000 ballots nationally—would have reversed fifty-five electoral votes from five states (Florida, Iowa, New Mexico, Oregon, and Wisconsin). Only in these close states, particularly Florida, did votes for minor candidacies of Ralph Nader and Pat Buchanan make a difference—but there they were still an immense influence.[13]

These candidates were successful in dividing the nation. Most of the urban industrial county and city areas cast their votes for Gore, but most of the rural counties cast their votes for Bush. Two Americas appear quite clearly, with competing visions on the role of government, values, morality, and the importance of character and leadership. All this, in part, was caused by two candidates who pledged to the American people that they would govern by bringing people together for compromise and conciliation. They were off to a slow start, and after election day nothing would be settled.

**Figure 17.2 Map of State Voting**

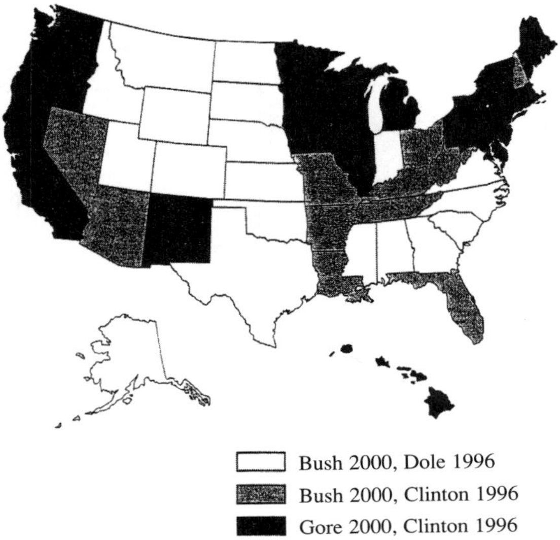

☐ Bush 2000, Dole 1996
▦ Bush 2000, Clinton 1996
■ Gore 2000, Clinton 1996

*Source:* Gerald M. Pomper. 2001. "The Presidental Election." In *The Election of 2000,* ed. Gerald M. Pomper. New York: Seven Bridges Press, p. 133. Reprinted by permission.

## The Postelection Phase

On election night, the media called the election for Gore, only to take back their projections. Vice President Gore telephoned Governor Bush to concede, only to withdraw his concession minutes later. It seems as though the electoral vote was too close to call, and although many states were close, all eyes were on Florida. George W. Bush's brother, Jeb, was governor, and Republicans controlled the Florida state legislature. Florida was the key because without it, Bush could not have ascended to the presidency. It became a wart to Gore because reports of voting irregularities were emanating from the state. There were accusations of illegal and confusing ballots; restrictions upon minority voting; questionable voter registration policies; the arbitrary counting of ballots, especially military ballots; voter fraud; and state government incompetence with respect to ensuring the people's right to vote.

In such an atmosphere, after millions of dollars had been expended, after thousands of campaign workers had given of their time, after interest groups had worked so hard on behalf of the candidates, neither Bush nor Gore could afford to let Florida go. The vice president simply had to contest the election results. He had won the popular vote, or so he believed. He *had* to pursue a recount strategy.[14]

The Bush lead in Florida after election day was approximately 1,784. However, after a machine recount in all of Florida's counties, Bush led by just 327 votes. Irregularities were reported in Palm Beach County, where Reform Party candidate Patrick Buchanan received more than 3,000 votes. That was an oddity, considering the heavily Jewish and African American county population. Voters used confusing punch card ballots there and elsewhere in Florida. Voter mistakes and other irregularities were inevitable.

Candidate Gore called for a manual recount of four selected counties in Florida. However, Secretary of State Katherine Harris, a Republican and George W. Bush campaign official, did not accept the manual recounts. Under her interpretation of Florida election law, all results were due in her office within one week. Only one contested county had met the deadline. In addition, overseas absentee ballots increased the Bush lead to 930 votes. The secretary of state was about to certify the election results, but the Gore legal team won a decision from the Florida State Supreme Court that eventually allowed the counting to continue.[15]

Controversy over counting rules erupted within the contested Florida counties. Standards for the counting of punch card ballots varied from county to county. Of the four counties in question, only Miami-Dade County failed to report its recounts, but Secretary of State Harris accepted only one additional county. Her decision gave Bush a lead of 537 votes, and Harris certified him as the winner of Florida's electoral votes and thus the presidency.[16]

However, the Florida Supreme Court was still hinting that it might permit a requested recount by the Gore legal team. The Bush legal team appealed to the U.S. Supreme Court. The Supreme Court reviewed the Florida State Supreme Court decision and sent it back down to the state court for review. The presumption was that the Florida State Supreme Court would stop the recounts after having reviewed its prior decision. At least, that was the direction the Supreme Court wanted.[17] In an act of defiance, the Florida State Supreme Court (populated with a Democratic majority) ruled in favor of a Gore appeal to continue the counting of ballots, not just in the originally contested four counties but now statewide. It also counted Gore votes previously not counted by Secretary of State Harris. Bush now led by only 154 votes.[18]

The Bush forces were worried because their slim lead was vanishing. They appealed to the U.S. Supreme Court (populated with seven justices appointed by Republican presidents) on the basis of an equal protection claim. They argued that the counting of ballots in the Florida counties was arbitrary and nonuniform and therefore a violation of the voter's right to equal protection. In essence, the Republican legal team was asking the federal court to rule against the Florida State Supreme Court. There is a certain amount of irony here because Republican presidents and candidates usually respect state decisions.

In a bitter five-to-four decision, *Bush v. Gore,* a divided Supreme Court ruled in favor of the Bush claim, effectively halting all recounts. The Court reasoned that such recounts violate the voter's guarantee of equal protection under the Constitution.[19] The Court attempted to rule narrowly and specifically limited their ruling to "present circumstances." However, some observers believe that this ruling will have wider implications, particularly in the upcoming fight over congressional redistricting.[20]

There were four bitter dissents to the ruling. These dissents exposed the partisanship and divided ideologies of the various members on the Court. The Court's decision was so unique and controversial that three justices decided to use other means to comment upon their ruling. Justice Rehnquist used a history lecture.[21] Justices Kennedy and Thomas used a congressional hearing.[22]

The actions in Florida spawned a class action suit by the National Association for the Advancement of Colored People (NAACP) claiming that African Americans were denied the right to vote in the November elections.[23] In June 2001, the U.S. Civil Rights Commission criticized the actions of Florida secretary of state Harris and Governor Jeb Bush for disparate voter treatment. The report noted 54 percent of the rejected votes cast in Florida were those of African Americans.[24]

All this was a footnote to a unique and historical election. The fact remained that George W. Bush became the forty-third president on January 20, 2001. President Bush had "negative coattails" in this election. His party lost three seats in the House of Representatives and four seats in the Senate. The Senate was now split 50-50, and both parties had to arrive at a power-sharing agreement.[25] Only a mere 136 days from the inauguration, the Senate made history. Vermont Republican senator James Jeffords announced that he was switching parties to become an independent and would vote with the Democrats, effectively giving them control of the Senate. President Bush became the first president in U.S. history to lose party control of one house of Congress between national elections. The implications and lessons of this election are still unfolding, but it is not too early to discuss a few of the more important ones.

## Significance and Lessons Learned

The 2000 presidential election affected the three major institutions of government. First, the presidency will continue to be a diminished institution in the future. Even before this historic election, the presidency was suffering from what some scholars have termed the post–Cold War syndrome and other problems confronting the modern presidency.[26] Divided government during most of the Clinton administration did not help increase the prestige of the presidency. Divisive budget battles, the Republican attempt to oust President Clinton via impeachment and trial in the Senate, and President Clinton's personal problems all contributed to the presidency's diminished prestige.

President Bush faced divided government, with the Democrats taking control of the Senate only 136 days into his administration. Bipartisanship and consensus building will be important, but presidents have never really been adept at practicing these skills.[27] As of 2003, the effects of the election are still present, especially in Congress.[28] The Bush administration must maneuver its agenda carefully through the congressional maze.

One specific example of diminished presidential power in recent years involves the process of judicial nominations. During the Clinton administration, the Republican-controlled Senate delayed confirming President Clinton's judicial nominees, which resulted in the appointment of moderate to conservative federal judges.[29] President Clinton sought to strike deals with the Republican majority and withdrew controversial (in the eyes of the Republican Senate) nominees. He thus ceded power and some control to the Republican Senate and its Judiciary Committee Chair, Senator Orrin Hatch of Utah.[30] With the Republicans now in control of the Senate, this scenario is changed for the Bush administration.

The Congress is now evenly divided, with a slim Republican majority in the House and slim Democrat control in the Senate. These two houses have different public policy agendas, yet reconciliation between these houses is necessary for public policy success. Divisive issues such as prescription drug reform, campaign finance reform, social security reform, and establishing a national energy policy will be prove to be difficult. The close presidential election further exacerbates these problems. Compounding that is the fact that President Bush has no real mandate from the people, and his failure to bring in greater numbers of Republican representatives and senators will ultimately harm his agenda. Moderate and maverick senators like John McCain and Jim Jeffords have already forced a vote on a campaign finance bill the Bush administration dislikes. They have also reduced and essentially backloaded many elements of the Bush tax plan. As a result, significant tax relief will now take a full decade to achieve.[31]

Despite these difficulties, President Bush is trying to reduce spending. However, his tax cuts and increased federal spending in the wake of September 11 have resulted in budget deficits. According to the Congressional Budget Office, the budget surplus has already evaporated into a $157 billion deficit for 2002.[32] Moderate Republicans and Democrats have shaped many bills in 2001, including the education bill. They have rejected public school vouchers, so coveted by the Bush administration, but increased funding for education programs.[33]

The Supreme Court may also suffer a drop in prestige because of the way in which it handled *Bush v. Gore*. Although its members claimed that their decision applied only to this specific case, it remains to be seen if they can hold back a movement for greater uniformity among the states concerning the education, registration, and tabulation of voters and votes in national elections. The appearance of partisanship created by their ruling in *Bush v. Gore*, along with the divided nature of Congress, promises to bring excitement to any Bush Supreme Court nomination.

## Reform

The 2000 election also affected the fundamental process of voting. The nation believed that strong voting rights and procedures were already in place. After all, people had died over the fight for voting rights in the 1960s. The result was the Voting Rights Act of 1965, which helped remove impediments to voting for minorities. The nation now knows how fragile its voting systems are. In any presidential election, possibly millions of votes go uncounted for various reasons such as voter error, confusing ballots, or poor voting instructions. Americans also know that minorities suffer the most in this type of environment. In response to the 2000 election, Florida has embarked upon voting and ballot reforms, but all states need to be active in this area.

To the extent that reform is necessary, public interest groups have been involved. The last election energized such groups and gave them a fundamental cause for organization and even litigation in this area.[34] Congress has examined the problem, and both houses conducted extensive hearings. After the House of Representatives failed to establish a special Select Committee on Election Reform in the early spring of 2001, former presidents Gerald Ford and Jimmy Carter, along with former senator Howard Baker and former White House counsel Lloyd Cutler, formed a National Commission on Federal Election Reform for the purpose of presenting recommendations to Congress by September 2001. Congress eventually passed an election reform bill in 2002, taking their advice into consideration when drafting the election reform package.

These are some of the more significant effects of the past presidential election. There will be others because the election represented the beginning of these reforms, not an ending. What are the lessons we can or should learn from the election?

First, candidates for the presidency of the United States should speak to the whole nation, not just selected states within an electoral battleground. To treat the nation as one large chess board is to divide, not unify it. Governing such a nation can become impossible. Second, candidates for the presidency should use all possible policy arguments, as well as legal and ethical means available, to win the election. In the 2000 election, Gore chose not to make economic success a primary issue. He failed to use an extremely popular President Clinton in the campaign because he wanted to put distance between himself and the flawed character of Bill Clinton. Bush also played it safe. His answers to policy questions were often vague and ambiguous. He promised that specifics would come after the election. The result was a winner without a mandate from the people and uncertainty about many of his policy proposals. This would also have been the case if Gore won. All this presents problems for governance. Why would anyone want to run for the presidency if winning implies the inability to govern? As the winner of the 2000 election will undoubtedly understand, winning is not everything.

The third general lesson highlighted by this election is the necessity of serious voting reform. The problem is not so much the electoral college (although Americans should reexamine this institution) but voting procedures in the states. Florida became the focus for voting irregularities, but all states have problems. Therefore, each state should conduct a review of its voter education, registration, ballot, vote-counting, and recounting procedures. More uniformity is needed across the nation in this regard. Indeed, if the battle for voting reform is joined, it might be one of this century's most noble efforts. As Ford, Carter, Baker, and Cutler note:

> In a democracy, few problems should set off as loud an alarm as this one. Government has a duty to provide a modern and reliable system that helps every registered citizen vote, and ensures that each vote counts. Elections must be open, honest and fair.[35]

How we handle this problem will speak volumes about our fundamental values as Americans. We cannot afford the luxury of complacency.

# Notes

## Introduction

1. For a discussion of political participation, see Verba and Nie 1972; Conway 2000.

2. Lau et al. 1999, 119–138; Wattenberg and Brains 1999, 891–899; Thurber, Nelson, and Dulio 2000; Goldstein et al. 2001.

3. Campbell and Trilling 1980; Clubb, Flanigan, and Zingale 1980; Petrocik 1981; Sundquist 1983; Keefe 1994.

4. Maisel 1999.

5. Campbell 1985, 357–376.

6. Davidson 1984; Williams and Morris 1987.

7. See Kousser 1984.

8. Diaz 1984.

9. Cronin 1996; Longley and Peirce 1999.

10. Pfiffner 1994.

11. The Twelfth Amendment was initiated in direct response to this controversy. The controversial election was also one of the factors that led to the eventual duel between Alexander Hamilton and Aaron Burr, in which Hamilton was killed.

12. Davidson and Oleszek 2002.

13. Butler and Cain 1992; Lublin 1997.

14. See the case studies in Thurber 2001; see also Herrnson 2001.

15. Nimmo 1970; Sabato 1981; Petracca 1989; Lavrakas and Traugott 2000.

16. Pomper and Lederman 1980.

17. See Thurber and Nelson 2000.

18. Agranoff 1972b; Herrnson 2000.

19. Reiter 1987.

## Part 1: Current Issues in Campaigns

1. Herrnson 1988, 2000.

2. Dinkin 1989; Medvic 2001.

3. Campbell and Dulio 2003.

4. Sabato and Larson 2002.

5. Kolodny 2000, 10; Bowler and Farrell 2000.

6. Kolodny 2000, 111.

7. Ibid.
8. See Thurber and Nelson 2000; Thurber, Nelson, and Dulio 2000.
9. Thurber 2000.
10. Kolodny 2000.
11. Mitchell 1992.
12. Schier 2000; Drinkard 1999, 1.
13. Mintz 2000, A21.

## Chapter 1

David A. Dulio would like to thank James A. Thurber and Candice J. Nelson for their continued support of this research. Their leadership of the "Improving Campaign Conduct" project at American University has been indispensable.

1. See the September 2, 1996, edition of *Time* magazine for articles on this subject.
2. Hiebert et al. 1971.
3. Sabato 1981.
4. Sabato and Simpson 1996; Nimmo 1970; Kelley 1956.
5. DeVries 1989, 21–25.
6. Dinkin 1989.
7. Ibid.
8. Herrnson 2000, 84.
9. Herrnson 1988.
10. Ibid., 26; see also Key 1964, 389–391.
11. Herrnson 1988, 26.
12. Ibid.
13. By only 1954, the electorate had already increased to over 100 million strong. See *Statistical Abstract of the United States, 1999* and *The National Data Book, 1999*, published by Brenan Press.
14. Salmore and Salmore 1985, 39.
15. Rosenbloom 1973, 50.
16. The question of measuring the number of professionals today is dealt with in a later discussion in this chapter.
17. Agranoff 1972a, 15.
18. Johnson-Cartee and Copeland 1997, xx.
19. For a full range of specialties, see Johnson 2001.
20. Dulio 2001.
21. These categories are borrowed from Johnson's (2000, 2001) work on consultants. He develops a fuller discussion of the differences between the three types of consultants mentioned here.
22. Nimmo 1970, 53.
23. Ibid, 88.
24. Johnson 2000, 40.
25. Some media consulting firms will both create the television spot and place the spot on the appropriate channel at the appropriate time. They might also act as time buyers. There is variation throughout the industry.
26. Recall that a main aspect of the definition of consultant presented in this chapter is that they work on a fee-for-service basis and are not full-time employees.
27. Author interview on February 24, 2000.
28. Johnson 2000.

29. This also contradicts some conventional wisdom surrounding political professionals. See Sabato (1981, 24–27) for claims that consultants pay little attention to party or ideology in their business.

30. The survey referred to was conducted by the Center for Congressional and Presidential Studies at American University, in conjunction with the "Improving Campaign Conduct" project, sponsored by the Pew Charitable Trusts. The survey was conducted in April 1999, was administered by Yankelovich Partners, and consisted of thirty-minute telephone interviews with 505 political consultants. Details about the survey can be found in Dulio 2001 or at the center's website at www.american.edu/ccps.

31. Some scholarly accounts of consulting also advance this assertion. See Sabato 1981.

32. Dulio 2001.

33. Republican consultant Robert Goodman, quoted in Sabato 1981, 36.

34. Quoted in Sabato 1981, 20. These data on political consultants are taken from a 1997 survey of the consulting industry also conducted as part of the "Improving Campaign Conduct" project at American University. This study was administered by the Pew Research Center for the People and the Press. See Thurber, Nelson, and Dulio 2000 and Thurber and Nelson 2000 for more details on this study.

35. Republican Douglas Bailey is quoted in Sabato 1981, 26.

36. Again, see the 1999 survey of consultants.

37. These figures were computed from *Campaigns and Elections* magazine's list of clients in the January 2001 issue. Some consultants did technical work only and did not contribute any strategic value.

38. Estimates of consultant use is really all we have at this time. The estimates reported here come from various sources—mostly surveys of candidate's campaigns—but they are the best scholars or journalists can do at the present time. Without turning to candidates' reports that are filed with the Federal Election Commission on how they spent their money during an election cycle, it is next to impossible to gauge exactly how many candidates for office employed consultants.

39. Goldenberg and Traugott 1984.

40. Medvic 2001.

41. Dulio 2001.

42. Herrnson 2000, Table 3.1.

43. Johnson 2000.

44. Ibid., 39.

45. Dulio 2001.

46. Personal communication on July 2, 2001.

47. For more information on these criticisms, see Blumenthal 1980; Petracca 1989, 11–14; Johnson-Cartee and Copeland 1997; and Sabato 1981, 7.

48. Marcus 2000, 1.

49. This report mentions that in the nation's top seventy-five media markets (484 television stations) at least $771 million was spent, but when the other 135 markets (roughly 800 stations) are factored into the calculation, the estimate nears the $1 billion figure. Alliance for Better Campaigns 2001; see www.bettercampaigns.org for a copy of the report.

50. This calculation adjusts for inflation.

51. Herrnson and Patterson 2000.

52. Media consultants do usually take a commission that ranges between 7 and 15 percent of the advertising time that is bought for the commercials they make. With many ad buys, the fee is not a small sum. However, critics overstate the amounts that make it to consultants in the form of profits.

53. Kamber 1997.

54. Clinger 1987, 727–748.

55. Kahn and Kenney 2000, 65.

56. I say alleged consequences because to a great extent, the scholarly literature is mixed in its conclusions about the effects of so-called negative advertising. There are studies that show that those who see negative ads are less likely to vote. However, there are also studies that show an increase in the likelihood of voting for those exposed to negative campaigning. For a full review of this literature, see Lau and Sigelman 2000.

57. Petracca 1989, 13.

58. See Jamieson 1992.

59. Jamieson, Waldman, and Sheerr 2000.

60. See Medvic 2001.

61. Jamieson, Waldman, and Sheerr 2000, 46.

62. Ibid.

## Chapter 2

1. There are a number of excellent studies of public or media polling, some of which also serve as good primers on the mechanics of polling. See, for example, Lavrakas and Traugott 2000; Traugott and Lavrakas 2000; Asher 1998; Mann and Orren 1992; and Cantril 1991.

2. The history of public opinion polling has been told in a number of books. Among the best are Converse 1987, and Herbst 1993.

3. Gallup and Rae 1940, 34–35; Smith 1990, 21–36.

4. Rubenstein 1995, 63.

5. "Landon" 1936, 5–6; "What Went Wrong?" 1936, 7–8.

6. Much hand-wringing occurred in the immediate aftermath of the *Digest*'s mistake. The magazine itself attempted to determine the source of the problem. Others who weighed in on the subject included Crossley 1937; Gosnell 1937; Robinson 1937; and Katz and Cantril 1937. See Squire 1988, 21–36; Rubenstein 1995, 63–68; Converse 1987.

7. The *Digest* had mailed ballots to people on telephone and automobile registration lists. This tel-auto sample frame was more Republican than the population at large. In addition, the poll suffered from a low response rate combined with a nonresponse bias (Squire 1988, 131.)

8. Rubenstein 1995, 66–67.

9. Converse 1987, 117.

10. Gallup and Rae 1940.

11. Rubenstein 1995, 72–79.

12. Kelley 1956, 39–66; Pitchell 1958, 11.

13. Nimmo 1970, 36.

14. See Perry 1968; Agranoff 1972a; Rosenbloom 1973; Napolitan 1999; Napolitan 1972.

15. Rosenbloom 1973, 51–53.

16. Medvic 2001.

17. Agranoff 1972b, 726.

18. As it settled into conventional wisdom in the late 1980s, the "decline of parties" thesis was probably exaggerated (for one of the earliest expressions of the thesis, see Broder 1972; Crotty 1984 offers a more scholarly take on the subject). Yet there was truth in the argument. And it is certainly no surprise that political

consulting began in California, a state with notoriously weak parties, following the Progressive Era. Nevertheless, the parties were able to adapt to "candidate-centered" politics in ways that make them essential actors in today's campaigns. See, for instance, Herrnson 1988; Maisel 1998; and Green and Shea 1999.

19. See Ware 1988, 10.

20. Jensen 1980, 54.

21. See Dexter 1954, 53–61.

22. Of course, Louis Harris had polled for the Kennedy campaign in 1960. Indeed, Hamilton (1995, 163) suggests that "it was Harris who truly spawned a new industry or profession in 1960 with the publicity surrounding his polling for the new president."

23. Harris 1963, 3–8.

24. King and Schnitzer 1968, 431–436.

25. Hamilton 1995, 165.

26. Goldenberg and Traugott 1984, 55.

27. Ibid, 54–56.

28. Hamilton 1995, 165.

29. My own data suggest that in 1992, 47.3 percent of all House candidates employed professional pollsters. See Medvic 2001; Herrnson 1998, 62.

30. Johnson 2001, 91.

31. Hamilton and Beattie 1999, 100.

32. Ibid, 98–99.

33. Ibid.

34. Ibid.

35. Ibid, 103.

36. Rivlin 1999, 2326.

37. Ibid.

38. Hamilton and Beattie 1999, 103.

39. Johnson 2001, 104.

40. Kolbert 1992, 18–20.

41. Ibid.

42. Quoted in ibid, 60.

43. Diamond and Bates 1992, 352–353.

44. Johnson 2001, 111–112.

45. Hamilton and Beattie 1999, 96.

46. Ibid, 97.

47. Author interview with Mark Mellman on July 17, 2000, Washington, D.C.

48. Harris 1963, 7.

49. Hamilton 1995, 166–167.

50. Ibid, 169.

51. Bradshaw 1995, 42.

52. Shea 1996, 150.

53. Ibid.

54. Shafer and Claggett (1995) argue that Democrats are stronger on what they call the "economic/welfare" factor and Republicans have an advantage on the "cultural/national factor."

55. See Medvic 2001.

56. Bolger and McInturff 1996, 70.

57. Ibid.

58. The AAPOR "Statement Condemning Push Polls" can be found on the Internet at www.aapor.org/ethics/pushpoll.html.

59. Bolger and McInturff 1996, 70.

60. See Couper (2000) for a full review of web polling systems.
61. Maguire and Ashford 2000, 68.
62. Ibid.
63. In fact, for a variety of reasons, Internet users may be more representative of voters as a group than of the population at large.
64. Estimate based on a July 1, 2001, figure of 167,421,299 Internet users. See 209.249.142.27/nnpm/owa/NRpublicreports.usageweekly.
65. For a list of the recruitment sources used, as well as a general discussion of the methodology of HOPL, see www.harrisinteractive.com/about/methodology.asp.
66. This is not to say that online polling does not have disadvantages. In fact, as Feld (2000) notes, push polling via the Internet can be done with ease, given the ability to "spam" (or send unsolicited mass e-mails). Cyber–push polling may soon be too tempting for some campaigns to resist.
67. Bowman 2000; Jacobs and Shapiro 2000.
68. Verba 1996, 1–7.
69. Luntz 1988, 227.
70. Even among adherents of the trustee model, the extent to which a representative is permitted to ignore public opinion is a matter of some debate.
71. Sabato 1981, 320.
72. Kolbert 1992, 72.
73. Hitchens 1994, 42–43.
74. Ibid.
75. Ibid.
76. Heclo 2000, 33.
77. Bryce 1891, 254.

## Chapter 3

1. Sweeney 1995, 14–29.
2. Lynn, Heinrich, and Hill 2001.
3. Lavrakas and Traugott 2000.
4. Wolfinger 1995, 181–191.
5. Hamilton 1995, 161–180.
6. Bradshaw 1995, 30–46.
7. Davies 1999.
8. Loomis 2001, 123–159.

## Chapter 4

1. The study was conducted by David B. Magleby of Brigham Young University. See the monograph at www.byu.edu/outsidemoney or the June 2001 edition of PS Online at www.aspsanet.org/psonline/.
2. Clymer 2000, A1.
3. Ibid.
4. Vigoda 2000, B01.
5. Canon 1990.
6. Kolodny 1998; Herrnson 1988.
7. Dwyre and Kolodny 2001.
8. Federal Elections Commission 2001b.

9. The figures were compiled by the authors from FEC data. See the FEC Web page at www.fec.gov.

10. Neil Oxman, telephone interview with authors, January 23, 2001.

11. Karin Johanson, political director, Democratic Congressional Campaign Committee, 2001. Interviewed by Jason Beal, Brigham Young University, January 10.

12. Joe Grace, telephone interview with authors, January 19, 2001.

13. FEC 2001b.

14. Peter Marinari, campaign manager for Stewart Greenleaf, 2000. Telephone interview with authors, November 15.

15. Ibid.

16. John Del Cecato, telephone interview with authors, December 21, 2000.

17. Oxman 2001.

18. Kolodny 1998.

19. Herrnson 2000, 128.

20. Diana White, telephone interview with authors, January 16, 2001.

21. Ibid.

22. FEC 2001b.

23. See the League of Conservation Voters press release on "LCV Action Fund's Environmental Champion's Campaign."

24. LCV and Andrew Werbrock, telephone interview with authors, January 16, 2000.

25. Andrew Englander, telephone interview with authors, December 20, 2000.

26. Gloria Totten, telephone interview with authors, December 20, 2000.

27. Ibid.

28. Ibid.

29. FEC, January 22, 2001.

30. Adam Spey, telephone interview with authors, December 12, 2000.

31. Ibid.

32. Ibid.

33. FEC, January 22, 2001.

34. Bernadette Budde, Business-Industry Political Action Committee (BIPAC). Interview with David Magleby, November 10, 2000.

## Part 2: Current Issues In Elections

1. Federal Election Commission 2000b.

2. "Uncounted ballots" are cast by voters but uncounted by election officials for whatever reason. "Unmarked ballots," sometimes termed the "undervote," may occur because the voter abstained or the recording device did not register the mark. "Overvoted ballots" record a vote in more than one place for a given office, but may occur because the voter clearly marked more names than allowed or when a voter places a legal mark next to a candidate's name and then writes the same name on the "write-in candidate" line on the ballot.

3. Recount officials identified a "punched chad" as punched all the way out; "hanging door chad" had one corner attached to the ballot; "swinging door chad" had two corners attached to the ballot; "pregnant chad" had a bulge but no punch through the ballot; and "dimpled chad" had an indentation on the ballot but no perforation. See Merzer et al. 2001.

4. See Herrnson 2000; Wolf 2000, A3.

5. Alvarez et al. 2001, www.vote.caltech.edu/#release.

6. Ibid., 7.

7. FEC 2000b.

8. See www.fec.gov/press/051501congfinact/p51501congfinact.html, accessed January 9, 2002.

9. Ibid.

# Chapter 6

1. Pomper 2001.

2. Schier 2000.

3. Ibid.

4. See Silbey 1991; McGerr 1986; Burnham 1982a.

5. McGerr 1986.

6. Campbell et al. 1960.

7. On realignment, see Burnham 1970; Key 1955, 3–18; Sundquist 1983.

8. Anderson 1976, 74–95.

9. See Hofstadter 1955; Burnham 1982b, 147–202.

10. Ladd 1978, 31–128.

11. Nie, Verba, and Petrocik 1976.

12. See Rae 1989; Brennan 1995.

13. See Shafer 1983.

14. Carter 1996.

15. Nie, Verba, and Petrocik 1976.

16. See Ehrenhalt 1991; Fenno 1978.

17. For information on Carter and the 1976 election, see Witcover.

18. Bibby 1980, 102–115.

19. Reichley 1985, 175–200.

20. Drew 1983.

21. See Peele 1984.

22. Sinclair 1995.

23. Rohde 1991.

24. Ranney 1983.

25. For information on Clinton and the "New Democrats" of the Democratic Leadership Council, see Baer 2000.

26. On the travails of U.S. conservatives in the early 1990s, see Lind 1996.

27. Rae 2001, 183–200.

28. Hill 1995, 38–401.

29. Gimpel 1996; Rae 1998.

30. On Gingrich's fall, see Baker 2000, 140–159.

31. Campbell and Rae 2000a.

32. Campbell and Rae 2000b.

33. On the 2000 nominating campaigns, see Mayer 2001.

# Chapter 7

1. Jacobson 1990; Krasno 1994.

2. Jacobson 1990; Connelly and Pitney 1994.

3. Herrnson 1998.

4. Farrar-Myers 2001.

5. Ibid.

6. McCain 2001, www.senate.gov/~mccain/cfrsumm.htm.

7. Farrar-Myers 1999, 261–278.

8. Cantor 1998.

9. Dwyre and Farrar-Myers 2001.

10. Ibid.

11. Ibid.

12. Quoted in a February 1, 1999, Common Cause press release titled, "Editorial Memorandum: Bipartisan Campaign Finance Reform Reintroduced; Reformers Ready to Capitalize on Majority Support and Push for Action."

13. Senator Jon Kyl (R-Ariz.), former senator William Roth (R-Del.), former senator Connie Mack (R-Fla.), Senator Richard Lugar (R-Ind.), former senator Spencer Abraham (R-Mich.), former senator Rod Grams (R-Minn.), former senator John D. Ashcroft (R-Mo.), Senator Trent Lott (R-Miss.), Senator Conrad Burns (R-Mont.), Senator Mike DeWine (R-Ohio), Senator Rick Santorum (R-Pa.), Senator Bill Frist (R-Tenn.), Senator Kay Bailey Hutchinson (R-Tx.), Senator Orrin Hatch (R-Utah), former senator Slade Gorton (R-Wash.), and Senator Craig Thomas (R-Wy.).

14. A greater need exists for supporting campaign finance reform in public opinion polls.

15. Elder 2001.

16. Gallup Poll 2001.

17. Elder 2001.

18. Gallup Poll 2001.

19. McCain 2001.

20. Dwyre and Farrar-Myers 2001.

21. Cochran 2001b; Cochran 2001c, 842.

22. Cochran 2001b; Cochran 2001c, 842.

23. Summary prepared by the offices of Representatives Shays and Meehan, February 14, 2002, available at www.house.gov/shays/hot/CFR.

24. Campaign Finance Institute Cyber Forum 2001.

25. The tax checkoff system is in decline in use, and public opinion shows less support for it as well. Not only are fewer people contributing to presidential campaigns via the $3 checkoff, but the money that is raised has not kept pace with inflation.

## Chapter 8

1. Key 1949, 10.

2. Black and Black 1987, 260–316; Bullock and Rozell 1998, 3–20.

3. Bullock and Rozell 1998, 20.

4. Lamis 1999, 4.

5. Quoted in Kohut 2000, 56.

6. Voter News Service exit polls may be found at msnbc.com/m/d2k/g/polls.asp.

7. Black and Black 1987.

8. Green et al. 1998.

9. The South in the Voter News Service exit polls includes the states of Oklahoma, Kentucky, and West Virginia, along with the eleven states of the old confederacy.

10. See Voter News Service exit polls, 2001.

11. Manuel 1998, 1A, 16A.

12. Shapiro 1998, 2A.

13. Kuzenski 1998, 33.

14. Edsall 1998, A4.
15. Quoted in Sack 1998, A16.
16. Swindell and Gaulden 1998, 1.
17. Kazee 1998, 144.
18. Alvarez 1998, 10.
19. Quoted in Dewar 1998, A23.
20. Luebke 1990.
21. Dewar 1998.
22. Colburn and de Haven-Smith 1999.
23. Follick 2000, 1.
24. Corrigan 2000, 61–69.
25. Quoted in Novak 2001, 21.

## Chapter 10

### *View 1*

1. In the appendix to this chapter, a copy of the notorious "butterfly ballot" used in Palm Beach County, Broward County's neighbor to the north, is shown. It had no formal or legal bearing on the Broward election. It simply added to the overall controversy in Florida's election.
2. Florida allows preregistration at age seventeen.
3. See the Division of Elections Opinion to Jane Carroll—DE0012 Manual Recount Procedures 102.11.1, Florida Statutes.
4. Florida attorney general opinion 00-65.
5. The name of the organization is Revitalizing Democracy in Florida—the Governor's Task Force on Election Procedures, Standards, and Technology, March 1, 2001.
6. Florida CS for SB1118-01, Florida Legislative Session.

### *View 2*

1. See "Make Every Vote Count," letter to the editor, *South Florida Sun-Sentinel,* February 26, 2001, 1.

## Part 3: Candidates and Voters

1. Herrnson 2000; Menefee-Libey 2000.
2. Ehrenhalt 1992.
3. Beiler 2000.
4. Davidson and Oleszek 2002, 420.

## Chapter 11

1. See "Election 2000: Senate Profiles" 2000, 2673–2678; see also http://library2.cqpress.com/cqweekly.

2. Hirschfeld 2001, 178–182.

3. See United Nations Development Program 1998.

4. Brophy-Baermann 2000; Canon and Herrnson 2000.

5. See Center for American Women and Politics 2000.

6. As a side note, the evidence that women comprise a smaller percentage of professionalized legislatures (e.g., those that pay higher salaries) is mixed, according to Darcy, Welch, and Clark 1994. Both Minnesota and Wisconsin have more professionalized legislatures, and a higher proportion of their legislators are women than the other four states studied here.

7. Rule 1987, 477–498, see 479; Rule 1981, 60–77.

8. Clark et al. 1984, 154.

9. Welch and Karnig 1979, 478–491.

10. Darcy, Welch, and Clark 1994.

11. Nechemias 1985, 119–131.

12. Nechemias 1987, 125–142.

13. Rule 1981.

14. Gertzog 1995.

15. Darcy and Schramm 1977, 1–12.

16. Darcy, Brewer, and Clay 1984, 67–78, see 70.

17. Clark et al. 1984.

18. Ibid, 145.

19. Newman 1994.

20. Ibid., 1–2; emphasis in original.

21. Darcy, Welch, and Clark 1994; see also Cook 1998.

22. Clark et al. 1984, 147.

23. Burrell 1988, 51–68; Burrell 1992, 493–508.

24. Carroll 1994.

25. Burrell 1985, 261.

26. Uhlaner and Schlozman 1986, 30–50, see 42.

27. Darcy, Welch, and Clark 1994.

28. Uhlaner and Schlozman 1986.

29. Mayhew 1974, 295–317.

30. Jacobson 1992.

31. Carey, Niemi, and Powell 1998, 271–300.

32. Schlesinger 1994.

33. Ibid.

34. Nebraska is the only legislature for which we have accurate data on prior elective office.

35. Bullock et al. 1999.

36. Conway, Steuernagel, and Ahern 1997.

37. Darcy, Welch, and Clark 1994.

38. Ibid.

39. In 2000, only fourteen women were serving in the South Dakota state legislature.

40. In early 2001, the author's team sent South Dakota state legislators and county commissioners a written questionnaire about their political experiences and plans. Sixty-eight of 105 legislators and 196 of 300 commissioners completed and returned the instrument.

41. Nechemias 1985.

42. Schlesinger 1994.

43. Conway, Steuernagel, and Ahern 1997.

44. Carroll 1994.

45. Maisel, Stone, and Maestas 2001.
46. Fowler and McClure 1989.
47. Ibid., 228.
48. Sigel 1996.
49. Beck 1991.
50. Welch and Thomas 1991.
51. Costantini 1990, 741–770.

## Chapter 12

1. For more on immigration from Mexico and U.S. immigration policy, see Andreas 2000.
2. Davidson and Oleszek 2000, 133.
3. Grofman, Handley, and Niemi 1992.
4. Southern Democrats agreed to provide enough Electoral College votes to allow Republican candidate Rutherford B. Hayes to become president in exchange for the withdrawal of union troops from the South and the general hands-off policy toward the South.
5. Rosenberg 1991.
6. By the Supreme Court in *Guinn v. United States.*
7. By the 1970 Voting Rights Act.
8. The Court did not overturn its use in state elections until *Harper v. Virginia State Board of Elections* in 1966.
9. Grofman, Handley, and Niemi 1992, 10.
10. Woodward 1971; Whitby 2000, 21.
11. Raines 1977, 337.
12. More than 6,500 such poll officials would be assigned.
13. Aside from nonvoting delegates representing Puerto Rico and Guam.
14. For additional information, see Balderama and Rodriguez 1998.
15. For more information, see García 2000.
16. Gómez-Quinones 1990, 104–105.
17. Davidson 1992, 35.
18. This term was named after Governor Elbridge Gerry of Massachusetts, who in 1811 signed into law a bill creating a district similar to a salamander—or a "gerrymander," according to political wags of the day.
19. Other electoral schemes to prevent the election of a minority official (known collectively as vote dilution) include switching from district to at-large voting, outlawing "single shot" voting, requiring a majority runoff, and moving state elections to off years. See Davidson 1992.
20. Grofman, Handley, and Niemi 1992, 26.
21. The Supreme Court also ruled that gerrymandering is illegal if it is used to dilute the power of minority voters, which was also forbidden by the Voting Rights Act of 1965.
22. See, for example, "High Court" 1993.
23. See, for example, "For Very Strange Bedfellows, Try Redistricting" 1995.
24. Cain and Miller 1998, 142.
25. Lublin 1997, 123.
26. Thernstrom 1987.
27. Reed 1988; for a rebuttal to these points, see Fraga 1992.
28. Skerry 1993.

29. See Cain and Miller (1998, 155–157) for recent litigation on this subject.

30. Three were originally elected from majority-minority districts that were later redrawn as majority-white districts because of a court order.

31. Calvo and Rosenstone 1989, 2.

32. Hero 1992, 8.

33. Ibid., 63.

34. Uhlaner, Cain, and Kiewiet 1987, i.

35. Wolfinger 1988.

36. DeSipio 1996.

37. Pachon 1987; de la Garza et al. 1992.

38. Jones-Correa 1998, 65.

39. Horner 2000.

40. These results are also reflected in the more recent Washington Post/Kaiser Family Foundation/Harvard University "National Survey on Latinos in America" poll. See also, de la Garza et al. 1992.

41. DeSipio, de la Garza, and Setzler 1999, 7.

42. The answers do not round to 100 because the answer "don't know" was not reported.

43. DeSipio, de la Garza, and Setzler 1999.

44. Data from Barker, Jones, and Tate 1998; Green 2000.

45. See de la Garza et al. 1992.

46. Green 2000.

47. DeSipio, de la Garza, and Setzler 1999, 9.

48. Horner 1999.

49. Verba and Nie 1972; Miller et al. 1981, 494–511; Shingles 1981, 76–91.

50. Verba and Nie 508; see also Miller et al. 1981, 494–511; Shingles 1981, 76–91.

51. Ellison and Gay 1989, 101–119.

52. Swain 1995, 11.

53. Whitby 2000, 8.

54. Swain 1995, 11.

55. Tate 1994, 51.

56. Data from Barker, Jones, and Tate 1998.

57. Weissberg 1978, 535–547.

58. Pitkin 1967.

59. Davidson 1992, 43.

60. National Association of Latino Elected Officials 2000.

61. Bositis 1997.

62. Hero 1992.

# Chapter 13

1. Center for the American Woman and Politics 2001.

2. Ibid.

3. Morris 1992; Weissman 1996.

4. Kahn 1994b, 162–195.

5. Graber 1997; Iyengar and Kinder 1987; Patterson 1980.

6. According to Gitlin (1980, 7), "media frames are persistent patterns of cognition, interpretation, and presentation, of selection, emphasis, and exclusion, by which symbol handlers routinely organize discourse, whether verbal or visual."

7. Morris 1992.

8. Braden 1996; Getlin and Evans 1992, 16–17; Mandel 1981; Morris 1992; Ross and Sreberny 2000; Weissman 1996; Witt, Paget, and Matthews 1994.

9. Miller 2001, 83–100.

10. Kahn 1994a, 154–173; Kahn 1996.

11. Kahn and Goldenberg 1991, 180–199; Kahn 1996; Kahn 1994a.

12. Kahn 1996.

13. Witt, Paget, and Matthews 1994.

14. Trent and Friedenberg 1991.

15. Lake 1990.

16. Smith 1997, 71–82, 77.

17. Rausch, Rozell, and Wilson 1999, 1–21.

18. Rausch, Rozell, and Wilson (1999), Kahn and Goldenberg (1991), and Kahn (1996, 1994a, 1994b) all use the September 1 through Election Day period; Smith (1997) uses forty days prior to the November election.

19. Center for the American Woman and Politics 2001.

20. Ibid.

21. Ibid.

22. Watson and Gordon 2003.

23. Kahn 1996, 1994a, 1994b.

24. Bystrom, Robertson, and Banwart 2000, 1999–2013.

25. Helderman, Carroll, and Olson 2000.

26. Devitt 1999.

27. Diamond and Bates 1992.

28. Lengle, Owen, and Sonner 1995, 370–383; Southwell 1986, 81–95.

29. Categorizing the issues in this way is consistent with the research by Kahn (1996).

30. Kahn 1996.

31. Smith 1997.

32. Ibid.

33. The source for this difference appears to be articles concerning her objectivity, partisan nature, and trustworthiness. The only major event at this time was Hoeven's request for a leave of absence from his job as head of the State Bank of North Dakota. Heitkamp was one of three members of the state's Industrial Commission that had to rule on his request. Heitkamp voted to deny the request. The story quickly became how "Heidi fired Hoeven."

# Chapter 14

1. Documents were provided by the Minnesota Secretary of State 1998.

2. Frank and Wagner 2001.

3. Kunkel 1998.

4. St. Cloud State University Survey was conducted in 1998.

5. Minnesota Secretary of State 1998.

6. Minnesota Campaign Finance and Public Disclosure Board 1999.

7. Ibid.

8. Backstrom 1998.

9. Ibid.

10. Backstrom 1998; Minnesota Secretary of State 1998.

11. Joseph A. Kunkle III's personal correspondence with the authors in 1999.

12. Ibid.

13. The "Minnesota Poll" was conducted by the *Star Tribune* in Minneapolis 1998.

14. The "Minnesota Poll" was taken in October 1998.

## Chapter 15

1. As quoted in Dewar 1998, A2. The last open seat election in New York had taken place in 1958.

2. Ibid.

3. Kirtzman 2000, 239.

4. Ibid.

5. Burger 1999, 5.

6. Grunwald 1999.

7. Kirtzman 2000, 240. Hillary Clinton sought out the advice of prominent New York political insiders such as Ickes, who had played a major role in David Dinkins's 1989 mayoral campaign in New York City and Bill Clinton's 1992 presidential campaign.

8. Ibid., 260.

9. Quoted in Duke 1999, A1. Regarding the FALN controversy, however, it should be noted that none of the Puerto Rican prisoners involved had been directly implicated in the bombings, yet most had received fifty-year sentences, and by the time President Clinton offered clemency, they had served roughly twenty years in jail.

10. Quoted in Barrett 2000, 165. Giuliani, who had been elected in 1993 and 1997, was ineligible to run for reelection in 2001.

11. Kirtzman 2000, 14. Giuliani had successfully prosecuted Stanley Friedman and three others for racketeering, conspiracy, and mail fraud. This case arose from Friedman's efforts to steer a contract for hand-held computers, for the City's Parking Violations Bureau, to a company in which he had a financial interest. The Queens borough president, Donald Manes, who was part of the scheme, committed suicide rather than face criminal charges. For more on this scandal and other scandals that buffeted the city government during Ed Koch's third term as mayor, see Newfield and Barrett 1988. Giuliani and Senator D'Amato had a long history marked by feud and disagreement. In 1989, D'Amato encouraged Ronald Lauder, the cosmetics heir, to challenge Giuliani for the Republican nomination for mayor. In addition to his feud with D'Amato, Giuliani had enraged Republicans by endorsing Democratic governor Mario Cuomo during his reelection bid in 1994.

12. Podhoretz 2000, 29.

13. Nagourney and Connelly 2000, A1.

14. Quoted in *Newsday* editorial 2000, A48.

15. Jakes 2000, A1.

16. Quoted in Janison and Palmer 2000, A3. The separation of Giuliani and Hanover was not surprising to most observers. Hanover, a newscaster and actress, had stopped appearing with her husband in public during his first term. An article written by Jennet Conant in *Vanity Fair* magazine titled "The Ghost and Mr. Giuliani" alleged that Giuliani was having an affair with a member of his staff and that the New York media had ignored the story; an affair that Hanover would make a veiled reference to in her own press conference following her husband's announcement. Both the Kirtzman and Barrett biographies examine the mayor's estrangement from his wife.

17. Barone and Ujifusa 1999. As a member of the House of Representatives, Lazio supported the Brady Bill, the assault weapons ban, the striker replacement

bill, and the Family Leave Act. He was also a supporter of the National Endowment for the Arts.

18. Riley 2000, A8.

19. The irony of Lazio's consideration for the Republican nomination for county executive in Nassau is that, if he had decided to run, he would have had to confront the "carpetbagger" issue. Lazio has lived his entire life in Suffolk County, the suburban county that lies to the east of Nassau County. Lazio replaced George J. Vojta, the former vice chairman of Bankers Trust, who had been president of the forum since April 1, 2000. When Vojta was hired, *American Banker* magazine reported that the "group is seeking to hire an experienced, high-profile Washington lobbyist." (See the article in the magazine, "Financial Services Forum Picks President," 2.). Lazio would appear to fit the bill.

20. Carolan and Keating 2000, A46. "Soft money" is the term used to describe contributions to national party committees that do not have to be reported to the Federal Elections Commission (and, depending on the law, not to state election authorities either) because they are supposed to be used for "party-building activity" rather than for a particular candidate. Often, these monies are used for "advocacy advertisements" or are conveyed to state party committees for their use.

21. Quoted in Kugler 2000, A38. The USS *Cole* was a naval ship that was bombed by terrorists while refueling in Aden, Yemen, on October 12, 2000. The attack killed seventeen crew members and injured thirty-nine others.

22. Quoted in Saul 2000, A26.

23. See Marist Institute of Public Opinion poll 2000.

24. Barone and Ujifusa 1999, 1088.

25. Quoted in Moore 2000, A17.

26. Quoted in Plaven 2000, A8.

27. Dolman 2000, A40.

28. Bumiller 2000, IV3.

29. Ibid.

30. Quoted in Nagourney and Connelly 2000, A1.

31. See Marist Institute poll 2001.

32. Lovett 2001, 2.

## Chapter 16

1. Jacobson 2001a.

2. Ibid.

3. Ibid.

4. Herrnson 2000; Gaddie and Bullock 2000.

5. Gaddie and Bullock (2000) estimate that, based on previous rates of Republican success in different types of open seat elections, Republicans would have realized a net gain of three open seats in 1994, rather than eighteen. Holding other outcomes constant, the result would have been a three-seat Democratic majority in the House.

6. Gilmour and Rothstein 1993, 345–365; Gaddie 1997, 675–686.

7. The normal vote is the average Republican share of the two-party presidential vote in the district for the previous two elections. Data for the computation of the normal vote were obtained from various editions of *The Almanac of American Politics*. It is worth noting that many normal vote measures incorporate data from a variety of other offices. However, Bond, Fleisher, and Talbert's (1997) analysis indicated that presidential-based normal vote measures and other normal

vote measures are highly correlated and that they produce almost identical relationships with dependent variables. Therefore, we opted for the simpler measure of the normal vote.

8. Gaddie and Bullock 2000.
9. Stone and Rappaport 2001.
10. Campbell 1997; Jacobson 2000.
11. Gaddie and Bullock 2000.
12. Gary Jacobson (2001) argues that there is no natural Republican majority in the U.S. House. Republicans are in the majority, but it is tenuous at best. We agree, though we would also posit that to the extent that the majority more typically belongs to the Democrats in this current system, it is a majority that will be far more vulnerable to partisan tides.
13. Corrado 2001.
14. Ibid.
15. Ibid.
16. Ibid.
17. Magleby 2001.
18. Ibid.
19. Jacobson 2001a.

## Chapter 17

1. Mayer 2001.
2. Balz 2000, A1, 11.
3. Glasser and Balz 2000, A1, 8.
4. Walsh 2000, A1, 18.
5. Mayer 2001.
6. Morin and Deane 2000, A1, 11.
7. Kaiser 2000, A12.
8. Erikson 2001, 29–52.
9. Mintz and Slevin 2001, A1, 20–21.
10. Eskew 2001, A17.
11. Erikson 2001, 43.
12. Ibid.
13. Pomper 2001, 133.
14. Von Drehele, Nakashima, Schmidt, and Connolly 2001, A1, 10–11.
15. Von Drehele, Becker, Nakashima, and Romano 2001, A1, 6–7.
16. Von Drehele, Becker, Nakashima, and Balz 2001, A1, 12–13.
17. Von Drehele, Balz, Grimaldi, and Schmidt 2001, A1, 12–13.
18. Von Drehele, Schmidt, Grimaldi, and Becker 2001, 16–17.
19. Von Drehele, Slevin, Balz, and Grimaldi 2001, A1.
20. Klain 2001, A12.
21. Lane 2001, A24.
22. Lane 2001, A13.
23. Pressley and Skipp 2001, A2.
24. Pierre and Slevin 2001, A1, 4.
25. Jacobson 2001b, 5–28.
26. Barger 1999.
27. Eksterowicz and Hastedt 1999.
28. O'Brien 2000.
29. Milbank 2001, A1, 18; Kessler 2001.

30. Eilperin 2001a, A6–7; Eilperin 2001, A23.
31. Dewar 2001a, A12–13.
32. Montgomery 2001, A10; see also the CBO online at www.cbo.gov/showdoc.
cfm?index=19448sequence=0.
33. Eilperin 2001a; 2001b.
34. Ford 2001.
35. Ford et al. 2001.

# Bibliography

Acuna, Rodolfo. 1972. *Occupied America: The Chicano's Struggle Toward Liberation.* San Francisco: Harper and Row.

Agranoff, Robert, ed. 1972a. *The New Style in Election Campaigns.* Boston: Holbrook Press.

————. 1972b. "Introduction/The New Style of Campaigning: The Decline of Party and the Rise of Candidate Centered Technology." In *The New Style in Election Campaigns*, ed. Robert Agranoff. Boston: Holbrook Press.

Alexander, Deborah, and Kristi Andersen. 1993. "Gender as a Factor in the Attribution of Leadership Traits." *Political Research Quarterly* 46: 527–545.

Alliance for Better Campaigns. 2001. "Gouging Democracy: How the Television Industry Profiteered on Campaign 2000." Washington, D.C.: Alliance for Better Campaigns, www.bettercampaigns.org.

Alter, Jonathan. 2001a. "A Beltway Bungee Jump." *Newsweek,* April 9, 30–31.

————. 2001b. "At Last, the Battle Is Joined." *Newsweek,* March 19, 31.

Alvarez, Lizette. 2001. "The Race Is Underway for Campaign Cash Before New Limits." *New York Times,* February 11, 11.

————. 1998. "Health Issue Dominates Senate Race." *New York Times,* July 5, 10.

Alvarez, R. Michael, Stephen Ansolabehere, Eric Antonsson, and Jehoshua Bruck. 2001. *Voting: What Is, What Could Be.* Cal Tech–MIT Voting Technology Project, www.vote.caltech.edu/#release.

American Banker. 2000. "Financial Services Forum Picks President." *American Banker,* March 17, 2.

Anderson, Kristi. 1976. "Generation, Partisan Shift, and Realignment: A Glance Back at the New Deal." In *The Changing American Voter*, ed. Norman H. Nie, Sidney Verba, and John R. Petrocik. Cambridge, Mass.: Harvard University Press, 74–95.

Andreas, Peter. 2000. *Border Games: Policing the U.S.-Mexico Divide.* Ithaca, N.Y.: Cornell University Press.

Ansolabehere, Stephen, Shanto Iyengar, Adam Simon, and Nicholas Valentino. 1994. "Does Attack Advertising Demobilize the Electorate?" *American Political Science Review* 88: 829–838.

Asher, Herbert. 1998. *Polling and the Public: What Every Citizen Should Know.* 4th ed. Washington, D.C.: Congressional Quarterly Press.

Backstrom, Charles H. 1998. "Conducting Elections in Minnesota." In *Perspectives on Minnesota Government and Politics,* ed. Steve Hoffman, Donald Ostrom, Homer Williamson, and Kay Wolsborn. Edina, Minn.: Burgess Publishing.

285

Baer, Denise. 1995. "Contemporary Strategy and Agenda Setting." In *Campaigns and Elections American Style*, ed. James A. Thurber and Candice J. Nelson. Boulder, Colo.: Westview Press.

Baer, Kenneth S. 2000. *Reinventing Democrats: The Politics of Liberalism from Reagan to Clinton*. Lawrence: University of Kansas Press.

Baker, Peter. 2000. *The Breach: Inside the Impeachment and Trial of William Jefferson Clinton*. New York: Scribner's.

Balderama, Francisco, and Raymond Rodriguez. 1998. *Decade of Betrayal: Mexican Repatriation in the 1930s*. Albuquerque: University of New Mexico Press.

Balz, Dan. 2001. "Awash in Money, Bush Needs Message." *Washington Post*, February 3, A1, 11.

Barger, H. M. 1999. "The Incredible Shrinking Image: From Cold War to Globalist Presidency." In *The Post–Cold War Presidency*, ed. Anthony J. Eksterowicz and Glenn P. Hastedt. Lanham, Md.: Rowman and Littlefield.

Barker, Lucius, Mack Jones, and Katherine Tate. 1998. *African Americans and the American Political System*. 4th ed. Englewood Cliffs, N.J.: Prentice-Hall.

Barone, Michael, and Grant Ujifusa. 1999. *Almanac of American Politics, 2000: The Senators, the Representatives, and the Governors: Their Records and Election Results, Their States and Districts*. Washington, D.C.: National Journal.

Barrett, Wayne. 2000. *Rudy: An Investigative Biography of Rudolph Giuliani*. New York: Basic Books.

Beck, Susan Abrams. 1991. "Rethinking Municipal Government: Gender Distinctions in Local Councils." In *Gender and Policymaking: Studies of Women in Office*, ed. Debra L. Dodson. New Brunswick, N.J.: Center for the American Woman and Politics, Eagleton Institute of Politics, Rutgers University.

Beiler, David. 2000. "Bama Bash: Endorsement Backlash Saves a Governor from Primary Defeat in Alabama in 1998." In *Campaigns and Elections: Contemporary Case Studies*, ed. Michael A. Bailey, Ronald A. Faucheux, Paul S. Herrnson, and Clyde Wilcox. Washington, D.C.: CQ Press.

Bender, Earl. 2001. Personal communication. July 2.

Berke, Richard L. 2001a. "Campaign Finance Overhaul May Enhance Influence of Big PACs." *New York Times*, April 2.

———. 2001b. "News Analysis: A New Approach for Party Chairman." *New York Times*, April 3, www.nytimes.com/2001/04/03/politics/03ASSE.html.

Bibby, John F. 1980. "Party Renewal in the Republican Party." In *Party Renewal in America: Theory and Practice*, ed. Gerald M. Pomper. New York: Praeger, 102–115.

Black, Earl, and Merle Black. 1987. *Politics and Society in the South*. Cambridge, Mass.: Harvard University Press.

Black, Merle. 1978. "Racial Composition of Congressional Districts and Support for Federal Voting Rights in the American South." *Social Science Quarterly* 59: 435–450.

Blumenthal, Sidney. 1980. *The Permanent Campaign: Inside the World of Elite Political Operatives*. Boston: Beacon Press.

Bolger, Glen, and Bill McInturff. 1996. "Push Polling Stinks." *Campaigns and Elections* (August): 70.

Bolton, Alexander. 2001a. "Breach of Civility Roils Reformers." *The Hill*, March 26, www.hillnews.com/news/nws_5.htm.

———. 2001b. "Daschle Advisor Warms Dems Against Campaign Reform." *The Hill*, April 2, www.hillnews.com.

———. 2001c. "Factions Imperil Campaign Bill." *The Hill*, January 25, www.hillnews.com/news/story_3.htm.

———. 2001d. "GOP and Dems in Money Race Before Reform Bill Takes Effect." *The Hill*, April 4, www.hillnews.com/news/nws_2.htm.

———. 2001e. "GOP Senators to Be Tracked on Fundraising." *The Hill*, April 4, www.hillnews.com/news/nws_1.htm.

———. 2001f. "Senate Dems Expect PAC Windfall." *The Hill*, June 18, www.hill-news.com/windfall.htm.

Bond, Jon R., Richard Fleisher, and Jeffrey C. Talbert. 1997. "The Experience Factor in Open Seat Congressional Elections, 1976–1994." *Political Research Quarterly* 50: 281–299.

Bositis, David A. 1997. *Black Elected Officials: A Statistical Summary, 1993–1997*. Washington, D.C.: Joint Center for Political and Economic Studies.

Bowman, Karlyn. 2000. "Polling to Campaign and to Govern." In *The Permanent Campaign and Its Future*, ed. Norman Ornstein and Thomas Mann. Washington, D.C.: American Enterprise Institute and Brookings Institution.

Bowler, Shaun, and David M. Farrell. 2000. "The Internationalization of Campaign Consultancy." In *Campaign Warriors: Political Consultants in Elections*, ed. James A. Thurber and Candice J. Nelson. Washington, D.C.: Brookings Institution.

Brace, Kimball, Bernard Grofman, and Lisa Handley. 1987. "Does Redistricting Aimed to Help Blacks Necessarily Help Republicans?" *Journal of Politics* 49: 169–185.

Brace, Kimball, Bernard Grofman, Lisa Handley, and Richard Niemi. 1988. "Minority Voting Equality: The 65 Percent Rule in Theory and Practice." *Law and Policy* 10: 43–62.

Braden, Maria. 1996. *Women Politicians and the Media*. Lexington: University Press of Kentucky.

Bradshaw, Joel. 1995. "Who Will Vote for You and Why: Designing Strategy and Theme." In *Campaigns and Elections American Style*, ed. James A. Thurber and Candice J. Nelson. Boulder, Colo.: Westview Press.

Bragg, Rick. 2000. "Campaign 2000: The Florida Race; 2 Candidates Eagerly Woo Moderates." *Washington Post*, A22.

Brennan, Mary C. 1995. *The Conservative Capture of the GOP*. Chapel Hill: University of North Carolina Press.

Bresnahan, John, and Amy Keller. 2001. "Ney's Bill Targets CBC." *Roll Call*, June 18, www.rollcall.com.

Broder, David. 2001a. "Campaign Finance Takes on a New Look for Democrats." *Arlington Star-Telegram*, February 21, 13B.

———. 2001b. "Here's the Hagel Alternative." *Arlington Star-Telegram*, March 11, 5E.

———. 2001c. "Reform: The Doubt." *Washington Post*, April 3, A21.

———. 1972. *The Party's Over: The Failure of Politics in America*. New York: Harper and Row.

Brophy-Baermann, Michelle. 2000. "Baldwin Defeats Musser in Wisconsin's Second District Race." In *The Roads to Congress, 1998*, ed. Robert Dewhirst and Sunil Ahuja. Belmont, Calif.: Wadsworth.

Browning, Rufus, Dale Rogers Marshall, and David H. Tabb. 1990. *Racial Politics in American Cities*. White Plains, N.Y.: Longman.

Bryce, James. 1891. *The American Commonwealth*. 2nd ed. London: Macmillan.

Budge, Ian, and Dennis J. Farlie. 1983. *Explaining and Predicting Elections: Issue Effects and Party Strategies in Twenty-Three Democracies*. London: Allen and Unwin.

Bullock, Charles S., III, Susan A. MacManus, Frances E. Akins, Laura Jane Hoffman, and Adam Newmark. 1999. "'Winning in My Own Back Yard': County

Government, School Board Positions Steadily More Attractive to Women Candidates." In *Women in Politics: Outsiders or Insiders?* ed. Lois Duke Whitaker. 3rd ed., Upper Saddle River, N.J.: Prentice-Hall.

Bullock, Charles S., III, and Mark Rozell. 1998. "Southern Politics at Century's End." In *New Politics of the Old South: An Introduction to Southern Politics,* ed. Charles S. Bullock III and Mark Rozell. Lanham, Md.: Rowman and Littlefield.

Bumiller, Elisabeth. 2000. "The Election: It Took a Woman; How Gender Helped Elect Hillary Clinton." *New York Times,* November 12, IV3.

Burger, Tim. 1999. "Dem: Hil May Seek Pat Seat." *New York Daily News,* January 4, 5.

Burnham, Walter Dean. 1982a. *The Current Crisis in American Politics.* New York: Oxford University Press.

———. 1982b. "The System of 1896: An Analysis." In *The Evolution of American Electoral Systems,* ed. Paul Kleppner. Westport, Conn.: Greenwood Press, 147–202.

———. 1970. *Critical Elections and the Mainsprings of American Politics.* New York: W. W. Norton.

Burrell, Barbara. 1992. "Women Candidates in Open-Seat Primaries for the U.S. House: 1968–1990." *Legislative Studies Quarterly* 17: 493–508.

———. 1988. "The Political Opportunity of Women Candidates for the U.S. House of Representatives in 1984." *Women and Politics* 8: 51–68.

———. 1985. "Women's and Men's Campaigns for the U.S. House of Representatives, 1972–1982: A Finance Gap?" *American Politics Quarterly* 13: 251–272.

Butler, David, and Bruce Cain. 1992. *Congressional Redistricting: Comparative and Theoretical Perspectives.* New York: Macmillan.

Bystrom, Dianne G., Terry A. Robertson, and Mary Christine Banwart. 2000. "Framing the Fight: An Analysis of Media Coverage of Female and Male Candidates in Primary Races for Governor and U.S. Senate in 2000." *American Behavioral Scientist* 44 (12), 1999–2013.

Cahalan, Don. 1989. "Comment: The *Digest* Poll Rides Again!" *Public Opinion Quarterly* 53: 129–133.

Cain, Bruce, and Kenneth Miller. 1998. "Voting Rights Mismatch: The Challenge of Applying the Voting Rights Act to 'Other Minorities.'" In *Voting Rights and Redistricting in the United States,* ed. Mark Rush. Westport, Conn.: Greenwood Press.

Calvo, Maria Antonia, and Steven J. Rosenstone. 1989. *Hispanic Political Participation.* San Antonio: Southwest Voter Research Institute.

Camarillo, Albert. 1979. *Chicanos in a Changing Society.* Cambridge, Mass.: Harvard University Press.

Campaign Finance Institute. 2001. "The Campaign Finance Institute Cyber-Forum: Parties Under McCain-Feingold." www.cfinst.org/parties/mf_responses.html, August.

Campbell, Angus, Philip Converse, Warren Miller, and Donald E. Stokes. 1960. *The American Voter.* New York: John Wiley and Sons.

Campbell, Bruce A., and Richard J. Trilling. 1980. *Realignment in American Politics: Toward a Theory.* Austin: University of Texas Press.

Campbell, Colton C., and David A. Dulio. 2003. "Campaigning Along the Information Highway." In *Congress and the Internet,* ed. James A. Thurber and Colton C. Campbell. Upper Saddle River, N.J.: Prentice-Hall.

Campbell, Colton C., and Nicol C. Rae. 2000a. "Ignoring Electoral Outcomes: House Judiciary Committee Republicans and the Clinton Impeachment." Paper presented at the annual meeting of the Midwest Political Science Association, Chicago, April 28–30.

————. 2000b. "Standing by Their Man: Congressional Democrats and the Clinton Impeachment." Paper presented at the annual meeting of the American Political Science Association, San Francisco, August 30–September 2.

Campbell, James C. 1997. *The Presidential Pulse of Congressional Elections.* Lexington: University of Kentucky Press.

Campbell, James E. 1985. "Sources of the New Deal Realignments: The Contributions of Conversion and Mobilization to Partisan Change." *Western Political Science Quarterly* 38 (September): 357–376.

Canon, David T. 1990. *Actors, Athletes, and Astronauts.* Chicago: University of Chicago Press.

Canon, David T., and Paul S. Herrnson. 2000. "Professionalism, Progressivism, and People Power." In *Campaigns and Elections: Contemporary Case Studies,* ed. Michael A. Bailey, Ronald A. Faucheux, Paul S. Herrnson, and Clyde Wilcox. Washington, D.C.: Congressional Quarterly Press.

Cantor, Joseph E. 2001a. *Campaign Finance Bills in the 107th Congress: Comparison of S.22 with S.27.* Washington, D.C.: CRS Report, March 23.

————. 2001b. *Campaign Finance Bills in the 107th Congress: Comparison of H.R. 380 with .27.* Washington, D.C.: CRS Report, February 16.

————. 2001c. *Campaign Financing: Highlights and Chronology of Current Federal Law.* Washington, D.C.: CRS Report, March 8.

————. 2001d. *Issue Brief—Campaign Financing.* Washington, D.C.: CRS Report, May 21.

————. 2001e. *Issue Brief—Campaign Finance.* Washington, D.C.: CRS Report, June 21.

————. 2001f. *CRS Issue Brief—Campaign Financing.* Washington, D.C.: CRS Report, October 16.

————. 1998. *Issue Brief—Campaign Finance.* Washington, D.C.: CRS Report, updated October 16.

Cantril, Albert H. 1991. *The Opinion Connection: Polling, Politics, and the Press.* Washington, D.C.: Congressional Quarterly Press.

Carelli, Richard. 2000. "Supreme Court Reaffirms States' Power to Limit Campaign Gifts." *Arlington Star-Telegram,* January 25, 9A.

Carey, John M., Richard G. Niemi, and Lynda W. Powell. 1998. "The Effects of Term Limits on State Legislatures." *Legislative Studies Quarterly* 23: 271–300.

Carolan, Matthew, and Raymond J. Keating. 2000. "Lazio Lost Because He Had No Clear Message to Voters." *Newsday,* November 14, A46.

Carroll, Susan, J. 1994. *Women as Candidates in American Politics.* 2nd ed. Bloomington: Indiana University Press.

————. 1987. *Women as Candidates in American Politics.* 3rd ed. Bloomington: Indiana University Press.

Carter, Dan T. 1996. *The Politics of Rage: George Wallace, the Origins of the New Conservatism and the Transformation of American Politics.* Baton Rouge: Louisiana State University Press.

Center for the American Woman and Politics. 2001. *Women in Elected Office 2001: Fact Sheet Summaries.* New Brunswick, N.J.: Eagleton Institute of Politics, Rutgers University.

————. 2000. Data file "States00," contained in MicroCase, version 4.5, Curriculum Plan Data Archive, 2000–2001, CD-ROM.

Clark, Cal, and Janet Clark. 1999. "The Gender Gap in 1996: More Meaning 'Than a Revenge of the Soccer Moms.'" In *Women in Politics: Outsiders or Insiders?* ed. Lois Duke Whitaker. 3rd ed. Upper Saddle River, N.J.: Prentice-Hall.

Clark, Janet, Robert Darcy, Susan Welch, and Margery Abrosius. 1984. "Women as Legislative Candidates in Six States." In *Political Women: Current Roles in*

*State and Local Government,* ed. Janet A. Flammang. Beverly Hills: Sage Publications.

Clinger, J. H. 1987. "The Clean Campaign Act of 1985: A Rational Solution to Negative Campaign Advertising Which the One-Hundredth Congress Should Reconsider." *Journal of Law and Politics* 3, no. 3: 727–748.

Clubb, Jerome M., William H. Flanigan, and Nancy H. Zingale. 1980. *Partisan Realignment: Voters, Parties, and Government in American History.* Beverly Hills: Sage Publications.

Clymer, Adam. 2001. "Justices Join Argument on Spending for Elections." *New York Times,* March 1, www.nytimes.com/clymer.

———. 2000. "The 2000 Campaign." *New York Times,* July 29, A1.

Cochran, John. 2001a. "Demand for Voting System Overhaul May Stall House Campaign Finance Bill." *Congressional Quarterly Weekly Report,* May 5, 1006–1007.

———. 2001b. "Some Democrats Express Concerns About Proposed Contributions Limits, Clouding Outlook for House Debate." *Congressional Quarterly Weekly Report,* June 9, 1365–1366.

———. 2001c. "Support of Campaign Finance Overhaul Collides with First Amendment Protection on Newspaper Editorial Boards." *Congressional Quarterly Weekly Report,* April 14, 842.

Colburn, David R., and Lance de Haven-Smith. 1999. *Government in the Sunshine State: Florida Since Statehood.* Gainesville: University Press of Florida.

Common Cause. 1999. "Editorial Memorandum: Bipartisan Campaign Finance Reform Reintroduced: Reformers Ready to Capitalize on Majority Support and Push for Early Action," February 1, www.commoncause.org.

Connelly, William F., Jr., and John J. Pitney Jr. 1994. *Congress's Permanent Minority? Republicans in the U.S. House.* Lanham, Md.: Rowman and Littlefield.

Conover, Pamela Johnston. 1988. "Feminists and the Gender Gap." *Journal of Politics* 50: 985–1010.

Converse, Jean. 1987. *Survey Research in the United States: Roots and Emergence, 1890–1960.* Berkeley: University of California Press.

Conway, M. Margaret. 2000. *Political Participation in America.* 2nd ed. Washington, D.C.: CQ Press.

Conway, M. Margaret, Gertrude A. Steuernagel, and David W. Ahern. 1997. *Women and Political Participation: Cultural Change in the Political Arena.* Washington, D.C.: CQ Press.

Cook, Elizabeth Adell. 1998. "Voter Reaction to Women Candidates." In *Women and Elective Office: Past, Present, and Future,* ed. Sue Thomas and Clyde Wilcox. New York: Oxford University Press.

———. 1994. "Voter Responses to Women Candidates." In *The Year of the Woman: Myths and Realities,* ed. Elizabeth Adell Cook, Sue Thomas, and Clyde Wilcox. Boulder, Colo.: Westview Press.

Cook, Rhodes. 2000. *How Congress Gets Elected.* Washington, D.C.: CQ Press.

Corrado, Anthony. 2001. "Financing the 2000 Elections." In *The Election of 2000.* ed. Gerald M. Pomper. New York: Chatham House.

Corrado, Anthony, Thomas E. Mann, Daniel R. Ortiz, Trevor Potter, and Frank J. Sorauf. 1997. *Campaign Finance Reform: A Sourcebook.* Washington, D.C.: Brookings Institution.

Corrigan, Matthew. 2000. "Top Down Republicanism in the South: A View from the Local Level." *State and Local Government Review* 32: 61–69.

Costantini, Edmond. 1990. "Political Women and Political Ambition: Closing the Gender Gap." *American Journal of Political Science* 34: 741–770.

Couper, Mick P. 2000. "Web Surveys: A Review of Issues and Approaches." *Public Opinion Quarterly* 64: 464–494.

Cronin, Thomas. 1996. "The Electoral College Controversy." In *The Choice of the People? Debating the Electoral College,* ed. Judith Best. Lanham, Md.: Rowman and Littlefield.

Crossley, Archibald M. 1937. "Straw Polls in 1936." *Public Opinion Quarterly* 1: 24–35.

Crotty, William. 1984. *American Parties in Decline.* 2nd ed. Boston: Little, Brown.

Culver, Chester J. 1999. *Iowa Official Register, 1999–2000.* Des Moines, Iowa: Secretary of State.

Daniel, Elizabeth. 2001. "Public Financing: Making It Work." *The National Voter* (June–July): 8–14.

Darcy, Robert, Margaret Brewer, and Judy Clay. 1984. "Women in the Oklahoma Political System: State Legislative Elections." *Social Science Journal* 21: 67–78.

Darcy, Robert, and Sarah Slavin Schramm. 1977. "When Women Run Against Men." *Public Opinion Quarterly* 41: 1–12.

Darcy, Robert, Susan Welch, and Janet Clark. 1994. *Women, Elections, and Representation.* 2nd ed. Lincoln: University of Nebraska Press.

Davidson, Chandler. 2000. "The Voting Rights Act: A Brief History." In *Controversies in Minority Voting: The Voting Rights Act in Perspective,* ed. Bernard Grofman and Chandler Davidson. Washington, D.C.: Brookings Institution.

———. 1984. *Minority Vote Dilution.* Washington, D.C.: Howard University Press.

Davidson, Roger, and Walter Oleszek. 2002. *Congress and Its Members.* 8th ed. Washington, D.C.: CQ Press.

Davies, Philip John. 1999. *U.S. Elections Today.* London: Manchester University Press.

De la Garza, Rodolfo, and Louis DeSipio. 1997. "Save the Baby, Change the Bathwater, and Scrub the Tub: Latino Electoral Participation After Twenty Years of Voting Rights Act Coverage." In *Latinos and the Political System,* ed. F. Chris Garcia. South Bend, Ind.: University of Notre Dame Press.

De la Garza, Rodolfo, Louis DeSipio, F. Chris Garcia, and Angelo Falcon. *Latino Voices: Mexican, Puerto Rican, and Cuban Perspectives on American Politics.* Boulder, Colo.: Westview Press.

DeSipio, Louis. 1996. *Counting on the Latino Vote: Latinos as a New Electorate.* Charlottesville: University Press of Virginia.

DeSipio, Louis, Rodolfo de la Garza, and Mark Setzler. 1999. "Awash in the Mainstream: Latinos and the 1996 Elections." In *Awash in the Mainstream: Latino Politics in the 1996 Elections,* ed. Rodolfo de la Garza and Louis DeSipio. Boulder, Colo.: Westview Press.

Devitt, James. 1999. *Framing Gender on the Campaign Trail: Women's Executive Leadership and the Press.* Washington, D.C.: Women's Leadership Fund.

De Vries, Walter. 1989. "American Campaign Consulting: Trends and Concerns." *PS: Political Science and Politics* (March): 21–25.

Dewar, Helen. 2001a. "Education Measure's Progress May Be a Unique Achievement." *Washington Post,* June 14, A12–13.

———. 2001b. "McCain, Feingold Turn to House." *Washington Post,* April 4, A4.

———. 1998a. "Moynihan to Leave Senate in 2000." *Washington Post,* November 7, A2.

———. 1998b. "Too Close to Call in North Carolina: Veteran Faircloth Battles Newcomer." *Washington Post,* October 29, A23.

Dexter, Lewis Anthony. 1954. "The Use of Public Opinion Polls by Political Party Organizations." *Public Opinion Quarterly* 18: 53–61.

Diamond, Edwin, and Stephen Bates. 1992. *The Spot: The Rise of Political Advertising on Television.* 3rd ed. Cambridge: MIT Press.

Dinkin, Robert J. 1989. *Campaigning in America: A History of Election Practices.* Westport, Conn.: Greenwood Press.

Dionne, E. J., Jr. 2001. "And the Delay." *Washington Post,* April 3, A21.

Dolman, Joseph. 2000. "Lazio Acting as If Upstate Is Out of State." *Newsday,* November 1, A40.

Drew, Elizabeth. 1983. *Politics and Money: The New Road to Corruption.* New York: Macmillan.

Drinkard, Jim. 1999. "E-politics: How the Net Is Transforming Grass-roots Campaigns." *USA Today,* August 31, 1.

Duke, Lynne. 1999. "First Lady Struggles with Learning Curve." *Washington Post,* September 11, A1.

Dulio, David A. 2001. *For Better or Worse? How Political Consultants Are Changing Elections in the United States.* Ph.D. diss., American University.

Dulio, David A., Colton C. Campbell, and Robert P. Watson. 2001. "The More Things Change, the More Things Stay the Same: Campaign Finance Reform in the United States." *Talking Politics* 13: 119–126.

Dulio, David A., and Robin Kolodny. 2001. "Political Parties and Political Consultants: Creating Alliances for Electoral Success." Paper presented at the annual meeting of the Western Political Science Association, March 15–17, Las Vegas, Nevada.

Dwyre, Diana, and Victoria A. Farrar-Myers. 2001. *Legislative Labyrinth: Congress and Campaign Finance Reform.* Washington, D.C.: CQ Press.

Dwyre, Diana, and Robin Kolodny. 2002. "Throwing Out the Rule Book: Party Financing of the 2000 Elections." In *Financing the 2000 Election,* ed. David B. Magleby. Washington, D.C.: Brookings Institution Press.

———. 2001. "Party Financing of the 2000 Elections." Presented at the annual meeting of the Western Political Science Association. Las Vegas, Nev., March 15–17.

Edsall, Thomas. 1998. "South Carolina Incumbent in Unexpected Tussle: Volatile Issues Threaten GOP Voter Base." *Washington Post,* September 30, A4.

Ehrenhalt, Alan. 1992. *The United States of Ambition: Politicians, Power, and the Pursuit of Office.* New York: Times Books.

Eilperin, Juliet. 2001a. "For Bush, Road to Restraining Spending Has Bumps." *Washington Post,* June 13, A6–7.

———. 2001b. "Losing Round 1, Democrats Counterpunch." *Washington Post,* March 26, A23.

Eksterowicz, Anthony J., and Glenn P. Hastedt. 1999. "The White House Legislative Liaison Office: An Opportunity for Inter-Branch Collaboration in the Post Cold War Era." In *The Post–Cold War Presidency,* ed. Anthony J. Eksterowicz and Glenn P. Hastedt. Lanham, Md.: Rowman and Littlefield.

Ekstrand, Laurie E., and William A. Eckert. 1981. "The Impact of Candidates' Sex on Voter Choice." *Western Political Quarterly* 34: 78–87.

Elder, Janet. 2001. "Poll Watch: Support for Campaign Reform Trumps Need for Tax Cuts." March 29, www.nytimes.com/2001/03/29/29POLL-WATCH.html.

"Election 2000: Senate Profiles." 2000. *Congressional Quarterly Weekly Report,* November 11, 2673–2678.

Ellison, Christopher, and David Gay. 1989. "Black Political Participation Revisited: A Test of Compensatory, Ethnic Community, and Public Arena Models." *Social Science Quarterly* 70: 101–119.

Elshtain, Jean Bethke. 1989. "Issues and Themes in the 1988 Campaign." In *The Elections of 1988,* ed. Michael Nelson. Washington, D.C.: CQ Press.

Encisco, Carmen, and Tracy North. 1995. *Hispanic Americans in Congress, 1822–1995*. Washington, D.C.: U.S. Government Printing Office.

Erikson, Robert S. 2001. "The 2000 Presidential Election in Historical Perspective." *Political Science Quarterly* 116: 29–52.

Eskew, Carter. 2001. "The Lessons of 2000." *Washington Post*, 30 January, A17.

Farrar-Myers, Victoria A. 2001. "Fundraiser-In-Chief: Bill Clinton's Legacy for Presidential Campaign Finance." In *The Presidency and the Law After Clinton*, ed. Michael Genovese and David Adler. Lawrence: University Press of Kansas.

———. 1999. "Strange Bedfellows: Organized Interests and Campaign Finance Reform." *American Review of Politics* 20: 261–278.

Farrell, David, Robin Kolodny, and Stephen Medvic. 2001. "Parties and Campaign Professionals in a Digital Age." *Harvard International Journal of Press/Politics* 6, no. 4.

Faucheux, Ronald A. 1999. "Hitting the Bull's Eye." *Campaigns and Elections* (July): 20–22, 24–25.

Federal Election Commission. 2001a. "FEC Reports on Congressional Financial Activity for 2000." Washington, D.C.: Federal Election Commission, May 15.

———. 2001b. "FEC Disclosure Database." www.fec.gov (January 22, 2001).

———. 2000a. "FEC Reports Increase in Party Fundraising for 2000." Washington, D.C.: Federal Election Commission, May 15.

———. 2000b. "History of the Voting System Standards Program." Washington, D.C.: Federal Election Commission.

Feld, Karl G. 2000. "What Are Push Polls, Anyway?" *Campaigns and Elections* (May): 62–63, 70.

Fenno, Richard J. 1978. *Home Style: House Members and Their Districts*. Boston: Little, Brown.

Foerstel, Karen. 2001a. "Election, Campaign Finance Issues Move Low-Profile Panel into Spotlight." *Congressional Quarterly Weekly Report*, June 2, 1298–1299.

———. 2001b. "Lott's Hold on Campaign Finance Bill a Non-Issue to Shays." *Congressional Quarterly Weekly Report*, May 19, 1125.

Foerstel, Karen, and John Cochran. 2001. "House Democrats' Tepid Response May Imperil McCain-Feingold." *Congressional Quarterly Weekly Report*, April 7, 776–780.

Follick, Joe. 2000. "Nelson Taps Panhandle Roots." *Tampa Tribune*, September 29, 1.

Fonder, Melanie. 2001. "For Key Lobbying, Senate Vote Was Just Beginning." *The Hill*, April 4, www.hillnews.com/news/nws_4.htm.

"For Very Strange Bedfellows, Try Redistricting." 1993. *New York Times*, July 23.

Ford, Gerald, James Carter, Howard Baker, and Lloyd Cutler. 2001. "Strengthening the Heart of Democracy." Editorial. *Washington Post*, March 22.

Fowler, Floyd J., Jr. 1993. *Survey Research Methods*. 2nd ed. Newbury Park, Calif.: Sage Publications.

Fowler, Linda L., and Robert D. McClure. 1989. *Political Ambition: Who Decides to Run for Congress*. New Haven: Yale University Press.

Fraga, Luis. 1992. "Latino Political Incorporation and the Voting Rights Act." In *Controversies in Minority Voting: The Voting Rights Act in Perspective*, ed. Bernard Grofman and Chandler Davidson. Washington, D.C.: Brookings Institution.

Frank, Stephen I., and Steven C. Wagner. 2001. *We Shocked the World: A Case Study of Jesse Ventura's Election as Governor of Minnesota*. Dallas: Harcourt College.

Gaddie, Ronald Keith. 1997. "Congressional Seat Swings: Revisiting Exposure in House Elections." *Political Research Quarterly* 50: 675–686.

Gaddie, Ronald Keith, and Charles S. Bullock III. 2000. *Elections to Open Seats in the U.S. House: Where the Action Is*. Lanham, Md.: Rowman and Littlefield.

Gallup, George, and Saul Forbes Rae. 1940. *The Pulse of Democracy*. New York: Simon and Schuster.

Gallup Poll. 2001. "Tuesday Briefing." March 20.

García, Ignacio M. 2000. *Viva Kennedy: Mexican Americans in Search of Camelot*. College Station: Texas A&M University Press.

Garcia, John A. 1997. "Political Participation: Resources and Involvement Among Latinos in the American Political System." In *Latinos and the Political System*, ed. F. Chris Garcia. South Bend, Ind.: University of Notre Dame Press.

Garcia, Mario T. 1989. *Mexican Americans*. New Haven, Conn.: Yale University Press.

Gertzog, Irwin N. 1995. *Congressional Women: Their Recruitment, Integration, and Behavior*. 2nd ed. Westport, Conn.: Praeger.

Getlin, Josh, and Heidi Evans. 1992. "Sex and Politics: Gender Bias Continues to Plague the Campaign Trail." *The Quill* 80, no. 20: 16–17.

Gilmour, John B., and Paul Rothstein. 1993. "Early Republican Retirement: A Cause of Democratic Dominance in the House of Representatives." *Legislative Studies Quarterly* 18: 345–365.

Gimpel, James G. 1996. *Legislating the Revolution: The Contract with America in Its First 100 Days*. Boston: Allen and Unwin.

Gitlin, Todd. 1980. *The Whole World Is Watching*. Berkeley: University of California Press.

Glasser, Susan. 2000a. "Hired Guns Fuel Fundraising Race." *Washington Post*, April 30, A1.

———. 2000b. "In Costly California Race, Control Was Key." *Washington Post*, May 1, A1.

———. 2000c. "Consultants Pursue Promising Web of New Business." *Washington Post*, May 3, A1.

Glasser, Susan B., and Dan Balz. 2000. "Bush Tries to Soothe Financiers." *Washington Post*, February 10, A1, 8.

Glick, Joseph A. 1999. "Focus Groups in Political Campaigns." In *The Manship School Guide to Political Communication*, ed. David D. Perlmutter. Baton Rouge: Louisiana State University Press.

Goldenberg, Edie N., and Michael W. Traugott. 1984. *Campaigning for Congress*. Washington, D.C.: CQ Press.

Goldstein, Kenneth M., Jonathan S. Krasno, Lee Bradford, and Daniel E. Seltz. 1998. "Going Negative: Attack Advertising in the 1998 Elections." In *Playing Hardball: Campaigning for the U.S. Congress*, ed. Paul S. Herrnson. Englewood Cliffs, N.J.: Prentice-Hall.

Gómez-Quinones, Juan. 1994. *Roots of Chicano Politics, 1600–1940*. Albuquerque: University of New Mexico Press.

———. 1990. *Chicano Politics: Reality and Promise, 1940–1990*. Albuquerque: University of New Mexico Press.

Gosnell, Harold F. 1937. "How Accurate Were the Polls?" *Public Opinion Quarterly* 1, no. 1: 97–105.

Graber, Doris. 1997. *Mass Media and American Politics*. Washington, D.C.: CQ Press.

Green, Eric. 2000. "Election 2000: Campaign Spotlight." Issue No. 44. Washington, D.C.: Office of International Information Programs, U.S. Department of State.

Green, John C., Lyman Kellestedt, Corwin Schmidt, and James Guth. 1998. "The Soul of the South: Religion and the New Electoral Order." In *New Politics of the Old South: An Introduction to Southern Politics*, ed. Charles C. Bullock III and Mark Rozell. Lanham, Md.: Rowman and Littlefield.

Green, John C., and Daniel M. Shea, ed. 1999. *The State of the Parties: The Changing Role of Contemporary American Parties.* Lanham, Md.: Rowman and Littlefield.

Grofman, Bernard, and Lisa Handley. 1989. "Minority Population and Black and Hispanic Congressional Success in the 1970s and 1980s." *American Politics Quarterly* 17: 436–445.

Grofman, Bernard, Lisa Handley, and Richard Niemi. 1992. *Minority Representation and the Quest for Voting Equality.* Cambridge, UK: Cambridge University Press.

Grunwald, Michael. 1999. "Hillary Clinton-for-Senate Hopes Alive." *Washington Post,* January 9, A2.

Hamilton, William R. 1995. "Political Polling: From the Beginning to the Center." In *Campaigns and Elections American Style,* ed. James A. Thurber and Candice J. Nelson. Boulder, Colo.: Westview Press.

Hamilton, William R., and Dave Beattie. 1999. "Modern Campaign Polling." In *The Manship School Guide to Political Communication,* ed. David D. Perlmutter. Baton Rouge: Louisiana State University Press.

Harris, Louis. 1963. "Polls and Politics in the United States." *Public Opinion Quarterly* 27: 3–8.

Hazeltine, Joyce. 1999. *Legislative Manual, South Dakota, 1999–2000.* Pierre, S.D.: Secretary of State.

Heclo, Hugh. 2000. "Campaigning and Governing: A Conspectus." In *The Permanent Campaign and Its Future,* ed. Norman Ornstein and Thomas Mann. Washington, D.C.: American Enterprise Institute and Brookings Institution.

Helderman, Caroline, Susan J. Carroll, and Stephanie Olson. 2000. "Gender Differences in Print Media Coverage of Presidential Candidates: Elizabeth Dole's Bid for the Republican Nomination." Paper presented at the annual meeting of the American Political Science Association, Washington, D.C.

Herbst, Susan. 1993. *Numbered Voices: How Opinion Polling Has Shaped American Politics.* Chicago: University of Chicago Press.

Hero, Rodney. 1992. *Latinos and the U.S. Political System.* Philadelphia, Pa.: Temple University Press.

Hero, Rodney, and Caroline Tolbert. 1995. "Latinos and Substantive Representation in the U.S. House of Representatives: Direct, Indirect, or Nonexistent?" *American Journal of Political Science* 39: 640–652.

Herrnson, Paul S. 2001. "Elections Are More Than Just a Game." In *Playing Hardball: Campaigning for the U.S. Congress,* ed. Paul S. Herrnson. Upper Saddle River, N.J.: Prentice-Hall.

———. 2000. *Congressional Elections: Campaigning at Home and in Washington.* 3rd ed. Washington, D.C.: CQ Press.

———. 1998. *Congressional Elections: Campaigning at Home and in Washington.* 2nd ed. Washington, D.C.: CQ Press.

———. 1988. *Party Campaigning in the 1980s.* Cambridge: Harvard University Press.

Herrnson, Paul S., and Kelly D. Patterson. 2000. "Agenda Setting and Campaign Advertising in Congressional Elections." In *Crowded Airwaves: Campaign Advertising in Elections,* ed. James A. Thurber, Candice J. Nelson, and David A. Dulio. Washington, D.C.: Brookings Institution Press.

Hiebert, Ray, Robert Jones, Ernest Lotito, and John Lorenz, ed. 1971. *The Political Image Merchants: Strategies in the New Politics.* Washington, D.C.: Acropolis Books.

"High Court Rules Racial Redistricting Could Violate Rights of White Voters." 1993. *Wall Street Journal,* June 29.

Hill, Kevin A. 1995. "Does the Creation of Majority Black Districts Aid Republicans? An Analysis of the 1992 Elections in Eight Southern States." *Journal of Politics* 57: 384–401.

Hirschfeld, Julie R. 2001. "Congress of Relative Newcomers Poses Challenge to Bush, Leadership." *Congressional Quarterly Weekly,* January 20, 178–182.

Hitchens, Christopher. 1994. "Voting in the Passive Voice." In *For the Sake of Argument: Essays and Minority Reports,* ed. Christopher Hitchens. London: Verso.

Hofstadter, Richard. 1955. *The Age of Reform: From Bryan to FDR.* New York: Alfred A. Knopf.

Horner, Louise. 2000. *Hispanic Americans: A Statistical Sourcebook.* Palo Alto, Calif.: Information Publications.

———. 1999. *Black Americans: A Statistical Sourcebook.* Palo Alto, Calif.: Information Publications.

Hosenball, Mark, and Bill Turque. 2001. "Torch Feels the Heat." *Newsweek,* April 2, 27.

Hurley, Patricia. 1989. "Partisan Representation and the Failure of Realignment in the 1980s." *American Journal of Political Science* 33: 240–261.

Iyengar, Shanto, and Donald R. Kinder. 1987. *News That Matters.* Chicago: University of Chicago Press.

Jacobs, Lawrence R., and Robert Y. Shapiro. 2000. *Politicians Don't Pander: Political Manipulation and the Loss of Democratic Responsiveness.* Chicago: University of Chicago Press.

———. 1994. "Issues, Candidate Image, and Priming: The Use of Private Polls in Kennedy's 1960 Presidential Campaign." *American Political Science Review* 88: 527–540.

Jacobson, Gary C. 2001a. "Congress: Elections and Stalemate." In *The Elections of 2000,* ed. Michael Nelson. Washington, D.C.: CQ Press.

———. 2001b. "A House and Senate Divided: The Clinton Legacy and the Congressional Elections of 2000." *Political Science Quarterly* 116: 5–28.

———. 2000. *The Politics of Congressional Elections.* 5th ed. New York: Harper Collins.

———. 1990. *The Electoral Origins of Divided Government.* Boulder, Colo.: Westview Press.

Jaeger, Alvin A. 1999. *North Dakota Blue Book, 1999–2000.* Bismarck, N.D.: Secretary of State.

Jakes, Lara. 2000. "Guiliani's Separation Clouds Senate Bid." *Albany Times Union,* May 11, A1.

Jamieson, Kathleen Hall. 1992. *Dirty Politics: Deception, Distraction, and Democracy.* New York: Oxford University Press.

Jamieson, Kathleen Hall, Paul Waldman, and Susan Sheerr. 2000. "Eliminate the Negative? Categories of Analysis for Political Advertisements." In *Crowded Airwaves: Campaign Advertising in Elections,* ed. James A. Thurber, Candice J. Nelson, and David A. Dulio. Washington, D.C.: Brookings Institution Press.

Janison, Dan, and Robert Palmer. 2000. "Guiliani's Decision: 'Not the Right Time': Citing Health, Guiliani Drops Out of Senate Race." *Newsday,* May 20, A3.

Jensen, Richard. 1980. "Democracy by the Numbers." *Public Opinion* (February–March): 53–59.

Johnson, Dennis W. 2001. *No Place for Amateurs: How Political Consultants Are Reshaping American Democracy.* New York: Routledge.

———. 2000. "The Business of Political Consulting." In *Campaign Warriors: Political Consultants in Elections,* ed. James A. Thurber and Candice J. Nelson. Washington, D.C.: Brookings Institution Press.

Johnson-Cartee, Karen S., and Gary A. Copeland. 1997. *Manipulation of the American Voter: Political Campaign Commercials.* Westport, Conn.: Praeger.

Jones, Mary Lynn F. 2001. "McCain and Hagel—Pals Up to a Point." www.hillnews.com/Jones, April 2.

Jones-Correa, Michael. 1998. *Between Two Nations: The Political Predicament of Latinos in New York City.* Ithaca, N.Y.: Cornell University Press.

Kahn, Kim Fridkin. 1996. *The Political Consequences of Being a Woman.* New York: Columbia University Press.

———. 1994a. "The Distorted Mirror: Press Coverage of Women Candidates for Statewide Office." *Journal of Politics* 56, no. 1: 154–173.

———. 1994b. "Does Gender Make a Difference? An Experimental Examination of Sex Stereotypes and Press Patterns in Statewide Campaigns." *American Journal of Political Science* 38, no. 1: 162–195.

Kahn, Kim Fridkin, and Edie N. Goldenberg. 1991. "Women Candidates in the News: An Examination of Gender Differences in U.S. Senate Campaign Coverage." *Public Opinion Quarterly* 55: 180–199.

Kahn, Kim Fridkin, and Patrick J. Kenney. 2000. "How Negative Campaigning Enhances Knowledge of Senate Elections." In *Crowded Airwaves: Campaign Advertising in Elections,* ed. James A. Thurber, Candice J. Nelson, and David A. Dulio. Washington, D.C.: Brookings Institution Press.

Kaid, Linda Lee, Chris Leland, and Susan Whitney. 1992. "The Impact of Televised Political Ads: Evoking Viewer Responses in the 1988 Presidential Campaign." *Southern Communication Journal* (Summer): 287.

Kaiser, Robert G. 2000. "Academics Say It's Elementary: Gore Wins." *Washington Post,* August 31, A12.

Kamber, Victor. 1997. *Poison Politics: Are Negative Campaigns Destroying Democracy?* New York: Plenum Press.

Kathlene, Lyn, Susan E. Clarke, and Barbara A. Fox. 1991. "Ways Women Politicians Are Making a Difference." In *Gender and Policymaking: Studies of Women in Office,* ed. Debra L. Dodson. New Brunswick, N.J.: Center for the American Woman and Politics, Eagleton Institute of Politics, Rutgers University.

Katz, Daniel, and Hadley Cantril. 1937. "Public Opinion Polls." *Sociometry* 1: 155–179.

Kazee, Thomas. 1998. "North Carolina: Conservatism, Traditionalism, and the GOP." In *New Politics of the Old South: An Introduction to Southern Politics,* ed. Charles S. Bullock III and Mark Rozell. Lanham, Md.: Rowman and Littlefield.

Keefe, William J. 1994. *Parties, Politics, and Public Policy in America.* 7th ed. Washington, D.C.: Congressional Quarterly Press.

Keller, Amy. 2001. "Losers Regroup in Reform Fight." *Roll Call,* April 2, www.rollcall.com.

Kelley, Matt. 2001. "Political Fund-Raisers Seeking New Ways to Keep Money Flowing." *Arlington Star-Telegram,* April 1, 4A.

Kelley, Stanley, Jr. 1956. *Professional Public Relations and Political Power.* Baltimore: Johns Hopkins University Press.

Kern, Montague. 1989. *30-Second Politics: Political Advertising in the Eighties.* New York: Praeger.

Kerr, Brinck, and Will Miller. 1997. "Latino Representation: It's Direct and Indirect." *American Journal of Political Science* 41: 1066–1071.

Kessler, Glenn. 2001. "Tax Cut Disappoints Conservatives, Who Decry Gimmicks, Trade Offs." *Washington Post,* June 7, A10–11.

Key, V. O. 1964. *Politics, Parties, and Pressure Groups.* New York: Thomas Y. Crowell.

———. 1955. "A Theory of Critical Elections." *Journal of Politics* 17: 3–18.

———. 1949. *Southern Politics in State and Nation.* Knoxville: University of Tennessee Press.

Kiffmeyer, Mary. 1999. *The Minnesota Legislative Manuals, 1999–2000.* Saint Paul, Minn.: Secretary of State.

King, Robert, and Martin Schnitzer. 1968. "Contemporary Use of Private Political Polling." *Public Opinion Quarterly* 32: 431–436.

Kirtzman, Andrew. 2000. *Rudy Guiliani: Emperor of the City.* New York: William Morrow.

Klain, Ronald A. 2001. "How Democrats Can Use *Bush v. Gore.*" *Washington Post,* March 22, A29.

Klein, Ethel. 1985. "The Gender Gap: Different Issues, Different Answers." *Brookings Review* 3: 33–37.

Kohut, John. 2000. "Is the South Up for Grabs? (Republican or Democrat?)" *World and I* 15: 56.

Kolbert, Elizabeth. 1992. "Test-Marketing a President." *New York Times Magazine,* August 30.

Kolodny, Robin. 2000. "Electoral Partnerships: Political Consultants and Political Parties." In *Campaign Warriors: Political Consultants in Elections,* ed. James A. Thurber and Candice J. Nelson. Washington, D.C.: Brookings Institution.

———. 1998. *Pursuing Majorities: Congressional Campaign Committees in American Politics.* Norman: University of Oklahoma Press.

Kousser, J. Morgan. 1984. "The Undermining of the First Reconstruction: Lessons for the Second." In *Minority Vote Dilution,* ed. Chandler Davidson. Washington, D.C.: Howard University Press.

Kousser, Thad, and Ray LaRaja. 2000. "Will a Soft Money Ban Stifle Political Competition? Theory and Evidence from the States." Paper presented at the annual meeting of the American Political Science Association, Washington, D.C., August.

Krasno, Jonathan S. 1994. *Challengers, Competition, and Reelection: Comparing Senate and House Elections.* New Haven, Conn.: Yale University Press.

Krueger, Richard A. 1994. *Focus Groups: A Practical Guide for Applied Research.* 2nd ed. Thousand Oaks, Calif.: Sage Publications.

Kugler, Sara. 2000. "Frenzied Race Takes Its Toll on Lazio." *Newsday,* November 8, A38.

Kuhnhenn, James. 2001. "Senate OKs Amendment to Help Rich Candidates' Rivals." *Arlington Star-Telegram,* March 21.

Kunin, Madeleine M. 1994. *Living a Political Life.* New York: Vintage Press.

Kunkel, Joseph A., III. 1998. "Political Parties in Minnesota." In *Perspectives on Minnesota Government and Politics,* ed. Steve Hoffman, Donald Ostrom, Homer Williamson, and Kay Wolsborn. Edina, Minn.: Burgess Publishing.

Kuzenski, John. 1998. "South Carolina: The Heart of GOP Realignment in the South." In *New Politics of the Old South: An Introduction to Southern Politics,* ed. Charles C. Bullock III and Mark Rozell. Lanham, Md.: Rowman and Littlefield.

Ladd, Everett Carl, Jr. 1978. *Transformations of the American Party System.* New York: W. W. Norton.

Lake, Celinda C. 1990. *Campaigning in a Different Voice.* Washington, D.C.: EMILY's List.

Lake, Celinda C., and Vincent J. Breglio. 1992. "Different Voices, Different Views: The Politics of Gender." In *The American Woman 1992–1993,* ed. Paula Ries and Anne J. Stone. New York: W.W. Norton.

Lamis, Alexander. 1999. *Southern Politics in the 1990s*. Baton Rouge: Louisiana State University Press.

"Landon, 1,293,669; Roosevelt, 972,897." 1936. *Literary Digest*, October 31, 5–6.

Lane, Charles. 2001a. "A Legal Battle on the Horizon." *Washington Post*, April 3, www.washingtonpost.com/04/03/01.

———. 2001b. "Rehnquist: Court Can Prevent a Crisis." *Washington Post*, January 19, A24.

———. 2001c. "2 Justices Defend Court's Intervention in Florida Dispute." *Washington Post*, March 30, A13.

Lau, Richard R., and Lee Sigelman. 2000. "Effectiveness of Negative Political Advertising." In *Crowded Airwaves: Campaign Advertising in Elections*, ed. James A. Thurber, Candice J. Nelson, and David A. Dulio. Washington, D.C.: Brookings Institution Press.

Lau, Richard R., Lee Sigelman, Caroline Heldman, and Paul Babbitt. 1999. "The Effects of Negative Political Advertisements: A Meta-Analytic Assessment." *American Political Science Review* 93: 119–138.

Lavrakas, Paul J., and Michael W. Traugott. 2000. *Election Polls, the News Media, and Democracy*. New York: Chatham House/Seven Bridges Press.

League of Conservation Voters. 2002. "LCV Action Fund's Environmental Champions Campaign." Washington, D.C.: League of Conservation Voters.

Lee, Barbara. 2001. *Keys to the Governor's Office*. Brookline, Mass.: Barbara Lee Family Foundation.

Lengle, James I., Diana Owen, and Molly W. Sonner. 1995. "Divisive Nominating Mechanisms and Democratic Electoral Prospects." *Journal of Politics* 57: 370–383.

Lewis, Carolyn, and Michele Verva. 1994. "Are Women for Women?" Paper presented at the annual conference of the Western Political Science Association.

Lind, Michael. 1996. *Up from Conservatism: Why the Right Is Wrong for America*. New York: Free Press.

Longley, Lawrence D., and Neal R. Peirce. 1999. *The Electoral College Primer, 2000*. New Haven, Conn.: Yale University Press.

Loomis, Burdett A. 2001. "Kansas's Third District: The 'Pros from Dover' Set Up Shop." In *The Battle for Congress: Consultants, Candidates, and Voters*, ed. James A. Thurber. Washington, D.C.: Brookings Institution, 123–159.

Lovett, Kenneth. 2001. "Lazio Lands Top Job at Think Tank." *New York Post*, May 3, 2.

Lowi, Theodore J., and Benjamin Ginsberg. 1994. *Democrats Return to Power: Politics and Policy in the Clinton Era*. New York: W. W. Norton.

Lublin, David. 1997. *The Paradox of Representation: Racial Gerrymandering and Minority Interests in Congress*. Princeton: Princeton University Press.

Luebke, Paul. 1990. *Tar Heel Politics*. Chapel Hill: University of North Carolina Press.

Luntz, Frank I. 1988. *Candidates, Consultants, and Campaigns: The Style and Substance of American Electioneering*. New York: Basil Blackwell.

Lynn, Laurence E., Jr., Carolyn J. Heinrich, and Carolyn J. Hill. 2001. *Improving Governance: A New Logic for Empirical Research*. Washington, D.C.: Georgetown University Press.

MacManus, Susan A., and Charles S. Bullock III. 1995. "Electing Women to Local Office." In *Gender in Urban Research*, ed. Judith A. Garber and Robyne S. Turner. Thousand Oaks, Calif.: Sage Publications.

Magleby, David B. 2001. "Outside Money in the 2000 Presidential Primaries and Congressional Elections." *PS Online*, June, www.apsanet.org/PS/june01/magleby.crm.

Maguire, Mark P., and Brad Ashford. 2000. "New Polling Technology: Cutting-Edge Internet Surveys." *Campaigns and Elections* (May).

Maisel, L. Sandy. 1999. *Parties and Elections in America: The Electoral Process.* Lanham, Md.: Rowman and Littlefield.

———. 1998. *The Parties Respond: Changes in American Parties and Campaigns.* Boulder, Colo.: Westview Press.

Maisel, L. Sandy, Walter F. Stone, and Cherie Maestas. 2001. "Quality Candidates to Congressional Incumbents: Can Better Candidates Be Found?" In *Playing Hardball: Campaigning for the U.S. Congress,* ed. Paul S. Herrnson. Upper Saddle River, N.J.: Prentice-Hall.

Mandel, Ruth. 1992. "Solid Gains for Women in the State Legislatures." Press release. New Brunswick, N.J.: Center for the American Woman and Politics.

———. 1981. *In the Running: The New Woman Candidate.* New York: Ticknor and Fields.

Mann, Thomas E., and Gary R. Orren, ed. 1992. *Media Polls in American Politics.* Washington, D.C.: Brookings Institution.

Manuel, Marlon. 1998. "Sigelman Knows Alabama Politics." *Atlanta Journal and Constitution,* November 8, 16A.

Marcus, Ruth. 2000. "Costliest Race Nears End; Bush, Gore Running Close; U.S. Campaigns Fuel $3 Billion in Spending." *Washington Post,* November 6, A1.

Marist Institute of Public Opinion. 2001. "New York's Two Senators and President Bush." Press release. Marist, N.Y.: Marist Institute of Public Opinion, April 9.

———. 2000. "Clinton vs. Lazio: In the Home Stretch." Press release. Marist, N.Y.: Marist Institute of Public Opinion, November 1.

Mayer, Kenneth R., and David T. Cannon. 1999. *The Dysfunctional Congress? Individual Roots of an Institutional Dilemma.* Boulder, Colo.: Westview Press.

Mayer, William G. 2001. "The Presidential Nominations." In *The Election of 2000,* ed. Gerald M. Pomper. New York: Chatham House.

Mayhew, David R. 1974. "Congressional Elections: The Case of the Vanishing Marginals." *Polity* 6: 295–317.

McCain, John. 2001. "The McCain-Feingold-Cochran Campaign Reform Bill." Washington, D.C.: Press release from the Office of Sen. McCain.

McDermott, Monika L. 1997. "Voting Cues in Low-Information Elections: Candidate Gender as a Social Information Variable in Contemporary United States Elections." *American Journal of Political Science* 41: 270–283.

McGerr, Michael E. 1986. *The Decline of Popular Politics: The American North, 1896–1926.* New York: Oxford University Press.

Medvic, Stephen K. 2001. *Political Consultants in U.S. Congressional Elections.* Columbus: Ohio State University Press.

Meier, Kenneth J., and Joseph Stewart Jr. 1991. *The Politics of Hispanic Education.* Albany: SUNY Press.

Menefee-Libey, David. 2000. *The Triumph of Campaign-Centered Politics.* New York: Chatham House.

Merzer, Martin. 2001. *Miami Herald Report: Democracy Held Hostage.* New York: St. Martin's Press.

Milbank, Dana. 2001. "Bush Signs Tax Bill into Law." *Washington Post,* June 8, A1, 18.

Milbrath, Lester W., and Madan Lal Goel. 1977. *Political Participation.* Chicago: Rand McNally College Publishing.

Miller, Arthur, Patricia Gurin, Gerald Gurin, and Oksana Malanchuk. 1981. "Group Consciousness and Political Participation." *American Journal of Political Science* 25: 494–511.

Miller, Geralyn. 2001. "Newspaper Coverage and Gender: An Analysis of the 1996 Illinois State Legislative House District Races." *Women and Politics* 22, no. 3: 83–100.

Minnesota Campaign Finance and Public Disclosure Board. 1999. *Candidate Filings.* St. Paul: State of Minnesota.

Minnesota Poll. 1998. *Star Tribune Tracking Poll.* Minneapolis.

Minnesota Secretary of State. 1998. *Official Election Vote Totals by County for Office of Governor, 1998.* St. Paul, Minn.: State of Minnesota.

Mintz, John. 2000. "Political Groups Scramble to Find E-mail Addresses of Likely Backers." *Washington Post,* October 22, A21.

Mintz, John, and Peter Slevin. 2001. "Disparities Marred Vote and Recount." *Washington Post,* June 1, A1, 20–21.

Mitchell, Alison. 2001a. "Senate Beats Challenge to McCain-Feingold." *New York Times,* March 27, www.nytimes.com/2001/03/27/politics/.

———. 2001b. "Senate Rejects Bush Plan to Curb Union and Corporate Donations." *New York Times,* March 27, www.nytimes.com/2001/03/22/politics/.

———. 2001c. "Campaign Finance Bill Passes in Senate, 59–41; House Foes Vow a Fight." *New York Times,* April 3, www.nytimes.com/2001/04/03/politics/03DONA.html.

———. 1999a. "6 Republicans Break Ranks on Campaign Finance Issue." *New York Times,* May 27, www.nytimes.com/2001/05/27/politics/.

———. 1999b. "As Campaign Finance Issue Shifts to House, a New Strategy Emerges." *New York Times,* April 4, www.nytimes.com/2001/04/04/politics/04DONA.html.

———. 1999c. "House Passes Bill with New Limits on Campaign Gifts." *New York Times,* September 15, www.nytimes.com/2001/09/15/politics/.

Mitchell, Greg. 1992. *The Campaign of the Century: Upton Sinclair's Race for Governor of California and the Birth of Media Politics.* New York: Random House.

Montejano, David. 1988. *Anglos and Mexicans in the Making of Texas, 1836–1986.* Austin: University of Texas Press.

Montgomery, David. 2001. "Simmering Election Anger Incites Rights Leaders." *Washington Post,* January 5, A10.

Moore, Elizabeth. 2000. "Upstate Economy at Last in Senate Race." *Newsday,* October 4, A17.

Morehouse, Sarah M. 2001. "The Political Pages." *Campaigns and Elections* (March).

Morin, R., and C. Deane. 2000. "Gore Takes Lead over Bush in Polls: Democrat Has Eased Doubts, Gained Edge on Key Issues." *Washington Post,* August 22, A1, 11.

Morris, Celia. 1992. *Storming the Statehouse.* New York: Macmillan.

Morris, Marie B. 2001. *527 Organizations: Reporting Requirements Imposed on Political Organizations After Enactment of P.L. 106-230.* Washington, D.C.: Congressional Research Service Report, March 19.

———. 2000. *527 Organizations: How the Difference in Tax and Election Laws Permit Certain Organizations to Engage in Issue Advocacy Without Public Disclosure and Proposals for Change.* Washington, D.C.: Congressional Research Service Report, September 7.

Mueller, Carol M., ed. 1988. *The Politics of the Gender Gap: The Social Construction of Political Influence.* Newbury Park, Calif: Sage Publications.

Nagourney, Adam, and Marjorie Connelly. 2000. "Guiliani's Ratings Drop over Actions in Dorismond Case." *New York Times,* April 7, A1.

Napolitan, Joseph. 1999. "Present at the Creation (of Modern Political Consulting)." In *The Manship School Guide to Political Communication,* ed. David D. Perlmutter. Baton Rouge: Louisiana State University Press.

———. 1972. *The Election Game and How to Win It.* New York: Doubleday.

National Association of Latino Elected Officials (NALEO). 2000. *2000 National Directory of Latino Elected Officials.* Washington, D.C.: NALEO Educational Fund.

*The National Data Book, 1999.* 1999. Baton Rouge, La.: Claitors Publishing.

Nebraska Legislature Online. 2001. http://www.unicam.state.ne.us/senators/senators.htm.

Nechemias, Carol. 1987. "Changes in the Election of Women to U.S. State Legislative Seats." *Legislative Studies Quarterly* 12: 125–142.

———. 1985. "Geographic Mobility and Women's Access to State Legislatures." *Western Political Quarterly* 38: 119–131.

Newman, Jody. 1994. *Perception and Reality: A Study Comparing the Success of Men and Women Candidates.* Washington, D.C.: National Women's Political Caucus.

*Newsday.* 2000. "Should Rudy Still Run for the Senate? It's His Call." *Newsday,* April 28, A48.

Newton, Christopher. 2001. "Campaign Finance Bill Is Doing Well, Sponsor Says." *Arlington Star-Telegram,* March 25, 4A.

Newton, Frank C. R., Olmedo Esteban, and Amado Padilla, eds. 1984. *Hispanics: Challenges and Opportunities.* New York: Ford Foundation.

Nie, Norman H., Sidney Verba, and John R. Petrocik, eds. 1976. *The Changing American Voter.* Cambridge, Mass.: Harvard University Press.

Nimmo, Dan. 1970. *The Political Persuaders: The Techniques of Modern Election Campaigns.* Englewood Cliffs, N.J.: Prentice-Hall.

Norris, Pippa. 1985. "The Gender Gap in Britain and America." *Parliamentary Affairs* 38: 192–201.

Novak, Robert. 2001. "Zell: Still a Democrat?" *Creator's Syndicate,* June 21.

O'Brien, David M. 2000. "Judicial Legacies: The Clinton Presidency and the Courts." In *The Clinton Legacy,* ed. Colin Campbell and Bert Rockman. New York: Chatham House Publishers.

Ornstein, Norman J. 2000. "Here's a Proposal on Campaign Finance That Bush, McCain, and the GOP Leadership Can Support." *Public Affairs Report,* September: 11.

O'Shaughnessey, Nicholas J. 1990. *The Phenomenon of Political Marketing.* New York: St. Martin's Press.

Patterson, Thomas E. 1980. *The Mass Media Election.* New York: Praeger.

Peele, Gillian. 1984. *Revival and Reaction: The Right in Contemporary America.* Oxford: Clarendon Press.

Perry, James M. 1968. *The New Politics: The Expanding Technology of Political Manipulation.* New York: Clarkson N. Potter.

Petracca, Mark. 1989. "Political Consultants and Democratic Governance." *PS: Political Science and Politics* 22, no. 1: 11–14.

Petrocik, John R. 1981. *Party Coalitions: Realignments and the Decline of the New Deal Party System.* Chicago: University of Chicago Press.

Pfiffner, James P. 1994. *The Modern Presidency.* New York: St. Martin's Press.

Pierre, Robert. E., and Peter Slevin. 2001. "Fla. Vote Rife with Disparities, Study Says." *Washington Post,* June 5, A1,4.

Pitchell, Robert J. 1958. "The Influence of Professional Campaign Management Firms in Partisan Elections in California." *Western Political Quarterly* 11: 278–300.

Pitkin, Hanna. 1967. *The Concept of Representation.* Berkeley: University of California Press.

Plaven, Liam. 2000. "A Tale of Two Cities: Utica, Elmira: A Split Economy; Lazio, Clinton Have Different Answers for Complex Region." *Newsday,* October 15, A8.

Podhoretz, John. 2000. "Rudy and His Enemies." *New York Post,* March 24, 29.

Pomper, Gerald M. 2001. "The Presidential Election." In *The Election of 2000,* ed. Gerald M. Pomper. New York: Chatham House.

Pomper, Gerald M., and Susan S. Lederman. 1980. *Elections in America: Control and Influence in Democratic Politics.* New York: Longman.

Popkin, Samuel L. 1994. *The Reasoning Voter: Communication and Persuasion in Presidential Campaigns.* 2nd ed. Chicago: University of Chicago Press.

Pressley, Sue A., and Catharine Skipp. 2001. "Class Action Suit Filed over Florida Election." *Washington Post,* January 11, A2.

Price, David E. 2000. *The Congressional Experience.* 2nd ed. Boulder, Colo.: Westview Press.

Rae, Nicol C. 2001. "Clinton and the Democrats: The President as Party Leader." In *The Postmodern Presidency: Bill Clinton's Legacy in U.S. Politics,* ed. Steven E. Schier. Pittsburgh: University of Pittsburgh Press, 183–200.

———. 1998. *Conservative Reformers: The Republican Freshman and the Lessons of the 104th Congress.* New York: M. E. Sharpe.

———. 1989. *The Decline and Fall of the Liberal Republicans: From 1952 to the Present.* New York: Oxford University Press.

Raines, Howell. 1977. *My Soul Is Rested.* New York: Putnam.

Ranney, Austin. 1983. *Channels of Power: The Impact of Television on American Politics.* New York: Basic Books.

Rausch, John David, Jr., and Mary S. Rausch. 1997. "Why Did West Virginia Voters Not Elect a Woman Governor?" *Comparative State Politics* 18, no. 3: 1–12.

Rausch, John David, Jr., Mark J. Rozell, and Harry L. Wilson. 1999. "When Women Lose: A Study of Media Coverage of Two Gubernatorial Campaigns." *Women and Politics* 20, no. 4: 1–21.

Reed, Adolph. 1988. "The Black Urban Regime: Structural Origins and Constraints." *Comparative Urban and Community Research* 1: 138–189.

Reichley, A. James. 1985. "The Rise of National Parties." In *The New Direction in American Politics,* ed. John E. Chubb and Paul E. Peterson. Washington, D.C.: Brookings Institution, 175–200.

Reiter, Howard L. 1987. *Parties and Elections in Corporate America.* New York: St. Martin's Press.

Richards, Ann, with Peter Knobler. 1989. *Straight for the Heart.* New York: Simon and Schuster.

Riley, John. 2000. "Poll: Lazio and Clinton Tied." *Newsday,* June 8, A8.

Rivlin, Allan. 1999. "Polling on a Deeper Level." *National Journal* 31: 2326–2327.

Robinson, Claude E. 1937. "Recent Developments in the Straw-Poll Field." *Public Opinion Quarterly* 1, no. 3: 45–56.

Rohde, David. 1991. *Parties and Leaders in the Postreform House.* Chicago: University of Chicago Press.

Rosenberg, Gerald. 1991. *The Hollow Hope: Can Courts Bring About Social Change?* Chicago: University of Chicago Press.

Rosenbloom, David Lee. 1973. *The Election Men: Professional Campaign Managers and American Democracy.* New York: Quadrangle Books.

Rosenthal, Cindy Simon. 1994. "When Girls Will Be Girls: The Gender Gap and Concepts of Representation." Paper presented at the annual meeting of the Western Political Science Association.

Ross, Karen, and Annabelle Sreberny. 2000. "Women in the House: Media Representation of British Politicians." In *Gender Politics and Communication,* ed. Annabelle Sreberny and Liesbet van Zoonen. Cresskill, N.J.: Hampton Press.

Rubenstein, Sondra Miller. 1995. *Surveying Public Opinion.* Belmont, Calif.: International Thomson Publishing.

Rule, Wilma. 1999. "Why Are More Women State Legislators?" In *Women in Politics: Outsiders or Insiders?* ed. Lois Duke Whitaker. 3rd ed. Upper Saddle River, N.J.: Prentice-Hall.

———. 1987. "Electoral Systems, Contextual Factors, and Women's Opportunity for Election to Parliament in Twenty-Three Democracies." *Western Political Quarterly* 40: 477–498.

———. 1981. "Why Women Don't Run: The Critical Contextual Factors in Women's Legislative Recruitment." *Western Political Quarterly* 34: 60–77.

Saad, Lydia. 1997. "No Public Outcry for Campaign Finance Reform." Gallup Organization Poll Press Release, February 22.

Sabato, Larry J. 2002. *The Party's Just Begun.* New York: Longman.

———. 1981. *The Rise of Political Consultants: New Ways of Winning Elections.* New York: Basic Books.

Sabato, Larry J., and Bruce Larson. 2002. *The Party's Just Begun.* 2nd ed. New York: Longman.

Sabato, Larry J., and Glenn R. Simpson. 1996. *Dirty Little Secrets: The Persistence of Corruption in American Politics.* New York: Times Books.

Sack, Kevin. 1998. "Two Democrats Hope Support for Lottery Will Help Break GOP Grip on the South." *New York Times,* September 27, A16.

Saint-Germaine, Michelle A. 1989. "Does Their Difference Make a Difference? The Impact of Women on Public Policy in the Arizona Legislature." *Social Science Quarterly* 70: 956–968.

Salmore, Stephen A., and Barbara G. Salmore. 1985. *Candidates, Parties, and Campaigns: Electoral Politics in America.* Washington, D.C.: CQ Press.

San Miguel, Guadalupe, Jr. 1987. *Let All of Them Take Heed: Mexican Americans and the Campaign for Educational Equality in Texas, 1910–1981.* Austin: University of Texas Press.

Sánchez, George. 1993. "Black Consciousness and Political Participation: The Missing Link." *American Political Science Review* 75: 76–91.

Sapiro, Virginia. 1981–1982. "If U.S. Senator Baker Were a Woman: An Experimental Study of Candidate Images." *Political Psychology* 3: 61–83.

Scicchitano, Michael J., and Richard Scher. 1998. "Florida Political Change: 1950–1996." In *New Politics of the Old South: An Introduction to Southern Politics,* ed. Charles Bullock III and Mark Rozell. Lanham, Md.: Rowman and Littlefield.

Schier, Steven E. 2000. *By Invitation Only: The Rise of Exclusive Politics in the United States.* Pittsburgh: University of Pittsburgh Press.

Schlesinger, Joseph A. 1994. *Political Parties and the Winning of Office.* Ann Arbor: University of Michigan Press.

Scope, Cindi Ross. 1998. "A Point by Point Comparison of Beasley, Hodges." Knight-Ridder News Service, September 11.

Shafer, Byron E. 1983. *Quiet Revolution: The Struggle for the Democratic Party and the Shaping of Post-Reform Politics.* New York: Russell Sage.

Shafer, Byron E., and William J. M. Claggett. 1995. *The Two Majorities: The Issue Context of Modern American Politics.* Baltimore: Johns Hopkins University Press.

Shaffrey, Mary, and Kerry L. Kantin. 2001. "House Coalition Seeks Reform Vote." January 31, www.hillnews.com/news/stort_8.htm.

Shapiro, Walter. 1998. "Alabama Democrat Has the Key to Success: Stay on Message." *USA Today,* October 2: 2A.

Shays, Christopher. 2001. "Statement of Rep. Christopher Shays (R-Conn.) on Introduction of the Bipartisan Campaign Finance Reform Act." Washington, D.C.: Office of Rep. Shays, press release, January 31.

Shea, Daniel M. 1996. *Campaign Craft: The Strategies, Tactics, and Art of Political Campaign Management.* Westport, Conn.: Praeger.

Shenon, Philip. 2001a. "Hard Money Becomes Focus of a Deal on Banning Soft." *New York Times,* March 24, www.nytimes.com/2001/03/24/politics/.

———. 2001b. "A Top GOP Senator Hints at Soft Money Compromise." *New York Times,* March 23, www.nytimes.com/2001/03/23/politics/.

Shingles, Richard. 1981. "Black Consciousness and Political Participation: The Missing Link." *American Political Science Review* 75: 76–91.

Sigel, Roberta S. 1996. *Ambition and Accommodation: How Women View Gender Relations.* Chicago: University of Chicago Press.

Sigelman, Lee, and Carol K. Sigelman. 1982. "Sexism, Racism, and Ageism in Voting Behavior: An Experimental Analysis." *Social Psychology Quarterly* 45: 263–269.

Silbey, Joel H. 1991. *The American Political Nation, 1838–1893.* Stanford: Stanford University Press.

Sinclair, Barbara. 1995. *Legislators, Leaders, and Lawmaking: The U.S. House of Representatives in the Postreform Era.* Baltimore: Johns Hopkins University Press.

Skerry, Peter. 1993. *Mexican Americans: The Ambivalent Minority.* Cambridge, Mass.: Harvard University Press.

Skocpol, Theda. 1997. *Boomerang: Health Care Reform and the Turn Against Government.* New York: W. W. Norton.

Smith, Kevin B. 1997. "When All's Fair: Signs of Parity in Media Coverage of Female Candidates." *Political Communication* 14: 71–82.

Smith, Tom W. 1990. "The First Straw? A Study of the Origins of Election Polls." *Public Opinion Quarterly* 54: 21–36.

Smith, Tom W., and Lance A. Selfa. 1992. "When Do Women Vote for Women?" *Public Perspective* (September–October): 30–31.

Southwell, Priscilla L. 1986. "The Politics of Disgruntlement: Nonvoting and Defection Among Supporters of Nomination Losers, 1968–1984." *Political Behavior* 8: 81–95.

Squire, Peverill. 1988. "Why the 1936 *Literary Digest* Poll Failed." *Public Opinion Quarterly* 52: 125–133.

St. Cloud State University Survey. 1998. *Annual Statewide Omnibus Survey.* St. Cloud, Minn.: SCSU.

Stambough, Stephen J., and Valerie R. O'Regan. 2000. "Cue Voting: Do Women Vote for Women Senate Candidates?" Paper presented at the annual meeting of the Western Political Science Association, San Jose, California, March 24–26, 2000.

Stanley, Harold, and Richard Niemi. 1999. *Vital Statistics on American Politics, 1999–2000.* Washington, D.C.: CQ Press.

*Statistical Abstract of the United States, 1999: The National Data Book.* 1999. Baton Rouge, La.: Claitors Publishing.

Stern, Philip M. 1988. *The Best Money Can Buy.* New York: Pantheon Books.

Stone, Walter J., and Ronald B. Rappaport. 2001. "It's Perot, Stupid! The Legacy of the 1992 Perot Movement in the Major-Party System, 1994–2000." *PS Online,* June, www.apsanet.org/PS/march01/stone.cfm.

Sundquist, James. L. 1983. *Dynamics of the Party System: Alignment and Realignment of Political Parties in the United States.* Washington, D.C.: Brookings Institution.

Swain, Carol. 1995. *Black Faces, Black Interests: The Representation of African Americans in Congress.* Cambridge, Mass.: Harvard University Press.

Sweeney, William R. 1995. "The Principles of Planning." In *Campaigns and Elections American Style,* ed. James A. Thurber and Candice J. Nelson. Boulder, Colo.: Westview Press, 14–29.

Swindell, Bill, and Sid Gaulden. 1998. "Women, Blacks, Republicans Played a Big Role." *Post and Courier,* November 5, 1.

Tate, Katherine. 1994. *From Protest to Politics: The New Black Voters in American Elections.* Cambridge, Mass.: Harvard University Press.

Taylor, Andrew, and John Cochran. 2001. "McCain-Feingold Tradeoffs Heighten Qualms Within Coalition." *Congressional Quarterly Weekly Report,* March 24, 647–652.

Taylor, Andrew, Derek Willis, and John Cochran. 2001. "McCain-Feingold Survives Hard Fight over Soft Money." *Congressional Quarterly Weekly Report,* March 31, 698–702.

Thernstrom, Abigail. 1987. *Whose Votes Count? Affirmative Action and Minority Voting Rights.* Cambridge, Mass.: Harvard University Press.

Thomas, Sue. 1994. "Women in State Legislatures: One Step at a Time." In *The Year of the Woman: Myths and Realities,* ed. Elizabeth Adell Cook, Sue Thomas, and Clyde Wilcox. Boulder, Colo.: Westview Press.

———. 1991. "Voting Patterns in the California Assembly: The Role of Gender." *Women and Politics* 53: 958–976.

Thurber, James A. 2000. "Introduction to the Study of Campaign Consultants." In *Campaign Warriors: Political Consultants in Elections,* ed. James A. Thurber and Candice J. Nelson. Washington, D.C.: Brookings Institution.

———. 1995. "The Transformation of American Campaigns." In *Campaigns and Elections American Style,* ed. James A. Thurber and Candice J. Nelson. Boulder, Colo.: Westview Press.

Thurber, James A., ed. 2001. *The Battle for Congress: Consultants, Candidates, and Voters.* Washington, D.C.: Brookings Institution.

Thurber, James A., and Candice J. Nelson, eds. 2000. *Campaign Warriors: Political Consultants in Elections.* Washington, D.C.: Brookings Institution.

Thurber, James A., Candice J. Nelson, and David A. Dulio, eds. 2000. *Crowded Airwaves: Campaign Advertising in Elections.* Washington, D.C.: Brookings Institution Press.

Traugott, Michael W., and Mee-Eun Kang. 2000. "Push Polls as Negative Persuasive Strategies." In *Election Polls, the News Media, and Democracy,* ed. Paul J. Lavrakas and Michael W. Traugott. New York: Chatham House/Seven Bridges Press.

Traugott, Michael W., and Paul J. Lavrakas. 2000. *The Voter's Guide to Election Polls.* 2nd ed. Chatham, N.J.: Chatham House.

Trent, Judith, and Robert Friedenberg. 1991. *Political Campaign Communication.* New York: Praeger.

Trish, Barbara. 1999. "Does Organization Matter? A Critical-Case Analysis from Recent Presidential Nomination Politics." *Presidential Studies Quarterly* 29: 873–895.

Uhlaner, Carole, Bruce Cain, and D. Roderick Kiewiet. 1987. "Political Participation of Ethnic Minorities in the 1980s." Social Science Working Paper 647. Pasadena, Calif.: California Institute of Technology.

Uhlaner, Carole Jean, and Kay Lehman Schlozman. 1986. "Candidate Gender and Congressional Campaign Receipts." *Journal of Politics* 48: 30–50.

United Nations Development Report. 1998. *Human Development Report.* Data file "Global99" contained in MicroCase, version 4.5, Curriculum Plan Data Archive, 2000–2001, CD-ROM.

Verba, Sidney. 1996. "The Citizen Respondent: Sample Surveys and American Democracy." *American Political Science Review* 90: 1–7.

Verba, Sidney, and Norman H. Nie. 1972. *Participation in America*. New York: Harper and Row.

Verba, Sidney, Kay Lehman Schlozman, and Henry Brady. 1995. *Voice and Equality: Civic Volunteerism in American Politics*. Cambridge, Mass.: Harvard University Press.

Vigoda, Ralph. 2000. "Hoeffel Credits the Ticket-Splitters." *Philadelphia Inquirer,* November 9, B01.

Von Drehele, David, Dan Balz, James V. Grimaldi, and Susan Schmidt. 2001. "For Gore Reasons to Hope Became Few." *Washington Post,* February 1, A1, 12–13.

Von Drehele, David, Jo Becker, Ellen Nakashima, and Dan Balz. 2001. "For Bush Camp, Some Momentum from a Memo." *Washington Post,* January 31, A1, 12–13.

Von Drehele, David, Jo Becker, Ellen Nakashima, and Lois Romano. 2001. "A 'Queen' Kept Clock Running." *Washington Post,* January 30, A1, 6–7.

Von Drehele, David, Ellen Nakashima, Susan Schmidt, and Ceci Connolly. 2001. "In Florida, Drawing the Battle Lines." *Washington Post,* January 29, A1, 10–11.

Von Drehele, David, Susan Schmidt, James V. Grimaldi, and Jo Becker. 2001. "In a Dark Hour, a Last Minute Reprieve." *Washington Post,* February 2, 16–17.

Von Drehele, David, Peter Slevin, Dan Balz, and James V. Grimaldi. 2001. "Endgame: The Bush Victory." *Washington Post,* February 3, A1.

Voter News Service exit polls. 2002. See www.msnbc.com/m/d2k/g/polls.asp.

Walsh, Edward. 2000. "A Would-Be Admiral Splashes into the Sea of Politics." *Washington Post,* January 21, A1, 18.

Ware, Alan. 1988. *The Breakdown of Democratic Party Organization, 1940–1980*. Oxford: Clarendon Press.

Watson, Robert P., and Ann Gordon. 2003. *Anticipating Madam President*. Boulder, Colo.: Lynne Rienner Publishers.

Wattenberg, Martin P., and Craig Leonard Brains. 1999. "Negative Campaign Advertising: Demobilizer or Mobilizer?" In *Crowded Airwaves: Campaign Advertising in Elections,* ed. James A. Thurber, Candice J. Nelson, and David A. Dulio. Washington, D.C.: Brookings Institution.

Weir, Sara J. 1999. "The Feminist Face of State Executive Leadership: Women as Governors." In *Women in Politics: Outsiders or Insiders?* ed. Lois Duke Whitaker. 3rd ed. Upper Saddle River, N.J.: Prentice-Hall.

Weissberg, Robert. 1978. "Collective vs. Dyadic Representation in Congress." *American Political Science Review* 72: 535–547.

Weissman, Art. 1996. *Christine Todd Whitman: The Making of a National Political Player*. New York: Carol Publishing.

Welch, Susan, and Albert K. Karnig. 1979. "Correlates of Female Office Holding in City Politics." *Journal of Politics* 41: 478–491.

Welch, Susan, and Lee Sigelman. 1982. "Changes in Public Attitudes Toward Women in Politics." *Social Science Quarterly* 63: 312–322.

Welch, Susan, and Sue Thomas. 1991. "Do Women in Public Office Make a Difference?" In *Gender and Policymaking: Studies of Women in Office,* ed. Debra L. Dodson. New Brunswick, N.J.: Center for the American Woman and Politics, Eagleton Institute of Politics, Rutgers University.

Werner, Emily. 1968. "Women in the State Legislatures." *Western Political Quarterly* 19: 40–50.

West, Darrell M. 1993. *Air Wars: Television Advertising in Election Campaigns, 1952–1992*. Washington, D.C.: Congressional Quarterly, Inc.

"What Went Wrong with the Polls?" 1936. *Literary Digest,* November 14, 7–8.

Whitby, Kenny. 2000. *The Color of Representation: Congressional Behavior and Black Interests.* Ann Arbor, Mich.: University of Michigan Press.

Williams, Eddie N., and Milton D. Morris. 1987. "Is the Electoral Process Stacked Against Minorities?" In *Elections American Style,* ed. A. James Reichley. Washington, D.C.: Brookings Institutions.

Wisconsin Legislative Reference Bureau. 2001. "Wisconsin State Legislature." Madison, Wis.: Joint Committee on Legislative Organization, Wisconsin State Legislature, www.legis.state.wi.us.

Witcover, Jules. 1976. *The Pursuit of the Presidency, 1972–1976.* New York: Viking Press.

Witt, Linda, Karen M. Paget, and Glenna Matthews. 1994. *Running as a Woman: Gender and Power in American Politics.* New York: Free Press.

Wolf, Richard. 2000. "Arizona Voters Click into History." *USA Today,* March 10, A3.

Wolfinger, Raymond. 1995. "The Promising Adolescence of Campaign Surveys." In *Campaigns and Elections American Style,* ed. James A. Thurber and Candice J. Nelson. Boulder, Colo.: Westview Press.

———. 1988. *Voter Turnout in California, 1974–1986.* Unpublished manuscript. Berkeley: State Data Program, University of California.

Woodward, C. Vann. 1971. *Origins of the New South, 1877–1913.* Baton Rouge: Louisiana State University Press.

# The Contributors

**Gary G. Aguiar** is assistant professor of political science at South Dakota State University, where he teaches courses in American politics. His research and publishing focus on the contextual role of racial, ethnic, and gender identity in subnational campaigns.

**Colton C. Campbell** is assistant professor at Florida International University. He is the author and coeditor of several books, most recently *Discharging Congress: Government by Commission.*

**Jane Carroll** ran for the position of Broward County (Fla.) supervisor of elections in 1968 and was elected to eight four-year terms; she retired on January 1, 2001, after having decided not to seek reelection in 2000.

**Matthew Corrigan** is associate professor of political science at the University of North Florida in Jacksonville. His research and publishing interests include electoral politics in the South and presidential public relations.

**Robert Dewhirst** is professor of political science at Northwest Missouri State University. His teaching and research specialties include Congress, the presidency, public policy, and media and politics.

**David A. Dulio** is assistant professor of political science at Oakland University in Michigan. He is coeditor of *Crowded Airwaves: Campaign Advertising in Elections,* and his research interests include campaigns and elections, political parties, and legislative politics.

**Anthony J. Eksterowicz** is professor of government at James Madison University. He is the author and coeditor of several publications. His most recent book is *The Presidential Companion,* with Robert P. Watson.

**Victoria A. Farrar-Myers** is assistant professor in the Department of Political Science at the University of Texas at Arlington. Her current research is in the areas of congressional leadership PACs and presidential foreign policy making.

**Stephen I. Frank,** professor of political science at St. Cloud State University, recently coauthored *"We Shocked the World!" A Case Study of Jesse Ventura's Election as Governor of Minnesota,* with Steven Wagner.

**Ronald Keith Gaddie** is associate professor of political science at the University of Oklahoma. He is the co-author of seven books, including, most recently, *Elections to Open Seats in the U.S. House: Where the Action Is,* with Charles S. Bullock III.

**Joan Karp** is the president of the League of Women Voters of South Palm Beach County, Florida, and has been a member of the League since 1965, first in Massachusetts and now in Florida.

**Robin Kolodny** is associate professor of political science at Temple University and author of *Pursuing Majorities: Congressional Campaign Committees in American Politics.*

**Jeffrey Kraus** is professor of political science at Wagner College in Staten Island, New York. He has written about political parties, campaign finance, and elections and has also managed and served as a consultant to a number of state and local political campaigns over the last ten years.

**David L. Leal** is assistant professor at the University of Texas at Austin. His research interests include Hispanic politics, campaigns and elections, and education policy. He has also been involved with a variety of senate and gubernatorial campaigns in capacities ranging from speechwriter to issues researcher.

**Stephen K. Medvic,** assistant professor of political science at Franklin and Marshall, is the author of *Political Consultants in U.S. Congressional Elections.*

**Valerie R. O'Regan** is assistant professor of political science at North Dakota State University. Her publications include the book *Gender Matters: Female Policymakers' Influence in Industrialized Nations.*

**Joseph W. Perkins Jr.** is a public relations executive in Montgomery, Alabama. His published writings are in the fields of interpersonal communications and media effects in society. Perkins has managed campaigns and specializes in political and public policy communication.

**Nicol C. Rae** is professor and chair of the Department of Political Science at Florida International University. Rae is a former American Political Science Association Congressional Fellow and the author of several books.

**Donna Simmons** was two-time campaign manager for Mississippi governor Musgrove and deputy chief of staff in the Musgrove administration. She has spent a decade working as a political professional providing consulting and campaign management to candidates at all levels, including U.S. representative John Arthur Evans Jr. (D-Miss.) and U.S. senator Mary Landrieu (D-La.).

**Stephen J. Stambough** is assistant professor of political science at North Dakota State University. His primary areas of research include electoral behavior, campaign strategies, and public policy.

**Sandra L. Suárez** is assistant professor of political science at Temple University. Focusing her research on interest group politics, business and government, and comparative economic development, she is the author of *Does Business Learn? Tax Breaks, Uncertainty and Political Strategies.*

**Steven C. Wagner,** professor of political science at St. Cloud State University, has written extensively on taxation and state politics, voting behavior, federal funding of local services, and organizational decisionmaking.

**Robert P. Watson,** founding editor of the journal *White House Studies,* has published fifteen books, most recently *Anticipating Madam President,* with Ann Gordon, and *The Presidential Companion,* with Anthony J. Eksterowicz. Formerly a member of the faculty at the University of Hawaii at Hilo, he is now associate professor at Florida Atlantic University.

**Joshua M. Whitman** is president of Panacea Consulting Group in Montgomery, Alabama, specializing in political, technology, and research consulting. Whitman is currently working on his Ph.D. in public administration from the joint program of Auburn University at Montgomery and Auburn University.

**Edward M. Yager Jr.** is associate professor of government at Western Kentucky University in Bowling Green. He worked in local government for five years in California before earning his Ph.D. in political science at the University of California at Santa Barbara.

# Index

# About the Book

Blending insightful scholarship with a "nuts and bolts" approach, *Campaigns and Elections* examines the electoral process at the local, state, and national levels.

The contributors—leading scholars, political professionals, and election administrators—focus on such current issues as the use of pollsters and political consultants, campaign finance reform, partisan politics, and the changing nature of both candidates and voters. Abundant case studies—including the contested election of George W. Bush—illustrate the text, and the editors' part introductions provide essential context. The resulting book is a perfect choice for any course dealing with political parties and elections.

**Robert P. Watson** is associate professor of political science at Florida Atlantic University. He is editor of the journal *White House Studies* and author of numerous books on gender and the presidency, including *The Presidents' Wives: Reassessing the Office of First Lady* and *Anticipating Madam President* (with Ann Gordon). **Colton C. Campbell** is assistant professor of political science at Florida International University. His extensive publications on contemporary U.S. politics include *Discharging Congress: Government by Commission* and *The Congressional Impeachment of Bill Clinton* (with Nicol Rae).